Acts Amid Pr

Acts Amid Precepts

The Aristotelian Logical Structure of
Thomas Aquinas's Moral Theory

KEVIN L. FLANNERY, S.J.

The Catholic University of America Press
Washington, D.C.

The paper used in this publication meets the minimum requirements of
American National Standards for Information Science—Permanence of
Paper for Printed Library materials,
ANSI Z39.48-1984.

∞

Library of Congress Cataloging-in-Publication Data
Flannery, Kevin L.
    Acts amid precepts : the Aristotelian logical
structure of Thomas Aquinas's moral theory / Kevin L.
Flannery.
        p. cm.
    Includes bibliographical references and index.
    ISBN 0-8132-0987-0 (cloth : alk. paper) —
    ISBN 0-8132-0988-9 (pbk. : alk. paper)
        1. Thomas, Aquinas, Saint, 1225?–1274—Ethics.
2. Thomas, Aquinas, Saint, 1225?–1274. Summa theologica. Prima secundae. Quaestio 94. 3. Ethics, Medieval.
4. Christian ethics—History—Middle Ages, 600–1500.
5. Aristotle. I. Title.
B765.T54 F55 2001
171´.2´092—dc21

Cover Illustration: *Sanctus Thomas Aquinas sua scripta ecclesiae tradit,*
painting by Ludovico Seitz. Courtesy of Musei Vaticani. This painting
shows Aristotle in the foreground handing his writing to St. Thomas
Aquinas, who in turn is presenting his own writings to an allegorical
figure of the Church.

"A man's friendship for himself is at bottom friendship toward the good."

ἡ αὑτοῦ πρὸς αὑτὸν φιλία ἀνάγεται πρὸς τὴν τοῦ ἀγαθοῦ

[Aristotle, *Eudemian Ethics* vii,6,1240b18].

For my father

CONTENTS

Acknowledgments, xi

Introduction, xiii

Abbreviations, Texts, Conventions, Sigla, xix

PART ONE: PRECEPTS

1. Acts Amid Precepts—I   3
[1] Practical reason and the practical syllogism, 5

[2] The characteristics of the practical syllogism, 8

[3] Means and component parts, 12

[4] Limits to looseness? 14

[5] The general structure of practical reason, 15

[6] The basis of the first principles of ethics, 19

2. The Precepts of Natural Law   25
[1] *Summa Theologiae* I–II q.94 a.2: the objections
and their responses, 26

[2] The *Sed contra*, 30

[3] The *per se*, 31

[4] The known *per se quoad nos*, 33

[5] A problem connected with the known *per se*, 36

[6] The theoretical order, 39

[7] The practical order, 41

[8] Less common common precepts? 45

[9] The point of a system of precepts, 48

3. The Derivation of Lower from Higher Principles   50
[1] Proper principles proved by prior principles, 51

[2] Countervailing indications, 54

[3] An alternative approach, 56

[4] Analysis and synthesis, 60

[5] Analysis in Thomas, 67

[6] Ethical applications, 71

[7] The development of an idea, 75

[8] Returning deposits, 79

4. Commensurability and Incommensurability   84

[1] Ordered series, common ideas, 86

[2] Some more anti-Platonic arguments, 90

[3] Aristotle's position, 93

[4] Synonyms and homonyms, 94

[5] Common ideas and analogy, 97

[6] Other complications, 100

[7] Ethico-political applications, 102

[8] Chancellors and slaves, 104

[9] Thomas's hierarchy of precepts, 105

PART TWO: ACTS

5. *Voluntas* Aristotelian and Thomistic   111

[1] The claims of Dom Lottin, 111

[2] *De malo* q.6: the body (first section), 116

[3] The first consideration, 119

[4] The second consideration, 120

[5] A list of major ideas, 123

[6] The predominance of *voluntas*, 124

[7] Rationality and freedom, 129

[8] Liberty of exercise and liberty of specification, 132

[9] God's influence on human action, 136

[10] The objections and their responses, 138

6. Practical Reason and Concrete Acts   144

[1] Aristotle's elenchic demonstration of PNC, 146

[2] *Metaphysics* iv,4, 147

[3] An elenchic demonstration of FPPR, 151

[4] Practical matter, practical form, 157

[5] Free choice and the stages of action, 162

7. The Principle of Double Effect and Fixed Paths   167

[1] *Summa Theologiae* II–II q.64 a.7, 168

[2] Indeterminacies, 172

[3] Goods in ancient practices, 177

[4] Resolving indeterminacies: hysterectomy and craniotomy, 183

[5] Resolving indeterminacies: the fat potholer, 185

[6] Law, 187

[7] Promoting and protecting goods, 191

8. Acts Amid Precepts—II   195

[1] More marks of the practical, 195

[2] A base in theoretical reason, 199

[3] Mapping on, 203

[4] The necessary and the contingent, 208

[5] An Aristotelian craft, 210

[6] Acts amid precepts, 216

[7] Analysis and natural deduction, 217

[8] The logic of localized analysis, 219

[9] The principle of double effect, again, 223

APPENDICES

Appendix A: *Summa Theologiae* I–II q.94 a.2
     (Latin, facing English translation), 228

Appendix B: The *per se* in Thomas Aquinas, 236

Appendix C: The dating of *De malo* q.6, 247

Appendix D: *De malo* q.6 (Latin, facing
     English translation), 250

Bibliography, 295

INDICES

Index of Aristolelian and Thomistic Passages Cited, 317

Index of Names, 323

Subject Index, 326

ACKNOWLEDGMENTS

In writing a book, one incurs many debts, few of which are ever adequately repaid; a beginning, however, is made by at least acknowledging what debts there are. My greatest is to Fr. Stephen Brock of the Pontifical University of the Holy Cross in Rome. Stephen read much of the book in draft and patiently commented more than once on some parts of it. His knowledge of St. Thomas and of Aristotle and the philosophical astuteness that he brings to their study never cease to astound me. I am also deeply grateful for his friendship, experienced not infrequently over plates of *spaghetti alle vongole*.

At a recent conference a speaker referred only half-jestingly to the "McInerny Identity Thesis"—i.e., the idea, attributed to Ralph McInerny, that Thomas *was* Aristotle. McInerny has played the odd man out for a good number of years among "traditional" Thomists by defending a slightly less radical form of the thesis attributed to him. If nothing else, with this book I shall provide him some company. This is an indication of the debt I owe to him intellectually. I am also much indebted to him personally for his encouragement.

I owe a great debt also to Germain Grisez, the first reading of whose article on *Summa Theologiae* [*ST*] I–II q.94 a.2 filled me with enormous consolation, as it began to dawn on me how one might make sense of ethics in a general way. Since that initial contact in print, I have come to know Germain and his wife Jeannette personally, and we have become friends. I hope they realize how much I value this friendship. In considering the intellectual debt, I am often reminded of Aristotle's remark near the beginning of the *Nicomachean Ethics:* "We had perhaps better consider the universal good and discuss thoroughly what is meant by it, although such an enquiry is made an uphill one by the fact that the Forms were introduced by friends of ours."

I owe similar debts to John and Marie Finnis and their family; to Robert George and his wife Cindy; to William and Patricia May; to Leon and Amy Kass; to Joseph M. Boyle, Jr., and to Patrick Lee. Other scholars who helped me include Kate Cleary, Gavin Colvert, Lawrence Dewan, Filippo Fabrocini, Anthony Fischer, Robert Gahl, William Joensen, Wolfgang Kluxen, Edward Mahoney, William Marshner, Mario Pangallo, Joseph Pilsner, Hayden Ramsey, and an anonymous referee for CUA Press. Many of my Jesuit confreres contributed intellectually and in other ways; they include Pierre Blet, Roberto Busa, Louis Caruana, Clarence Gallagher, Carlo Huber, Marc Leclerc, Paul Mankowski, John Michael McDermott, Paul McNellis, Peter Ryan, Niko Sprokel, and Maksimilijan Žitnik. Fr. Sprokel read the entire manuscript very carefully and presented me with a long list of very welcome corrections. Professor Kluxen's comments were also very helpful and encouraging. I used ideas contained in the book in a number of courses taught at the Gregorian University, receiving in the process helpful suggestions and criticisms from many students, including Charles Alfarone, Christopher Altieri, Dana Begley, Thomas Berg, William Donovan, Lorenz Festin, John Keenan, Hugh MacKenzie, Patrick Messina, Philip Miller, Francis Njoku, Stephen Wang, and Hagos Woldeselassie. I was also greatly aided by the kind assistance of José Palacios of the Gregorian University Library. I am also very grateful to Sara Bianchini, Sr. Mary Sarah Braun, Marina Cianconi, John Flynn, Jonathan Jones, and Paraic Maher for help in the final preparation of the book.

I am very grateful to the staff at The Catholic University of America Press, and especially to David McGonagle and to Susan Needham, for their kindness and for the care with which they saw this book through the press, and to Elizabeth Benevides.

I thank Georgetown University Press for permission to re-use material that appears in chapter 6. I thank the Leonine Commission for permission to reproduce their text (with line numbers) of *De malo* q.6. In writing this book, I have often made use of Fr. Roberto Busa's CD version of Thomas's *Opera omnia*. I have also received invaluable help from the Centro di Calcolo at the Gregorian University.

I owe a special debt of friendship to the Santamarias of Melbourne, Australia, and especially to Joseph and Soonie Santamaria and their family, and to the paterfamilias, now deceased, B. A. Santamaria. Finally, I thank my own family, especially my mother, for their unfailing love.

INTRODUCTION

The idea from which this book has grown has been with me for as long as I have been interested in philosophy. It is the idea that, in certain circumstances, an act can be morally upright, even if the agent knows that it will be accompanied by an unwelcome and (in some sense) evil effect. The idea struck me as correct and even luminous right from the beginning, its air of paradox only serving to heighten its luminosity. If one can bring about an evil effect and yet still be acting morally, there must be something very important about that radius of attention excluding the evil effect but including the good. Within the radius one finds what one is doing; outside of it are mere "side-effects." How does this work? What determines the dimensions of the radius? It is not the agent who does this, although it is all about what he is doing at the moment—i.e., about his intention. And yet neither can we say that the act's dimensions are set by purely physical considerations. The radius that appears in performing or considering an act is a "spiritual" thing, in the sense Thomas Aquinas sometimes applies to something having existence solely within the realm of intellect.

After many, many abortive attempts to answer such questions about the nature of intention, the answer I have come up with is that, in order to understand an act, we have to set it within the culture within which it is performed. It is culture whence comes an act's meaning, at least when it is an act of some cultural significance—as when it is part of a complex cultural phenomenon such as medicine. It is culture which provides the missing element in the modern analysis of acts, which has tended in its investigations to consider acts in isolation. This is not to say, however, that ethics depends on cultures in a relativistic sense. The context within which an act is performed is just one factor among many which go into its accurate analysis.

The great Aristotelian commentator Alexander of Aphrodisias, in his commentary on the *Prior Analytics*, speaks about the value of indicating at the beginning of a work its aim and purpose:

[T]hose who know what each thing you say refers to learn more easily than those who do not know. The difference between such learners is like that between people walking along the same road, when some know the destination to be reached and others are ignorant of it: those who know walk with more ease and accomplish their purpose without exhaustion, whereas those who are ignorant tend to tire.

I am aware, of course, that the readers of this book will not necessarily be "learners"; nonetheless, for the reasons Alexander gives, it will be useful at this point to give a description of the layout and plan of the book.

I have divided it into two parts, each containing four chapters, Part One bearing the heading "Precepts," Part Two the heading "Acts." These headings are intended to indicate the emphasis of three of the four chapters of either part, the first and the last chapters of the book alike being about the general thesis and bearing therefore the title "Acts Amid Precepts" (I and II).

Chapter 1 is a defense of Thomas from criticisms made by Martha Nussbaum. Nussbaum regards Thomas as a "deductivist," putting forward a moral theory characterized by moral absolutes derived from a supernatural source —and therefore not Aristotelian. I argue that she has both Aristotle and Thomas wrong. Aristotle and Thomas both accept moral absolutes, even with respect to particular acts, and both recognize a supernatural source (and object) of ethics. I argue that an Aristotelian ethical theory must be understood as having the general structure of an Aristotelian science. The moral analysis of particular acts involves, therefore, recognizing that acts are part of a larger structure, made up of analogues of first principles, theorems, definitions, etc. I hasten to add that Nussbaum's writings are more the occasion of, than the reason for, this chapter. I single her out as an adversary only because she articulates a common approach to Aristotle (and Thomas) in an especially clear manner. She has made important contributions to our understanding of Aristotle's ethical doctrines and to their application within the modern context.

Chapter 2 ("The Precepts of Natural Law") is an exegesis of *Summa theologiae, prima secundae,* question 94, article 2, probably the most important of Thomas's writings for understanding his conception of natural law.

Germain Grisez published in 1965 a very influential exegesis of the same article. I eagerly embrace Grisez's insight, derived from *ST* I–II q.94 a.2, that the basic human goods are of supreme importance in practical reason and therefore in natural law; but I argue that Thomas's main concern in *ST* I–II q.94 a.2 is to demonstrate that the structure of practical reason is parallel to that found in theoretical reason—i.e., to that found in an Aristotelian science.

Chapter 3 ("The Derivation of Lower from Higher Principles") comes back to the issue, raised by Nussbaum and others, of Thomas's alleged "deductivism." There are actually a couple of issues involved here, although they are closely related. The first is whether Thomas held that the lower sciences and disciplines, including ethics, receive their proper principles from the supreme science of metaphysics, as conclusions derived from principles. Without denying that the proper principles might be conclusions of arguments within metaphysics, I argue in favor of the autonomous intelligibility of the lower sciences and disciplines. The second issue is how we are to understand Thomas's talk of the derivation of lower ethical precepts from higher ones. I argue that the derived precepts are not derived from the higher in the sense that they are contained *in* them and then drawn out, which would be for the precepts of natural law to be "derived from on high" in a way that not only Professor Nussbaum finds objectionable. In the ancient world, as I argue, such pure derivation was not even employed in that model of theoretical sciences, geometry, which used instead a double methodology of analysis/synthesis, the analysis part involving the positing of that which is to be proved and providing the very material in terms of which a geometrical system grows. I argue that there are solid indications that Thomas recognized the role played in ethics by this analysis/synthesis methodology. Pursuing this line of thought, I argue that even derived ethical precepts are posited as responses to particular concrete situations. This means that the precepts of natural law are, in a certain sense, positive (i.e., posited) law.

Chapter 4 ("Commensurability and Incommensurability") addresses an issue in the interpretation of *ST* I–II q.94 a.2, where Thomas apparently recognizes a hierarchy of precepts corresponding to goods desired and sought. Does this mean that his ethical theory can be employed in a consequentialist way, whereby one weighs one good or prospect of good against another in order to decide which of several options is the morally correct one? Since the

Thomistic corpus does not contain a sustained treatment of commensuration, I develop the argument by examining some ideas in Aristotle's philosophy of mathematics, arguing ultimately that he would regard such weighing
of goods as confused. If Thomas follows Aristotle in this respect (and there is
good reason to believe he does), we need not worry that he might be a consequentialist.

Chapter 5 initiates, as I have said, the discussion of acts, as opposed to precepts. Entitled "*Voluntas* Aristotelian and Thomistic," it is about Thomas's *De
malo* [*De ma.*] q.6 and the very slippery issues first introduced into Thomistic
circles by the Benedictine Odon Lottin—issues having to do with the relationship between will (or *voluntas*) and intellect. I argue that it is impossible
to decide whether Lottin is right or not but that, by methodically reconsidering the arguments set out in *De ma.* q.6, we can show that those who attempt
to use Lottin's ideas to argue that Thomas turned away from the Aristotelian
tradition and toward a more modern approach are mistaken. This is, in effect, an argument for the close relationship in Thomas's ethics between will
and intellect, for it is a characteristically modern tendency to argue that what
a person wills to do with an act enjoys precedence over what he understands
himself "objectively" to be doing. This chapter is necessary for my overall argument, especially in this second part, since so much of it depends on the
idea, which I attribute to Thomas, that will never operates independently of
intellect—and since so many scholars deny this interdependence.

Chapter 6 ("Practical Reason and Concrete Acts") is an attempt to take seriously Thomas's statement in *ST* I–II q.94 a.2 that the first principle of practical reason ("good is to be done and pursued and evil avoided") is parallel to
the first principle in theoretical reason (or the principle of non-contradiction).[1] It offers, that is, an "elenchic demonstration" of the first principle of
practical reason modelled upon the similar demonstration of the principle of
non-contradiction in Aristotle's *Metaphysics,* book 4. Since the first principle
of practical reason has a definite place in the structure of practical reason, we
therefore gain some insight into the way in which acts are to be situated
among precepts.

Like Aristotle's demonstration, the demonstration of its practical equiva-

---

1. A large part of Chapter 6 appeared in Robert P. George, ed. (1998), although with some differences; see Flannery (1998b). What appears here does so with permission.

lent depends on the principle's opponent's "making a signification"—in this case, his identifying a *prosequendum,* a definite thing to be pursued. The understanding of human action that results from this approach is in harmony with the ideas put forward in Chapter 5, for here too intellect and will are seen as closely bound up with one another. I speak in this connection of the matter and form of human action—i.e., of the necessity of conceiving of human action in terms of concrete acts. I speak also of the bearing that all this has upon our conception of free choice.

Chapter 7 ("The Principle of Double Effect and Fixed Paths") argues that some of the difficulties that have plagued interpreters of the principle of double effect can be resolved by allowing another factor into the principle's analysis, a factor discernable in the *locus classicus* for the principle, *ST* II–II q.64 a.7. This factor is the idea that the ethical world has among its basic elements fixed paths of behavior, an idea very much present in the ethical theories of Plato and Aristotle. These fixed paths include, besides the legitimate practices of crafts such as medicine, statesmanship, and soldiering, also laws in general.

This latter point naturally provokes the objection that the theory proposed might be too "legalistic." I deflect this charge by arguing that the law involved has nothing to do with the merely legal but represents a more ancient approach to law, according to which positive law and morality (i.e., natural law) are intimately tied up with each other, so that the laws at issue are necessarily just laws. I argue, finally, that determining when a good is being attacked involves the "back and forth" movement characteristic of the analysis/synthesis method. Ethical precepts must first be posited and then shown to be consistent with the larger system of practices, laws, and higher precepts.

Finally, Chapter 8 ("Acts Amid Precepts—II") puts particular acts, as represented by practical syllogisms, into the context of practical reason in general, which includes the various precepts of natural law and the practices that make up the various crafts. I try to do this with some logical precision, at times making use of ideas and techniques developed in modern systems of natural deduction, although the logical system depicted is basically Aristotle's. Some of what is said in this chapter goes beyond what is found in either Aristotle or Thomas; but that seems only appropriate for a final chapter. This book is not an exercise in antiquarianism. We read—and write—books of philosophy in order to help us deal with philosophical questions which concern us.

I have included also a number of appendices, two of which, B and C, are investigations of matters pertinent to but not part of the general argument of the book. Appendix B attempts to settle the difficult question of how Thomas understands *per se* predications, of which he speaks in *ST* I–II q.94 a.2. Appendix C contains a textual analysis of *De ma.* q.6 and, to some extent, *De veritate*, q.24 a.1. I argue, on textual grounds, that *De ma.* q.6 cannot have been written after 1259. If correct, this would be an important finding, since *De ma.* q.6, often associated with the Paris condemnations of 1270, has been employed in establishing the chronology of Thomas's philosophical career.

ABBREVIATIONS, TEXTS, CONVENTIONS, SIGLA

[See the Bibliography, Primary Sources, for abbreviations of works by authors other than Thomas, Aristotle, and Plato.

Certain abbreviations (e.g., *in En, in Metaph.*) in standard usage refer to works by Thomas and also to works by other authors. Where such abbreviations are used, the text will make it apparent whose work is being cited.]

Thomas Aquinas

De carit.: De caritate. In *Quaestiones disputatae,* vol. 2, pp. 753–91, R. Spiazzi, P. Bazzi, M. Calcaterra; T. S. Centi, E. Odetto, and P. M. Pession (eds.), Turin/Rome: Marietti (1953).

De div.nom.: In librum Beati Dionysii De divinis nominibus expositio, C. Pera (ed.), Turin/Rome: Marietti (1950).

De ma.: Quaestiones disputatae de malo. Opera omnia, vol. 23, Rome/Louvain: Leonine Commission/Librairie Philosophique J. Vrin (1982).

De pot.: De potentia. In *Quaestiones disputatae,* vol. 2, pp. 7–276, P. Pession (ed.), Turin/Rome: Marietti (1953).

De princ.nat.: De principiis naturae ad Fratrem Sylvestrum. Opera omnia: vol. 43, pp. 1–47. Rome: Leonine Commission/Editori di San Tommaso (1976).

De ver.: Quaestiones disputatae de veritate. Opera omnia, vol. 22, Rome: Leonine Commission/Editori di San Tommaso (1970–1975).

in I Tim.: Super primam epistolam ad Timotheum lectura. In *Super epistolas S. Pauli lectura,* vol. 2, R. Cai (ed.), Turin/Rome: Marietti (1953).

in An.post.: Expositio libri Posteriorum. Opera omnia, vol. I*, part 2,
Rome/Paris: Leonine Commission/Librairie Philosophique J. Vrin (1989).
(This is the Leonine Commission's second edition of *in An.post.,* the first
having been published in 1882.)

in De an.: Sententia libri De anima. Opera omnia, vol. 45, part 1, Rome/Paris:
Leonine Commission/Librairie Philosophique J. Vrin (1984). (Note that
chapter divisions here are different from the Marietti edition.)

in De cael.: In libros Aristotelis De caelo et mundo expositio. Opera omnia, vol.
3, pp. 1–257, Rome: Leonine Commission (1886).

in De hebdom.: Expositio libri Boetii de ebdomadibus. Opera omnia, vol. 50, pp.
231–94, Rome/Paris: Leonine Commission/Les Éditions du CERF (1992).

in EN: Sententia libri Ethicorum. Opera omnia, vol. 47, Rome: Leonine
Commission (1969).

in Int.: Expositio libri Peryermenias. Opera omnia, vol. I*, part 1, Rome/Paris:
Leonine Commission/Librairie Philosophique J. Vrin (1989).

in Lib.caus.: In Librum de causis expositio, C. Pera (ed.), Turin/Rome: Marietti
(1955).

in Metaph.: In duodecim libros Metaphysicorum Aristotelis expositio, A. M.
Pirotta (ed.), Turin/Rome: Marietti (1950).

in Phys.: In octos libros Physicorum Aristotelis expositio, P. M. Maggiòlo (ed.),
Turin/Rome: Marietti (1965) [contains Leonine Commission text of 1884].

in Pol.: Sententia libri Politicorum. Opera omnia, vol. 48, Rome: Leonine
Commission (1971).

in Rom.: Super epistolam ad Romanos lectura. In *Super epistolas S. Pauli lectura,* R. Cai (ed.), Turin/Rome: Marietti (1953).

*in Sent.: Commentum in quatuor libros Sententiarum Magistri Petri Lombardi.
Opera omnia,* vols. 6–7, Parma: *typis Petri Fiaccadori* (1856–1858).

in Trin.: Super Boetium De Trinitate. Opera omnia, vol. 50, pp. 1–230,
Rome/Paris: Leonine Commission/Les Éditions du CERF, 1992.

Perf.: De perfectione vitae spiritualis. In *Opuscula theologica,* vol. 2, pp. 111–53,
R. M. Spiazzi (ed.), Turin/Rome: Marietti (1954).

Quodl.: Quaestiones de quolibet. Opera omnia, vol. 25, Rome/Paris: Leonine
Commission/Les Éditions du CERF (1996).

SCG: Summa contra gentiles, C. Pera, P. Marc, P. Caramello (eds.), 3 vols., Turin/Rome: Marietti (1961). (Vols. 2 and 3 contain the Leonine Commission text, revised.)

ST: Summa theologiae, Turin/Rome: Marietti (1948). (Contains the Leonine Commission text.)

Tab.: Tabula libri Ethicorum. Opera omnia, vol. 48, pp. B1–B172. Rome: Leonine Commission (1971).

The texts of Thomas used are those of the Leonine Commission, when such are available, although I usually change the Leonine orthography to standard Latin orthography. (In Appendix D, however, where I give the entire Leonine text of *De ma.* q.6, I retain their orthography.) In cases where a Leonine edition does not exist, I use the Marietti text, with the exception of the commentary on Peter Lombard's *Sentences,* where I use the Parma edition (see above).

Where a Leonine edition exists and where exact line numbers are indicated and would be useful, I give in a citation the book number, the *lectio* or *capitulum* number, and the line numbers, followed by the reference to the more commonly available Marietti edition (if the Marietti edition includes division numbers). Thus, a typical citation to Thomas's commentary on Aristotle's *Nicomachean Ethics* would be written: *in EN* lb.1 lect.6 ll.98–105 (§80). The symbol § always indicates a Marietti division.

In citing Thomas's *Summa theologiae,* I use the standard method. Thus, '*ST* I q.12 a.2 ad 3' = first part *(prima pars),* question 12, article 2, the response to the third objection; '*ST* I–II q.94 a.2' = first part of the second part *(prima secundae),* question 94, article 2; '*ST* II–II q.100 a.5 c' = second part of the second part *(secunda secundae),* question 100, article 5, body *(corpus)* of the article; '*ST* III' = third part *(tertia pars);* etc., etc.

A typical reference to the commentary on the *Sentences* runs: *in Sent.* lb.4 d.22 q.1 a.2. The reference is to the commentary on the fourth book, distinction 22, question 1, article 2. In citing *in Sent.,* I also occasionally use the abbreviation 'sol.', which refers to a solution to a subquestion and includes the responses (ad 1, ad 2, etc.).

Aristotle

An.post. = *Posterior Analytics*   *MM* = *Magna moralia*
An.pr. = *Prior Analytics*   *PA* = *De partibus animalium*
Cael. = *De Caelo*   *Phys.* = *Physics*
Cat. = *Categories*   *Poet.* = *Poetics*
De an. = *De anima*   *Pol.* = *Politics*
EE = *Eudemian Ethics*[1]   *Protr.* = *Protrepticus*
EN = *Nicomachean Ethics*   *Rhet.* = *Rhetoric*
Int. = *De interpretatione*   *SE* = *Sophistici elenchi*
MA = *De motu animalium*   *Top.* = *Topics*
Metaph. = *Metaphysics*

Plato

Chrm. = *Charmides*   *Lg.* = *Laws*   *R.* = *Republic*
Cra. = *Cratylus*   *Men.* = *Meno*   *Sph.* = *Sophist*
Euthd. = *Euthydemus*   *Phd.* = *Phaedo*   *Ti.* = *Timaeus*
Grg. = *Gorgias*   *Phlb.* = *Philebus*
La. = *Laches*   *Prt.* = *Protagoras*

For the Greek text of the works of Plato and Aristotle I have used the latest Oxford Classical Texts, when available. For *De motu animalium,* I have used Nussbaum (1978). For the *Magna moralia,* I have used Susemihl (1883). For *Protrepticus,* I have used Düring (1969). For many of the translations from Aristotle, I have made use of the *Revised Oxford Translation* [=Barnes (1984); see abbreviation below]. For translations of *An.post.,* I have made use of Barnes's revised translation [in Barnes (1994 <1975>) (see bibliography)]. For translations of Plato, I have made use of the Loeb series. For translations from Thomas's *Summa theologiae,* I have made use of the old Dominican translation, first published in 1911 (London: Burns, Oates and Washbourne), revised in 1920 (reprint: Westminster, Maryland: Christian Classics, 1981). Often I use my own translations; occasionally I alter a published translation without further comment.

---

1. In some codices, *EE* vii,13–15 = *EE* viii,1–3. I employ the latter numbering system—i.e., recognizing an eighth book.

Other abbreviations

Other abbreviations used (some already mentioned) are the following:

a.: article

c: *corpus* (body of an article or solution)

cap.: *capitulum* (chapter)

col.: column

d.: distinction

ll.: lines

lb.: *liber* (book)

lect.: *lectio* (a section in a commentary)

n.: number

obj.: objection

Pat.Gr.: *Patrologia Graeca* (Migne)

Pat.Lat.: *Patrologia Latina* (Migne)

PDE: the principle of double effect

q.: question

ROT: *The Complete Works of Aristotle: the Revised Oxford Translation* [=Barnes (1984)]

sol.: *solutio* (solution, as in Thomas's *in Sent.*)

un.: *unicus* (e.g., a question in one article)

§: a Marietti division

Conventions

I adopt the convention, now common within philosophical circles, of reserving double inverted commas (". . .") for genuine quotations and "scare quotes," single inverted commas ('. . .') for all other appropriate uses, such as the mention of a term or concept.

In order to keep italic text to a minimum, quotations in foreign languages but written in the Latin alphabet appear in double inverted commas. When I (as opposed to another) employ a foreign word or phrase written in the Latin alphabet, or when I employ a transliterated Greek word or phrase, or when I am discussing particular Latin words or phrases, I use italics.

The terms 'principle' and 'precept' occur often in the book. 'Principle' is the wider of the two concepts and refers to the starting points of an Aristotelian science or discipline; 'precepts' are the principles of practical reason and of natural law.

The expression *per se notum* also occurs many times, especially in chapter 2. Because it occurs so often and since (for reasons explained in chapter 2) I do not wish to translate it, I use the phrase *per se notum* as if it were English—that is, I make no attempt to change the ending of *notum* to match the number or (supposed) gender of that to which it refers, unless that to which it refers is itself in Latin.

When I speak of chapters and sections (e.g., "chapter 3, sections [4] to [6]") without further specification, the reference is to chapters and sections of this book.

SIGLA USED IN CHAPTER 2

Chapter 2 contains two sets of sigla, one representing the tiers of principles in theoretical reason, the other the tiers of precepts in practical reason. It will be useful to have these sigla, set out apart.

The tiers of theoretical reason

[e] = other principles

[d] = proper principles

[c] = common axioms

[b] = PNC (principle of non-contradiction)

[a] = being

The tiers of natural law

$[\delta^3]$ = natural law precepts pertaining to rationality <9>

$[\delta^2]$ = natural law precepts pertaining to life <8>

$[\delta^1]$ = natural law precepts pertaining to being <7>

$[\gamma]$ = common precepts

$[\beta]$ = FPPR (first principle of practical reason)

$[\alpha]$ = good

Precepts

CHAPTER 1

ACTS AMID PRECEPTS—I

I N H E R B O O K on Aristotle's *De motu animalium,* Martha Nussbaum depicts, in order to oppose it, a certain approach to Aristotle's moral theory. According to this approach, "practical principles form a closed, consistent deductive system, beginning with a priori first principles concerning
the essence or nature of man. These principles are objectively valid, independently of the desires and judgments of human agents." This system is notable not least for its lack of freedom, for below the *a priori* first principles is
found "a closed, consistent hierarchy of rules of practice, covering both the
moral and non-moral sides of human life, down to the smallest details: the
decision to eat some candy, the need to make a cloak." In order to know what
to do in a particular situation, one need only "subsume the situation under
the relevant rule, plug it into the right place in the hierarchy." There can be no
conflicts within this system: "Since it is to be a consistent system, there should
be no incommensurable claims. In every situation there will be one appropriate response, and for every right action only one most appropriate justification."[1]

Nussbaum associates this approach with Thomas Aquinas—or, at least,
with certain Thomists and, in particular, Jacques Maritain.[2] These thinkers,

1. Nussbaum (1978), pp. 166–67. See also Nelson (1992), pp. 8–11.
2. "The desire to establish such a deductive science has been a powerful and pervasive one in
philosophy, but perhaps the most striking example of an attempt to associate Aristotle with moral
deductivism has been the Aristotelianism of Aquinas and the tradition of Christian exegesis descending from it" [Nussbaum (1978), p. 168]. (She then cites Maritain (1943) [=Maritain (1947
<1942>)].) In a note, however, she adds: "I am not claiming that the deductivist position I sketch
is a correct exegesis of [Aquinas's] position" [p. 169, n. 9].

whom she dubs "deductivists," hold that ethical norms are established not by man but by God. According to Thomas, she says, "all laws, insofar as they partake of right reason, are derived from the eternal law." Moreover, all knowledge of moral truth is "a kind of reflection and participation of the eternal law, which is the unchangeable truth."[3] Continues Nussbaum:

> In Maritain's striking analogy, we are all pianos, which will produce the proper sounds only if tuned to an external and objective standard of pitch.... If a piano does not produce the right sounds, it "must be tuned, or discarded as worthless." The aim of ethical science would be, then, to attain to knowledge of the heavenly first principles and the system of prescriptions following from them—ultimately to complete this system so that it offers a coherent set of rules governing every possible human situation.[4]

Aristotle, on the other hand, according to Nussbaum, recognizes no such objective standard of human morality. His ethical methodology is not deductivist, and he allows that irreconcilable conflicts are possible, even within his system of ethics itself.

> There is, as far as we know, no "true life-plan," just as there are no ideal pianos or heavenly tuning-forks. There are, nonetheless, pianos that are well and badly tuned according to a public and (let us suppose) generally agreed standard. And there are men whose lives can be agreed by rational men to be good or bad, without appeal to extra-human values.... We retain throughout our lives an interest in defending and explaining our actions to our fellow human beings—defending them not as good *simpliciter,* but as good actions for the sort of being both we and they are, components of or means to a good human life.[5]

General rules, says Nussbaum, have a certain usefulness as "rules of thumb," but they cannot be considered "objectively valid norms" or "laws of nature."[6] The decisions made in particular cases have a claim on us prior to that of the

---

3. Nussbaum (1978), pp. 168–69. For the first quotation, Nussbaum cites *ST* I–II q.93 a.3. She gives q.93 a.1 as her source for the words "a kind of reflection and participation of the eternal law, which is the unchangeable truth." They come actually from article 2.

4. Nussbaum (1978), pp. 168–69. The quoted remark about the pianos is at Maritain (1947 <1942>), pp. 63–64. It must be said, even at the outset, that Maritain—and particularly the book that Nussbaum cites, his *Les droits de l'homme et la loi naturelle*—is an extremely unlikely candidate for the sort of criticism she directs at him. That book, first published in 1942—that is, during World War II—is a virtual paean to human liberty, containing as an appendix the 1929 *Déclaration internationale des droits de l'homme.* Nowhere in the book does Maritain present anything like the deductive scheme Nussbaum attributes to him.

5. Nussbaum (1978), p. 219.

6. Nussbaum (1978), p. 199.

rules themselves: "there is no fixity," she says; ". . . even the 'naturally just' is *kinēton*, revisable; no imaginable set of precepts could adequately cover the indefinite matter of the practical."[7]

What is important in human affairs is the conversation *about* ethics. Aristotle addresses himself, says Nussbaum, to "reflective men":

He suggests that for such men a sorting-out of the questions with which the *Ethics* will deal *will* make a difference—not because it will put them in touch with the a priori, but because, as archers, they will thereby get a clearer view of the target at which they are aiming (1094a33-34). What we ought to be after in ethics, he suggests, is a broad consensus among the mature and reflective, an ordering of their moral intuitions through reasoned adjustment of competing considerations—a theory very much like Rawls's notion of "wide reflective equilibrium," which explicitly rejects appeals to the a priori, but also insists that a non-relativistic agreement can be reached among rational men.[8]

Nussbaum raises a number of interesting and important issues, many of which are addressed in this book. The scope of this chapter, however, is much more limited. My aim is to sketch out a correct account of Aristotle's conception of practical reason. In doing this, I also show, I believe, that Aristotle is less Rawlsian and more Thomistic than Nussbaum makes him out to be. I argue that Aristotle does recognize objective, exceptionless moral principles and that they are to be associated, even according to Aristotle, with the divine.

[1] Practical reason and the practical syllogism

I start, however, with something that Nussbaum certainly has right—and that is her rejection of D. J. Allan's understanding of the practical syllogism in Aristotle. Allan's position is actually a fairly complex theory having to do not only with the practical syllogism but also with the development of Aristotle's ideas about the nature of practical reason. It is important to enter into some of the details of this theory since Nussbaum's position (which she shares with several other modern Aristotelians) is in many ways a reaction to it.

Allan contends that when Aristotle wrote *EN* iii he had not yet fully developed his understanding of practical reason. Consider, for instance, *EN* iii,2,

7. Nussbaum (1978), p. 214; see also pp. 210–20.
8. Nussbaum (1978), p. 105; in a note, Nussbaum cites Rawls (1971), pp. 20-21 and 48–53.

where Aristotle explains that there is a difference between choice [*prohairesis*] and wish [*boulēsis*]. Wish can be for things that are impossible; choice cannot be. Also: ". . . wish relates rather to the end, choice to the means [*ta pros to telos*]; for instance, we wish to be healthy, but we choose the acts which will make us healthy, and we wish to be happy and say we do, but we cannot well say we choose to be so; for, in general, choice seems to relate to the things that are in our own power."[9] This might be read, says Allan, as if Aristotle were saying that all human action might be analyzed according to the means-end model. Obviously, some actions can be: a cobbler who wishes to make a shoe (his end) reaches for his awl (the means). But it is not necessarily the case that, for instance, a man who chooses to perform a courageous act does so because he wishes something ulterior to being courageous in that particular act.

By the time he writes *EN* vi, according to Allan, Aristotle has successfully separated choice and deliberation—and also narrowed his understanding of practical reason. Deliberation is limited to instrumental thinking, i.e., the determination of means to ends; it is intellectual and, therefore, "not a distinctive operation of the *practical* reason."[10] Choice, on the other hand—or, more properly, "choice with no ulterior end in view"—has to do with "the man's general aim or policy, reflecting his disposition of character."[11] Choice, thus conceived, properly pertains to practical reason; it is the basis of ethics itself, as opposed to the mere thinking that a man might do about how to get to where he wants to be.

This distinction enters into Aristotle's *De motu animalium* [*MA*], says Allan. In chapter vii of that work, Aristotle runs through, in staccato fashion, a number of practical syllogisms:

Whenever someone thinks that every man should take walks, and that he is a man, at once he takes a walk. Or if he thinks that no man should take a walk now, and that he

9. *EN* iii,2,1111b26–30: . . . ἡ μὲν βούλησις τοῦ τέλους ἐστὶ μᾶλλον, ἡ δὲ προαίρεσις τῶν πρὸς τὸ τέλος, οἷον ὑγιαίνειν βουλόμεθα, προαιρούμεθα δὲ δι' ὧν ὑγιανοῦμεν, καὶ εὐδαιμονεῖν βουλόμεθα μὲν καὶ φαμέν, προαιρούμεθα δὲ λέγειν οὐχ ἁρμόζει· ὅλως γὰρ ἔοικεν ἡ προαίρεσις περὶ τὰ ἐφ' ἡμῖν εἶναι. I use here the original Ross translation [Ross (1925)] since Ross translates the phrase τῶν πρὸς τὸ τέλος as Allan would: i.e., as "means." More on this below.

10. Allan (1955), p. 328 [emphasis by Allan]. See also Allan (1953), pp. 124–25.

11. Allan (1955), p. 338–39. See also p. 332: "practical reasoning is allied to, or expressed in, habitual desire." As support for his understanding of choice [*prohairesis*], Allan cites *EN* vi,12,1144a19.

is a man, at once he remains at rest. . . . I should make something good; a house is something good. At once he makes a house. I need covering, a cloak is a covering: I need a cloak. What I need, I have to make; I need a cloak. I have to make a cloak. And the conclusion, the "I have to make a cloak," is an action.[12]

At the end of this section, Aristotle says: "Now, that the action is the conclusion, is clear. And as for the premisses of action, they are of two kinds— through the good and through the possible."[13] Allan claims to find in this latter remark Aristotle's identification of two types of practical syllogism: one pertaining to instrumental thinking, the other to overall "disposition of character." Although Aristotle speaks here of premisses, says Allan, he is really identifying types of syllogism, the type being determined by the major premiss, which might be either "of the possible" or "of the good." A premiss "of the possible," explains Allan, starts from the desirability of some end and leads to the performance of some action as means; a premiss "of the good" starts from "the notion of a general rule to be realized in a series of actions, which severally are good, not as means, but as constituents [of the good sought]."[14]

There are a number of problems with this theory of Allan's, which have led to its being universally repudiated by present-day Aristotelian scholars. Anthony Kenny, for instance, points to a number of passages in which Aristotle does associate practical reason with deliberation.[15] The main problem, however, is that the series of syllogisms in *MA* vii do not divide up in the way that Allan suggests they should, i.e., into those that concern the good and those that identify means. Says Nussbaum:

The passage cannot bear this interpretation. Context indicates that Aristotle, having once again told us his position on the nature of the practical conclusion in *all* these examples (701a22–23), is going on to make a correspondingly general remark about the nature of the premisses. Allan implies that there can be a practical syllogism concerned only with naming a good, without any specification of how it is possible to realize that good, and that, on the other hand, there can be practical reasoning issuing in

---

12. *MA* vii,701a13–20; the translation is Nussbaum's [Nussbaum (1978), p. 40].

13. *MA* vii,701a22–25 (Nussbaum).

14. Allan (1955), pp. 330–31.

15. Kenny (1979), p. 118. Kenny also accuses Allan of confusing "a distinction between two kinds of *premisses* with a distinction between two kinds of *syllogism*" [Kenny (1979), p. 119, his emphasis].

action that begins with the mere naming of a possibility. But the "walk" example, which Allan cites as exemplary of a syllogism of the good, has a minor premiss ("he is a man") that indicates that it is *possible* for him to realize the major; and the "cloak" example begins with the statement of a desire for covering and aims, as much as any of the other examples, at some good for the agent.[16]

In other words, although, as Nussbaum acknowledges, there are important differences among practical syllogisms, they are regarded in *MA* vii as belonging to one general type—i.e., they all involve, in some sense, getting to a good. This criticism of Allan is decisive and compelling.[17]

[2] The characteristics of the practical syllogism

What difference does this gathering of all practical syllogisms into one general type make for one's conception of practical reason and ethics? In order to answer this question, we need to know more about what a practical syllogism is—i.e., what are its characteristics or, at least, what are some of its major ones. At this point I depart somewhat from Nussbaum's account in order to rely more directly on Anthony Kenny, who, to my mind, has done the most in recent years to improve our understanding of the practical syllogism. His account of the practical syllogism is by no means incompatible with Nussbaum's general approach; indeed, in several ways it provides better support for it than Nussbaum's own account.[18]

Since the practical syllogism is a piece of reasoning about goods, it has a peculiar structure and a peculiar logic. Let us consider again the "cloak syllogism" from *MA*: "I need covering, a cloak is a covering: I need a cloak. What I need, I have to make; I need a cloak. I have to make a cloak. And the conclusion, the 'I have to make a cloak,' is an action" [*MA* vii,701a17–20]. Normally—that is, in Aristotle's *Prior* and *Posterior Analytics*—when one be-

---

16. Nussbaum (1978), pp. 189–90.

17. Among Allan's modern critics are also Wiggins and Cooper. Wiggins writes: "The walk syllogism like the next syllogism would have to be treated as a dummy syllogism, a mere variable in any case. For even if Allan's distinction between two kinds of syllogism could stand, the syllogism would be an idiotic example of either" [Wiggins (1980 <1975–1976>), p. 229]. In Cooper (1986 <1975>), see pp. 2–5, 25 (n. 27), 47 (especially n. 57).

18. See Burnyeat (1981), p. 188, where he complains that Nussbaum relies too heavily on von Wright (e.g. *The Varieties of Goodness*) and not enough on Kenny in her analysis of the Aristotelian practical syllogism. He notes, for instance, that she persists in speaking of entailment, although entailment in the usual sense is not at work in the practical syllogism.

gins the process of constructing syllogisms, one has a supply of propositions, potential premises. Combinations of these premises, provided that the premisses fall into valid "moods" (Barbara, Celarent, etc.), *produce* conclusions.[19] This same "direction" of activity is in evidence in any proof in any book of modern logic. First the premises are set out (along with abbreviations for rules employed, etc.); the proof then finishes with its conclusion. That we say of the conclusion that it *follows* (from the premises) has a certain extra-logical appropriateness.

The most characteristic feature of the practical syllogism is that it proceeds in quite a different direction. Consider the following two syllogisms, the first {A} a standard "deductive" syllogism, the second {B} one of the practical syllogisms we have already seen:

{A}   Needed-thing holds of every coveRing.
      coveRing holds of every cloaK
      Thus, Needed-thing holds of every cloaK

{B}   coveRing leads to Need-satisfaction
      cloaK leads to coveRing
      Thus, cloaK leads to Need-satisfaction

Syllogism {A} clearly has a downward direction. One might say that its point is to "nail down" the truth in this particular instance: if **N** holds of every **R**, and **R** holds of every **K**, then **K** cannot get out from under **N** since it is under **R** and **R** is under **N**.[20] But in syllogism {B}, the point is to get *to* the "major term," the satisfaction of a need (the need for warmth).[21] That is, in {A} the "direction" is like this:

19. See *An.pr.* i,28. For the valid syllogistic moods, see chapter 8, section [2]. Note that at *MA* vii,701a11 Aristotle speaks of "putting together" a theoretical syllogism from its premises. At *Phys.* ii,3,195a18–19, he speaks of the premises of a syllogism as the (apparently) material cause of a conclusion. Alexander of Aphrodisias interprets this passage as suggesting that the premises are the efficient causes of the conclusion [in Simplicius, *in Phys.* (vol. 9) 320.1–11]. On Alexander's understanding, see Flannery (1995d), pp. 142–44.

20. This is not incompatible with what I argue in Appendix B—i.e., that the general direction of the {4}-{1}-{2} structure is upwards, at least as regards the major premise and the conclusion. Aristotle, however, can maintain that causation is in fact teleological (and, therefore, in a sense practical) without denying that finding out about the teleological character of nature is a matter of "nailing things down."

21. For the idea of the direction in which a piece of reasoning proceeds, see Hintikka and Remes (1974), pp. xiv, 11, 38, etc. "In the Middle Ages and in much of the later literature, analysis is simply identified with proceeding 'upstream,' in a direction contrary to that of logical or causal

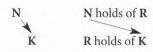

Whereas, in {B} the "direction" is like this:

The basic unit of ethical thinking is, therefore, nothing like: 'ought-not-to-do holds of every killing of the innocent; killing of the innocent holds of every act of abortion; therefore, ought-not-to-do holds of every act of abortion.' The basic unit is rather more like: 'Life is part of human flourishing; protecting children promotes human life; protect children.' Under this understanding, therefore, ethics has more to do with human flourishing than with following rules for the sake of following rules.[22]

Another major peculiarity of the practical syllogism is that it does not entail (i.e., necessitate) its conclusion. Suppose that one's practical reasoning consists in this (abbreviated) practical syllogism: 'covering meets my need; a cloak gives me a covering; I get a cloak.' But suppose also that all the cloaks are contaminated by poisonous insects. Practically speaking, one is not bound to get a cloak. One can, if one wants, get a blanket (presuming that the blankets are not contaminated). This characteristic of the practical syllogism is often referred to as its "defeasibility": the conclusion of a practical syllogism is "defeatable" by extraneous factors.[23] This cannot happen in theoretical reason. If it is the case that 'A holds of B' and 'B holds of C,' then 'A holds of

---

implications, while synthesis is identified with proceeding 'downstream' along a sequence of logical inferences or causal connections" (p. 11). I discuss analysis and synthesis in chapters 3 and 8.

22. Kenny makes the point about the direction of practical reason somewhat differently. In practical reason, he notes, one begins with where one wants to go ("I need covering"), and then casts about for ways ("means") to get there ("a cloak is a covering: I need a cloak"). In normal— i.e., non-practical logic—to say 'if p then q,' then to affirm q, and then (as a consequence) to affirm p, is a fallacy: the fallacy known as "affirming the consequent." But in a practical syllogism one reasons in just that way: one begins with q ('I need a covering'), then asserts 'if p then q' ('if I make a cloak, I shall have a covering'), then "asserts" p ('I must make a cloak'). See Kenny (1975), pp. 70, 83.

23. Kenny (1975), pp. 92ff.; also Geach (1972), p. 286. Chisholm formalizes the defeasibility of obligation in Chisholm (1978 <1974>).

C' follows, whatever else may be the case in the universe. The practical syllo-gism does not work like that.[24]

Kenny has pointed out that, also in theoretical reason, no one is *forced* by the laws of logic to draw a conclusion.[25] If it is the case that 'A holds of B' and 'B holds of C,' a particular individual might not see—or might be unwilling to draw—the conclusion that 'A holds of C'; and he can do this without vio-lating any logical law. But this does not go against the idea that a practical syl-logism is defeasible in a characteristic way. In the first place, in the theoretical sphere, even if a particular individual does not see or is unwilling to draw a particular conclusion, the conclusion does follow. This does not happen in the practical sphere, since in the practical sphere there is no such thing as a conclusion that no one actually draws, for the conclusion to a practical syllo-gism is an action (or, at least, a choice).[26] Secondly, even if in a certain sense a theoretical syllogism is defeasible—i.e., insofar as a person, without violating any law of logic, might not draw the proper conclusion—a certain stigma at-taches to one who does not draw the conclusion: he is considered dull-witted or, in any case, very stubborn. No such stigma attaches in practical reason. Indeed, allowing for the defeasibility of practical syllogisms is part of being practically reasonable. Thus, whatever the truth of Kenny's point, the practi-cal syllogism is defeasible in a characteristic way.

Both these aspects of the practical syllogism—its peculiar "direction" and its defeasibility—allow us to speak of a general difference between the practi-cal syllogism and the better-known, standard, theoretical syllogism. The latter,

24. See *ST* I–II q.13 a.6 ad 1 and ad 2. In ad 2, Aquinas associates the necessity of the practical syllogism with hypothetical necessity. See also *De ver.* q.22 a.6 ad 4.

25. Kenny (1979), p. 144; also Nussbaum (1978), p. 342. The point is basically a Wittgensteinian one: see Wittgenstein (1978 <1956>), p. 50 (§34); Wittgenstein (1968 <1953>), §201. See also Flannery and Moser (1985), *passim*. As Nussbaum points out, Aristotle himself makes the point at *An.pr.* ii,21,67a33ff.

26. Perhaps too we could say this: that the defeasibility of theoretical deduction that Kenny talks about is actually in the practical sphere. According to this conception, the conclusion would (in the theoretical sphere) follow but the person would choose (in the practical sphere) not to as-sent to it. There are problems, however, with such an approach—but not uninteresting ones. It might mean, for instance, that theoretical reason would, strictly speaking, involve no *seeking* of answers. This would be consistent with Barnes's interpretation of Aristotelian science, according to which *An.post.* "does not describe how scientists do, or ought to, *acquire* knowledge: it offers a model of how teachers ought to *impart* knowledge" [Barnes (1969), p. 138, emphasis his]. See also Barnes (1981) and Barnes's partial retraction of the thesis of Barnes (1969) in Barnes (1994 <1975>), pp. xviii–xx.

suggests Kenny, is "truth preserving," whereas the former is "good preserving." That is, in the standard syllogism, the truth of the premisses ensures the truth of the conclusion. In the practical syllogism, they ensure (as best they can) that we get to where we are going. It establishes a link between a goal and an action in such a way that the good of the goal is preserved in the action.[27]

[3] Means and component parts

Fairly obviously, then, rejecting Allan's approach and accepting that of Nussbaum and Kenny is going to have wide-ranging repercussions within one's understanding of Aristotelian ethics, for it means that something like means-end reasoning, with its orientation toward goods rather than toward the acceptance of rules, becomes the dominant pattern of moral reasoning. Ethics comes to have more of an "upward" direction, as opposed to the "top-down" direction than Allan conceives of when he speaks of "actions . . . subsumed by intuition under general rules."[28] No longer is the conscious pursuit of goods put in a compartment separate from properly-speaking ethical considerations, as in Allan; the practical syllogism becomes the central type of practical reasoning. This, combined with the practical syllogism's defeasibility, introduces into ethics a certain welcome looseness—in short, the freedom that Nussbaum claims is missing under the "deductivist" understanding.

But does not the Nussbaum-Kenny approach also present certain problems? If the types of practical syllogism in *MA* vii are not distinct in the way that Allan suggests, are we to say that *EN* iii, where Aristotle seems to regard ethics quite generally as a matter of performing actions in order to gain an ulterior good, represents his considered opinion? Like Allan, we recoil from this, believing that at least something in morals must be less business-like and

---

27. Kenny (1979), pp. 128, 144–46. The expressions "truth preserving" and "good preserving" (borrowed from Kenny) are not completely satisfactory since, with a practical syllogism, one is not necessarily seeking to *preserve* anything but, more properly, to get to some good which is not yet. Also, it needs to be acknowledged—what shall be discussed several times in this book—that practical reason is not unconnected with issues of truth. "Dicendum, quod theoricus sive speculativus intellectus in hoc proprie ab operativo sive practico distinguitur, quod speculativus habet pro fine veritatem quam considerat, practicus vero veritatem consideratam ordinat in operationem tamquam in finem" [*in Trin.* q.5 a.1 c ll.93–98]. When making this point, Thomas invariably cites Aristotle's *De an.* iii,10,433a14–15 and *Metaph.* ii,1,993b20–21. See also *ST* I q.14 a.16 c; *De ver.* q.3 a.3 c. I discuss the relationship between practical and theoretical syllogisms in a fairly formal way in chapter 8.

28. Allan (1955), p. 336.

calculating. And, in any case, it is quite incompatible with the distinction that Aristotle insists upon elsewhere between making *(poiēsis)* and action *(praxis)*—only the latter (which has itself as its end) pertaining to ethics proper.[29] Unless we are simply to say that Aristotle in *EN* iii is being inconsistent, there must be a way of understanding both types of practical syllogism as sharing a similar structure without having to say that all of ethics is a matter of pursuing an extrinsic end.

And, indeed, there is recoverable from Aristotle's writings just such a way of associating—without regarding as identical—means-end reasoning and the reasoning we do when we simply act well and morally, with no ulterior motive. It is recoverable from the very phrase which initially led Allan to say that *EN* iii was earlier than *EN* vi and which, in the *EN* iii passage quoted above, was translated as "the means."[30] The phrase *ta pros to telos* need not be so translated but admits also of a "vaguer" meaning, signifying not so much "means to an end" as "things that are for the end."[31] So understood, the phrase might comprise also constituent parts of the end. The potion (i.e., the means) that a doctor prescribes for a patient is among the "things that are for the end" *(ta pros to telos)*, which end is his patient's health. But health itself is also among the "things that are for the end" of any person insofar as he seeks health as a constituent part of happiness.[32] Similarly, we might get on a bus (i.e., take that means) in order to visit a friend; but we visit the friend because we realize it is part of living well and morally. We do not regard friendship as a means to happiness in the sense that, if it did not get us there, we would cease to engage in it. Happiness, i.e., the good life, is *in* friendship. We pursue friendship for its own sake.

---

29. *EN* vi,5,1140b6–7: τῆς μὲν γὰρ ποιήσεως ἕτερον τὸ τέλος, τῆς δὲ πράξεως οὐκ ἂν εἴη· ἔστι γὰρ αὐτὴ ἡ εὐπραξία τέλος. See also *MM* i,34,1197a4–10.

30. See above, note 9. This understanding of *ta pros to telos* is also found, for instance, at Grant (1885), vol. 2, pp. 25–26; Stewart (1892), vol. 1, pp. 248–49; and Rackham (1975 <1934>), p. 131 (translation of *EN* iii,2,1111b27). Aristotle uses the phrase at *EN* iii,2,1111b27, iii,3,1113a14–15, iii,5,1113b4, vi,13,1145a6; see also *EN* vi,9,1142b29–33.

31. Hardie (1968), p. 256. See also Greenwood (1973 <1909>), pp. 46–48.

32. *EN* vi,12,1144a3–5 (also vi,13,1145a6–11); *EE* viii,3,1249b9–13. There have not been wanting interpreters of Thomas who regard most of the moral life as means to an ulterior end. See, for instance, Lottin (1924), p. 339, n. 1: "Le but de la vie spirituelle, écrit saint Thomas, est de s'unir à Dieu par la charité et de s'y disposer par la purification du coeur. Tout le reste n'est qu'un moyen." Lottin cites *Quodl.* V q.10 a.1 [19] ll.94–95 (§112) [= Lottin's *Quodl.* 5 a.19], although Thomas's words ("omnia . . . alia quae sunt spiritualis vitae, ordinantur . . . sicut in finem") can certainly be read in a non-instrumental way.

We can analyze actions involved in friendship by means of the practical syllogism since they involve a sort of aiming at the good. (The friendly visit is also defeasible since, given certain circumstances, one might not make it and still be a friend.) But this "aiming at the good" is not the artful sort of aiming which falls short of fully ethical behavior (see *EN* ii,4). The good of friendship is inherent in being a friend itself; it is nothing other than being a friend. This close relationship between good and concrete behavior in which it is embedded is characteristically Aristotelian.

[4] Limits to looseness?

The looseness of the practical syllogism, as depicted by Kenny and Nussbaum, accords well with a good number of places in Aristotle where he speaks about the improvisational character of practical reasoning—places where he acknowledges that there is much in human ethics which is not determinable in advance (a fact which allows room, incidentally, for free choice and human creativity). In *EN* ii,2, for instance, we read:

[M]atters concerned with conduct and questions of what is good for us have no fixity, any more than matters of health. The general account being of this nature, the account of particular cases is yet more lacking in exactness; for they do not fall under any art or set of precepts, but the agents themselves must in each case consider what is appropriate to the occasion, as happens also in the art of medicine or of navigation.[33]

He characterizes those who would demand exactness in ethics as uneducated: "for it is the mark of an educated man to look for precision in each class of things just so far as the nature of the thing admits: it is evidently equally foolish to accept probable reasoning from a mathematician and to demand from a rhetorician demonstrative proofs."[34] All these citations show that for Aristotle ethics is a dynamic enterprise in which all the answers are not given in advance—even potentially. Ethics requires, indeed, the reflection and moral instincts of good men, whose decisions and deliberations are more like the actions of an artist than those of an applier of rules.

---

33. *EN* ii,2,1104a3–10. For other places where Aristotle talks about the imprecision of ethics, see *EN* i,3,1094b19–22; see also *EN* i,7,1098a26–29, *EN* ii,2,1103b34–1104a10, etc., etc.

34. *EN* i,3,1094b23–27. Thomas takes the same approach. Not only does he, in his commentary on the *Ethics*, expound the Aristotelian position accurately, but in the *Summa theologiae* he cites the remark approvingly and uses the idea often: *in EN* lb.1 lect.3 ll.70–93 (§36); *ST* I–II q.96 a.1 ad 3; *ST* II–II q.47 a.9 ad 2; q.60 a.3 ad 1; q.70 a.2.

But there is a problem with this approach if we push it so far as to say that, according to Aristotle, there are no fixed rules of conduct. For despite his many caveats about the imprecision of ethics, Aristotle also says quite straightforwardly that

[n]ot every action nor every passion admits of a mean; for some have names that already imply badness, e.g. spite, shamelessness, envy, and in the case of actions, adultery, theft, murder. For all of these and suchlike things imply by their names that they are themselves bad, and not the excesses or deficiencies of them. It is not possible, then, ever to be right with regard to them; one must always be wrong. Nor does goodness or badness with regard to such things depend on committing adultery with the right woman, at the right time, and in the right way, but simply to do any of them is to go wrong.[35]

How to explain this? How to reconcile this passage—and other similar passages—with Aristotle's repeated cautions against fixity in ethics? The solution comes in a consideration of the structure of practical reason itself.

[5] The general structure of practical reason

Although within practical reason, as we have seen, the reasoning process is decidedly different from what we find in theoretical reason, the general structure of practical reason is still that of an Aristotelian science. We receive indications of this in Aristotle's selection of vocabulary and examples. In *An.post.*, for example, as part of an extended argument to the effect that universal demonstrations are better than particular ones, he employs, side-by-side, examples drawn from geometry and from the practical realm.[36] In the same

35. *EN* ii,6,1107a8–17. See also *EN* iii,1,1110a26–27, where Aristotle says that "some acts, perhaps, we cannot be forced to do, but ought rather to face death after the most fearful sufferings." See also *EE* ii,3,1221b18–26. Some modern interpreters have argued (usually with respect to the *EN* ii,6 passage) that Aristotle is making a logical or formal point: i.e., he is saying simply that *terms* such as 'adultery,' 'murder,' etc., have pejorative connotations (see for example [Hardie (1968), p. 137]), what they refer to being another matter. For a good criticism of this approach, see Finnis (1991b), pp. 31–37. Finnis points out that Hardie "does not tell us how to read the sentence, 'Goodness or badness with regard to such things does not depend on committing adultery with the right woman, at the right time, and in the right way'" [Finnis (1991b), p. 32]. Finnis makes the same point with regard to *EE* ii,3,1221b20–21, where Aristotle says, "A man is not an adulterer through having intercourse with married women more than he ought (there is no such thing): that is already a vice." Finnis's argument also includes an interesting treatment of remarks by Aspasius and "the Scholiast," the latter's remarks having been discussed by Albert the Great, Robert Grosseteste, and Thomas. See also Finnis (1998), pp. 163–70.

36 *An.post.* i,24,85a20ff., particularly 85b30–86a3.

work, in the midst of a discussion of how to identify things that are predicated "in what a thing is" (such as are necessary for demonstrations), Aristotle
introduces an argument about different senses of the word 'pride' [*megalop-
suchia*].[37] In *EN* he uses the language of the syllogistic when discussing the
deliberations of the *akratēs*, and he uses the language of demonstration when
discussing the good habits necessary for the study of ethics.[38]

Most importantly of all, however, Aristotle speaks repeatedly of first principles *(archai)* or sometimes "the first principle" *(archē)* of practical reason as
parallel to the first principles of theoretical reason. In *EN* vi,5 for instance,
while discussing various differences between *phronēsis* and more theoretical
knowledge, he remarks that the person who becomes morally corrupt does
not lose grip of beliefs such as the belief that triangles have angles equal to
two right angles but rather of beliefs about what is to be done. "For the principles [*archai*] of the things that are done consist in that for the sake of which
they are to be done" [1140b16–17]. And in *EN* vii,8, he remarks that "excellence and vice respectively preserve and destroy the first principle [*archē*],
and, in actions, that for the sake of which is the first principle, as the hypotheses are in mathematics" [1151a15–17]. According to Aristotle, the major
structurally related difference between practical and theoretical reason is that

37. *An.post.* i,13,97b15–25; see also Thomas's *in An.post.* lb.2 lect.16 ll.39–65 (§554). At *in
An.post.* lb.1 lect.44 ll.317–50 (§406), while discussing Aristotle's remark that acumen (ἀγχίνοια
or, in William of Moerbeke's Latin, *solercia*) is a certain facility in finding middle terms [*media*],
Thomas notes that Aristotle's examples are taken from both the practical and the theoretical
spheres (ll.347–50). Thomas also suggests a number of times in *in An.post.* that the structure of
sciences comes from practical concerns, rather than vice-versa. In the *prooemium*, for instance, he
begins by saying that it is the peculiar characteristic of man to direct his own acts by mean of reason: "nihil enim aliud ars esse videtur, quam certa ordinatio rationis, quomodo per determinata
media ad debitum finem actus humani perveniatur" [*in An.post.* lb.1 lect.1 ll.9–12 (§1)]. He then
goes on to include under this rubric all the various sciences, arts, and disciplines—including
those discussed in the *Posterior Analytics* and *Nicomachean Ethics* (and also in *Topics, Rhetoric,*
and *Poetics,* etc.) [lb.1 lect.1 ll.75ff. (§6)]. See also *in An.post.* lb.1 lect.41 ll.136–141 (§362): ". . . est
autem cuiuslibet scientiae finis sive terminus genus circa quod est scientia, quia in speculativis
scientiis nihil aliud quaeritur quam cognitio generis subiecti, in practicis autem scientiis intenditur quasi finis constructio ipsius subiecti"; also lb.1 lect.4 ll.137–39 (§36): "definit syllogismum
demonstrativum per comparationem ad finem suum, qui est scire"; also lb.1 lect.41 ll.162–64
(§363): "ad cuius evidentiam considerandum est quod, sicut iam dictum est, progressus scientiae
consistit in quodam motu rationis discurrentis ab uno in aliud."
38. *EN* vii,3,1146b35–1147a10; i,4,1095a30ff. See also *EN* iii,3,1112b20–24: "the person who deliberates seems to inquire and analyse . . . as though he were analysing a geometrical construction"
(I discuss this passage in chapter 3). See also *EE* ii,6,1222b15–42, ii,10,1227a8–9 and ii,11,1227b28–30;
also *MM* i,10,1187a29–b11; also *Phys.* ii,3,194b32–34 and ii,9,200a15–30—cited by Thomas at *ST*
I–II q.13 a.3 c.

the goods at which we aim are more closely connected with experience than are their theoretical counterparts.[39] We could obviously add that practical reasoning has an upward direction and that its "derivations" are not strictly speaking derivations at all. But practical reason's actual structure is the same as theoretical reason's: the whole edifice depends on the first principles—which are the ends, i.e., the goods that humans seek.

If then within ethics much is indeterminate and awaits the prudent judgment of the wise but certain other things are absolutely ruled out, it would seem reasonable to associate these latter with ethics' first principles. The geometer, says Aristotle, does not and ought not to provide arguments for the first principles of geometry since this would be to step out of geometry itself: he would not be acting *qua* geometer [*An.post.* i,12,77b3–15]. Geometry itself can proceed effectively only if it assumes that certain ideas, certain concepts are fixed [*An.post.* i,2,72a25–72b4]. So also in ethics. The student of ethics must already have a grasp of the first principles; otherwise "his study will be vain and unprofitable" [*EN* i,3,1095a5]. The moral predicament of the person who grows corrupt through seeking pleasure and avoiding all pain is precisely that he ceases to perceive the *archai* [*EN* vi,5,1140b16–20]. The person who is merely weak of will (the *akratēs*) is better off than the one who is totally corrupt (the *akolastos*) since "the best thing in him, the first principle, is preserved" [*EN* vii,8,1151a25–26]. The closer a person's bad behavior impinges upon ethical first principles, the more serious it is, for the very sense of ethics depends on them.

If this is right—i.e., that the essentially dynamic activity of ethics takes place against an enduring background—we would expect to find passages in Aristotle where he restricts the scope of his observations about the flexibility and imprecision of ethics. And, indeed, we do find just that. The first section

---

39. *EN* vi,11,1143b4–5: ἀρχαὶ γὰρ τοῦ οὗ ἕνεκα αὗται· ἐκ τῶν καθ' ἕκαστα γὰρ τὰ καθόλου· τούτων οὖν ἔχειν δεῖ αἴσθησιν, αὕτη δ' ἐστὶ νοῦς; see also i,4,1095a30–b13, especially 1095b4–8: διὸ δεῖ τοῖς ἔθεσιν ἦχθαι καλῶς τὸν περὶ καλῶν καὶ δικαίων καὶ ὅλως τῶν πολιτικῶν ἀκουσόμενον ἱκανῶς. ἀρχὴ γὰρ τὸ ὅτι, καὶ εἰ τοῦτο φαίνοιτο ἀρκούντως, οὐδὲν προσδεήσει τοῦ διότι· ὁ δὲ τοιοῦτος ἔχει ἢ λάβοι ἂν ἀρχὰς ῥαδίως. Note the ambiguity in the last phrase about whether, as a well-brought-up youth, one begins with the *archai* or goes to them. Stewart argues (with respect to the first passage) that "The sharp contrast drawn between the νοῦς θεωρητικός and the νοῦς πρακτικός . . . is indeed very misleading. A καθόλου is at first dimly seen *by each* in the material setting of the καθ' ἕκαστα belonging to its sphere; and *each*, using its own peculiar method—νοῦς θεωρητικός using ἐπαγωγή and νοῦς πρακτικός using ἐθισμός—comes to apprehend its καθόλου more clearly" [Stewart (1892), vol. 2, p. 93; emphasis his].

of *EN* ix,2 is taken up by a discussion of various things in the practical life that are not easily decidable. After asserting that a certain degree of precision *is* possible with respect to the question whether to pay back a debt rather than help a friend, Aristotle says: "But perhaps even this is not always true; e.g. should a man who has been ransomed out of the hands of brigands ransom his ransomer in return, whoever he may be (or pay him if he has not been captured but requests payment), or should he ransom his own father?" [*EN* ix,2,1164b33–65a1]. What is required here is prudence—a certain weighing of factors, attending to how it feels as one option is contemplated rather than another. If one's father is not in grave danger, one might feel obliged to pay back the debt first. But if the person owed the debt is a crook and has rescued one for selfish or evil motives, one might not be obliged to pay him back at all [1165a5–10]. Then Aristotle says: "*As we have said therefore many times, reasonings about feelings and actions have the definiteness corresponding to that about which they treat.*"[40] As we have seen, Aristotle has, indeed, over the course of these lectures on ethics, often asserted that ethics does not admit of precision. Here at 1165a12–14 he tells us what he had in mind in making these assertions: cases tending toward one end of the scale and calling for an educated estimate or prognostication rather than the application of an invariable rule.

The closer a case approaches the first principles, the less room for doubt there will be. When speaking about ethics' indeterminacy, Aristotle often draws a parallel with medicine, which similarly must often make decisions based not on fixed rules but on the weighing of factors peculiar to the case at hand.[41] But, although many things in medicine fall into this class—for example, whether in a particular instance to operate or to attempt to cure with drugs—there are other things that are quite clear. A doctor ought not to cut off a patient's head, for example. In the above-quoted passage in which Aristotle says that some matters "have no fixity, any more than matters of health," we do not interpret him as denying that such fixed medical principles exist. So neither ought we to interpret him as saying that there are no fixed

---

40. ὅπερ οὖν πολλάκις εἴρηται, οἱ περὶ τὰ πάθη καὶ τὰς πράξεις λόγοι ὁμοίως ἔχουσι τὸ ὡρισμένον τοῖς περὶ ἅ εἰσιν[1165a12–14; my emphasis].

41. See note 33; Aristotle makes the comparison with medicine at *EN* ii,2,1104a4–5 and also 1104a9–10 (quoted above).

principles in ethics—especially since a number of times he makes mention of them.

[6] The basis of the first principles of ethics

So, *pace* Nussbaum, some "general rules" in Aristotle are more than mere "rules of thumb"; they can even be considered "objectively valid norms" or "laws of nature." What then can we say of Nussbaum's other contention, that Aristotelian ethics has nothing to do with attunement to something beyond humanity—nothing to do, that is, with attunement to the divine?

It will have been noticed, no doubt, that, when (as reported above) Aristotle speaks about the stability of the first principles of a science like geometry, he does not deny outright that they are revisable. He says only that "for the principles, the geometer as geometer should not supply an argument" [*An.post.* i,12,77b5–6] and that the person who wishes to work within a science must be "familiar with the principles and be better convinced of them than of what is being proved" [i,2,72a37–39]. But can it be shown that Aristotle thought the first principles of at least practical reason are fixed and secure? One might want to argue by straightforward citation that, since in the *Posterior Analytics* Aristotle describes first principles in general as necessary [i,6,74b5], they are not revisable; but this would only shift the argument to the much-disputed question, whether Aristotle is presenting in *An.post.* a model for the actual prosecution of science or a model of the ideal science. If the latter, then someone might argue that, on the way to the forever-receding ideal science, first principles are always revisable, if not by the geometer then by someone else, and that talk about fixed principles in Aristotle is therefore an illusion.[42]

---

42. I am inclined, in fact, to believe that *An.post.* does in some sense present a model of the perfect science. This is also Thomas's position. See *in An.post.* lb.1 lect.4 ll.149–53 (§36), where he says that Aristotle's remark "by scientific I mean [a syllogism] in virtue of which, by having it, we understand something" [*An.post.* i,2,71b18–19] is made "lest by 'scientific syllogism' anyone understand that which some science *uses*" (my emphasis) ["dicens quod scientialis syllogismus dicitur, secundum quem scimus in quantum ipsum habemus, ne forte aliquis syllogismum scientialem intelligeret quo aliqua scientia uteretur"]. The concept 'to use' [*uti*] is a central one in Thomas. He defines it at *ST* I–II q.16 a.1 c by saying, "The use of a thing implies the application of that thing to an operation." At *in Sent.* lb.1 d.1 q.1 a.2 c, he recognizes a number of different meanings of the word, noting especially its employment with respect to things that are ordered toward the attaining of some end. This can involve a number of operations (or faculties), he says, including reason: "the first is the operation of reason as it predetermines an end and orders and directs to-

Is there not, however, another way to show that at least some first principles are fixed? As we have noted, the geometer, *qua* geometer, does not question his own first principles. Aristotle discusses this idea about the particular
sciences a number of times in his metaphysics, for it is to that discipline or
science that the principles of the other sciences especially pertain.

All these sciences [he says] mark off some particular being—some genus, and enquire
into this, but not into being simply nor *qua* being, nor do they offer any discussion of
the essence of the things of which they treat; but starting from the essence—some
making it plain to the senses, others assuming it as a hypothesis—they then demonstrate, more or less cogently, the essential attributes of the genus with which they deal.
[*Metaph.* vi,1,1025b7–13]

It is the task of metaphysics—or the science of being *qua* being—to consider
these things that the other sciences use but do not treat of: i.e., their first
principles [1025b3]. As we shall see in chapter 3, this does not mean that the
particular sciences are incomplete before the metaphysician comes along to
"ground" their first principles. This is part of Aristotle's reason for saying that
the geometer *qua* geometer does not provide arguments for geometry's first
principles: a science has an intelligibility all its own. It does, however, mean
that, although a science certainly contains knowledge of its own first principles, it cannot produce it [*An.post.* i,1]. The particular sciences depend upon
first principles, not first principles upon the sciences. Thus, the sciences look
to something beyond themselves. Sometimes this "something beyond" is
found in the sensible world; sometimes it is simply a new and different hypothesis—such as that parallel lines *do* meet.[43] But, in whatever type of case, a
principle is not proved within the science upon which it comes to bear.

We can say a similar thing about practical reason—i.e., that it receives
support from beyond itself, even while this support corresponds to some-

---

ward it" ["Prima est operatio rationis praestituentis finem et ordinantis et dirigentis in ipsum"].
This language is quite similar to what we find in the *prooemium* to *in An.post.* where Thomas describes the origins of science as a practical pursuit (see especially lb.1 lect.1 ll.8&13 (§1)). For the
controversy regarding the applicability of the *Posterior Analytics* to scientific investigation, see
MacIntyre (1990a), pp. 23ff.; Barnes (1969), *passim*; Barnes (1994 <1975>), pp. xviii–xx; see also
the discussion of more recent work on p. xx of the latter.
    43. Aristotle discusses the non-convergence of parallel lines (i.e., what became Euclid's fifth
postulate) at *An.post.* i,12,77b22–24; see also *An.pr.* ii,16,65a4–5; ii,17,66a13. In the *Posterior
Analytics* passage he says that the denial of the postulate is a paralogism, but a peculiar one: it is
in a sense geometrical and in another sense non-geometrical. See Toth (1997), *passim*.

thing within. This is partly the reason for Aristotle's inclusion of an extended discussion of leverage at the beginning of *De motu animalium* (in connection with which, it will be remembered, Nussbaum develops her interpretation of Aristotle's ethics). He begins by noting that, when an animal moves, we must always conceive of something remaining steady—at least relatively. If a person bends an arm, for instance, the elbow serves as the fulcrum, about which the movement is effected [*MA* i]. But such internal points of rest require also external ones: "For just as there must be something immovable within the animal, if it is to be moved, so even more must there be something immovable outside it, by supporting itself upon which that which is moved moves" [*MA* ii,698b12–15]. He uses as an example the ease with which a boat is moved if one pushes against the mast from outside with a pole, as opposed to pushing against the mast while inside the boat [*MA* ii,698b21–24].

Aristotle goes on to apply these various conceits to the movement of animals and, in particular, to the movement of the human soul. Just as all inanimate things are moved by some other thing, so also the motions of animate things "have a limit"—i.e., the explanation of these motions stops at "that for the sake of which." "For all living things both move and are moved for the sake of something, so that this is the limit of all their movement—that for the sake of which" [*MA* vi,700b15–16]. These limits, says Aristotle, are the objects of desire and intellect; that is, they are not just any objects of the intellect but those which motivate: the practical goods [700b23–28]. Included among them would also be the apparent good and the pleasant, since they do motivate animals [700b28–29]. Together, these goods constitute the first principles of the motion of the soul, the first principles of practical reason.[44] They are the fulcra—the "limits"—of the practical life.

The first principles of practical reason are, like those of the particular sciences, investigated by metaphysics—i.e., by wisdom or first philosophy. But there is an important difference. The first principles of practical reason *are*

---

44. *MA* vi,700b10; this point is made more expansively at *EE* i,8,1218b7–24. In commenting on *MA* vi and while considering the end of practical reason (τὸ τῶν πρακτῶν τέλος—*MA* vi,700b25), Michael of Ephesus mentions especially "the products of crafts" (τὸ τέλος πρακτόν, ὡς ἐπὶ τῶν τεχναστῶν καὶ ἄλλων τινῶν, τούτων καὶ τὸ τέλος προαιρετόν ...) [*in MA* 113.25–26; see also 116.4–5]. This is consistent with what is argued especially in chapters 7 and 8 of the present work—i.e., that the practical good is found in the various substructures of practical reason, which include the crafts.

also, in a certain sense, the first principles of metaphysics. Says Aristotle in *Metaph.* i,2:

And the science that knows to what end each thing must be done is the most authoritative of the sciences, and more authoritative than any ancillary science; and this end is the good in each class, and in general the supreme good in the whole of nature. Judged by all the tests we have mentioned, then, the name in question [i.e., 'wisdom'] falls to the same science; this must be a science that investigates the first principles and causes; for the good, i.e. that for the sake of which, is one of the causes. [*Metaph.* i,2,982b4–b10]

Aristotle is speaking here, of course, about metaphysics, the science "that investigates the first principles and causes." It is true that, in a certain sense, the first principles of practical reason are not the absolutely highest principles, for practical reason is primarily occupied with human goods and "man is not the best thing in the universe" [*EN* vi,7,1141a21–22]; but, as the quotation shows, even the pursuit of human goods is linked to the pursuit of the supreme good.[45]

Aristotle addresses this issue also at the beginning of *Metaph.* xii,10, where he asks how the nature of the universe contains "the good—that is, the highest good: whether as something separate and by itself, or as the order of the parts" [1075a11–13]. His answer is that it is contained in both ways, as the good that a general seeks is contained in his subordinates, who seek the goals that he determines, but especially in himself: "for he does not depend on the order but it depends on him" [1075a15].

This special status of the first principles of practical reason, linked as they are to the supreme good, means for Aristotle that they are in some sense divine. Properly speaking, we do not praise the gods, he says in *EN* i,12, for they stand outside the system of human achievement; rather, we bless them and

45. This is, of course, not to say that Aristotle does not distinguish the concerns of metaphysics (or "wisdom") from practical concerns. He discusses this matter extensively in *EN* vi. The relationship between metaphysics and prudence [*phronēsis*] is like that between health and medicine. Prudence "is not *supreme* over wisdom, i.e., over the superior part of us, any more than the art of medicine is over health; for it does not use it but provides for its coming into being; it issues orders, then, for its sake but not to it" [*EN* vi,13,1145a6–9; emphasis in ROT]. To maintain the primacy of *phronēsis* over *sophia* "would be like saying that the art of politics rules the gods because it issues orders about all the affairs of state" [1145a10–11]. (Here too it is apparent that human goods are connected with the divine.) For Thomas's understanding of the relationship between metaphysics and the other disciplines see *in Sent.* lb.1 *prologus* q.1 a.2; see also Dewan (1997); see also chapter 3, sections [1] to [3].

call them happy. "So too with good things; no one praises happiness as he does justice; rather, he blesses it, as being something more divine and better."[46] Justice [*to dikaion*] is praised because, even if it is a constituent part of happiness, it is still linked to actions that have an end. Happiness, on the other hand, *is* the end. It is a first principle, says Aristotle; "it is for the sake of this that we all do everything else, and the first principle and cause of goods is, we claim, something prized and divine" [1102a2–4].

It is likely that Aristotle did regard the first principles of the particular sciences as revisable, for it is hardly possible to be an active scientist and not realize that sometimes an adjusted principle will improve an explanation. It is one of the theoretical advantages of understanding the *Posterior Analytics* as a model of the ideal science that it allows for such revision without creating great difficulties in the interpretation of Aristotle.[47] But we cannot regard the first principles of practical reason as revisable. They are the most basic things regarded by humans as good or worth pursuing—knowledge, life, play, practical reasonableness, etc.; and such things do not vary.[48] We shall never come across a person seeking an entirely new and unheard of basic human good. Indeed, if we did, how would we know what he was doing? How could we make sense of it? In any case, that Aristotle regarded the first principles of practical reason as unrevisable is quite apparent, not only from his identifying them with the first principles of metaphysics itself, but also from his associating them with the divine, for the latter, although certainly dynamic, is, to his mind, constant and invariable.[49]

To conclude, then, Professor Nussbaum maintains, as we have seen, that Aristotle's ethical approach is "very much like Rawls's notion of 'wide reflective equilibrium,' which explicitly rejects appeals to the a priori," i.e., which explicitly rejects moral absolutes and has nothing to do with "heavenly first principles" to which our souls might be attuned. We can see now, I believe,

---

46. ὁμοίως δὲ καὶ τῶν ἀγαθῶν· οὐδεὶς γὰρ τὴν εὐδαιμονίαν ἐπαινεῖ καθάπερ τὸ δίκαιον, ἀλλ᾽ ὡς θειότερόν τι καὶ βέλτιον μακαρίζει [1101b25–27].

47. See above, note 42.

48. Even if a person pursues an only apparent good, that which he seeks is still to be found, in some sense, among the things that all men seek. One who, for instance, pursues culinary delight thinking it constitutes true happiness, goes against human nature; but his pursuit is not entirely unnatural. The desire for personal survival upon which it is based is universal; it is one of the unrevisable principles of human nature.

49. See Flannery (1997), p. 77.

that this claim is false. This is not to say that Nussbaum has not made a significant contribution to our understanding of Aristotelian practical reason. Aristotelian practical reason, as she has shown, is a much more fluid thing than is conceived of by some Aristotelian and Thomistic scholars. Nonetheless, there is discernible a certain stability within this fluidity, for practical reason derives leverage from its own first principles.

CHAPTER 2

THE PRECEPTS OF NATURAL LAW

ARTICLE 2, QUESTION 94 of the *prima secundae* of the *Summa theologiae,* on "Whether natural law contains many precepts or one only," is perhaps the most important of Thomas's writings for understanding his conception of natural law.[1] It has also been important for contemporary ethical thought, since it stands at the basis of the very influential natural law theory put forward by Germain Grisez, Joseph Boyle, Jr., John Finnis, William May, Robert George, and Patrick Lee (among others).[2]

The key document in this regard is an article published by Grisez in 1965. There Grisez explains that, according to *ST* I–II q.94 a.2, "the primary precepts of practical reason" and of natural law—which precepts correspond to inclinations such as the inclination to conserve one's own being, the inclination toward the union of male and female, the inclination to know the truth

1. Recent useful secondary literature regarding *ST* I–II q.94 a.2 includes S. Brock (1991); Gómez-Lobo (1985); Finnis (1998), pp. 79–94; Grisez (1988a); Hittinger (1987), especially pp. 30–48; Johnstone (1986); Lee (1997); Lottin (1924); McInerny (1980) [see also reply in Finnis and Grisez (1981)]; McInerny (1984) and (1992), especially pp. 184–92; Rhonheimer (1987), pp. 76–84, 235–39 and (1994), pp. 545–50; Schultz (1985), (1986), (1987), (1988a), and (1988b); Van Overbeke (1957), especially pp. 452–74; also see the controversy between Veatch (1981) and Finnis (1981). Appendix A of the present work contains a deliberately literal translation of *ST* I–II q.94 a.2, to which are also added numerals in pointed brackets (<1>, <2>, <3>, etc.), which correspond to references in this chapter. Appendix A also gives the Latin text of the Leonine Commission.

2. See Finnis (1983), (1991b), and (1998); Finnis, Boyle, and Grisez (1987); George (1993); Lee (1996); May (1991). Grisez has written three volumes of a projected four-volume work on Christian ethics: Grisez (1983), (1993), and (1997). There is "selected bibliography" of pertinent writings by Grisez, Boyle, and Finnis at the end of Grisez, Boyle, and Finnis (1987) (pp. 148–51). George (1998) is a Festschrift for Grisez, which (unlike many such) contains several discussions of his work.

about God—are *per se notum quoad nos* (literally, "known in themselves in relation to us").[3] Because these self-evident precepts are the primary precepts, morality is ultimately a matter of protecting them. As Grisez puts it in a later work, the "basic principle of morality" is: "In voluntarily acting for human goods and avoiding what is opposed to them, one ought to choose and otherwise will those and only those possibilities whose willing is compatible with a will toward integral human fulfillment."[4]

The purpose of this chapter is not to argue against Grisez's interpretation, with which I have no substantial disagreement, but to bring into relief an aspect of *ST* I–II q.94 a.2 that Grisez largely ignores. Thomas is not primarily interested there in the self-evidence of ethical precepts. He introduces the idea of the *per se notum*—in a very perfunctory and incomplete manner (as Grisez acknowledges)—because it allows him to depict natural law as possessing the same general structure as an Aristotelian science.

This gives us a somewhat different understanding of natural law than we find in Grisez. The basic goods of practical reason are still of supreme importance—i.e., they are still the basis of the practical life and we ought, therefore, always to act for them and avoid what is opposed to them. But also important is the scheme itself. As I argue more extensively in chapters 7 and 8, the analysis of actions still involves establishing whether they constitute attacks on basic goods, but this is done by situating them within the ordered system of precepts which is natural law. Our task, however, in this chapter is simply to understand what Thomas is saying in *ST* I–II q.94 a.2, in particular with respect to precepts and principles.

[1] *ST* I–II q.94 a.2: the objections and their responses

The first thing to take notice of is the nature of the three objections, since this determines the general configuration of the article itself. Each argues that

---

3. As noted in the Introduction, because the phrase *per se notum* occurs so often in this book, I use it as if it were English, making no attempt to change the ending of *notum* to match the number or gender of that to which it refers, unless that to which it refers is itself in Latin.

An extremely worthwhile study of Thomas's development with respect to primary and secondary precepts is Armstrong (1966). Armstrong considers extensively the secondary literature on this topic up to the time in which he writes, much of it in French; also, his pp. 28–55 are devoted to "the concept of 'self-evidence'" in Thomas. On the *per se notum* in Thomas, see also Tuninetti (1996), especially pp. 11–26. For a summary of Armstrong's work, see Nelson (1992), pp. 18–23.

4. Grisez (1983), p. 205; also Grisez (1964), p. 83. See also Grisez, Boyle, and Finnis (1987), pp. 121–29; also Finnis (1970), p. 366.

natural law can contain only one precept.[5] Thomas's strategy is not to reject this notion outright but to show that in a way it is right, in a way wrong. There are many precepts of natural law, although they share "a single common source" (ad 2). It is also clear that, in order to show this, he must oppose the strict unitarian view. All are agreed, it seems, that natural law in some sense contains one precept; but all are not agreed that it also contains many.

The first objection makes a technical point about the definition of law. Law, it says, "is contained in the genus of precept." Thomas has argued this point just previously, in *ST* I–II q.92 a.2, where the first objection is that law cannot be fourfold. That is, it cannot be ordering, prohibiting, permitting, and punishing; rather, it has to be simply precept. Thomas, in fact, largely agrees with this point, saying that, once we realize that also prohibitions (etc.) have the intelligibility of goods, we can lump all four of these characterizations together: "Since to cease from evil has something of the intelligibility of a good [*quandam rationem boni*], thus also a prohibition has something of the intelligibility of a precept. In this respect, taking 'precept' in the broad sense, law in general is said to be a precept" [*ST* I–II q.92 a.2 ad 1]. Picking up on Thomas's association of law with precept, the first objection in *ST* I–II q.94 a.2 argues that this would give us many natural laws. Since animal is the genus of man and man the species of Socrates and Plato, Socrates and Plato, besides being both animals, are also both men. Similarly, if precept were the genus of natural law and natural law the species of various precepts, it would follow that the various precepts, besides being precepts, would also all be natural laws. But, so the objection goes, this is absurd; there must therefore be just one precept of natural law.

Thomas's way of dealing with this issue is typically Aristotelian. The various precepts of natural law, he says, "insofar as they are referred to a single first precept, have the intelligibility [*rationem*] of a single natural law."

5. Lottin notes that the thirteenth and fourteenth centuries were greatly influenced by the school of Anselm of Laon, which made of natural law the primitive law of human nature, anterior to the more detailed prescriptions of the Decalogue. Natural law became, thus, the pure obligation to do good and avoid evil: "quelques principes primordiaux" [Lottin (1931 <1924–1926>), p. 98; see also Lottin (1942–1960), vol. 5, p. 88]. Lottin also notes that the issue of the possible plurality of precepts was discussed by Albert the Great [Lottin (1931 <1924–1926>), pp. 99,118]. See also Lottin (1954), pp. 177–78, where he connects the issue of the "objective extension of the natural law" (i.e., beyond a fundamental *ratio naturalis*) with the issue of there being various grades of natural law precepts. (I discuss grades of precepts below.) See also Van Overbeke (1957), pp. 450–52.

Thomas is denying here that 'precept' is a genus and indicating why nonetheless the various precepts might rightly be called precepts of the natural law.
The correctness of the predication depends not on a genus-species relationship but on a different type of relationship, which relates the various types of
precept to one central precept, while allowing that the various precepts are
precepts in their own right.[6] This relationship is an Aristotelian *pros hen* ("toward one") relationship.[7] The one central precept "toward which" the others
are oriented and from which they receive their intelligibility as natural law is,
as we shall see, the first principle of practical reason (FPPR).

This trans-generic conception of precept is closely related to Aristotle's
conception of "the good."[8] According to Thomas, "it is of the intelligibility of
a precept that it bear with it order with respect to an end: insofar, that is, as it
prescribes what is necessary or expedient for reaching an end."[9] Anywhere we
find something moving naturally toward an end (or good), we find a precept.
Thus, there are precepts in law, since law brings a people to justice (its proper
end); but for the same reason there are also precepts corresponding to the
natural inclinations of man: the desire to work, to eat, to procreate, to protect
oneself with weapons, etc.[10] Goods, however, are goods in their own right and
not because they participate in some good that stands above them. Although
it is true that seeking, for instance, the good of personal survival can be understood as a way of seeking happiness or *eudaimonia* or even God, seeking
personal survival has full intelligibility on its own.[11] To adapt and apply an

6. We might note that, in *ST* I–II q.92 a.2 ad 1, Thomas is careful not to say that natural law is
a species within the genus of precept. He speaks there in very tentative terms: a prohibition has a
"*certain* intelligibility of a precept"; "taking 'precept' in the *broad* sense, *in general* law is said to be
a precept." "Ad primum ergo dicendum quod, sicut cessare a malo habet quandam rationem
boni, ita etiam prohibitio habet quandam rationem praecepti. Et secundum hoc, large accipiendo
praeceptum, universaliter lex praeceptum dicitur."

7. See *EN* i,6,1096b27–28; also *Metaph.* iv,2,1003a33; also *in EN* lb.1 lect.7 ll.198–213 (§96); also
Owens (1978), pp. 107–35, especially 118–23; and Owen (1960).

8. See, for instance, *EN* i,4,1095a26–28 and *EN* i,6; also *Top.* i,15,107a3–17; also, in the present
book, Chapter 4, sections [1] and [2]. Note, on the other hand, that *Cat.* xi,14a23–5 suggests that
good is a genus. See also *Metaph.* xii,10,1075a11–15. In Thomas, see *in EN* lb.1 lect.6 ll.125–48 (§81).
See also Grisez (1965), pp. 199–200.

9. *ST* I–II q.99 a.1 c. See also *ST* I–II q.90 a.2 ad 1; q.92 a.2; q.99 a.5 c; q.100 a.5; *ST* II–II q.44
a.1 c. On Thomas's conception of the good, see Gallagher (1994a), pp. 38–47; see also McInerny
(1992), pp. 103–6.

10. *Quodl.* VII q.7 a.1 [17] (§157); see also *ST* I–II q.5 a.5 ad 1; q.95 a.1 c.

11. See *in EN* lb.1 lect.1 ll.173–83 (§11): "Ipsum autem tendere in bonum est appetere bonum,
unde et actum dixit appetere bonum in quantum tendit in bonum. Non autem est unum bonum

observation of Aristotle's, a person striving for personal survival and told of some distinct and higher good supposedly involved in his striving, might well ask of what use it might be in explaining what he is doing.[12]

The second objection begins by admitting that the "natural law follows upon human nature," but it seeks to rein the point in. How shall we consider human nature? it asks. We must consider it either as a unity or in its particularity. But if we consider human nature in all its particularity, we are going to have to say that a lot of lawless things like greed and sex and gluttony are *precepts* of natural law. But that is absurd; thus, there can be only one precept of natural law, a precept that applies to human nature as a unity.

This objection is basically a "puritanical" one, of a sort known also in Aristotle's day.[13] Law is reasonable, the concupiscible parts of man are not. Since the concupiscible parts are many and reason one, law must be of reason alone and single. Thomas's approach to this is to show, in the body of the article, how the lower propensities fit into the general order of human nature— or, more precisely, how they "pertain" to the ordered structure of moral precepts. Rationality, indeed, *is* order, according to Thomas. He begins his commentary on the *Nichomachean Ethics* by saying:

As the Philosopher [Aristotle] says at the beginning of the *Metaphysics*, it belongs to the wise man to order. The explanation of this is that wisdom is the most powerful perfection of reason, whose chief characteristic is to know order. For, although the sensitive powers know some things in an absolute sense, to know the order of one thing with respect to another is proper to the intellect or to reason.[14]

---

in quod omnia tendunt, ut infra dicetur, et ideo non describitur hic aliquod unum bonum, sed bonum communiter sumptum; quia autem nihil est bonum nisi in quantum est quaedam similitudo et participatio summi boni, ipsum summum bonum quodam modo appetitur in quolibet bono et sic potest dici quod unum bonum est quod omnia appetunt."

12. "It is hard . . . to see how a weaver or a carpenter will be benefited in regard to his own craft by knowing this 'good itself,' or how the man who has viewed the Idea itself will be a better doctor or general thereby. For a doctor seems not even to study health in this way, but the health of man, or perhaps the health of a particular man; for it is individuals that he is healing" [*EN* i,6,1097a8–14]. Some would argue that Thomas's understanding of how finite goods participate in divine goodness is Neoplatonic. This is not an opinion that I share, but I cannot go into the matter here. On the whole issue, see Te Velde (1995); see also Henle (1956).

13. See for instance *EN* x,2,1172b35–x,3,1173b31. See also Gosling and Taylor (1982), *passim*.

14. *in EN* lb.1 lect.1 ll.1–6 (§1). See also *Metaph.* i,2,982a17–19 and *in Metaph.* §42; also the *prooemium* to the latter work. Order is another of those things that cannot be considered genera, since the ordered things are be found in all of reality: "ea in quibus invenitur prius et posterius non videntur esse unius ordinis et per consequens nec aequaliter unam ideam participare" [*in EN* lb.1 lect.6 ll.106–8 (§80)]. The latter remark concerns *EN* i,6,1096a17ff.; see also *Metaph.*

Once Thomas has brought the second objector to see that also the concupiscible parts of man pertain to an ordered scheme (i.e., that they are at least potentially law-abiding), he will have met his objection.

The third objection is readily seen to fit into this overall scheme. Thomas's interlocutor says that law is reasonable and reason in man is one. "Thus there is just one precept of natural law." Thomas's reply is that natural law can contain many precepts and man and reason still be one, since the various precepts are not reduced but "*referred* to a single first precept," so that they have "the intelligibility of a single natural law." Again, the emphasis is on diversity rather than unity.

[2] The *Sed contra*

In the *Sed contra* ("On the other hand") section of the article, Thomas introduces for the first time a parallel between practical and theoretical reason, saying that the precepts of natural law are like the indemonstrable first principles of demonstrations. It is worth noticing that he speaks of practical reason's "precepts" but of theoretical reason's "principles."[15] He does this, it seems, in order to mark verbally the distinction between practical and theoretical reason. Behind this distinction lies the idea that politics, for instance, is different from physics since the former and not the latter is concerned immediately with action.

The relationship between practical and theoretical reason is discussed in chapters 6 and 8 of this book, so we will not go into the matter extensively here. More important in the present context is the fact that Thomas draws a parallel between the precepts of natural law and the *first* principles of theoretical reason.[16] Although it often happens in Thomas that the *Sed contra* does

---

iii,3,999a6–14 (and Thomas's commentary, *in Metaph.* §§437–38). I discuss the *prius et posterius* extensively in Chapter 4.

15. As noted above (p. xxiii), however, the term 'principle' includes within its connotation precepts; thus, Thomas sometimes speaks of precepts as principles, although never vice versa. Cp. Grisez (1965), p. 178.

16. The word *principium* can have a very wide meaning, taking in not only propositions but also definitions in the sense of the constitution of things spoken of in scientific demonstrations, the matter and form of substances, etc., etc. [see Schuster (1933), pp. 48–49]. In short, it can bear all the meanings that Aristotle's ἀρχή bears. See, for instance, *An.post.* ii,19,99b17ff., and see especially *Metaph.* v,1. In *ST* I–II q.94 a.2, however, *principium* refers to a proposition of the sort that can be used in demonstrations. Not all *principia* are *principia prima*: *ST* I–II q.6 a.1 ad 1; also *ST* I q.33 a.1; also *in An.post.* lb.1 lect.20 ll.10–14 (§167): "Circa primum duo facit: primo ostendit

not contain his considered opinion of the matter at hand, in this case it clearly does, for the body of the article begins with the same idea.[17] Does he mean
to suggest that only the highest precepts of practical reason, which are known
naturally, belong to natural law? It would seem so, although there are other
places where he employs a wider sense of the term natural law.[18]

[3] The *per se*

We come now to the body of the article. As already noted, Thomas repeats
(in <1>) what is found in the *Sed contra*, again observing the precept/princi-
ple distinction, but his primary interest here is in the way precepts and first
principles are similar. They are such, he says, because they are both *per se notum*.[19]

In section <2> Thomas explains this concept, noting that there are two
ways of being known *per se: secundum se* and *quoad nos*. Being known *per se
secundum se* and *quoad nos* are not incompatible, as is clear from *ST* I q.2 a.1
c, where Thomas says that "something can be known *per se* in two ways: one
way is *secundum se* but not *quoad nos;* the other is *secundum se* and *quoad
nos*."[20] He goes on in the same article to say that the first principles of
demonstrations are known *per se quoad nos* but that certain other concep-

---

quomodo se habent demonstrativae scientiae circa prima principia inter communia; secundo
quomodo se habent communiter circa omnia principia communia." Cajetan also recognizes a
difference between common principles (sometime he calls these *prima principia simpliciter*) and
first principles [Cajetan, *apud ST* I–II q.94 a.1—Leonine large format edition]. He holds that second-order first principles are not *per se nota quoad omnes*. Lottin laments Thomas's lack of consistency in speaking of secondary precepts of the natural law [Lottin (1954), pp. 178–85]. See also
Lottin (1950); also Armstrong (1966), pp. 56–114.

17. See Elders's essay, "Structure et fonction de l'argument *sed contra* dans la *Somme
théologique* de saint Thomas Aquin" [Elders (1987), vol. 2, pp. 147–66, especially pp. 160–62].

18. See, for instance, *ST* I–II q.94 a.4 c, where he says that, although the precept "goods en-
trusted to another should be restored to their owner" belongs to natural law, it sometimes fails to
apply and it is sometimes (i.e., where "reason is perverted by passion, or evil habit, or an evil disposition of nature") not known. See also *ST* I–II q.94 a.5–6; also q.95 a.4 ad 1: "[I]us gentium est
quidem aliquo modo naturale homini, secundum quod est rationalis, inquantum derivatur a lege
naturali per modum conclusionis quae non est multum remota a principiis. Unde de facili in
huiusmodi homines consenserunt. Distinguitur tamen a lege naturali, maxime ab eo quod est
omnibus animalibus communis."

19. Some aspects of Thomas's understanding of *per se* predications are controversial—in particular, his position on how the different types of *per se* predications identified by Aristotle in
An.post. i,4, come into demonstrations. Since entering into the associated textual and exegetical
problems would needlessly interrupt the flow of the present argument, I perform that task in
Appendix B.

20. See also *in An.post.* lb.1 lect.4 ll.292–312 (§43bis).

tions are known *per se* only to the wise.[21] Thus, the concepts 'known *per se quoad nos*' and 'known *per se secundum se*' are distinct, inasmuch as something can be known *per se secundum se* without being known *per se quoad nos* (i.e., it can be known *solis sapientibus*), although that which is known *per se quoad nos* is also known *per se secundum se*.[22]

That Thomas does not hesitate to use very strong expressions such as *per se notum secundum se* of that which is known only to the wise is consistent with the idea, which he shares with Aristotle, that something is known in the fullest sense and most certainly when it is known in the way that the wise know things.[23] This is quite contrary to most modern approaches, according to which we can only really be sure of the sort of information that is available to all: sense data. Thomas would not deny that this is knowledge; but he would insist that it is not the most central and important case of knowledge. Knowledge, simply speaking, is not that which man shares with animals but that which characterizes man as man: scientific knowledge—the more sophisticated and refined, the better. Although, clearly, knowledge for Aristotle and Thomas is an epistemological notion, for knowledge comes from demonstrations and demonstrations are based on what is "true and primitive and immediate and more familiar than and prior to and explanatory of conclusions" [*An.post.* i,2,71b20–22], it is not such in the modern, post-Cartesian sense. Thomas and Aristotle are interested not so much in fending off scepticism as in depicting the structure of knowledge or science. What they regard as certainly known and even known to all does not always correspond to modern conceptions, for they begin their consideration with a different conception of "what cannot be doubted."[24]

21. The examples he uses are very similar to those of *ST* I–II q.94 a.2. That is, he says that *homo est animal* is known *per se* because its predicate inheres in the intelligibility of the subject. Such also, he says, are the first principles of demonstrations whose terms are known to all: "ens et non ens, totum et pars, et similia." His example of something known *per se solis sapientibus* is "incorporalia in loco non esse."

22. For many of the distinctions discussed here, see Tuninetti (1996), chapter 1; see also McInerny (1992), pp. 113–14.

23. See the *prooemium* to the commentary on the *Metaphysics,* where Thomas argues that metaphysics (i.e., *sapientia*) is the highest science. It is the highest because it is more "intellectual"—that is, it is about things that are "maximally intelligible." Things are maximally intelligible if the intellect achieves certainty from them, and the intellect achieves certainty insofar as it knows the causes of things. The most intelligible things are, therefore, the causes—the higher the cause, the more the intelligibility. Since it belongs primarily to the wise to know causes, knowledge in the fullest sense belongs especially to the wise.

24. A word about the "self-evident" and the known *per se.* Thomas is concerned in *ST* I–II

[4] The known *per se quoad nos*

Let us look more closely at the 'known *per se quoad nos*,' for doing so will provide clarification (and confirmation) of the points just made. As Thomas himself acknowledges,[25] Aristotle offers two seemingly contradictory analyses of this phrase.

One comes in the *Posterior Analytics,* where he writes:

> I call prior and more familiar in relation to us items that are nearer to perception, prior and more familiar *simpliciter* items that are further away. What is most universal [*ta katholou*] is furthest away, and the particulars [*ta kath hekasta*] are nearest—these are opposite to each other. [*An.post.* i,2,72a1–5]

The other comes in the *Physics:*

> Now what is to us plain and clear at first is rather confused masses, the elements and principles of which become known to us later by analysis. Thus we must advance from universals [*ek tōn katholou*] to particulars [*epi ta kath hekasta*]; for it is a whole that is more knowable to sense-perception, and a universal is a kind of whole, comprehending many things within it, like parts. [*Phys.* i,1,184a23–26]

Aristotle appears to be saying (1) that we start with particulars that are known *per se quoad nos* and proceed toward universals that are known *simpliciter* (or *secundum se*),[26] (2) that we start with universals that are known *per*

---

q.94 a.2 with things that are already known. Translating 'known *per se*' with 'self-evident' (or similar locutions) tends to obscure this fact: something that is self-evident is not necessarily *known*. Part of the meaning of the expression 'self-evident' is the idea that, *if* someone comes across a thing or a proposition or whatever, he will see it as true—not that he already does so. This is not to deny, however, that 'known *per se*' is for Thomas an epistemological concept; it is only to say that, unlike many post-Cartesian philosophers, he is not especially interested in the question whether we *can* know. He presumes that certain things are known and then occupies himself with determining where in the ordered scheme of knowledge these things are to be located. It is a mark of the epistemological (but not necessarily Cartesian) character of both the 'known *per se quoad nos*' and the 'known *per se secundum se*' that Thomas says in <2> that, although the proposition 'man is rational' is "known *per se* with respect to its nature" (i.e., it is known *per se secundum se*), to one who does not know what man is, it is not known *per se*—i.e., to him. On the type of epistemological investigation one finds in *ST* I–II q.94 a.2, see Schuster (1933), pp. 46 (and also pp. 49–50, 52). Schuster notes that Thomas never "auf metaphysische Erörterungen verzichtet." See also Jenkins (1997), pp. 11–50, for the non-Cartesian character of Aristotelian (and Thomistic) science. See also Nelson (1992), p. 20; also Preller (1967), p. 82.

25.*in An.post.* lb.1 lect.4 ll.256–80 (§43); *in Phys.* lb.1 lect.1 n.8 (§8).

26. The word *simpliciter* in the *An.post.* passage has a different meaning than the one in section <4> of *ST* I–II q.94 a.2 ("ens est primum quod cadit in apprehensione simpliciter") where "simpliciter" comes quite close to meaning *quoad nos*. See Thomas's *in Phys.* lb.1 lect.1 n.8 (§8): "Contrarium autem huic videtur esse quod dicit Philosophus in I Poster., quod singularia sunt

se quoad nos and proceed toward particulars that are better known than the universals.

Thomas reconciles these two approaches by saying that Aristotle is using different senses of the words 'universal' and 'particular.'[27] In the *Posterior Analytics*, a universal is that which explains more things, as when a scientist has a general explanation of a large number of phenomena; the particulars, on the other hand, are sensible individuals. In the *Physics*, however, universals are genera and particulars are not sensible individuals but "species." When a person has a general (i.e., generic) grasp of a concept, without yet being able to distinguish the species that fall within in it, he has less knowledge, properly speaking, than the person who has knowledge of the species. To employ Aristotle's example in *Physics*, a person who can use the word 'circle' might not yet understand the definition [*horismos*] of circle, which specifies its "defining principles"—i.e., that it is "that surface which extends equally from the middle every way."[28] In other words, according to the *Physics* approach, one grows in knowledge as one learns to specify the various elements that constitute the intelligibility or essence of something. In this context these elements are the "species."[29]

Which understanding of *per se notum quoad nos* is Thomas employing in *ST* I–II q.94 a.2? If one attends to the examples that he adduces when speaking of that which is *per se notum quoad nos*—"every whole is greater than its part" or "those things that are equal to one and the same thing are equal to each other"—it seems unlikely that he could have in mind the *Posterior*

magis nota quoad nos, universalia vero naturae sive simpliciter" (the reference is to *An.post.* i,2,72a1–5). See also *An.post.* i,1,71a28–29 and (more generally) i,1,71a24–i,2,72a7 (with Thomas's commentary: *in An.post.* lb.1 lectiones 3–4 (§§22–43). Note that Aristotle also uses the word *simpliciter* (or rather ἁπλῶς) at *Phys.* i,1,184a18. At *in Sent.* lb.4 d.49 q.3 a.5 sol.1, certain *delectationes* are judged to be better known either *simpliciter* or *quoad nos*. The lower delights are better known *quoad nos*, the higher *simpliciter*. See also *in EN* lb.1 lect.4 §52 ll.121–22 ("quaedam simpliciter et quoad naturam").

27. Thomas speaks actually of *singularia*, but for the sake of consistency with the above translations, I shall speak of particulars instead of singulars.

28. *Phys.* i,1,184b2–3; see also *Rhet.* iii,6,1407b27–28. Ross thinks that the talk of particulars at *Phys.* i,1,184b2–3 refers to "the various senses of an ambiguous term" [Ross (1936), p. 458]. Thomas, however, understands the particulars to be "principia definientia" or "principia definiti" [*in Phys.* lb.1 lect.1 n.10 (§10)]. Charlton has this same understanding, the provenance of which he traces to Philoponus [Charlton (1992), p. 52].

29. Aristotle uses another example as well: a child calls every male it encounters 'father.' It has a tentative grasp on the concept 'man' without being able to distinguish the various men within that class.

Analytics understanding. These examples are not sensible individuals, as in the commentary on the *Posterior Analytics,* but are clearly propositional. This finding is confirmed by turning to Thomas's commentary on Boethius's *De hebdomadibus,* from which latter work the examples come. There, Thomas says of that which is grasped by all that it is something "common and indeterminate"—as is said also in the *Physics.*[30] In *ST* I–II q.94 a.2, therefore, the things that are known *per se quoad nos* are things that are grasped by all in an indeterminate way—that is to say, without the knowers necessarily having a very scientific understanding of that which they have grasped in an initial way.[31]

This is consistent with the approach suggested just above, according to which Thomas's epistemological presuppositions are different from our own. He maintains that that which is *per se notum quoad nos* is actually rather tenuously known, although such knowledge can be solidified or "tied down" as one grows in knowledge of a science or the sciences.[32] Applying this to ethics, at the beginning of the process, a moral agent has some grasp of the highest precepts. At the end of the process, as the wise or good person, he understands them *as* first precepts—which is to understand that they are more important for the system itself than the less general precepts. He understands, that is, in a practical way, how the various parts of the discipline of ethics, including its lower precepts, fit together and also how the higher precepts are specified by the lower ones.

---

30. *in De hebdom.* lect.2 l.20 (§21). Note also that at *in Metaph.* §595 Thomas associates the propositions known as *per se quoad nos* mentioned by Boethius with Aristotle's *Physics.* On Boethius and the *per se notum* and its use in the Middle Ages, see Tuninetti (1996), pp. 48–67; also see McInerny (1990), pp. 199–202.

31. In his commentary on *Metaph.* ii,1,993b6–7 ("the fact that we can have a whole truth and not the particular part we aim at shows the difficulty of [knowledge]"), Thomas connects the growth in knowledge implied in *Phys.* i,1, i.e., progress from the confused universal to a distinct knowledge of its parts, with the method of analysis (i.e., *resolutio*): "Est autem duplex via procedendi ad cognitionem veritatis. Una quidem per modum resolutionis, secundum quam procedimus a compositis ad simplicia, et a toto ad partem, sicut dicitur in primo Physicorum, quod confusa sunt prius nobis nota. Et in hac via perficitur cognitio veritatis, quando pervenitur ad singulas partes distincte cognoscendas. Alia est via compositionis, per quam procedimus a simplicibus ad composita . . ." [*in Metaph.* §278; see also S. E Dolan (1950), pp. 39–40]. I discuss the method of analysis/synthesis in chapters 3 and 8.

32. This idea of growth in knowledge as a process of "tying down" information within a system of knowledge comes from Plato's *Meno.* See 97e5–98a6 where Socrates deplores the

[5] A problem connected with the known *per se*

These ideas help us past a number of interpretational problems. For instance, Thomas says in *ST* I–II q.94 a.2 <2> that the proposition 'man is rational' is known *per se secundum se* and not *quoad nos*. But 'man is rational' does not seem to require an expert to understand it. Further, as we have already noted, Thomas cites as examples of what is known *per se quoad nos* the propositions 'every whole is greater than its part' and 'those things that are equal to one and the same thing are equal to each other.' The first seems fine: if a child does not know that a whole is larger than its parts, it will not know to break off a piece of its food in order to get it into its mouth; and all children (we might presume) know to break up their food. On the other hand, the proposition 'those things that are equal to one and the same thing are equal to each other' is a fairly sophisticated mathematical idea. Can this really be said to be known *per se quoad nos?*[33]

In fact, both these propositions are found among the "common notions" of Euclid's *Elements*. What we might call the "equals axiom" ('those things that are equal to one and the same thing are equal to each other') is his first common notion; the "part-whole axiom" ('every whole is greater than its part') is the eighth.[34] So, although the part-whole axiom seems more obvious (or known *per se quoad nos*) than the equals axiom, according to the tra-

---

slipperiness and unreliability of true opinion: "And to what am I referring in all this? To true opinions. For these, so long as they stay with us, are a fine possession, and effect all that is good; but they do not care to stay for long, and run away out of the human soul, and thus are of no great value until one makes them fast with causal reasoning. And this process, friend Meno, is recollection, as in our previous talk we have agreed. But when once they are fastened, in the first place they turn into knowledge, and in the second, are abiding." This approach (shorn of the notion of recollection) is taken over by Aristotle in his *Posterior Analytics* [see Barnes (1994 <1975>), p. 88]. "All teaching and learning of an intellectual kind," says Aristotle, "proceed from pre-existent knowledge" [*An.post.* i,1,71a1–2]. Although we know—and must know—certain things when we start out on the path of learning, knowledge in the proper sense (i.e., knowledge *simpliciter*) is knowledge that is tied down by means of a larger system of interconnected deductions and initial insights.

33. McInerny makes a similar point with respect to the principle of non-contradiction and the first principle of practical reason [McInerny (1984), p. 136]; see also McInerny (1992), pp. 115–16, 122–25.

34. Euclid, *Elem.* i (10.1–12). The list of the common notions was tampered with over the centuries [Mueller (1974), pp. 65–66; Heath (1981 <1921>), vol. 1, p. 361] but the first and eighth are fairly well attested. Heath argues that probably the eighth (which he calls the fifth) is a generalization "from particular inferences found in Euclid and . . . inserted after his time" [Heath (1981 <1921>), vol. 1, p. 376]. See also Heath (1956 <1925>), vol. 1, pp. 221–23, 232.

dition within which Thomas is writing they are on more or less the same level.[35]

But what level are they on? That is not as obvious as it might seem. One's first inclination is to say simply that they are both alike mathematical (or geometrical) axioms. They are that, of course, but even in Euclid they are set apart from the definitions and postulates, the building blocks of his geometrical system. The equals axiom and the part-whole axiom occur in scattered places in Aristotle, and he also uses with reference to them (or, at least, to their type) the word 'common': "Of the items used in the demonstrative sciences some are proper to each science and others common—but common by analogy, since they are only useful insofar as they bear on the kind under the science. Proper: e.g. that a line is *such-and-such,* and straight so-and-so. Common: e.g. that if equals are removed from equals, the remainders are equal."[36] Aristotle's point here is that certain axioms are common not so much in the sense that they are known commonly by all (although he does also hold this)[37] but that their role is not limited to one science. For example, as Aristotle notes, the axiom 'if equals are removed from equals, the remainders are equal,' besides coming into mathematics also comes into the science of being *qua* being (i.e., metaphysics).[38] This general employment of the "common axioms" (as they have come to be called) is also found in Thomas, who employs the equals axiom in a discussion of the equality that exists in God, noting explicitly that quantity comprises not just "dimensive quantity" but also "quantity of virtue."[39]

Again, therefore, we see that it is best to be cautious about phrases like *per se notum quoad nos.* Although it is true that 'known *per se*' is an epistemological notion, the common axioms that Thomas takes from Boethius owe their status as common axioms as much to their position within Aristotle's organi-

35. At *in Metaph.* §605, Thomas suggests that the part-whole axiom is more basic than the equals axiom. (Note, however, that in Euclid the part-whole axiom is the eighth common notion and the equals axiom the first.) But even Thomas presumes that the two axioms are of the same general class—i.e., they are not of separate classes as would be a proposition known to all and a proposition known only to experts.

36. *An.post.* i,10,76a37–41 [emphasis in Barnes (1994 <1975>)]. The principle 'if equals are removed from equals, the remainders are equal' is Euclid's third common notion [*Elem.* i (10.4–5)].

37. *SE* i,11,172a27–36; *Metaph.* iii,1,995b8; 2,996b27–29; iv,3,1005a19–29; see also Barnes (1994 <1975>), p. 99.

38. *Metaph.* xi,4,1061b19–21. He says that it is "common to all quantities."

39. *ST* I q.42 a.1; see especially obj.3.

zational scheme of all knowledge as to anything else.[40] They are presupposed by several sciences and *therefore* count as more basic, more "common." Thomas is quite explicit about all this in the commentary on the *Posterior Analytics*, where he notes that "the genus of immediate propositions is twofold."

For [*nam*] those immediate propositions that consist of terms that are primary and common, such as 'being' and 'not being,' 'equal' and 'unequal,' are primary and immediate propositions—as, for instance, 'it does not happen that the same is and is not,' 'those things that are equal to one and the same thing are equal to each other,' and similar things. The immediate propositions that involve terms that are posterior and less common are posterior with respect to the first, as for instance that 'a triangle is a figure,' or that 'man is animal.'[41]

Here the word 'common' does not mean 'common to everybody.' As he says just above this passage, the order of the immediate propositions is "according to the *order* of terms."[42] If the secondary immediate propositions are "more

40. Note that Thomas himself associates the part-whole axiom with the senses: "[E]a quae per se nobis nota sunt, efficiuntur nota statim per sensum; sicut visis toto et parte, statim cognoscimus quod omne totum est majus sua parte sine aliqua inquisitione. Unde Philosophus: principia cognoscimus dum terminos cognoscimus" [*in Sent.* lb.1 d.3 q.1 a.2 c; the reference to Aristotle is apparently to *An.post.* i,11,7a26–35 [see *in An.post.* lb.1 lect.20 ll.142–44 (§171): "veritas principiorum communium est manifesta ex cognitione terminorum communium, ut entis et non entis, totius et partis, et similium," which is a comment on 77a30; see also i,10,76b36–37]. This does not, however, undermine my point that in epistemological matters Thomas (and Aristotle) tend to think first of a proposition's place in the overall scheme of knowledge. See above, note 24. See especially Thomas's *in An.post.* lb.1 lect.4 ll.233–55 (§42), where Aristotle's remark [*An.post.* i,2,72a2–3] about proximity to the senses is given a broad interpretation. See also *in An.post.* lb.1 lect.18 ll.1–17 (§149), where Thomas interprets Aristotle's "It is difficult to know whether you know something or not" [*An.pr.* i,9,76a26] as meaning "[I]t is difficult to know whether or not we know by means of proper principles—which is the sole way of truly knowing" (ll.8–10). On this see MacIntyre (1990a), p. 13: "The contrast with Cartesianism could not be sharper." At *in Metaph.* §692–707, Thomas discusses what we would today call epistemological issues; the corresponding passage in Aristotle is *Metaph.* iv,5,1010b1ff. See also Barnes (1994 <1975>), p. 97, who acknowledges that the axioms of a science must be "self-explanatory" and that some of them have to be believed and then says: "but the later notion that the axioms of a science must be in some way evidently and patently true is not at all Aristotelian."

41. "Nam illae propositiones immediatae quae consistunt in terminis primis et communibus, sicut est 'ens' et 'non ens,' 'aequale' et 'inaequale,' 'totum' et 'pars,' sunt primae et immediatae propositiones, <sicut> quod: 'non contingit idem esse et non esse', et, 'quae uni et eidem sunt aequalia, sibi invicem sunt aequalia,' et similia; immediatae autem propositiones quae sunt circa posteriores terminos et minus communes, sunt posteriores respectu primarum, sicut quod: 'triangulus est figura,' vel quod 'homo est animal'" [*in An.post.* lb.1 lect.43 ll.252–65 (§392)]. Note that, at *in An.post.* lb.1 lect.44 ll.103–18 (§399), Thomas accepts as at least a possible interpretation of *An.post.* i,33,89a3–4 that Aristotle is speaking about contingent immediate propositions.

42. "ordo immediatarum propositionum secundum ordinem terminorum" [*in An.post.* lb.1 lect.43 ll.251–52 (§392)].

posterior and less common" than the primary, the primary are less posterior and, therefore, more common than the secondary. In short, the common axioms are more basic because other bits of knowledge depend on them rather than vice versa.[43]

[6] The theoretical order

We return once again, to the detailed exegesis of *ST* I–II q.94 a.2. We have now a good understanding of paragraph <2>—i.e., the paragraph where Thomas discusses the distinction, *per se notum quoad nos/per se notum secundum se*. At the beginning of <3> he introduces a concept essential for his undermining the objections—and, in particular, objection 2. "Among those things . . . that fall within the apprehension of all, a certain *order* is discovered" (my emphasis). Up until now he has been discussing the various distinctions within theoretical knowledge without really engaging the issues at hand. With the introduction of the idea of order, he begins to close in on those issues, for if theoretical reason is ordered (we might even say, "law-abiding"), why cannot practical reason also be such?

Thomas offers in <3> a thumbnail sketch of the order of theoretical reason:

43. There is one other bit of evidence we might adduce in order to show that what is primarily at issue with the *per se notum* is the position of a proposition within a science. As is explained in Appendix B, Thomas follows Aristotle in identifying different types of *per se* propositions. The type to which the proposition 'man is rational' would seem to belong is the first (i.e., type {1}), since that type involves a predicate that pertains to the essence of the subject and 'rational' belongs to the essence (or definition) of man. However, the example that Thomas gives in *in An.post.* lb.1 lect.10 ll.34–35 (§84) for {1}—'line' is predicated of triangle—appears to be quite different from 'man is rational' for the latter is true and 'triangles are lines' is false.

This difficulty is surmounted, however, once one recalls that in the *Posterior Analytics* Aristotle is interested primarily in setting out the logical structure of science (or sciences), which means that he (along with Thomas) is interested in organizing terms, rules, etc., in such a way that someone might see how they all fit together [see Barnes (1969), (1981); also Barnes (1994 <1975>), pp. xviii–xx, MacIntyre (1990a)]. Thus, to say that a particular term is predicated of a subject is not to make reference to a proposition but to indicate the relationship between the two terms in a particular Aristotelian science. Thomas's (and Aristotle's) remark that 'line' is predicated of triangle has no connection with the false proposition 'triangles are lines' but refers rather to the truth that 'line' is essential to there being a triangle.

Also, some pages after the passage in Thomas's commentary on the *Posterior Analytics* just considered, he stipulates that predications that cannot be part of a demonstration are not predicates at all [*in An.post.* lb.1 lect.33 ll.121–41 (§282); see also *An.post.* i,22,83a14ff.]. Clearly, although subjects and predicates are among the elements of an Aristotelian science, the *per se* relationship of which Thomas speaks so much in *ST* I–II q.94 a.2 has little to do with language—or with propositions *qua* propositions. The issue is always the structure of knowledge.

For that which falls first within apprehension is being,[44] the comprehension of which is included in whatever a person apprehends. And therefore the first indemonstrable principle is that 'to affirm and simultaneously to deny is not [to be done],' which is founded upon the intelligibility of being and not-being; and on this principle all others are founded, as is said in the fourth book of the *Metaphysics*.

On first examination, one discerns three tiers in this order. The first principle of theoretical reason is 'to affirm and simultaneously to deny is not [to be done]'—or the principle of non-contradiction (PNC). On this principle "all others are founded"; while PNC itself is "founded upon the intelligibility of being and not-being"—or simply being.[45]

But are these all the tiers that ought to—or can—be posited? We already know that the common axioms are of a different class from the proper principles, so within the class of principles founded on PNC, we can identify at least two tiers. Are there more? Thomas says that, "on this principle [that is, on PNC] all others are founded." He puts no restriction upon this: i.e., he does not say that only first principles are founded on PNC but that all principles are. This is confirmed by what immediately follows: "as is said in the fourth book of the *Metaphysics*."[46] Central to Aristotle's argument in that section of the *Metaphysics* is the idea that every proposition depends in some sense on PNC. Thomas's point here in *ST* I–II q.94 a.2 is restricted to princi-

---

44. One asks oneself whether Thomas is reserving the concept of 'falling first within apprehension' for being (and the good), the concept of *per se notum* (in one way or the other) for principles. This would be consistent with the way he defines the types of *per se notum* in <2>—i.e., in terms of subjects and predicates.

45. Thomas uses '*fundor supra* + accusative' for the relation of PNC to being but '*fundor super* + ablative' for the relation of the other principles to PNC. I have marked this distinction in the translation by using 'founded upon' for '*fundor supra* + accusative' and 'founded on' for '*fundor super* + ablative.' At *in Metaph.* §§603–6, Thomas discusses these relations. They both appear to come down to a type of dependence: "Et quia hoc principium, impossibile est esse et non esse simul, dependet ex intellectu entis, sicut hoc principium, omne totum est maius sua parte, ex intellectu totius et partis: ideo hoc etiam principium est naturaliter primum in secunda operatione intellectus, scilicet componentis et dividentis. Nec aliquis potest secundum hanc operationem intellectus aliquid intelligere, nisi hoc principio intellecto. Sicut enim totum et partes non intelliguntur nisi intellecto ente, ita nec hoc principium omne totum est maius sua parte, nisi intellecto praedicto principio firmissimo" [*in Metaph.* §605; see also §49]. I suspect that the difference between the two has to do with a reluctance on Thomas's part to say that the "other principles" are properly speaking founded *upon* (i.e., "on top of") PNC, since PNC does not really interpose itself between the other principles and being.

46. The Leonine Commission edition of the *Summa theologiae*, at *ST* I–II q.94 a.2 (paragraph <4>), makes reference to Thomas's *in Metaph.* lb.4 lect.6 [=§§596–610; see especially §603].

ples; nonetheless, it is clear that he is expanding the scope of the order of theoretical reason beyond its first principles.[47]

In his commentary on the *Metaphysics,* Thomas says that the first thing in "the understanding of indivisibles" is being.[48] It is there, i.e., in the grasp of "quiddities," that being is discovered. These indivisibles are the objects of referring expressions (or significations—*Metaph.* iv,4,1006a21) such as that uttered by the denier of PNC and which serve as the basis of Aristotle's refutation in *Metaph.* iv,4 of such a denier's position.[49] So, we ought not to think of the first tier within the order of theoretical reason as a single mass of being. It is discovered *in* individual existing things.

[7] The practical order

We have identified within theoretical reason at least five tiers. What we might call tier [a] contains being (or beings); tier [b] contains PNC; tier [c] contains the common axioms (which are, of course, first principles); tier [d] contains proper first principles of the various sciences and disciplines; tier [e] contains other principles (i.e., principles that are not first principles).[50]

The order of practical reason, discussed in sections <4> through <9>, ought to be similar to that of theoretical reason since Thomas's argument depends upon there being a parallel between the two. Thomas says that "just as

47. In his commentary on the *Metaphysics,* Thomas says that "every demonstration reduces its propositions to this proposition" (i.e., to PNC): "Et propter hoc omnes demonstrationes reducunt suas propositiones in hanc propositionem, sicut in ultimam opinionem omnibus communem" [*in Metaph.* §603 (*ad Metaph.* iv,3,1005b18)]. Immediately afterwards, however, he extends the idea to all uses of the intellect: "Nec aliquis potest secundum hanc operationem intellectus aliquid intelligere, nisi hoc principio intellecto" [*in Metaph.* §605]. See Schuster (1933), p. 53.

48. *in Metaph.* §605: "duplex sit operatio intellectus: una, qua cognoscit quod quid est, quae vocatur indivisibilium intelligentia . . . : in prima quidem operatione est aliquod primum, quod cadit in conceptione intellectus, scilicet hoc quod dico ens; nec aliquid hac operatione potest mente concipi, nisi intelligatur ens." The phrase "the understanding of indivisibles" ["indivisibilium intelligentia"] comes from *De an.* iii,6,430a26 ('Η . . . τῶν ἀδιαιρέτων νόησις) See *in De an.* lb.3 cap.5 ll.7–13 (§746): "Dicit ergo primo quod una operatio intellectus est secundum quod intelligit indivisibilia, puta cum intelligit hominem aut bovem aut aliquid aliud incomplexorum, et haec intelligentia est in his circa quae non est falsum, tum quia incomplexa neque sunt vera neque falsa, tum quia intellectus non decipitur in quod quid est . . ." See also *in An.post.* lb.1 lect.36 ll.231–62 (§318), where Thomas associates indivisibles, the *per se notum* and intellect (νοῦς); see also *in An.post.* lb.1 lect.44 ll.40–73 (§397).

49. See chapter 6, sections [1] and [2], of the present work.

50. I have set out the tiers of theoretical (and also practical) reason near the beginning of the present volume in "Abbreviations, Texts, Conventions, Sigla."

. . . being is the first thing that falls within apprehension *simpliciter,* so good is the first thing that falls within the apprehension of practical reason . . .". Thus, practical reason's first tier—let us call it [α]—would contain the "intelligibility of good." As with tier [a] of theoretical reason, we should understand this to be referring not to any generic good but to that which is discovered in the various goods that are the ends of the various entities in the world and their capacities, powers, etc.[51] If the goods aimed at were objects of reference as in theoretical reason, we might call them correspondingly "indivisibles."

Next, in [β], comes the "first principle in practical reason" (or FPPR), "good is to be done and pursued and evil avoided." On FPPR "are founded all the other precepts of the law of nature," says Thomas, "so that clearly all those things that are to be done and avoided, which practical reason apprehends naturally to be human goods, pertain to the precepts of the law of nature." The phrase "are founded all the other precepts" ["fundantur omnia alia praecepta"] is clearly parallel to the phrase "all others are founded" ["omnia alia fundantur"] in the discussion of theoretical reason (<3>).

In [γ], we locate analogues to the common axioms: let us call these "common precepts." What are the common precepts? At *ST* I–II q.100 a.3, in discussing the relationship of the Decalogue to other precepts of the Old Law, Thomas says:

Consequently two types of precepts are not reckoned among the precepts of the decalogue: those that are primary and common, which require no other promulgation than their being written in natural reason as if known *per se*—for instance, 'ill is to be done to no one,' and others of this sort. And again those that through the diligent enquiry of the wise are discovered to be in accord with reason . . .

'Ill is to be done to no one' is therefore a common precept—although, apparently, it is just one of several.[52] In another place, Thomas suggests that 'one should act rationally' is also a common precept, derived from which is the

---

51. I do not wish to deny that tier [α] refers to the *ratio boni in commune* [*ST* I q.5 a.1] but only to make the anti-Platonic point that the good is not a genus from which individual practices get their character as good [see Gallagher (1994a), pp. 38–47]. Individual practices *are* good (in their own right), although they may be considered not unlike other goods insofar as they all stand in an analogical relationship. See McInerny (1968a). See also *EN* i,6, especially 1097a8–9 (and above, note 8); and Thomas, *in EN* lb.1 lect.6 ll.149–68 (§82); also lect.8.

52. The precepts "nulli esse nocendum" and "non esse aliquid iniuste agendum" are mentioned at *in De.an.* lb.3 cap.9 ll.108–10 (§826) as first principles that we cannot fail to know.

precept that one ought to return deposits.[53] And elsewhere he speaks of the two "great commandments" about love of God and love of neighbor as known *per se quoad nos*.[54]

It is not hard to see these four as parallel to the common axioms. 'One should act rationally' comes quite near in the practical sphere to being tautological: one might as well say that 'rationally, one should act rationally.' Moreover, it is clearly a precept upon which many other precepts depend, so it is "common" in the relevant sense. Similar things can be said about the precept 'ill is to be done to no one.' Thomas is interested in goods quite generally; harming a good is a direct contradiction of FPPR no matter whose good it is.[55] Not doing ill to anyone is, therefore, a very general way in which one avoids such moral self-contradiction, just as the part-whole axiom is one very general way of not falling into theoretical contradiction.

The two great commandments are also fairly easily handled. Take love of

53. *ST* I–II q.94 a.4. The precept about returning deposits or loans is not known *per se quoad nos* and fails in particular cases. "Apud omnes enim hoc rectum est et verum, ut secundum rationem agatur. Ex hoc autem principio sequitur quasi conclusio propria, quod deposita sint reddenda. Et hoc quidem ut in pluribus verum est, sed potest in aliquo casu contingere quod sit damnosum, et per consequens irrationabile, si deposita reddantur; puta si aliquis petat ad impugnandam patriam. Et hoc tanto magis invenitur deficere, quanto magis ad particularia descenditur, puta si dicatur quod deposita sunt reddenda cum tali cautione, vel tali modo, quanto enim plures conditiones particulares apponuntur, tanto pluribus modis poterit deficere, ut non sit rectum vel in reddendo vel in non reddendo." On returning deposits and the place of such principles within natural law, see Lottin (1924), pp. 351–56.

In ad 1 of this same article Thomas mentions the "golden rule" ("do to others as you would be done by"); but it is not clear whether he regards this as a common precept. The saying is attributed to Gratian, and Thomas says only that it belongs to the natural law; that is, it is "*de lege naturae*." In *ST* I–II q.99 a.1 ad 3, Thomas is again willing to accept the golden rule as part of natural law, but only insofar as it can be assimilated to Aristotle's ethical theory (and in particular *EN* ix,4,1166a1–2). He says that it is "implicitly contained in" the precept about love of neighbor (which, as we shall see, is a common precept). Thomas mentions the golden rule at *in Sent.* lb.4 d.33 q.1 a.1 ad 8 as "a precept of natural law," but his concern there is to downplay its applicability. Thomas holds that polygamy, although against the natural law, is not completely contrary to it. An objection would have it that polygamy is completely against natural law since the golden rule is part of natural law and no man wants his wife to have a second husband. Thomas replies that the rule ought not to be applied in this case.

54. *ST* I–II q.100 a.11; also q.100 a.3 ad 1. Cp. Grisez (1965), p. 172, including n. 13; see also May (1991), pp. 49–50. See also *SCG* lb.3 cap.117. See Armstrong (1966), pp. 40–41, who says that precepts such as "one ought to live according to reason" ["secundum rationem esse vivendum," *De ver.* q.16 a.1 ad 9 ll.336–37] and "thou shalt love the Lord thy God" are "not self-evident to all people, [but] may nonetheless be self-evident in themselves."

55. Thomas's ability to move back and forth easily between talk about personal good and talk about the good of one's neighbor is bound up with Aristotle's conception that a friend is another self: see *EN* ix,4,1166a10–b2, ix,8,1168a28–1169b2. See Thomas, *Perf.* §562 and *ST* II–II q.25 a.12. On contradiction in the practical sphere, see chapter 6 of the present work; see also Flannery (1995e).

God first. Thomas holds that God's existence is not known *per se quoad nos*;[56] so our knowledge that he is to be loved does not necessarily include the precise knowledge that that which we naturally love and desire is God. On the other hand, "to know in something universal, i.e., in an obscure way, that God exists is naturally implanted in us, insofar, that is, as God is man's happiness."[57] Everyone naturally seeks happiness *in* something—some identifying this with wealth, others with prestige, etc.; and, since happiness is God, no matter what each calls happiness, they also seek God unawares, "just as to see that someone is approaching is not to see that Peter is, although it is Peter who is approaching."[58] Thus, the commandment 'God is to be loved' is quite a general precept and qualifies as "common." It is not, however, so general as to be identical with FPPR, since it represents a particular aspect of the pursuit of good: i.e., that thing which a person seeks *as* his god, dedicating himself to the pursuit of wealth, prestige, etc.—or to the love of God.

Thomas makes a similar move with respect to the commandment 'Thou shalt love thy neighbor as thyself.' He maintains, that is, that love of neighbor is essentially love of God. "The aspect [*ratio*] under which our neighbor is to be loved is God, for what we ought to love in our neighbor is that he be in

56. *ST* I q.2 aa.1&2. In his exposition of *ST* I–II q.94 a.2, Grisez mentions the precept "God should be loved above all," arguing that it is a precept that not everyone knows but that it is "objectively self-evident" [Grisez (1965), p. 172]. Thus, for him, it would not be among the common precepts.

57. See *ST* I q.2 a.1 ad 1: "[D]icendum quod cognoscere Deum esse in aliquo communi, sub quadam confusione, est nobis naturaliter insertum, inquantum scilicet Deus est hominis beatitudo, homo enim naturaliter desiderat beatitudinem, et quod naturaliter desideratur ab homine, naturaliter cognoscitur ab eodem." See also *ST* I–II q.89 a.6, where Thomas is considering whether it is possible for a youth to sin venially before sinning mortally. In his response to objection 3, he argues that in the first moments of discretion a person commits a sin of omission by not turning toward God. But he would so turn (were he to do it) in his first thought of himself and his end: "Primum enim quod occurrit homini discretionem habenti est quod de seipso cogitet, ad quem alia ordinet sicut ad finem, finis enim est prior in intentione. Et ideo hoc est tempus pro quo obligatur ex Dei praecepto affirmativo, quo Dominus dicit, convertimini ad me, et ego convertar ad vos" [Zechariah 1.3].

58. In *ST* I q.2 a.1 ad 1, Thomas says of our knowledge of God (which is "sub quadam confusione"), "Sed hoc non est simpliciter cognoscere Deum esse; sicut cognoscere venientem, non est cognoscere Petrum, quamvis sit Petrus veniens." The approach taken here is that by means of which Thomas, at *in EN* lb.7 lect.13 ll.155–68 (§1511), interprets *EN* vii,13,1153b31–32. See also *SCG* lb.3 cap.38 (§2161); also *De ver.* q.22 a.2 c ("Deus propter quod est primum efficiens agit in omni agente, ita propter hoc quod est ultimus finis appetitur in omni fine; sed hoc est appetere ipsum Deum implicite . . ." [ll.55–58]); also *in Trin.* q.1 a.3 ll.180–89 ("non tamen oportet quod [Deus] sit primus in cognitione mentis humanae. . . . Cognoscitur autem a principio, et intenditur in quadam generalitate, prout mens appetit se bene esse et bene vivere; quod tunc solum est ei cum Deum habet." See also Dewan (1997), p. 563.

God. Thus is it clear that we love our neighbor by specifically the same act as we love God. And so the habit of charity extends not only to love of God but also to love of neighbor."[59] Love of neighbor, he says, is less general than love of God, but they are both accomplished by the same act, just as "the act of vision by means of which we see light is specifically the same as that by which we see color under the aspect [*ratio*] of light."[60] Thomas apparently regards this species identity of the two great commandments as sufficient warrant to assert that also the second is a common precept. He does so with reason, for the latter is presupposed by a large number of more specific moral precepts: 'do not steal,' 'pay your income tax,' 'don't turn right on red,' etc.[61]

[8] Less common common precepts?

Let us make a brief survey of our results so far with respect to the ordering of theoretical and practical reason. In [a] and [α] are located being and good respectively. Neither is strictly speaking principle (or precept), since the *first* principles in both spheres (i.e., PNC and FPPR) are founded upon them; they are rather the objects of PNC and FPPR (and other things as well, as we shall see). In [b] and [β] are located PNC and FPPR themselves; in [c] and [γ], are the common axioms and the common precepts we have discussed thus far. Are there, besides the common precepts, "proper precepts," analogues of the proper (first) principles beyond which we must go in order to arrive at "all the other precepts"? It would seem to be incorrect to posit such principles since within practical reason there do not exist different sciences possessing proper first principles.[62]

59. *ST* II–II q.25 a.1 c. See also *ST* I–II q.99 a.1 ad 2 ["in dilectione enim proximi includitur etiam Dei dilectio, quando proximus diligitur propter Deum"]; II–II q.25 a.12; *Perf.* §562; *in Sent.* lb.3 d.30 q.1 a.4 c ["dilectio Dei est causa et ratio dilectionis proximi; unde dilectio Dei includitur virtute in dilectione proximi sicut causa in effectu, et dilectio proximi includitur in dilectione Dei sicut effectus in causa potestate"] and lb.3 d.37 q.1 a.1 sol.2 ad 2. See also Finnis (1998), p. 314.

60. *ST* II–II q.25 a.1: ". . . sicut est eadem specie visio qua videtur lumen, et qua videtur color secundum luminis rationem." See also *Perf.* §626. In the latter and in ad 2 of *ST* II–II q.25 a.1, Thomas says that love of God is the more general good, under which is found love of neighbor. At *in Sent.* lb.3 d.37 q.1 a.2 sol.2 ad 2, however, he compares the commandment about love of neighbor to PNC: as PNC stands with respect to more particular principles, he says, so this commandment stands with respect to the more special precepts.

61. I would not deny that there is a *certain* ranking even among the common precepts. For instance, 'one should act rationally' seems to be more general than 'ill is to be done to no one'; and Thomas says that love of God is more general than love of neighbor. As we have seen (above, note 35), Thomas himself suggests that the part-whole common axiom is more basic than the equals common axiom.

62. Stephen Brock, however, has pointed out to me that in Thomas's ethics we have general

Thomas speaks in *ST* I–II q.94 a.2 of some precepts that appear less general than the common precepts already identified. That is, he speaks in <7>,
<8>, and <9> of precepts having to do with the inclinations to conserve one's
being, precepts having to do with the preservation of species, precepts having
to do with our rational nature.[63] He formulates two of the latter category:
"those things that concern an inclination of this sort pertain to natural law,
with the result that man ought to avoid ignorance [and] ought not to offend
those with whom he must deal" <9>. These two could be regarded as of
roughly equal generality with 'ill is to be done to no one' and 'one should act
rationally,' except that "man ought to avoid ignorance" needs to be read in its
context as 'man ought to avoid ignorance about God,' for it corresponds to
the "natural inclination to know the truth about God," and "[man] ought not
to offend those with whom one must deal" ["quod alios non offendat cum
quibus debet conversari"] is about avoiding a specific type of ill: ill done to
family, colleagues, neighbors, etc.

The precepts of <7> and <8>, none of which actually receives a formulation, are, if anything, less general than those in <9>. Thomas speaks in <7> of
"those things"—or, perhaps, "those precepts"—"by means of which the life of
a man is conserved (and the contrary impeded)" and in <8> of those things
(or precepts) "which nature teaches all animals—as, for instance, the union

---

principles, concerned with human conduct in general, and also proper ones, concerned with special *virtues* (I–II q.94 a.3). Perhaps the corresponding difference in matter is enough to give us
something like proper precepts.

63. Among the precepts of <7> would be found at least some of the precepts about eating,
working, and self-defense mentioned or alluded to at *Quodl.* VII q.7 a.1 c (§157). Thomas refers
there to Aristotle's *PA* iv,10,687a23ff. (note that Thomas speaks of *PA* iv as "XIV *De animalibus*":
l.133), which argues that the means of self-defense that animals have naturally, man selects for
himself. Thomas speaks in this respect of the role of reason ["homini in his non providit, quia
ipse est praeditus ratione" (ll.128–29)], which notion does not appear explicitly in the Aristotelian
text. (See above, note 10.)

Among the precepts of <8> would be precepts to the effect that procreation is to be pursued,
acts contrary to this good to be avoided. There is also involved here a familial aspect, for Thomas
speaks (in <8>) about "the raising of offspring ["educatio liberorum"]." At *ST* II–II q.154 a.2 c,
Thomas says that fornication is contra-life. (Fornication, he says, is a mortal sin since it is "a sin
that is committed directly against the life of a man. For simple fornication involves a disorder
that tends toward the harm of the one who is to be born of such a sexual union.") Although
Thomas says that this issue pertains to reason [*ST* II–II q.154 a.2 ad 2], he need not be interpreted
as saying that sex-related precepts belong among the precepts of <9>. Thomas's general point in
ST I–II q.94 a.2 is that the lower inclinations are all subject to natural law insofar as they are under reason. But this does not mean that he cannot *then* go on to show that "with respect to the
order of natural inclinations, there is an order of the precepts of the law of nature" (<6>).

of male and female, the raising of offspring." If the precepts having to do with, for instance, raising offspring are a subclass of the precepts pertaining to man *qua* animal, they are not at the highest level of generality.

One is tempted, therefore, to say that the precepts of <7>, <8>, and <9> are not *per se notum quoad nos* but rather *per se notum secundum se*. Thomas introduces this distinction into *ST* I–II q.94 a.2 itself; the presence of precepts *per se notum secundum se* in <7>, <8>, and <9> might be his reason for doing so.[64] But there are many passages where he says clearly enough that the precepts corresponding to the basic human inclinations are known to everyone. Here in *ST* I–II q.94 a.2, for instance, he says, "[A]ll those things that are to be done and avoided, which practical reason apprehends naturally to be human goods, pertain to the precepts of the law of nature" <5>.[65] The most reasonable thing to do is, I think, to posit another tier of "less common" common precepts, *per se notum quoad nos*. Let us call it tier [δ]. Tier [δ] would actually comprise three sub-tiers, corresponding to the order Thomas sets out in <7>, <8>, and <9>.[66]

64. Speaking of the "speziellen Prinzipien des Naturgesetzes" (which he associates with <7>, <8>, and <9>), Schuster remarks, "Es mag also zweifelhaft sein, ob diese abgeleiteten Sätze ohne weiteres *per se notae* sind *quoad omnes*, weil die Begriffe vielleicht nicht allen bekannt sind, aber dann sind sie wenigstens *per se notae quoad se*" [Schuster (1933), p. 63]. On this issue, see Armstrong (1966), pp. 51–55. See also McInerny (1992), pp. 125–30; also Rhonheimer (1987), pp. 224–39. Some important texts (as Armstrong notes, pp. 62ff.) are found at *Suppl.* q.65 aa.1–2 [=*in Sent.* lb.4 d.33 q.1 aa.1–2]. See also Van Overbeke (1957), pp. 450–70, especially 457–58; also Lottin (1954), pp. 176–88.

65. See also, for instance, *ST* II–II q.154 a.12 c: "Principia autem rationis sunt ea quae sunt secundum naturam, nam ratio, praesuppositis his quae a natura determinata, disponit alia secundum quod convenit. Et hoc apparet tam in speculativis quam in operativis. Et ideo, sicut in speculativis error circa ea quorum cognitio est homini naturaliter indita, est gravissimus et turpissimus; ita in agendis agere contra ea quae sunt secundum naturam determinata, est gravissimum et turpissimum. Quia ergo in vitiis quae sunt contra naturam transgreditur homo id quod est secundum naturam determinatum circa usum venereum, inde est quod in tali materia hoc peccatum est gravissimum." See also *in Sent.* lb.1 d.48 q.1 a.4 c; lb.4 d.26 q.1 a.1 c. See Finnis (1998), pp. 79–86. Grisez asks, "Why has Aquinas introduced the distinction between objective self-evidence and self-evidence to us? I think he does so simply to clarify the meaning of 'self-evident,' for he wishes to deal with practical principles that are self-evident in the latter, and fuller, of the two possible senses" [Grisez (1965), p. 173]. This seems to be right. See also McInerny (1984), pp. 135 and 142.

66. Van Overbeke cites *ST* I–II q.10 a.1, which appears to put the precepts pertaining to reason first: "[H]omo vult non solum obiectum voluntatis, sed etiam alia quae conveniunt aliis potentiis, ut cognitionem veri, quae convenit intellectui; et esse et vivere et alia huiusmodi, quae respiciunt consistentiam naturalem; quae omnia comprehenduntur sub obiecto voluntatis, sicut quaedam particularia bona." He says of *ST* I–II q.10 a.1 that "it is evident that, in this respect, this article does not have the precision nor the end of article 2 of question 94" [Van Overbeke (1957), p. 457;

That completes Thomas's sketch of the order of practical reason. As mentioned above, having set it out, he has an answer to the objections posed at the beginning of the article. It is now apparent that the order presumably recognized by all as existing in the theoretical reason exists also in practical reason. This is an order that takes in also the most basic inclinations, uniting them with the most fundamental practical principle, FPPR. It is possible, thus, for Thomas to affirm that natural law contains many precepts. This is not to countenance chaos within the realm of precepts but to recognize that natural law is a complex but ordered whole.

[9] The point of a system of precepts

Why is this important? What difference does it make that Thomas is so much concerned about the structural aspect of practical reason? Grisez and Thomas both hold that immoral acts are immoral because they involve damage to basic human goods. The issue between them is, how we know when a basic human good has been damaged, or even directly attacked. Grisez has made several attempts to determine when an action is damaging to a basic good—none of them, in my opinion, successful.[67] What counts as an attack on a basic good is left indeterminate in a number of crucial cases. By contrast, if we begin where Thomas begins—that is, with the structure of practical reason—we find ourselves in the position of at least knowing how to proceed in seeking answers to such questions. In order to know whether an action is an attack on a basic good, we must situate it within the context of the system to which it belongs: i.e., within natural law. This involves the often not simple task of determining whether a particular law or professional practice within a society is immoral (i.e., contrary to natural law). (See chapters 7 and 8.) But if and when that can be done, we have a determinate answer to the question whether an action does damage to a human good.

This is an answer that emerges from the systematic depiction of natural

---

emphasis his]. Van Overbeke does not think that Thomas's way of setting out the order of natural inclinations in *ST* I–II q.94 a.2 need be regarded as sacrosanct [Van Overbeke (1957), p. 469]; similarly, see also Hall (1994), pp. 32–33. See also Armstrong (1966), pp. 46–51. Finnis says that the hierarchy suggested in <7>, <8>, <9> "sets a questionable example." "In ethical reflection," he says, "the threefold order should be set aside as an irrelevant schematization" [Finnis (1980), pp. 94–95]. I discuss the significance and possible uses of the hierarchy in chapter 4.

67. See, for instance, Grisez (1970), which Grisez is no longer willing to defend; see also Grisez and Boyle (1979), pp. 381–92. I argue at Flannery (1993b), pp. 500–502, that Grisez and Boyle (1979), pp. 381–92, is inadequate as a theory. For more on this issue, see chapter 7.

law that we find in *ST* I–II q.94 a.2; it does not depend in the first instance upon epistemological considerations, even though the structure of the system does depend upon such considerations. On its own, the idea that human goods are apprehended by all does not get us very far. As we saw above, such knowledge is "confused" and "indeterminate" to those who have little knowledge of the system to which these goods belong. Once, however, a person has dwelt within and worked within the system for a period of time in a knowing manner, tracing connections among the various precepts and among the various levels of natural law, etc., he has a better appreciation and understanding of these goods and what they require of us. His knowledge is more certain, in the Aristotelian and Thomistic sense. In particular cases where "on the spot" prudence is required, he will have developed a "knack" for knowing when an action would be right and when wrong.[68] In cases where a law or practice must be fixed, he will have an ample supply of background knowledge pertaining to how such questions have been determined in the past, how to avoid contradictions and incoherencies within a system of laws, etc., and thus be better able to say when a law would be and when it would not be in accordance with natural law. I am not saying that such an approach is incompatible with what Grisez and colleagues do or hold; but I do think that Thomas's way of presenting natural law in *ST* I–II q.94 a.2 provides a more perspicuous view of the various factors required for the sound application of natural law than one can derive from Grisez's exegesis.

A number of other issues also emerge from *ST* I–II q.94 a.2. One has to do with the commensurability of goods. If the precepts of natural law are, as Thomas says, ordered, does this mean that his system is compatible with the type of consequentialism that weighs one consideration against another in order to determine the right thing to do? I confront this issue in chapter 4. A second issue has more directly to do with moral absolutes. If the precepts associated with basic human inclinations are located at some distance from the higher principles of practical reason, as Thomas suggests, they would seem at least possibly to allow of exceptions, as does the precept about returning deposits, on account of its distance from the highest principles.[69] I confront this issue in chapter 3, section [8].

68. See *EN* ii,9; see also *ST* II–II q.2 a.3 ad 2. See also D'Arcy (1961), pp. 34–36.
69. See above, note 53.

THE DERIVATION OF LOWER FROM HIGHER PRINCIPLES

A s w e s a w in chapter 1, Thomas has been accused occasionally of a sort of "top-down deductivism," in which lower principles are derived from higher in the sense that, once the highest precepts are in place, it is simply a matter of spinning out the lower principles as conclusions.[1] I addressed some aspects of this general issue in chapter 1, but it raises further questions. I would like to consider in this chapter two such questions: first, whether or in what sense Thomas regarded the proper principles of the various sciences and disciplines as derived from metaphysics ("first philosophy"); secondly, whether or in what sense he regarded the lower precepts of natural law as derived from the higher.[2] In addressing this second question, I introduce a number of connected topics: one has to do with the scientific method of analysis/synthesis, another with the distinction between natural and positive law, another with the nature of the "exceptions" to some lower precepts such as the precept to return to their owners things left in one's custody.

---

1. See Nelson (1992), pp. 18–23 (and, in fact, *passim*); also Armstrong (1966), especially pp. 38–41; also D'Arcy (1961), pp. 50–55; also Nussbaum (1978), pp. 168–69.

2. I maintain in this chapter the verbal distinction, set out in the Introduction and based on what Thomas says in *ST* I–II q.94 a.2, between precepts (the starting points of practical reason) and principles (primarily, the starting points of theoretical reason but including also precepts). In theoretical reason, there exist principles that are common to the various particular disciplines; these are called the 'common axioms,' as opposed to the 'proper principles' of the particular disciplines (see chapter 2, section [5]). Following Thomas, I sometimes also refer to the common axioms simply as 'common principles.' In practical reason, there also exist principles (i.e., precepts) that are common (see chapter 2, section [7]). These I call 'common precepts.'

[1] Proper principles proved by prior principles

There are passages in his commentary on the *Posterior Analytics* in which Thomas suggests that the proper principles of the various sciences or disciplines are proved by the common axioms. In *lectio* 17 of the first book, for instance, he comments on Aristotle's remark at *An.post.* i,9,76a16–18, "If this, it is clear that it does not belong to each to demonstrate proper principles; for those will be principles of everything, and understanding of them will be proper to everything."[3]

First [Aristotle] draws a conclusion, saying that "if this" is true—that is, that demonstrations in the individual sciences do not come about from common principles [76a14–15] and again that the principles of the sciences have something prior to them which is common [76a15]—"it is clear that it does not belong to each (science) to demonstrate (its) proper principles"; "for those" prior "principles," through which the proper principles of the individual sciences can be proved, are the common principles of all, and that science which considers such common principles is "proper to all"— that is, it stands toward those things that are common to all as the other particular sciences stand toward those things that are proper <to them>.[4]

There are a number of obscurities in Thomas's argument here, some of which I shall discuss below; nonetheless, Thomas has not infrequently been inter-

---

3. I translate here the Latin of James of Venice upon which Thomas is commenting: "Si autem hoc, manifestum est quod non est uniuscuiusque propria principia demonstrare; erunt enim illa omnium principia, et scientia illorum propria omnibus." This differs significantly from the modern received text of Aristotle. The revision of James by William of Moerbeke, which Thomas begins to use exclusively at *in An.post.* lb.1 lect.27 (although he had it in front of him even earlier in the commentary—see lb.1 lect.6 ll.76–79), is more accurate. In particular, at *An.post.* i,9,76a16–17, instead of "it does not belong to each to demonstrate proper principles" [*non est uniuscuiusque demonstrare principia propria*], William has "the proper principles of anything cannot be demonstrated" [*non est propria uniuscuiusque principia demonstrare*]. The full text of the pertinent passage in William's version is as follows: "Si autem manifestum hoc, manifestum est et quod non est propria uniuscuiusque principia demonstrare; erunt enim illa omnium principia, et scientia illorum domina omnium." (For William's version, see the Leonine Commission's 1989 edition of *in An.post.*, p. 258.)

4. "Primo inducit conclusionem, dicens quod, 'si hoc' verum est, scilicet quod demonstrationes in singulis scientiis non fiunt ex communibus principiis, et iterum quod principia scientiarum habent aliquid prius qua est commune, 'manifestum est quod non est' uniuscuiusque 'scientiae demonstrare principia' sua 'propria'; 'illa enim principia' priora, per quae possent probari singularum scientiarum propria principia, sunt communia 'principia omnium,' et illa scientia, quae considerat huiusmodi principia communia, est 'propria omnibus,' id est ita se habet ad ea quae sunt communia omnibus sicut se habent aliae scientiae particulares ad ea quae sunt propria" [*in An.post.*, lb.1 lect.17 ll.94–107 (§146)]. In his immediately subsequent remarks, he discusses "the preeminence of this science that considers the common things, that is first philosophy" (or metaphysics) [ll.117–18].

preted as saying that, since no particular science or discipline is in a position to prove its own (proper) principles, "the task falls rather to a supreme science, first philosophy, which has for its object the principles of all things."[5] Thomas, therefore, appears to be saying that the proper principles can be proved through the common principles.

Jacopo Zabarella, the sixteenth-century Aristotelian commentator, offers a similar interpretation of *An.post.* i,9,76a15–25. This is part of it:

Furthermore, it is to be noted that Aristotle does not deny that the metaphysician is able to prove the principles of the other sciences—for that cannot be denied—but he only denies that within those sciences to which the principles belong it is possible for this to occur. For, from metaphysical principles, the principles of geometry can be proved—as can, in fact, the very subject matter of geometry—not however in geometry itself but in metaphysics, as we too have asserted elsewhere.[6]

Alfonso Gómez-Lobo rejects this (as he calls it) "traditional" interpretation of Aristotle, which he associates also with Thomas.[7] According to Aristotle, he

---

5. Mignucci (1975), p. 178. See also Mansion, S. (1946), p. 144, n. 42 (who cites also translations by Mure and Tricot and the commentary by Philoponus: *in An.post.* 119.12–19). With respect to Thomas, she remarks, "L'interprétation de saint Thomas est donc à rejeter: la philosophie première ne fournit pas la preuve de ces principes et leur caractère indémontrable n'est pas seulement relatif à la science dans laquelle ils sont principes. Aristot ne croit pas que la métaphysique doive s'immiscer dans le domaine de chaque science."

6. Zabarella, *in An.post.* 781CD. "Praeterea notandum est, Aristotelem non negare metaphysicum posse probare aliarum scientiarum principia, id enim negari non potest, sed solum negare, quod in illis scientiis, quarum sunt principia, id fieri queat: ex principiis enim metaphysicis possunt probari principia geometrica, atque adeo ipsum geometriae subjectum, non tamen in ipsa geometria, sed in metaphysica, sicut alibi quoque declaravimus." (The latter reference is to his *De praecogn.* c. 14, pp. 527–30.)

7. Gómez-Lobo cites not Thomas's commentary on the *Posterior Analytics* but his commentary on *Metaph.*—in particular, *in Metaph.* §1149, which treats of *Metaph.* vi,1,1025b7–13. The Aristotelian passage reads: "All these [particular] sciences mark off some particular being—some genus, and enquire into this, but not into being simply nor *qua* being, nor do they offer any discussion of the essence of the things of which they treat; but starting from the essence [*to ti esti*]— some making it plain to the senses, others assuming it as an essence—they then demonstrate, more or less cogently, the essential attributes of the genus with which they deal." Thomas's commentary reads, in part, "But other sciences accept the essence [*quod quid est*] of their own subject by supposition from some other science, as geometry accepts what magnitude is from the first philosopher." Gómez-Lobo acknowledges that Thomas does not here espouse the stronger view that metaphysics proves the principles of the particular disciplines (i.e., the view Gómez-Lobo attributes to Zabarella) but only that it "hands down the principles to the particular disciplines" [Gómez-Lobo (1978), p. 184]. It is clear, however, that he wants to connect Thomas with the "traditional view." His case would be stronger using *in An.post.* §146. Another text he might have adduced is *in Trin.* q.6 a.1 ll.383–95: "Haec autem sunt de quibus scientia divina considerat, ut supra dictum est, scilicet substantiae separatae, et communia omnibus entibus; unde patet quod sua consideratio est maxime intellectualis. Et exinde etiam est quod *ipsa largitur principia omnibus*

argues, in the ideal scheme of things, each discipline minds its own business, having nothing to do with the affairs of the others (unless, of course, one discipline happens to be subordinate to another—see *An.post.* i,9,76a9–10). In particular, metaphysics "conducts discussions," but never gives demonstrations, of that which concerns *it*. He compares this view of the relationship between first philosophy and the particular disciplines to the ascending side of Platonic dialectic as depicted in *Republic* book vi, where hypotheses—always offered tentatively—are "destroyed" by way of Socratic criticism. The traditional view, on the other hand, is more like the corresponding descending side of dialectic, in which the philosopher proceeds "downward to the conclusion, making no use whatever of any object of sense but only of pure ideas moving on through ideas to ideas and ending with ideas" [*R.* vi,511b8–c2].[8]

This way of attempting to derive everything from metaphysical principles is, indeed, common in Neoplatonism. Proclus, for instance, in proposition 72 of his *Elements of Theology,* argues that "All those things among the participants that have the character of substrates [*hupokeimena*] proceed from more complete and more universal causes." As part of a corollary to the corresponding proof, he says, "From these remarks, it is apparent why matter, which takes its origin from the One, is in itself bereft of form . . .". "The One" here is a metaphysical principle, invoked also by Plato; indeed, in Platonism in general it is identified with God himself. It is apparent that in proposition 72 Proclus is attempting to derive even the material substrate of the world from the highest transcendent principle.[9]

---

aliis scientiis, in quantum intellectualis consideratio est principium rationalis, propter quod dicitur prima philosophia; et nihilominus ipsa addiscitur post physicam et ceteras scientias, in quantum consideratio intellectualis est terminus rationalis, propter quod dicitur metaphysica quasi trans physicam, quia post physicam resolvendo occurrit."

8. Gómez-Lobo (1978), pp. 188. In *R.* vi,510–11, Plato speaks of an upward methodological phase in which reason employs assumptions as "underpinnings, footings, and springboards so to speak, to enable it to rise to that which requires no assumption and is the starting point of all . . .". Having reached this starting point (or *archē*), reason then proceeds in the other direction. It is tempting to identify the geometrical method of synthesis (of which I shall speak more below) especially with the downward path of *R.* vi,510–11. There are difficulties, however, with any attempt to associate it with either the upward or the downward path, as Robinson has shown [Robinson (1953), pp. 146–79]. See also Robinson (1937).

9. The *Elements of Theology,* says E. R. Dodds, is "an attempt to supply the comprehensive scheme of reality desiderated by Plato in the seventh book of the *Republic*—to exhibit, that is to say, all forms of true Being as necessary consequences derived in conformity with certain general laws from a single ἀρχή" [Proclus, *Elem.,* p. x]. Although in other works Proclus often bases himself upon the writings of Plato or an oracular saying, "in the *Elements of Theology,*" notes Dodds, "Proclus has adopted, at least in appearance, the method of pure *a priori* deduction known to the

[2] Countervailing indications

Although Thomas does say things that suggest that the various particular disciplines receive their principles from metaphysics, there are other passages where he says things incompatible with this notion. For instance, in the very *lectio* where he speaks of those "prior 'principles,' through which the proper principles of the individual sciences can be proved," he says that "it does not do to use things that are true and immediate to demonstrate something, for in this way it would be possible to demonstrate something as Bryson demonstrated 'tetragonism,' i.e., the squaring of the circle, showing by means of certain common principles that something squared is equal to a circle."[10]

Thomas also notes, with respect to Bryson's method, that there is a disparity between the subject matter of common principles and the subject matter of the particular discipline in which such a proof might be attempted, so that, even if a person might at the end of such a proof know something, he would have only *per accidens* knowledge. Thomas says, moreover, that the logical distance between the common principles and the particular disciplines is too great to allow for *per se* knowledge.[11] If there were a causative deductive chain from metaphysics down into the particular disciplines, there would not be such a disparity of subject matter or the logical distance of which Thomas speaks.[12]

Book 1, *lectio* 43 raises similar doubts. The corresponding passage in the *Posterior Analytics* is obscure, but for us the important thing is not what

---

ancient mathematicians as synthesis and familiar to us from Euclid and Spinoza" [Proclus, *Elem.*, p. xi]. I speak about the method of synthesis below.

10. *in An.post.* lb.1 lect.17 ll.20–25 (§144): "non sufficit ex veris et immediatis aliquid demonstrare, quia sic contingeret aliquid demonstrare sicut Brisso demonstravit tetragonismum, id est quadraturam circuli, ostendens aliquod quadratum esse circulo equale per aliqua principia communia . . .". On Bryson, see Heath (1981 <1921>), vol. 1, pp. 223–25. Thomas's "tetragonismum" translates Aristotle's τὸν τετραγωνισμόν at *An.post.* i,7,75b41.

11. *in An.post.* lb.1 lect.17 ll.19–52 (§144); see also lect.20 ll.92–103 (§170). In the latter Thomas says that the various sciences "communicate in" the common principles insofar as they use them as principles from which they demonstrate, but they do not use them as that *about* which they demonstrate (i.e., as subjects) nor as that *which* they demonstrate (i.e., as conclusions). See also Thomas's *in Phys.* lb.8 lect.5 n.3 (§1006) ("omnes artes et scientiae utuntur motu").

12. As if to ensure this disparity of subject matter, Aristotle at one point says that the common principles come down into the particular disciplines only in analogical form [*An.post.* i,10,76a38–9; see also *Metaph.* xi,4,1061b17–19]. See *in An.post.* lb.1 lect.18 ll.72–81 §154 (note particularly ll.78–81: "'utile est' accipere huiusmodi principia in scientiis quantum pertinet ad genus subjectum quod contineatur sub illa 'scientia'").

Aristotle meant but what Thomas makes of the passage. In a general consideration of the idea that all things are derived from the same principles, Aristotle says that someone might understand this to mean that anything is proved from everything.[13] Thomas, following Aristotle, says that this would be absurd: it happens neither when it is a question of the most apparent mathematical ideas nor when it is a question of reducing propositions *to* first principles by analysis.[14] In both these cases, "we know that a further conclusion is demonstrated, another immediate proposition having been co-assumed."[15] An alternative interpretation of the phrase 'all things are derived from the same principles' is then proposed. Perhaps it refers only to *primary* immediate propositions (that is, to the common principles), the secondary immediate (proper) propositions being co-assumed in order to demonstrate the diverse conclusions. Thomas writes:

And so, in order to exclude this, [Aristotle] says that, "if someone says that it is the primary immediate propositions which are" those "principles" [88b20–21] from which all are demonstrated, he ought to consider that nonetheless "in each genus" there has to be "one" principle or one immediate proposition, first in its genus, not first *simpliciter.* And from that which is first *simpliciter,* the proper principle of this genus having been co-assumed, it is necessary <that things> in this genus be demonstrated. And thus it is not possible for everything to be demonstrated from only common principles; but it is necessary to co-accept proper <principles>, which are different for different things.[16]

13. *An.post.* i,32,88b15–16. Thomas says of this remark, "Si aliquis quaerens omnium eadem esse principia, hoc intendat dicere quod 'quodlibet' demonstretur ex quolibet" [*in An.post.* lb.1 lect.43 ll.227–28 (§391)].

14. In the Latin of *An.post.* i,33,88b17–18, upon which Thomas was commenting, "Neque enim in manifestis mathematibus hoc fit, neque in resolutione possibile est."

15. Commenting on the phrase "Immediatae enim propositiones principia sunt, altera autem conclusio fit coaccepta propositione immediata" [*An.post.* i,33,88b18–20], Thomas remarks: "videmus autem quod demonstratur alia 'conclusio,' coassumpta 'immediata propositione' alia" [*in An.post.* lb.1 lect.43 ll.241–42 (§391)]. The idea is that, since a particular demonstration depends on a particular co-assumed premiss, it cannot be that anything is proved from *anything* (see above, note 13).

16. *in An.post.* lb.1 lect.43 ll.268–80 (§392): "Et ideo ad hoc excludendum dicit quod, 'si aliquis dicat primas immediatas propositiones has esse' illa 'principia' ex quibus omnia demonstrantur, considerare debet quod nihilominus 'in unoquoque genere' oportet esse 'unum' principium vel unam propositionem immediatam primam in illo genere, non primam simpliciter, et quod ex illa quae est prima simpliciter, coassumpto isto principio proprio huius generis, oportebit in hoc genere demonstrari; et ita non ex solis communibus principiis possunt omnia demonstrari, sed oportet etiam coaccipere propria, quae sunt diversa diversorum." See also Schuster (1933), pp. 53–54: "Eine inhaltliche Ableitung aber ohne Zuhilfenahme von *principia propria* ist nach Thomas für die spezielleren Sätze nicht möglich."

In other words, even if the principles from which everything is derived are limited to the common principles, a proper principle will still have to be added on in order to derive anything within the particular discipline. But, one immediately asks, if the proper principles are derived *from* the common, why would they have to be added *to* them? It is clear that Thomas's comment in *lectio* 17 about proper principles being proved through prior principles requires some interpretation.

[3] An alternative approach

At *An.post.* i,12,77b5–6, Aristotle says that a geometer does not offer arguments about the first principles of geometry "insofar as he is a geometer." Commenting upon this, Thomas remarks, "[Aristotle] says, 'insofar as he is a geometer,' because it is possible in some science for the principles of this science to be proved, insofar as this science takes on the trappings of the other science, as when the geometer proves his principles by assuming the form of a first philosopher."[17] This remark provides us with an entry into the interpretation we require, for it tells us something about how Thomas conceives of the relationship between the proper principles and metaphysics. Although in some sense the proper principles can be "proved" in metaphysics, we don't *get* them from there, as if something wanting was being supplied from on high. The idea is rather that, *if* we want to have a more philosophical understanding of the principles of a discipline, we shall have to perform such investigations in their proper field of study.[18] It is quite possible that a geometer will not be interested in metaphysical discussions about the nature of lines and points; he can still be a perfectly good geometer—even the best of geometers.

This is certainly consistent with Aristotle. Anyone who has read the *Metaphysics* knows that it contains no proofs of the proper principles of the lower sciences and disciplines—nor is there even talk of such proofs as a possible task to be completed. Principles of the lower disciplines appear not infrequently in the *Metaphysics*; but, when they are not employed as mere examples, they are invariably examined as "givens." In book xiii, for instance,

---

17. *in An.post.* lb.1 lect.21 ll.74–79 (§177): "Dicit autem, 'secundum quod geometer est,' quia contingit in aliqua scientia probari principia illius scientiae, in quantum illa scientia assumit ea quae sunt alterius scientiae; sicut si geometra probet sua principia secundum quod assumit formam philosophi primi."

18. "[Q]uia quod quid est proprie pertinet ad scientiam quae est de substantia, scilicet ad philosophiam primam, a qua omnes aliae hoc accipiunt" [*in An.post.* lb.1 lect.18 ll.44–47 (§152)].

where (as we shall see in chapter 4) Aristotle treats of the principles of mathematics (the concepts of 'unit,' 'successor,' etc.), he is clearly speaking about things already assumed by him and his audience to exist or to be true. He views his task not as providing mathematics with its own principles but as sorting out what mathematics sets before him. Indeed, *Metaph.* xiii can be viewed as an argument against the idea that mathematical principles and procedures require metaphysical "grounding" (to use the common modern expression). The fact that the same thing can be both a "double" and also a "half" (Socrates might be twice the size of his chair but half the size of his house) need not (as in Plato) drive us to speculation about a primordial Oneness and a primordial Twoness. Mathematics simply *works* like that: at one moment we can halve something, a moment later we can double it. Thomas's commentary on the *Metaphysics* reflects this same lack of concern about shoring up the lower disciplines.

If, then, all that Thomas means when he speaks of proving proper principles is that *qua* metaphysician a person might study them, there is no danger that he regards them as being derived from metaphysics in the Neoplatonic manner. If in a sense a lower discipline receives its principles from metaphysics, it is just as accurate to say that metaphysics receives the same principles from the lower discipline, for it cannot do its job of sorting out these principles and correctly characterizing them without first having been given that which requires this treatment.

We begin at this point to understand Thomas's use of the language of "proving" with respect to the investigation that metaphysics sometimes conducts of the proper principles. It may very well be that a principle of one science appears as the conclusion of a syllogism in another (e.g. metaphysics), but this does not mean that the former science depends on the latter for its proper intelligibility. If metaphysics did not exist, geometry would not lack one ounce of rigor. Of course, it is also true that did the subject matter of metaphysics—being *qua* being—not exist, geometry would not exist at all and in that sense geometry is dependent on metaphysics. But geometry requires no metaphysical grounding. It is complete—or, at least, can be completed—on its own.

An example will be useful. Thomas says in his commentary on the *Posterior Analytics* that there are certain propositions that cannot be proved except by means of the principles of another science; and thus it is necessary that they be assumed in this science, although they are proved by means of the principles of the other science. For instance, a geometer assumes that a straight line leads from point to point, and a natural scientist proves this, showing that between any two points there is an intermediate line.[19]

Let us grant the basic presuppositions of this argument. Sir Thomas Heath has shown that, as a matter of fact it is not at all easy from within geometry to prove that, if two straight lines have the same end points, they must coincide along their entire length.[20] And one can make an intelligent guess as to how Thomas might argue that Euclid's first postulate can be proved within natural science: he might argue (presumably within the science of physics) that there must exist a shortest route that an object might take between two points. What interests us, however, is not so much the technical accuracy of all this but rather how Thomas understands the relationship between the two sciences. They are independent of one another in the sense that they involve disparate subject matter. Geometry is about abstract, mathematical constructions; physics is about the movement of physical bodies. The physical proof of Euclid's first postulate does not *belong* in geometry, so it could not be filling a gap in it. Geometry, therefore, does not depend on physics, even though one of its principles might be studied profitably within physics. A similar thing might be said of the relationship between any science or discipline and metaphysics. They make sense on their own, although there is nothing to prevent—and often much to be gained by—a metaphysical investigation of their proper principles.

Gómez-Lobo insists that metaphysics is concerned with *its* proper subject matter and he cites the opening lines of *Metaph.* iv: "There is a science that investigates being as being and the attributes that belong to this in virtue of its own nature."[21] We can now see that this is not incompatible with Thomas's

19. *in An.post.* lb.1 lect.5 ll.145–52 (§50): "Sunt enim quaedam propositiones, quae non possunt probari nisi per principia alterius scientiae, et ideo oportet quod in illa scientia supponantur, licet probentur per principia alterius scientiae; sicut a puncto ad punctum rectam lineam ducere supponit geometra et probat naturalis, ostendens quod inter quaelibet duo puncta sit linea media." Thomas is alluding here to Euclid's first postulate, Ἡιτήσθω ἀπὸ παντὸς σημείου ἐπὶ πᾶν σημεῖον εὐθεῖαν γραμμὴν ἀγαγεῖν [*Elem.* i,8.7–8] ("Let the following be postulated: 1. To draw a straight line from any point to any point" [Heath (1956 <1925>), vol. 1, p. 154]).

20. Heath (1956 <1925>), vol. 1, pp. 195ff.

21. *Metaph.* iv,1,1003a21–22; he also cites *Metaph.* vi,1,1026a31–32 [Gómez-Lobo (1978), p. 192; see also p. 186].

position. Moreover, it is not incompatible with what Thomas says in the passage that presented our problem in the first place. For just after remarking that the prior principles,

through which the proper principles of the individual sciences can be proved, are the common principles of all, and that science which considers such common principles is "proper to all"—that is, it stands toward those things that are common to all as the other particular sciences stand toward those things that are proper <to them>,[22]

Thomas also says,

Just as the subject of arithmetic is number and therefore arithmetic treats of those things that are proper to number, similarly, first philosophy, which treats of all principles, has for its subject being, which is common to all; and therefore it treats of those things that are proper to being (which are common to all things) as if they were proper to itself.[23]

In other words, Thomas, like Aristotle, insists that the subject matter of metaphysics is being *qua* being. Metaphysics does not study numbers *qua* numbers—that would be to study quite a foreign subject matter; it studies numbers, rather, *qua* beings. It does not, therefore, prove the principles of mathematics for it, as if the mathematics depended on metaphysics. Rather, metaphysics discusses such principles as part of its proper subject matter—i.e., under the rubric of being *qua* being. This subject matter is quite distinct from the subject matter of mathematics.[24]

22. See above, note 4.

23. "Sicut enim subiectum arismeticae sit numerus et ideo arismetica considerat ea quae sunt propria numeri, similiter prima philosophia, quae considerat communia principia, habet pro subiecto ens, quod est commune ad omnia, et ideo considerat ea quae sunt propria entis, quae sunt omnibus communia, tanquam propria sibi" [*in An.post.* lb.1 lect.17 ll.107–14 (§146)].

24. According to both Aristotle and Thomas, sciences and other disciplines are individuated with respect to their subject matter, which is also to be associated with their genus. See, for instance, Aristotle's *An.post.* i,7, which begins with the words, "Thus you cannot prove anything by crossing from another kind [ἐξ ἄλλου γένους]—e.g. something geometrical by arithmetic" [75a38–39]. See also *An.post.* i,28,87a38; see also Hintikka (1972), pp. 61–62. Says Thomas, "Dicit ergo [Philosophus] primo: ex quo demonstratio est ex his quae sunt 'per se,' 'ergo' manifestum est quod non contingit 'demonstrare descendentem' vel procedentem 'ex alio genere' in aliud genus, sicut non contingit quod geometra ex propriis principiis demonstret aliquid descendens in arismeticalia" [*in An.post.* lb.1 lect.15 ll.25–30 (§128)]. Even super- and subordinate disciplines, according to Aristotle and Thomas, are distinguished one from another by their subject matter. Optics, for instance, stands toward geometry as one thing under another [θάτερον ὑπὸ θάτερον—*An.post.* i,13,78b36–37]. Geometry, however, studies the *propter quid,* optics the *quia.* "Here it is for the empirical scientists to know the fact and for the mathematical scientists to know the reason why. The latter possess demonstrations which give the explanations, and often

Again, if this is correct, it sounds very much like the Gómez-Lobo understanding of what goes on in metaphysics. We find in Thomas's metaphysics
discussions of proper principles but no pretensions that the business of the
particular disciplines actually starts in metaphysics and then funnels down to
them in a deductive way, giving them a metaphysical certainty they lack.
Thus, Gómez-Lobo's objections to the "traditional" understanding of the relationship between metaphysics and the proper principles do not apply to
Thomas.[25]

[4] Analysis and synthesis

That brings us to the second question mentioned at the beginning of this
chapter: whether or in what sense Thomas regarded the lower precepts of
natural law as derived from the higher. Before, however, embarking upon that
question properly speaking, I would like to say something about the scientific
methodology of analysis/synthesis as employed in the ancient world. I do so
with a view to using these ideas here in order to explain Thomas's comments
on the relationship between higher and lower precept. They will also be of
use in chapter 8, where I attempt to bring more precision to our understanding of the structure of practical reason.

The primary source for our understanding of this double method of

---

they do not know the fact—just as people who study universals often do not know some of the
particulars through lack of observation" [*An.post.* i,13,79a2–6]. Barnes, however, calls attention to
difficulties in establishing criteria according to which the material or genus of one discipline
might be different from that of another [Barnes (1994 <1975>), pp. 131, 158–62, 195–96]. See also
Nussbaum (1978), pp. 108ff.; Kung (1982); McKirahan (1992), pp. 50–63.

25. Nor in fact do they apply to Zabarella, to whom Gómez-Lobo attributes the stronger version of the traditional understanding [Gómez-Lobo (1978), p. 184; see also above note 7].
Although Zabarella does say, as Gómez-Lobo notes, that "from the principles of metaphysics, the
principles of geometry can be proved" (see above, note 6), he also says with respect to the same
passage in Aristotle, "facta illatione, consequens ab Aristotele ita deducitur, si propria alicuius scientiae principia in eadem scientia demonstrantur, necesse est id fieri vel per alia eiusdem scientiae principia, vel per aliena, vel per communia: at nullum horum fieri potest, ergo nulla ratione
possunt demonstrari" [*in An.post.* 779E, see also 781A]. Note though that Zabarella's restrictions
only apply to the proper principles being proved *within* their respective sciences (as in note 6). In
this connection, he uses a phrase similar to Thomas's, saying that if, for example, the natural scientist wishes to answer challenges about the principles of natural science, he must do this not as a
natural philosopher but "ut indutum habitu Metaphysicae" [781D]. This separation between
metaphysics and the other sciences means, says Zabarella, that the others are not subalternate to
metaphysics ["subalternatas Metaphysicae": 781DE]. By this he does not mean that they are not
subordinate to metaphysics—for in this same comment he speaks much of the preeminence of
"the divine science" on which the other sciences "depend" [780CD]—but that they are not subalternate in the way that music is subalternate to arithmetic. See his *De praecogn.* 527B–530C.

analysis and synthesis is the fourth century (A.D.) mathematician Pappus of Alexandria. "Analysis," he writes,

takes that which is sought as if it were admitted and passes from it through its successive consequences [διὰ τῶν ἑξῆς ἀκολούθων] to something that is admitted as the result of synthesis: for in analysis we assume that which is sought as if it were (already) done, and we inquire what it is from which this results, and again what is the antecedent cause of the latter, and so on, until by so retracing our steps we come upon something already known or belonging to the class of first principles, and such a method we call analysis as being solution backwards [ἀνάπαλιν λύσιν].

But in synthesis, reversing the process, we take as already done that which was last arrived at in the analysis and, by arranging in their natural order as consequences [ἑπόμενα] what were before antecedents, and successively connecting them one with another, we arrive finally at the construction of what was sought; and this we call synthesis.[26]

There are some obscurities in this passage, although the general lines of the method described are readily apparent. In synthesis, one works from that which is already known or from first principles, through their "consequences" ("successively connecting them one with another" in their natural order), until one arrives at the conclusion originally desired. In analysis, one works in the opposite direction, "against the flow," from the conclusion sought up toward the accepted principles.[27]

The obscurities have to do mainly with how this latter journey is accomplished. If one interprets the words διὰ τῶν ἑξῆς ἀκολούθων ("through its successive consequences") as meaning that in analysis one seeks to derive propositions that follow from the conclusion for which a proof is sought until one arrives at the accepted principles, one drastically limits the possible

26. Pappus Alexandrinus, *Collec.* vii,634.11–23. Translation taken from Heath's translation of Euclid's *Elements* [Heath (1956 <1925>), vol. 1, p. 138]. See also Hintikka and Remes (1974), pp. 8–10; also Jones (1986), vol. 2, pp. 376–80 (Greek text in vol. 1, p. 83). A classic article on Pappus's remarks on analysis/synthesis is Gulley (1958).

27. Hintikka and Remes study a geometrical proof involving both analysis and synthesis by Pappus [Hintikka and Remes (1974), pp. 22–30], identifying parts within analysis and synthesis, of which the "resolution" (part of analysis) is fairly important. It deals with the auxiliary constructions required in the analysis phase (one has to show that they are independent of the desired outcome, τὸ ζητούμενον) [Hintikka and Remes (1974), pp. 43, 49–69]. Below I discuss the significance of constructions in analysis; following Hintikka and Remes, I also argue that the opposite "directions" of analysis and synthesis are not their essential features. For a good, succinct summary (and criticism) of the Hintikka/Remes argument, see Mueller (1976).

uses of the method since, unless one is operating in a field where most implications are mutual (as in mathematics or geometry), one is unlikely ever to arrive at the accepted principles. This problem is solved and the analysis/synthesis method rendered more useful if one interprets the word ἀκόλουθον as meaning not 'consequence' but rather (more widely) 'concomitant.' If q follows from p, it is not necessarily the case that p follows from q, but p is certainly consistent with q. Thus, analysis would involve searching for a step, related to and not inconsistent with the step where one stands, and from that step seeking another, and so on, the whole series leading in what looks to be the direction of the accepted principles. If and when one reaches the accepted principles, one can return in the synthesis phase along the same path, making sure that each of the conclusions follows from its premises.[28]

DIAGRAM 1

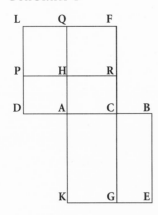

Although it is a fairly complicated matter, I give now an example of geometrical analysis and synthesis. (It will be useful also for the argument of chapter 8.) The example is a proof of the first proposition of Euclid's *Elements*, book xiii. *Elem.* xiii,1 says, "If a straight line be cut in extreme and mean ratio, the square on the greater segment added to the half of the whole is five times the square of the half."[29] Diagram 1 is necessary in order to follow the proof.

Line AB is "the line be cut in extreme and mean ratio." This latter expression means that, cutting a line at a point (here C), as the whole line stands to the greater segment, so the greater stands to the

28. On the meaning of ἀκόλουθον and ἑπόμενον in Aristotle, see Mueller (1976), pp. 161–62; Brandon (1978); Hintikka (1973), pp. 41–55.

29. Heath (1956 <1925>), vol. 3, pp. 440–42; Ἐὰν εὐθεῖα γραμμὴ ἄκρον καὶ μέσον λόγον τμηθῇ, τὸ μεῖζον τμῆμα προσλαβὸν τὴν ἡμίσειαν τῆς ὅλης πενταπλάσιον δύναται τοῦ ἀπὸ τῆς ἡμισείας τετραγώνου [*Elem.* xiii,1 (248.2–5)]. The "greater segment added to the half of the whole" is line DC. The square on DC is the square DF. (I will use this means of identification—identifying, that is, squares by means of the end points of their diagonals.) The proof of *Elem.* xiii,1 given here is based on some remarks found in the text of the *Elements* just after xiii,1, which mention (and use) analysis and synthesis [see Heath (1956 <1925>), vol. 3, pp. 442–43; see also Robinson (1969 <1936>), pp. 9–11]. Heath regards them as interpolated. (Eudoxus, Theaetetus, Theon, and Heron have been suggested as possible authors.) The remarks are now found in Appendix I to vol. 4 of Heiberg's edition of *Elem.*, pp. 365–68.

less.[30] In other words, if AC (as in the diagram) is the greater segment and CB the smaller, the ratio between AB and AC is the same as that between AC and CB. The line DA is stipulated to be half the length of AB. The proposition to be proved is, therefore, that the square constructed using DC as one of its sides (i.e., the square DF) is five times the size of the square constructed using DA as one of its sides (i.e., the square DH).

<hr>

ANALYSIS

[1] We assume what is to be proved: i.e., that the square DF is five times the size of square DH.

[2] We note too that square DF equals the square DH + the square that one could construct on line AC + twice the rectangle constructed using lines DA and AC. (This is proved at *Elem.* ii,4.)[31]

[3] Since square DF = 5 x square DH and since square DF = square DH + the square one could construct on line AC + twice the rectangle constructed using lines DA and AC, using subtraction we can say that the square one could construct on line AC + twice the rectangle constructed using lines DA and AC is equal to 4 x square DH.

[4] But, since line AB, as stipulated, is twice line DA, the rectangle constructed using lines AB and AC is twice the rectangle constructed using lines DA and AC.

[5] Moreover, the square one could construct on line AC equals the rectangle constructed using lines AB and CB, since, as is proved at *Elem.* vi,17, "if three straight lines be proportional, the rectangle contained by the extremes is equal to the square on the mean."[32]

<hr>

30. Ἄκρον καὶ μέσον λόγον εὐθεῖα τετμῆσθαι λέγεται, ὅταν ᾖ ὡς ἡ ὅλη πρὸς τὸ μεῖζον τμῆμα, οὕτως τὸ μεῖζον πρὸς τὸ ἔλαττον [*Elem.* vi,df.3 (72.8–10)]; "A straight line is said to have been cut in extreme and mean ratio when, as the whole line is to the greater segment, so is the greater to the less" [Heath (1956 <1925>), vol. 2, p. 188].

31. It is also fairly obvious from studying the diagram itself. Since DH is a square and the sides AH and HP are therefore equal, the lines HQ and HR are also equal and figure HF is a square. But, since line HR is equal to line AC, the square HF is equal to the square that would be constructed on line AC. Given the equality of lines DA, AH, and HP and given too the equality of lines AC, HR, and HQ, it is clear that the "rectangle constructed using line DA and AC" must be equal to rectangle AR and also to rectangle PQ. Thus, within square DF we have the square DH; we have there also the square HF, which equals the square "one could construct on line AC," and we have two rectangles equal to "the rectangle constructed using line DA and AC."

32. Heath (1956 <1925>), vol. 2, p. 228; Ἐὰν τρεῖς εὐθεῖαι ἀνάλογον ὦσιν, τὸ ὑπὸ τῶν ἄκρων περιεχόμενον ὀρθογώνιον ἴσον ἐστὶ τῷ ἀπὸ τῆς μέσης τετραγώνῳ . . . [*Elem.* vi,17 (122.2–4)]. Since line AB is cut in the mean and the extreme ratio, the lines AB, AC, CB are proportional, AB and CB being the extremes and AC being the mean.

[6] Therefore, since (as concluded in [3]) the square one could construct on line AC + twice the rectangle constructed using lines DA and AC are equal to 4 x square DH, we can say that the rectangle constructed using lines AB and AC + the rectangle constructed using lines AB and CB equals four times the square DH.

[7] But, as is shown at *Elem*. ii,2, the rectangle constructed using lines AB and AC + the rectangle constructed using lines AB and CB equals the square constructed on (and below) line AB in the diagram.[33]

[8] Thus, combining [6] and [7], the square constructed on line AB is equal to four times the square DH.

[9] And this is clearly the case since, as stipulated, line AB is twice the length of DA.[34]

SYNTHESIS

{9} Line AB is twice the length of DA,

{8} which means that the square constructed on line AB is equal to four times the square constructed on line AD (= square DH).

{7} But we know (from *Elem*. ii,2) that the square constructed on line AB is equal to the rectangle constructed using lines AB and AC + the rectangle constructed using lines AB and CB.

{6} Thus, the rectangle constructed using lines AB and AC + the rectangle constructed using lines AB and CB, together equal four times the square DH.

{5} Applying *Elem*. vi,17, we can say that the rectangle constructed using lines AB and CB equals the square one could construct on line AC.

33. "If a straight line be cut at random, the rectangle contained by the whole and both of the segments is equal to the square on the whole" Heath (1956 <1925>), vol. 1, p. 376]; Ἐὰν εὐθεῖα γραμμὴ τμηθῇ, ὡς ἔτυχεν, τὸ ὑπὸ τῆς ὅλης καὶ ἑκατέρου τῶν τμημάτων περιεχόμενον ὀρθογώνιον ἴσον ἐστὶ τῷ ἀπὸ τῆς ὅλης τετραγώνῳ [*Elem*. ii,2 (120.20–23)]. The rectangle KC is equal to the rectangle constructed using lines AB and AC; the rectangle GB is equal to the rectangle constructed using lines AB and CB. Rectangles KC and GB combined are the square on line AB.

34. Those used to dealing with symbols may find the following synopsis of the analysis useful:

[1] $\square$DF = 5x $\square$DH
[2] $\square$DF = $\square$DH + $\square$onAC + 2x(DA,AC) [*Elem*. ii,4]
[3] $\square$onAC + 2x(DA,AC) = 4x $\square$DH [subtraction]
[4] (AB,AC) = 2x(DA,AC) [AB = 2x DA]
[5] (AB,CB) = $\square$onAC [*Elem*. vi,17]
[6] (AB,AC) + (AB,CB) = 4x $\square$DH [3], [4], [5]
[7] (AB,AC) + (AB,CB) = $\square$onAB [*Elem*. ii,2]
[8] $\square$onAB = 4x $\square$DH
[9] Apparent, since AB = 2x DA.

{4} We also know that the rectangle constructed using lines AB and AC is twice the rectangle constructed using lines DA and AC (since line AB is twice line DA).

{3} From {6}, {5} and {4}, therefore, we can conclude that the square one could construct on line AC + twice the rectangle constructed using lines DA and AC is equal to 4 x square DH.

{2} Applying *Elem.* ii,4, we can say that the square DH + the square one could construct on line AC + twice the rectangle constructed using lines DA and AC = the square DF.

{1} But, since, as concluded in {3}, the square one could construct on line AC + twice the rectangle constructed using lines DA and AC is equal to 4 x square DH and since (from {2}) square DF = the square DH + the square one could construct on line AC + twice the rectangle constructed using lines DA and AC, we know that the square DF is five times the square DH. And this was the proposition to be proved.

The first part of this proof, i.e., the analysis, is the more useful for our present purposes, since it gives us the more striking image of how reasoning of this type works. It shows that even geometrical reasoning need not be simply a matter of deducing conclusions from higher principles. Such indeed does occur in the synthesis phase, which, in the above proof, is obviously a re-tracing and re-checking of the steps taken in the analysis; but that which allows a deductive system to grow in a particular direction is analysis. A geometer, or perhaps even an astronomer or engineer, gets the idea that a particular theorem might be useful if true, and set out to prove it: i.e., to link it up to the principles of geometry. As we shall see more clearly in the coming pages (especially chapters 5 and 6), one cannot will without willing *something*— i.e., something presented by the intellect to the will. Similarly, even strictly-speaking deductive systems such as geometry do not grow without there first being an idea about which it might grow. This is represented in the above proof in step [1], the assumption that the square DF is five times the size of square DH.

Such added, or non-deduced, material is also present in the diagram itself. In Euclid, just after the introduction of *Elem.* xiii,1, we find a brief description (or specification) of the line mentioned in the proposition—i.e., line AB, which is cut at C and extended half its own distance by line DA—and a restatement of the proposition, "I say that the square on CD is five times the square on AD." Euclid then adds, "For let the squares AE, DF, be described on AB, DC, and let the figure DF be drawn; let FC be carried through to G."[35] In the above proof I have also added lines AQ and PR. With such a construction before him, the geometer can begin to visualize how a proof might be devised: he knows that square DF is supposed to be 5 times DH; having worked some other proofs within the system (such as that of *Elem.* vi,17), he knows that there is relationship between the line AC (i.e., the mean of three proportional lines) and rectangle GB (which is equal to the rectangle that would result if lines AC and CB were used as sides), etc. Given, then, a desired outcome, a diagram and an ample supply of background knowledge, the geometer attempts, by trial and error, to work his way toward the accepted principles.

Jaakko Hintikka and Unto Remes are very articulate and insightful about the philosophical significance of analysis.[36] Analysis, they note, is "a method of discovery, not one of proof."[37] Scholarly treatments of analysis and synthesis, especially in the Middle Ages, have tended to overemphasize the "direction" in which analysis proceeds, i.e., the fact that it goes "against the flow" of what one finds in synthesis.[38] This is still to look at analysis as merely the passing from one proposition to another. Viewing analysis in this way, one does not see the role that the structure of the proposition to be proved plays in the process itself. "Clearly the 'secret' of the method of analysis is to use in some sense the structure of the theorem to be proved . . . to find a proof for it."[39]

Also important is the construction or diagram employed. Speaking of the absence of a "decision procedure" for geometry once it reaches a certain level of complexity, they remark,

the failure of the analytical method as a foolproof discovery procedure has to be explained by reference to the need of constructions (auxiliary individuals). . . . What [the geometer] must analyze is not a unique figure determined completely by the theorem or problem at hand, but a figure amplified by constructions in the finding of

35. (Heath 1956 <1925>), vol. 3, p. 440; Ἀναγεγράφθωσαν γὰρ ἀπὸ τῶν ΑΒ, ΔΓ τετράγωνα τὰ ΑΕ, ΔΖ, καὶ καταγεγράφθω ἐν τῷ ΔΖ τὸ σχῆμα, καὶ διήχθω ἡ ΖΓ ἐπὶ τὸ Η [*Elem.* xiii,1 (248.11–13)].
36. The method has been practiced more widely than in the ancient world. See in Crombie (1994), for example, pp. 282–94, 1185–90; see also Berti (1983).
37. Hintikka and Remes (1974), p. 7. See also S. E. Dolan (1950), p. 41; see also Rhonheimer (1987), pp. 216–23; also Rhonheimer (1994), p. 553.
38. Hintikka and Remes (1974), p. 11.
39. Hintikka and Remes (1974), p. 33.

which (as Leibniz already saw—see *Nouveaux essais* IV,xvii,3) "the greatest art" of an analyst typically consists.[40]

[5] Analysis in Thomas

So then, even a deductive system such as geometry is not purely a matter of deriving conclusions from principles, further conclusions from those conclusions, etc. A geometrical system grows by positing paths along which it might be developed. Such positing might easily be passed over as unimportant or incidental to the science of geometry itself; and, once the synthesis is set out, a person might wonder, Why retain the analysis phase at all? But, in fact, the added, non-deduced material plays an important role in the system itself. One cannot go forward—or, at least, go very far forward—without such material.

Can we say for sure that Thomas knew the analysis/synthesis method? We can, for references to the method are found throughout his writings. In the *prima secundae* of the *Summa theologiae,* for instance, having explained that metaphysics considers the highest causes, he says, "thus, it properly judges and puts in order all things since it is not possible to have a perfect and universal judgment other than through resolution to first causes."[41] (In Latin, ἀνάλυσις becomes *resolutio;* σύνθεσις becomes *compositio.*) In the same part of the *Summa,* he speaks (very interestingly) of analysis as a series of courts: "so long as there remains a yet higher principle, the question can be submitted to it: wherefore the judgment is still in suspense, the final judgment not being yet pronounced."[42]

---

40. Hintikka and Remes (1974), pp. 133–34. The two scholars explain what is essential to analysis: (i) one studies interrelationships of geometrical objects in a given configuration; (ii) one uses maximal information. (They also identify a third essential part of analysis (iii): the construction of auxiliary figures [Hintikka and Remes (1974), p. 44].) "Principle (ii)," they say, "implies that analysis cannot be thought of as a stepwise journey *either* from [the premisses to the desired conclusion] or from [the desired conclusion to the premisses]" [Hintikka and Remes (1974), p. 38; emphasis theirs]. (See also Hintikka and Remes (1976), pp. 267–71.) They draw a contrast between the analysis of deductive steps (which is linear) and the analysis of figures, which "takes the form of a more complicated network of connections" [Hintikka and Remes (1974), p. 39].

41. "Unde convenienter iudicat et ordinat de omnibus, quia iudicium perfectum et universale haberi non potest nisi per resolutionem ad primas causas" [*ST* I–II q.57 a.2 c]. In ad 2 of this article Thomas talks about the relationship of metaphysics (*sapientia*) to *scientia* and *intellectus*. "Et utrumque dependet a sapientia sicut a principalissimo, quae sub se continet et intellectum et scientiam, ut de conclusionibus scientiarum diiudicans, et de principiis earundem."

42. *ST* I–II q.74 a.7 c: "Quandiu enim remanet aliquod principium altius, adhuc per ipsum

In *De veritate,* Thomas speaks of analysis in connection with geometry (although he applies these ideas more generally). As long as an analysis has not been performed, a person apprehends something only as a probability, as someone does who has only heard something from others and therefore cannot apply this knowledge to other situations and problems.

> If someone does not know how to deduce the conclusions of geometry from the principles, he does not have the settled disposition [*habitum*] of geometry, but whatever conclusions of geometry he knows he knows as one believing a teacher. Just so, he needs to be instructed about individual matters: he is incapable of proceeding from some things to others in a reliable manner, the resolution to first principles not having been made.[43]

Two questions later, he makes it apparent that analysis in a sense both begins and ends with the principles. It is true (as we have been arguing) that the initial incentive to perform an analysis comes with the proposition to be proved and thus the general configuration of the problem to be considered is set by this proposition; but no one thinks to do an analysis unless he knows there are principles into which the proposition might be resolved.[44] We should not

---

potest examinari id de quo quaeritur: unde adhuc est suspensum iudicium, quasi nondum data finali sententia." Thomas takes a similarly interesting approach at *in Trin.* q.1 a.3 ll.155–56: lower principles are said to be *certified* by higher ones. See also *ST* I–II, where he says that nothing is firm in practical reason "nisi per resolutionem ad prima principia" [q.90 a.2 ad 3].

43. *De ver.* q.12 a.1 c ll.190–203 (§109): "[Q]uamdiu enim non fit resolutio cognitorum in sua principia cognitio non firmatur in uno, sed apprehendit ea quae cognoscit secundum probabilitatem quamdam utpote ab aliis dicta, unde necesse habet de singulis acceptionem ab aliis habere. Sicut si aliquis nesciret geometriae conclusiones ex principiis deducere habitum geometriae non haberet, sed quaecumque de conclusionibus geometriae sciret apprehenderet quasi credens docenti, et sic indigeret ut de singulis instrueretur: non enim posset ex quibusdam in alia pervenire firmiter, non facta resolutione in prima principia."

44. *De ver.* q.14 a.1 c ll.168–76 (§128): "[E]x ipsa enim collatione principiorum ad conclusiones assentit conclusionibus resolvendo eas in principia et ibi figitur motus cogitantis et quietatur; in scientia enim motus rationis incipit ab intellectu principiorum et ad eumdem terminatur per viam resolutionis, et sic non habet assensum et cogitationem quasi ex aequo, sed cogitatio inducit ad assensum et assensus cogitationem quietat." Other discussions of *resolutio* (sometimes explicitly paired with *compositio*) are found at, for example, *in Sent.* lb.2 d.9 q.1 a.8 ad 1; lb.4 d.9 q.1 a.4 sol.1 c ("judicium enim perfectum haberi non potest de aliqua cognitione, nisi per resolutionem ad principium unde cognitio ortum habet"); *SCG* lb.3 cap.41 (§2182); lb.3 cap.47 (§2243); *in De cael.* lb.2 lect.4 n.4 (§333) ("Et primo assignat eam per viam compositionis, procedendo a primo ad ultimum quod quaeritur; secundo per viam resolutionis, procedendo ab ultimo quod quaeritur usque ad primum"). There are also many references to the analysis/synthesis method in the commentary on the *Posterior Analytics*—e.g., *in An.post.* lb.1 lect.43 ll.240–41 (§391) (discussed above), lb.2 lect.4 ll.20–21 (§444)—and in the commentary on the *Metaphysics* (e.g., *in Metaph., proem.,* where he says that metaphysics is called metaphysics "in quantum considerat ens et ea quae consequuntur ipsum. Haec enim transphysica inveniuntur in via resolutionis, sicut magis

overemphasize, therefore, the role of the material in terms of which a science or discipline grows. In the end, it is always a matter of connecting the new material up with the higher principles.

But, someone might ask, can we legitimately apply a method developed within a mathematical science in the field of ethics? Neither Aristotle nor Thomas hesitates to do so. In the *Nicomachean Ethics,* having explained that those who deliberate begin with the end they wish to reach and cast about for means to get there, Aristotle says: "For the person who deliberates seems to inquire and analyze in the way described as though he were analyzing a geometrical construction (not all inquiry appears to be deliberation—for instance mathematical inquiries—but all deliberation is inquiry), and what is last in the order of analysis seems to be first in the order of becoming."[45] Thomas alludes to this remark often. For instance, in the *Summa contra gentiles,* speaking about the difference between the souls of sinful persons and those of the saints in heaven, he remarks:

---

communia post minus communia"; also §278, where he notes that the principles toward which we move in analysis "confusa sunt prius nobis nota"). On some of these texts and on some others, see Aertsen (1989).

45. *EN* iii,3,1112b20–24. On the use of the words ἀνάλυσις, ἀναλύειν, etc., in Aristotle, see Einarson (1936), pp. 36–39; see also Allan (1961) and Narcy (1978). See now also the very useful Byrne (1997), of which I became aware only after the present book was largely completed.

Thomas comments on *EN* iii,3,1112b20–24 as follows: "Et dicit quod ideo causa quae est prima in operatione est ultima in inventione, quia ille qui consiliatur videtur inquirere, sicut dictum est, per modum resolutionis cuiusdam. Quemadmodum diagramma, id est descriptio geometrica in qua qui vult probare aliquam conclusionem oportet quod resolvat conclusionem in principia quousque pervenit ad principia prima indemonstrabilia" [*in EN* lb.3 lect.8 ll.61–69 (§476); see also ll.73–77 and ll.88–92 (§477)]. Elders [Elders (1987), vol. 2, p. 51] points to a comment in the same commentary that seems to say the opposite: "Et quia secundum artem demonstrativae scientiae, oportet principia esse conformia conclusionibus, amabile est et optabile, de talibus, idest tam variabilibus, tractatum facientes, et ex similibus procedentes ostendere veritatem, primo quidem grosse idest applicando universalia principia et simplicia ad singularia et composita, in quibus est actus; necessarium est enim in qualibet operativa scientia ut procedatur modo compositivo, e contrario autem in scientia speculativa necesse est ut procedatur modo resolutivo, resolvendo composita in principia simplicia. Deinde oportet ostendere veritatem figuraliter, idest verisimiliter; et hoc est procedere ex propriis principiis huius scientiae. Nam scientia moralis est de actibus voluntariis: voluntatis autem motivum est, non solum bonum, sed apparens bonum" [*in EN* lb.1 lect.3 ll.47–63 (§35)]. In speaking here, however, of the synthetic mode ["modo compositivo"] Thomas is clearly not speaking about the deductive mode found in the second part of a geometrical proof, since Aristotle's point in *EN* i,3 (which Thomas faithfully interprets in his commentary) is that ethics has not the deductive rigor that the speculative sciences have. Thomas is speaking rather of the initial, "common and indeterminate" grasp we have of practical reason's first precepts (see chapter 2, section [5]). With such an indeterminate grasp of the good, a person sets out to discover means of getting to it—which is to proceed "modo resolutivo," as he says in *in EN* lb.3 lect.8 (above).

Our intellect can err with respect to certain conclusions before a resolution to first principles comes about, the resolution to which once completed, knowledge of the conclusions is had, which knowledge cannot be false. But as stands a principle of demonstration in speculative matters, so stands an end in appetitive matters. As long, therefore, as we have not achieved the ultimate end, our will can be corrupted—but not once it has arrived at the enjoyment of the ultimate end, for it is desirable for its own sake, as the first principles of demonstrations are known in themselves.[46]

This text is especially interesting insofar as it applies the concept of being *per se notum* ("known in themselves") to practical ends. (See chapter 2, sections [3] and [4].)

An article in the *Summa theologiae* devoted to deliberation (or "counsel") comes close to quoting the above passage from *EN* iii,2:

In every inquiry one must begin from some principle. And if this principle precedes both in knowledge and in being, the process is not analytic, but synthetic: because to proceed from cause to effect is to proceed synthetically, since causes are more simple than effects.[47] But if that which precedes in knowledge is later in the order of being, the process is one of analysis, as when our judgment deals with effects, which by analysis we trace to their simple causes.[48]

Thomas goes on to argue that counsel is analytic and then, of course, to answer objections. His answers to two of these tell us much about how he conceived of analysis, as it operates in practical reason. Both objection 2 and objection 3 argue that the order of counsel should be determined by temporal

---

46. "Intellectus noster circa conclusiones aliquas errare potest antequam in prima principia resolutio fiat, in quae resolutione iam facta, scientia de conclusionibus habetur, quae falsa esse non potest. Sicut autem se habet principium demonstrationis in speculativis, ita se habet finis in appetitivis. Quandiu igitur finem ultimum non consequimur, voluntas nostra potest perverti: non autem postquam ad fruitionem ultimi finis pervenerit, quod est propter se ipsum desiderabile, sicut ultima principia demonstrationum sunt per se nota" [*SCG* lb.4 cap.92 (§4263)].

47. Pappus, as seen at the end of the above quotation from his *Collec.* vii, argues that the word ἀνάλυσις does not signify a breaking up into smaller parts but "a solution backwards": i.e., an ἀνάπαλιν λύσις [Pappus Alexandrinus, *Collec.* vii,634.18]. Árpád K. Szabó accepts the etymology of Pappus (translating ἀνάπαλιν λύσις as "untying again, a solution backwards") and holds that the word ἀνάλυσις signifies an undoing or relaxing of what was previously bound [Szabó (1974), p. 119]. Hintikka and Remes disagree with Szabó, defending the view that, at least in Aristotle and Proclus, ἀνάλυσις means 'breaking up' or 'taking apart' [Hintikka and Remes (1974), pp. 131–32].

48. *ST* I–II q.14 a.5 c: "Respondeo dicendum quod in omni inquisitione oportet incipere ab aliquo principio. Quod quidem si, sicut est prius in cognitione, ita etiam sit prius in esse, non est processus resolutorius, sed magis compositivus, procedere enim a causis in effectus, est processus compositivus, nam causae sunt simpliciores effectibus. Si autem id quod est prius in cognitione, sit posterius in esse, est processus resolutorius, utpote cum de effectibus manifestis iudicamus, resolvendo in causas simplices."

considerations. Reason, argues objection 2, "proceeds from things that precede to things that follow"; therefore, "in taking counsel one should proceed
from the past and present to the future: which is not an analytical process."
Objection 3 argues similarly that "the inquiry of counsel should begin from
things present."[49]

One might have thought that, since he holds that the practical syllogism
proceeds from that which might be done at one moment to that which comes
after it and so on until one arrives at the end, Thomas would be in agreement
as to the temporal consideration. But he is not. He responds that "Reason begins with that which is first according to reason, but not always with that
which is first in point of time."[50] He clearly does not mean that counsel begins with the principles, for that would be synthetic reasoning and the whole
point of this article is to show that counsel "procedet ordine resolutorio." He
must have in mind, therefore, the way in which we test out, i.e., posit, alternative stratagems, until, through a process often characterized by fits and starts,
we arrive at a solution: a path up to the principles. It is clear, therefore, that
here too—i.e., even in the reverse direction of analysis—the process is not a
step-to-next-step process but, rather, a matter of hypothesis and even invention.

[6] Ethical applications

We come now, more properly speaking, to the second question mentioned
at the beginning of this chapter: In what sense did Thomas consider lower
precepts of natural law to be derived from higher? There can be little doubt
that he did recognize some such logical relationship between the two, for he
speaks of derivation in this respect in *ST* I–II q.95 a.2.[51] There, having asked
"whether every humanly posited law is derived from natural law" and having

---

49. "Praeterea, consilium est inquisitio rationis. Sed ratio a prioribus incipit, et ad posteriora
devenit, secundum convenientiorem ordinem cum igitur praeterita sint priora praesentibus, et
praesentia priora futuris, in consiliando videtur esse procedendum a praesentibus et praeteritis in
futura. Quod non pertinet ad ordinem resolutorium. Ergo in consiliis non servatur ordo resolutorius.

Praeterea, consilium non est nisi de his quae sunt nobis possibilia, ut dicitur in iii Ethic. Sed
an sit nobis aliquid possibile, perpenditur ex eo quod possumus facere, vel non possumus facere,
ut perveniamus in illud. Ergo in inquisitione consilii a praesentibus incipere oportet."

50. "Ad secundum dicendum quod ratio incipit ab eo quod est prius secundum rationem,
non autem semper ab eo quod est prius tempore."

51. Other passages in which Thomas speaks of deriving lower principles include: *ST* I–II q.91
a.3, where he says that the natural law goes from the more general to the more particular as one

noted that according to Augustine "every humanly posited law has something of the intelligibility of law insofar as it is derived from the law of nature," he says:

But it is to be noted that something can be derived from the natural law in two ways: one, as conclusions are from principles; another, as particular determinations from certain things that are common. The first way is similar to that in which, in the sciences, demonstrative conclusions are produced from principles. The second way is similar to that whereby, in the arts, common forms are made determinate with respect to something special, as an artificer needs to determine the common form of a house to this or that shape of a house.

Certain things, therefore, are derived from the common principles of the law of nature in the manner of conclusions, as for instance 'one must not kill' can be derived as a sort of conclusion from 'ill is to be done to no one.' Certain things, however, <are derived> in the manner of a determination, as for instance the law of nature has it that he who does wrong should be punished; but that he should be punished by such and such a penalty, this is a particular determination of the law of nature.[52]

---

goes from principles to conclusions ["... sicut in ratione speculativa ex principiis indemonstra-bilibus naturaliter cognitis producuntur conclusiones diversarum scientiarum, quarum cognitio non est nobis naturaliter indita, sed per industriam rationis inventa; ita etiam ex praeceptis legis naturalis, quasi ex quibusdam principiis communibus et indemonstrabilibus, necesse est quod ratio humana procedat ad aliqua magis particulariter disponenda"] and *ST* I–II q.94 a.4 ["Apud omnes enim hoc rectum est et verum, ut secundum rationem agatur. Ex hoc autem principio sequitur quasi conclusio propria, quod deposita sint reddenda"]. I discuss this latter article below. On many of the relevant texts, see Rhonheimer (1987), pp. 224–39.

52. I give the entire body here:

"Respondeo dicendum quod, sicut Augustinus dicit, in I De lib. arb., non videtur esse lex, quae iusta non fuerit. Unde inquantum habet de iustitia, intantum habet de virtute legis. In rebus autem humanis dicitur esse aliquid iustum ex eo quod est rectum secundum regulam rationis. Rationis autem prima regula est lex naturae, ut ex supradictis patet. Unde omnis lex humanitus posita intantum habet de ratione legis, inquantum a lege naturae derivatur. Si vero in aliquo, a lege naturali discordet, iam non erit lex sed legis corruptio.

Sed sciendum est quod a lege naturali dupliciter potest aliquid derivari, uno modo, sicut conclusiones ex principiis; alio modo, sicut determinationes quaedam aliquorum communium. Primus quidem modus est similis ei quo in scientiis ex principiis conclusiones demonstrativae producuntur. Secundo vero modo simile est quod in artibus formae communes determinantur ad aliquid speciale, sicut artifex formam communem domus necesse est quod determinet ad hanc vel illam domus figuram.

Derivantur ergo quaedam a principiis communibus legis naturae per modum conclusionum, sicut hoc quod est non esse occidendum, ut conclusio quaedam derivari potest ab eo quod est nulli esse malum faciendum. Quaedam vero per modum determinationis, sicut lex naturae habet quod ille qui peccat, puniatur; sed quod tali poena puniatur, hoc est quaedam determinatio legis naturae.

Utraque igitur inveniuntur in lege humana posita. Sed ea quae sunt primi modi, continentur

It would appear that Thomas is acknowledging here that ethics does sometimes involve added material ("a particular determination") but that, for the most part, it proceeds by synthesis (as "demonstrative conclusions are produced from principles"). If this is the case, then Neoplatonic methods apply at least with respect to the less particular precepts of the natural law. In fact, however, it is precisely this *locus classicus* for the "derivation" of ethical precepts which provides our best evidence that even the relatively higher precepts enjoy a certain independence from those yet higher than them.

In *ST* I–II q.95 a.2, Thomas identifies two types of precepts: (1) precepts that involve no arbitrariness since they are located close up to the common precepts and (2) lower precepts that do involve arbitrariness.[53] The central issue in the article is whether even the arbitrary determinations communicate in the natural law. Thomas's answer is yes. To use a modern example, when Italy, for instance, determines that the sentence for drunk driving shall be permanent loss of one's driver's license and the United States opts for temporary suspension, the connection with natural law may not be the most direct or the strongest but it does exist—since protection of life pertains to natural law and such arbitrary determinations are specific ways of protecting life. This is all quite clear in the article and, at least in the present context, uncontroversial. But, as is so often the case in Thomas, the interesting thing is not so much the central issue he puts forward but rather what he presupposes. In particular, he presupposes in q.95 a.2 that *both* types of derivation involve "posited law."[54] Consider the lines that immediately follow those just quoted:

---

lege humana non tanquam sint solum lege posita, sed habent etiam aliquid vigoris ex lege naturali. Sed ea quae sunt secundi modi, ex sola lege humana vigorem habent."

53. Here and in what follows the word 'arbitrary' (with its derivatives) is used in its legal sense; that is to say, it bears no negative connotations but merely signifies that a precept is (to some degree) dependent upon human willing. On *ST* I–II q.95 a.2 and related texts, see Armstrong (1966), pp. 93–98.

54. Says John Finnis, citing *ST* I–II q.95 a.2 [Finnis (1996), p. 212, n. 38], "Aquinas treats his here-favoured phrase *lex humanitus posita* as synonymous with *lex humana posita* and with *ius positivum* (see obj. 2) and *lex positiva* (see ad 3); the very next article (a.3) settles down to talking of *lex positiva* as synonymous with *lex humana*." See also *ST* I–II q.95 a.4: "dividitur ius positivum in ius gentium et ius civile, secundum duos modos quibus aliquid derivatur a lege naturae, ut supra dictum est"—the latter being a reference to q.95 a.2 which, as we shall see shortly, argues that *lex* is *humanitus posita* in two ways. Although often *lex posita* is translated 'positive law,' in what follows I use the more literal translation since the idea of positing a law is important for my argument. For the difference between natural and positive law, see *ST* II–II q.57 a.2. Note that in Thomas there is also such a thing as divine posited (i.e., positive) law: "Si autem lex sit divinitus posita, auctoritate divina dispensatio fieri potest" [*SCG* lb.3 cap.125 (§2986)].

"Both, therefore, are found in human posited law. But those things that are of the first way are contained in human law not as if they were only contained in posited law, but they have also something of their force from the law of nature. But those things that are of the second way have their force from human law alone."[55] What interests *us* here is that the precept 'one must not kill'— which is certainly well-embedded in natural law—in the very article in which it is said to be derived from a higher principle, is also said to be posited.[56]

What is so important about its being posited? It shows that Thomas has in mind something other than mere derivation. Deriving and positing are quite different procedures. In positing, one knows a higher principle (perhaps only in a practical way) and, when faced with a situation to which the higher principle is pertinent, posits a law that has a certain independence of the first. Suppose that there was no way that a human being could ever be killed. A lawmaker would not think of positing the precept 'one must not kill.' This shows that part of the law depends on the particular circumstances in which the higher principle applies—here, an aspect of human nature. On the other hand, in deriving 'all Greeks are mortals' from 'all men are mortals' and 'all Greeks are men,' nothing new is added—except to identify what it is that follows. The proposition 'all Greeks are mortal' is contained *in* the premisses from which it is derived.[57]

So, although on its surface the point of the first quotation from *ST* I–II q.95 a.2 would seem to be that "the first way" involves derivation ("derived from the common principles . . . in the manner of conclusions") while "the

55. It is possible to construe the first sentence ("Utraque igitur inveniuntur in lege humana posita") as, "Both . . . are found posited in human law," but the succeeding sentence would seem to rule this out, as would the apparently equivalent phrase "lex humanitus posita" (see, for instance, the title). In any case, that Thomas is interested at this point in posited law is apparent in the second sentence, "Sed ea quae sunt primi modi, continentur lege humana non tanquam sint solum lege posita." Thomas Gilby's translation (which renders "in lege humana posita" as "in human positive law") appends to the phrase a footnote which begins: "The Low Latin term *positivus* signified what was accidental and imposed, not essential and inherent. So positive laws, though they should not contradict, are not prolongations of inherently moral precepts" [Gilby (1966), pp. 102–7, in particular p. 106, note f].

56. This has been obscured in the older Dominican translation of the *Summa theologiae* (see "Abbreviations, Texts, Conventions, Sigla," near the beginning of the present volume) where we find, "Accordingly, both modes of derivation are found in the human law. But those things that are derived in the first way, are contained in human law not as emanating therefrom exclusively, but have some force from the natural law also. But those things that are derived in the second way, have no other force than that of human law."

57. See Armstrong (1966), p. 92–93, 181; also Nelson (1992), pp. 21–23.

second way" involves positing ("a particular determination of the law of nature"), the second quotation makes it clear that both ways are positings—just
as both are in some sense derivations. This combination of positive and logical factors is, of course, reminiscent of the analysis/synthesis method presented above: even geometry, as we saw, is not simply a matter of manipulating
axioms and first principles but involves tracing the logical connections from
posited conclusions to principles, and back again.

[7] The development of an idea

The conception of laws as things posited is an ancient one, the classical
Greek word for what lawmakers do being *nomothetein* ("to posit law").[58] But
traditionally—that is, apparently until Thomas's more mature thought—that
which was posited had been sharply distinguished from that which was according to nature. One finds this sharp distinction in Aristotle's *Phys.* iii, for
instance, where all objects are said to be in space, which has an up and a
down, a left and a right, etc.—and which distinctions hold, says Aristotle,
"not only in relation to us and by posit, but also in the whole itself."[59]

---

58. Aristotle uses the phrase "positings of laws" [τὰς τῶν νόμων θέσεις] at *Pol.* iv,1,1289a22.
The expression is a common one. The core idea is that laws are human products, although not
necessarily arbitrary ones. At *An.post.* i,2,72a14ff., Aristotle introduces posits (*theseis*) as elements
of scientific demonstrations (whose premisses are always true and necessary). Barnes notes that
the "classification of principles undertaken in this section [i.e., 72a14ff.] is treated again in
An.post. i,10. . . . The distinction between axioms and posits is identical with that drawn at
An.post. i,10,76a37–b2 between 'common' and 'proper principles' . . ." [Barnes (1994 <1975>), p.
99].

59. *Phys.* iii,5,205b33–34: καὶ ταῦτα οὐ μόνον πρὸς ἡμᾶς καὶ θέσει, ἀλλὰ καὶ ἐν αὐτῷ τῷ
ὅλῳ διώρισται. This remark is interpreted by Simplicius and also apparently by Alexander of
Aphrodisias as making a distinction between what is "by posit" and what is "according to nature"
[Simplicius, *in Phys.* iii,489.12–24]. Simplicius cites Alexander's lost work "Against the Epicurian
Zenobius" and also Aristotle's *Cael.* iv,1 (see in the latter especially 308a22). Bonitz, however, notes
that others understand the word θέσει at *Phys.* iii,5,205b34 in the local sense [Bonitz (1961
<1870>) 327b17–18].
    John Finnis has called to my attention a passage in Aulus Gellius where a distinction is drawn
between words that have the meanings they do "by nature" [φύσει] and those that have them "by
posit" [θέσει] [*Noct.Att.* x,4; see Finnis (1996), p. 207, n. 3]. The distinction is here attributed to
Nigidius Figulus (d.45 B.C.; Gellius gives his Greek words in his own Latin text); but the passage
itself says that "the [Greek] philosophers *often* raised the question whether words [τὰ ὀνόματα]
are by nature or by posit." Gellius perhaps has in mind Plato's *Cratylus*, although one finds the
distinction applied to words as early as the Presocratic Democritus: see Diels and Kranz (1951) 68
B 26, where we find the distinction τὰ ὀνόματα φύσει καὶ θέσει. (This latter passage was also
pointed out to me by Finnis.)
    Klibansky attributes the arrival in the West of the distinction *iustitia naturalis/iustitia positiva*
(and *ius positivum/ius naturale*) to the commentary by Calcidius on Plato's *Timaeus* [Klibansky
(1982 <1939, 1943>), p. 74]. See Calcidius, *in Ti.* vi,59.18–20.

The distinction appears also in Thomas's earlier writings. In his commentary on Peter Lombard's *Sentences* (written c.1255), for instance, he writes:

... there are two types of precept: that is, of natural law and of positive law. By a precept of natural law are prohibited those things in themselves wrong; but by the precepts of positive law are prohibited those things that might be occasions of wrongs— or some things are prescribed that are ordered toward a virtue that the framer [*positor*] of a law intends to encourage. And for this reason positive law is derived from natural, as Cicero says.[60]

We see here many of the ideas put forward in *ST* I–II q.95 a.2, but positive law is kept separate from natural law in the sense that no precept of natural law is positive law.

By the time he wrote the third book of the *Summa contra gentiles*,[61] Thomas appears to have developed the view that also precepts very closely connected with the natural law are posited laws. In a chapter having to do with the permanence of marriage, he remarks:

Thus, since law is instituted for the common good, it is proper that those things that pertain to generation be ordered before other laws, both divine and human. Moreover,

---

60. *in Sent.* lb.4 d.15 q.3 a.1 sol.4 c: "[D]uplex est praeceptum, scilicet juris naturalis et juris positivi. Praecepto juris naturalis prohibentur ea quae sunt secundum se mala; sed praeceptis juris positivi prohibentur ea quae possunt esse occasiones malorum; vel praecipiuntur aliqua ordinantia ad virtutem, quam legis positor inducere intendit; et propter hoc, jus positivum, ut dicit Tullius, est a naturali derivatum . . .". The Parma edition of *in Sent.* gives Cicero's *De inv.* ii,65 as the reference. Speaking of legal controversies (i.e., the *pars negotialis* of a constitution—i,14; ii,62), Cicero remarks: "Initium ergo eius [i.e., of the *ius* in such cases] ab natura ductum videtur; quaedem autem ex utilitatis ratione aut perspicua nobis aut obscura in consuetudinem uenisse; post autem adprobata quaedam a consuetundine aut uero utilia uisa legibus esse firmata. Ac naturae quidem ius esse, quod nobis non opinio, sed quaedam innata uis adferat, ut religionem, pietatem, gratiam, uindicationem, obseruantiam, ueritatem" [*De inv.* ii,65]. In *De inventione*, see also ii,160–62 ("Naturae ius est quod non opinio genuit, sed quaedam innata uis inseuit, ut religionem, pietatem, gratiam, uindicationem, obseruantiam, ueritatem" [161]). Cicero's *De inventione* is cited in a similar connection at *in Sent.* lb.3 d.37 q.1 a.3 c and a.4 ad 2. See also *in Sent.* lb.4 d.15 q.3 a.2 sol.1.

61. "We know that before leaving Paris he had embarked on the great work which rapidly acquired the title, *Summa contra gentiles*. He completed it at his leisure, it seems, between leaving Paris in 1259 and starting the *Summa theologiae* in about 1266" [Tugwell (1988), p. 251—note omitted]. It is worthy of remark, however, that in his commentary on 1 Tim., Thomas makes an observation very similar to what we have just seen at *in Sent.* lb.4. That is, at *in I Tim.* cap.1 lect.3 (§25), he says: "Cum autem sit duplex ius, scilicet naturale et positivum, naturali repugnat quod secundum se est malum, positivo autem repugnat quod est malum quia prohibitum." It is generally acknowledged that the commentary on 1 Tim. belongs to the first period during which Thomas commented on the Bible: i.e., the years 1259 to 1268, according to Cai and Mandonnet; 1265 to 1268, according to Torrell. See Cai (1953), vol. 1, p. vi; Torrell (1996 <1993>), pp. 250, 340; see also Weisheipl (1983 <1974>), pp. 372–73, who gives the first period as the years 1259 to 1265.

it is proper that posited laws proceed from natural instinct, if they are human <laws>; for, as in the demonstrative sciences, every human construct [*inventio*] takes its beginning from principles naturally known.[62]

Thomas has here apparently moved away from the separation of posited (i.e., positive) from natural law, which separation characterized not only his commentary on the *Sentences* but also the legal tradition of the twelfth and early thirteenth centuries.[63]

But Thomas is clear even in the commentary on the *Sentences* that lower precepts of natural law are not derived from the corresponding higher principles in a strictly logical way. Peter Lombard says that to be understood somehow within the sixth commandment is a prohibition not only of adultery but also of any sexual conduct outside of marriage. An objection says in reply that such lesser offenses are not contained in the greater and are therefore not prohibited. Thomas's reply to the objection is as follows:

[A]lthough the prohibition of a minor wrong is not included in the greater wrong in the syllogistic way (as it is possible to argue), if the greater wrong is to be rejected, so also is the lesser wrong. For it is included in the way in which those things that come forth from the seeds found in nature are contained in their seminal principles. For just as nature proceeds from tiny seeds into giant trees, so law proceeds from those things that are in their beginning and just budding, into other things that are sometimes more difficult and more perfect. And thus the legislator [i.e., God] by prohibiting adultery prohibits simple fornication, and by prohibiting false testimony prohibits every type of lie, and by prohibiting theft prohibits every base gain—and so on with respect to other things.[64]

62. "Unde, cum lex instituatur ad bonum commune, ea quae pertinent ad generationem, prae aliis oportet legibus ordinari et divinis et humanis. Leges autem positae oportet quod ex naturali instinctu procedant, si humanae sunt: sicut etiam in scientiis demonstrativis omnis humana inventio ex principiis naturaliter cognitis initium sumit" [*SCG* lb.3 cap.123 (§2965)].

63. See Finnis (1996), pp. 195–96. Finnis cites Hugh of St. Victor, William of Conches, and Thierry of Chartres. See also Aubert (1955), pp. 105–8.

64. ". . . quod quamvis prohibitio minoris mali in magis malo non includatur via syllogistica, ut argui possit, si magis malum dimittendum est, quod et minus malum; includitur tamen eo modo quo ea quae ex seminibus naturae progrediuntur, in rationibus seminalibus continentur. Sicut enim natura ex parvis seminibus in maximas arbores proficit, ita etiam et lex ex his quae in principio et in promptu sunt, in alia procedit, quae sunt quandoque difficiliora et perfectiora; et ideo legislator per prohibitionem moechiae prohibuit fornicationem simplicem, et per falsum testimonium prohibuit omne mendacium, et per furtum prohibuit omnem turpem quaestum, et sic de aliis" [*in Sent.* lb.3 d.37 q.1 a.2 sol.1 ad 2].

Thomas is well aware of the issue whether the derivation of lower principles is derivation in the strict "syllogistic" sense. Moreover, the lower principles involved here are by no means the "particular determinations from common things" spoken of as the second way in *ST* I–II q.95 a.2. That is, they are not like the determination that an offender "should be punished by such and such a penalty"; they are precepts of natural law, albeit less close to the source of natural law than some others.

Slightly later in the same section of the commentary of the *Sentences*, Thomas draws a parallel between the way lower practical principles are derived from higher and the way that their theoretical counterparts are. An objection argues that the full intention of the lawmaker is contained in the precept 'love thy neighbor' and therefore the rest of the Decalogue is unnecessary. Thomas replies:

[L]ove of neighbor is like the primary root of observing the precepts . . . ; thus, it occupies the place of the first principle in the <theoretical> disciplines. Thus, just as the other principles closer to particular conditions are placed there, after the first principle to which, as is said in *Metaph.* iv, everything is reduced (that is to say, that the affirmation and the negation are not verified of the same thing), so also in the law, beyond love of neighbor, it is necessary to place certain special precepts that guide particular acts.[65]

Thomas is saying here that ethical principles are reduced to the first principle of practical reason in the same way that lower principles in the theoretical sphere are reduced to the principle of non-contradiction. We have already seen that such reduction is not simply a matter of deducing. I have translated the words "ponuntur alia principia" as "the other principles . . . are *placed*" and the words "oportuit poni aliqua specialia praecepta" as "it is necessary to *place* certain other precepts" since it sounds better in English. But I might just as well have spoken of positing either set of laws.

---

65. ". . . quod dilectio proximi est sicut prima radix observandi praecepta . . . ; unde tenet locum primi principii in disciplinis. Unde sicut ibi post primum principium, ad quod omnia reducuntur, ut dicitur in IV Metaph. (scilicet quod affirmatio et negatio non verificatur de eodem), ponuntur alia principia magis propinqua particularibus conditionibus; ita etiam in lege praeter dilectionem proximi oportuit poni aliqua specialia praecepta quae dirigerent in particularibus actibus" [*in Sent.* lb.3 d.37 q.1 a.2 sol.2 ad 2]. The Aristotelian reference appears to be to *Metaph.* iv,3,1005b32–34). See Thomas's *in Metaph.* §603: "Et propter hoc omnes demonstrationes reducunt suas propositiones in hanc propositionem, sicut in ultimam opinionem omnibus communem: ipsa enim est naturaliter principium et dignitas omnium dignitatum." See D'Arcy (1961), pp. 52–53.

[8] Returning deposits

We are now in a position to confront an issue mentioned at the end of chapter 2. In chapter 2, it was acknowledged that the precepts associated with the basic human inclinations are, according to Thomas, located farther down within the structure of practical reason than is sometimes realized. This raises the question whether even they would therefore allow of exceptions, as does, for example, the precept about returning deposits, precisely on account of its distance from the highest principles.[66] If not, how do we distinguish (what we might call) "basic-inclination precepts" from (what we might call) "deposit-type precepts"?

We find in Thomas a remarkable array of images intended to explain this latter distinction. In *in Sent.* lb.3, he divides "natural things" into three categories: those occurring always, those occurring frequently, those occurring rarely. The first category causes the other two and they can be reduced to it: the celestial motions affect the weather, and both of these cause chance happenings, as when "a man, either because of the rain or something else of that sort which is reducible to the motion of the heavens, has occasion to be digging in a field and there discovers a treasure." It is the same, Thomas says, with laws. Some inhere in reason itself and are binding always. "There are some laws, however, which, as what they are, contain the reason why they ought to be observed, although, certain things occurring, their observance is impeded—e.g., 'a deposit ought to be returned to the depositor' is impeded when a sword is to be returned to a furious depositor."[67] In the same article, he answers an objection to the effect that the precepts of law cannot be reduced to the precepts of the decalogue as if to a cause since "the effect remains while the cause remains. But certain precepts of the law are altered even while these precepts [of the Decalogue] remain." Thomas replies:

Those precepts of the law that are altered had their reason for being observed not from the substance of the thing done but from certain circumstantial causes, such as that it

---

66. See chapter 2, note 53.

67. *in Sent.* lb.3 d.37 q.1 a.3 c: "Quaedam vero leges sunt quae secundum id quod sunt, habent rationem ut observari debeant, quamvis aliquibus concurrentibus earum observatio impediatur; sicut quod depositum reddatur deponenti, impeditur quando gladius furioso deponenti reddendus esset." Thomas expands this theory of the causal relationship between different levels of reality in *in Metaph.* §§1207ff.

was necessary by certain signs to prefigure the mystery of our redemption, or some-thing of that sort. Thus, these causes having desisted, the reduction of these precepts to the natural precepts does not remain.[68]

Also, in his commentary on *EN*, picking up on a remark by Aristotle at *EN* v,7,1134bh33–35, Thomas notes that according to nature most people are right-handed, although we also find people who are ambidextrous—"and so also with those things that are naturally just, such as that deposits ought to be returned, which is to be observed for the most part, although in a few cases it is altered."[69]

These images provide us with a general orientation toward the problem; but otherwise, due to the contrary ideas they elicit, they are not terribly help-ful. Ambidexterity is certainly not a suspension of the laws of nature and nei-ther is the chance discovery of treasure; and, although one might argue that ambidexterity is a matter of chance, it involves a different sort of chance than finding a treasure—one more tied to natural events and laws. Moreover, these images clash with another current of argument also found in Thomas. A few *lectiones* after the remark just quoted about ambidexterity, he speaks of "pec-catum in natura rei," which makes it impossible for precepts to apply univer-sally; and again he cites the example of returning deposits [*in EN* lb.5 lect.16 ll.116–29 (§1085)]. The idea occurs again, in more clearly moral terms, in *ST* II–II, where Thomas remarks that man has a mutable nature so that that which is natural to him might sometimes not occur.

As, for instance, the returning of a deposit to the depositor is according to natural equality: and, if things were such that human nature were always upright, this would have to be observed always. But since sometimes it happens that a man's will is de-

---

68. *in Sent.* lb.3 d.37 q.1 a.3 ad 3: "Ad tertium dicendum, quod illa praecepta legis quae mutata sunt, observantiae suae rationem habebant non ex ipsa substantia facti, sed ex aliquibus circum-stantibus causis, sicut quod oportebat nostrae redemptionis mysterium aliquibus signis praefigu-rare, vel aliquid hujusmodi; unde cessantibus his causis, non manet reductio istorum praecepto-rum ad praecepta naturalia." The third objection reads: "Praeterea, manente causa, manet effec-tus. Sed quaedam praecepta legis mutata sunt illis praeceptis manentibus. Ergo non reducuntur ad ista sicut ad causam."

69. "Ea enim quae sunt naturalia apud nos sunt quidem eodem modo ut in pluribus, sed ut in paucioribus deficiunt; sicut naturale est quod pars dextra sit vigorosior quam sinistra, et hoc in pluribus habet veritatem; et tamen contingit ut in paucioribus aliquos fieri ambidextros, qui sin-istram manum habent ita valentem ut dextram: ita etiam et ea quae sunt naturaliter iusta, ut puta depositum esse reddendum, ut in pluribus est observandum, sed ut in paucioribus mutatur" [*in EN* lb.5 lect.12 ll.187–96 (§1028)].

praved, there are cases in which a deposit should not be returned, lest the man having the perverse will make evil use of it . . . .[70]

Whereas previously the lower precepts were represented as even miraculous, here they are the consequence of sin. None of this is to say that these various images are utterly irreconcilable or useless but only that their radically diverse connotations do not help us toward a clear understanding of the nature of deposit-type precepts.

More useful are Thomas's remarks about the position of deposit-type precepts within the ordered system of practical reason. Particularly useful, indeed, is *ST* I–II q.94 a.4, where he notes that, although both theoretical and practical reason proceed from common principles to proper ones, in practical reason this descent has a more appreciable effect.

Practical reason, however, is occupied with contingent matters, about which human actions are concerned; and consequently, although there is a certain necessity in general principles, the more one descends to matters of detail, the more frequently one encounter defects. . . . For it is right and true, according to all, that one ought to act according to reason: and from this principle it follows, as though a proper conclusion, that deposits are to be returned. And this indeed is true for the majority of cases; but it may happen in a particular case that it would be injurious, and therefore irrational, for deposits to be returned—for instance, if someone makes the request for the purpose of fighting against one's country. And this principle will be found to fail the more one descends into detail—e.g., if it is said that the deposits are to be restored with such and such a stipulation, or in such and such a way. For the greater the number of conditions added, the greater are the number of ways in which the principle may fail, so that it would not be right either to return a deposit or not to return it.[71]

This passage is useful not simply because of what it says about the position of deposit-type precepts but also because of what it says about how posi-

---

70. "Sicut naturalem aequalitatem habet ut deponenti depositum reddatur: et si ita esset quod natura humana semper esset recta, hoc esset semper servandum. Sed quia quandoque contingit quod voluntas hominis depravatur, est aliquis casus in quo depositum non est reddendum, ne homo perversam voluntatem habens male eo utatur, ut puta si furiosus vel hostis reipublicae arma deposita reposcat" [*ST* II–II q.57 a.2 ad 1]. See also *ST* I–II q.4 a.4 c; also *ST* II–II q.51 a.4 c, where Thomas compares exceptions to the deposit precept to "monstruosi partus animalium."

71. "Sed ratio practica negotiatur circa contingentia, in quibus sunt operationes humanae, et ideo, etsi in communibus sit aliqua necessitas, quanto magis ad propria descenditur, tanto magis invenitur defectus. . . . Apud omnes enim hoc rectum est et verum, ut secundum rationem agatur. Ex hoc autem principio sequitur quasi conclusio propria, quod deposita sint reddenda. Et hoc quidem ut in pluribus verum est, sed potest in aliquo casu contingere quod sit damnosum, et

tion bears upon the precepts themselves. It does not say that, as we go down the scale, precepts get progressively weaker. We cannot derive from an ordering a scale of reliability according to which, as it might be imagined, FPPR has a zero percent failure rate, the common precepts a 2 percent rate, the natural law precepts associated with the inclinations a 10 percent rate, and so on. In fact, a deposit-type precept has the same moral force (derived from FPPR) as a basic-inclination precept. The difference is that, because basic-inclination precepts are closer to the first principles of practical reason, they do not admit of the morally significant conditions that deposit-type precepts do. Take the example of adultery, with regard to which, according to Aristotle, "it is not possible ever to be right" [*EN* ii,6,1107a14–15]. This is so, presumably, because adultery attacks a basic good (the object of a basic inclination). It makes no *sense*, says Aristotle, to add conditions: "Nor does goodness or badness with regard to such things depend on committing adultery with the right woman, at the right time, and in the right way, but simply to do any of them is to go wrong" [1107a15–17].

With deposit-type precepts, on the other hand, because they are not positioned so close to the first principles, one can specify morally significant conditions. If one were a lawmaker for Athens, one might indeed specify that a deposit is to be returned provided that it is not a weapon and the depositor is not out of his mind. But even if one does not impose such conditions, one can intend them, knowing how it is that laws are applied and knowing too that one's more simplified law will be so applied. Moreover, a particular contract might specify that a deposit is to be returned if the depositor asks for it after six months; and this could be recognized, at a higher level, as a legal contract. The lawmaker can be understood as intending this, too, although, in a certain very literal sense, it seems to contradict the precept 'deposits are to be returned.'[72]

---

per consequens irrationabile, si deposita reddantur; puta si aliquis petat ad impugnandam patriam. Et hoc tanto magis invenitur deficere, quanto magis ad particularia descenditur, puta si dicatur quod deposita sunt reddenda cum tali cautione, vel tali modo, quanto enim plures conditiones particulares apponuntur, tanto pluribus modis poterit deficere, ut non sit rectum vel in reddendo vel in non reddendo."

72. Thomas speaks in a number of places about deposit-type precepts conforming or not conforming to the intention of the lawmaker: e.g., *in Sent.* lb.3 d.33 q.3 a.4 sol.5 ad 5; lb.3 d.37 q.1 a.4 c ("Si quando vero possunt salva intentione legis praeteriri, tunc est licitum dispensare . . ."); lb.4 d.15 q.3 a.1 sol.4 ad 3; *ST* I–II q.96 a.6 ad 2. Thomas also speaks of "going beyond the letter of the law" ("praetermissis verbis legis") [*ST* II–II q.120 a.1], asserting that to follow the letter can, in

It is clear that Thomas's way of understanding deposit-type precepts and their moral force is much tied up with his conception of the way they are derived from higher precepts. They are not found *in* the higher precepts; rather, their derivation has to do with the particular circumstances in which the higher precepts are applied. They are added to the higher precepts, although they are also in accordance with them.[73] The particular circumstances that matter morally become more numerous as one moves down within the hierarchy of the precepts, so that nearer the bottom the precepts are relatively imprecise measures. Or, rather, they would be such were it not known also that they are intended as "Lesbian rules" which adapt themselves to particular circumstances.[74]

Deposit-type precepts are, then, in a sense, just as binding as any other precepts, although, given the way they sometimes must be formulated and taking such formulations literally, they are not so binding. The difference between basic-inclination and deposit-type precepts is that, with the latter, there is more occasion for such inexact formulation.

---

fact, sometimes be immoral. On this idea in Roman law (to which Thomas alludes in ad 1), see Aubert (1955), pp. 80–81. Many of Thomas's ideas in these respects can also be traced back to Aristotle's *EN* v,10.

73. Thomas employs this conception in *ST* I–II q.93 a.3. In considering the question "Whether every law is derived from the eternal law," he remarks: "In all movers that are ordered one to the other, it is necessary that the power of the second mover be derived from the power of the first mover, for the second mover does not move except insofar as it is moved by the first." He goes on then to speak of "secondary governors" deriving the plan (*ratio*) of governing from "the governor in chief" and of manual workers who derive a *ratio* from an architect. The conception of derivation being used here is not simply one in which there is a premiss (or premisses) from which a conclusion is deduced but one in which, in the first place, there is a higher law and then at a lower level another act or insight in accordance with the higher law but adapted to more particular circumstances.

74. See *EN* v,10,1137b29–31, where Aristotle discusses "Lesbian rules." See also Thomas, *in EN* lb.5 lect.16 ll.173–84 (§1088); *in Sent.* lb.3 d.37 q.1 a.4 obj.1; *Tab.* B118.48–53.

CHAPTER 4

COMMENSURABILITY AND INCOMMENSURABILITY

W E SAW in chapter 2 that, in setting out the structure of natural law, Thomas posits various levels of precepts. At the base of the scheme, at least as far as precepts or principles go, is the first principle of practical reason (FPPR), "good is to be done and pursued and evil avoided," on which "are founded all the other precepts of the law of nature."[1] Among these other precepts are, in the next tier, the common precepts such as that 'ill is to be done to no one' and 'one should act rationally.' The next three tiers (or subtiers), according to Thomas (*ST* I–II q.94 a.2 <7>, <8>, <9>), contain respectively precepts pertaining to being, precepts pertaining to life, and precepts pertaining to rationality.

The appearance of such an ordered scheme raises a number of issues, especially for those engaged in debates about whether one can engage in consequentialist commensuration. If the precepts mentioned by Thomas in *ST* I–II q.94 a.2 <7>, <8>, <9> are ordered, does this not suggest that one can or even should weigh the different prospects there related, one against the other, when deciding what to do? Or, conversely, are not people who take into consideration hierarchies, such as one finds in *ST* I–II q.94 a.2, commensurating?[2]

---

1. *ST* I–II q.94 a.2 <5>. The ordered scheme of precepts is given in "Abbreviations, Texts, Conventions, Sigla," on p. xxiv. A translation of *ST* I–II q.94 a.2, with accompanying paragraph markers (<1>, <2>, etc.), is found in Appendix A.

2. Richard McCormick holds that in making choices people employ a hierarchy of goods and therefore do employ a sort of commensuration [McCormick (1978), pp. 227–28,251–53]. On this argument, see Grisez (1983), pp. 156–57. Russell Hittinger has criticized Grisez and colleagues for

Unfortunately, there is not to be found in Thomas an extended treatment of commensurability. The most likely place to have found such a treatment would have been in a commentary on books 13 and 14 of the *Metaphysics,* where Aristotle deals with the philosophy of mathematics and, in particular, with counting and ordering; but Thomas never got past the twelfth book in his commentary on the *Metaphysics.*[3] Instead, therefore, of studying Thomas directly, I devote the major part of this chapter to expounding Aristotle's ideas on commensurability, especially as found in *Metaph.* xiii and the *Categories.*[4] Having set out pertinent aspects of Aristotle's theory of counting and ordering, I then make some remarks about how these ideas can be applied in the practical sphere, concluding with some remarks about how, in the light of them, we can understand the hierarchy of precepts Thomas sets out in *ST* I–II q.94 a.2.

---

not taking sufficiently into account Thomas's hierarchy of goods [Hittinger (1987), pp. 74–92]. For a critique of Hittinger's "critique of the new natural law theory," see George (1988), pp. 1407–29; for Grisez's own reply, see Grisez (1988b). Grisez's most sustained argument against consequentialism is found in Grisez (1978). See also Luban (1990) and Finnis's response to Luban and others in Finnis (1990a), (1990b), and (1990c), but especially (1990a), p. 10; see also Finnis (1983), pp. 89–90. See also McKim and Simpson (1988) and Boyle, Grisez, and Finnis (1990). On incommensurability, see also D. Brock (1973).

3. The commentary on the twelfth book finishes (§2663) with a doxology, suggesting that Thomas deliberately stopped at that point. See Mansion, A. (1925), pp. 278–79; but see also Pelster (1936), p. 380, n. 7, who cites *in Metaph.* §2488, *In secunda secundum opinionem aliorum, sequenti libri, ibi, "De sensibili quidem igitur substantia,"* the latter being a quotation from the beginning of *Metaph.* xiii (1,1076a8). On "the problem of the last books" in Thomas's commentary, see, besides Mansion and Pelster, also Rowan (1995 <1961>), pp. xxii–xxiv.

In this chapter, I normally use the word 'count' (or 'counting,' etc.), to mean the procedure of "counting up"—e.g., counting the number of men in a room. It is a central contention of this chapter that counting up is a different procedure from ordering (i.e., putting things in an order). There is another sense of counting according to which one simply runs through the natural numbers (1,2,3,4, etc.). The context usually makes it apparent which meaning of 'counting' I am employing; where there is danger of ambiguity, I speak of the former procedure as 'counting up,' the latter as 'counting off.'

One might argue that counting up is not such a distinct procedure as I am suggesting, since counting up involves an ordering and also a counting off. In counting up the number of men in a room, one goes through, in order, part of the series of natural numbers; i.e., one counts off. I do not deny this latter point but do insist that even still the procedures are distinct. One *uses* the ordered natural numbers in order to count up—one does not put them in order; and, similarly, one counts off *in order to* count up.

4. We do, however, find a number of remarks especially in Thomas's commentaries on Aristotle confirming that he is in general agreement with the Aristotelian approach. I will indicate some of these in the footnotes.

[1] Ordered series, common ideas

I start, however, with a remark in the *Nicomachean Ethics*. In chapter 6 of the first book of that work, having first announced that he intends to oppose the conception of a universal good held by certain "friends" who had introduced the Forms, Aristotle uses against them an *ad hominem* argument in order to show that, according to their own mathematical theories, there cannot be a highest genus of the good.

The men who introduced this doctrine did not posit Ideas of classes within which they recognized priority and posteriority (which is the reason why they did not maintain the existence of an Idea embracing all numbers); but things are called good both in the category of substance and in that of quality and in that of relation, and that which is *per se,* i.e. substance, is prior in nature to the relative (for the latter is like an offshoot and accident of what is); so that there could not be a common Idea set over all these goods.[5]

Aristotle does not name the philosophers he has in mind, but they certainly include Plato himself and perhaps Xenocrates who, unlike Plato's other major disciple Speusippus, accepted the existence of Forms.[6]

Although the idea played a central role in his philosophy of mathematics, it would appear that Plato, along with those who shared his opinions on this point, maintained the principle that, wherever there is an ordered series, there cannot be a common idea [*koinē idea*] that holds of all the members of the series. He recognizes, that is, the principle, 'ordered series ⇒ no common idea': 'if there is an ordered series, its members do not fall under a single common idea.'[7] It is worth noting that this principle is, according to both

---

5. *EN* i,6,1096a17–23. *EE* i,8,1218a1–15 is a parallel passage with some important differences; on these, see Woods (1992), p. 70. See *Metaph.* xiv,1,1088b2–4, where Aristotle also makes the point that the category of substance is prior to the others. Thomas, commenting on the *EN* i,6 passage, speaks of a number of anti-Platonic arguments, of which, he says, the first "sumitur ex ipsa positione Platonicorum, qui non faciebant aliquam ideam in illis generibus in quibus invenitur prius et posterius; sicut patet in numeris, nam binarius naturaliter prior est ternario et sic inde, et ideo non dicebant Platonici quod numerus communis esset quaedam idea separata, ponebant autem singulos numeros ideales separatos, puta binarium, ternarium et similia. Et huius ratio est, quia ea in quibus invenitur prius et posterius, non videntur esse unius ordinis et per consequens nec aequaliter unam ideam participare" [*in EN* lb.1 lect.6 ll.98–108 (§80)].

6. See Gauthier and Jolif (1958–1959), ad 1096a13–14 (vol. 2, pp. 36–37); see also Annas (1976), pp. 75–76.

7. Michael Pakaluk gets a very similar point out of the very difficult passage at *EN* i,6,1096a34–b5: "And one might ask the question, what in the world they [i.e., certain Platonists]

Aristotle and Plato, an extremely general one, applying right across the board of the categories. So, I shall be calling it and similar principles 'axioms.'

Aristotle is by no means denying here that there could be a hierarchy of goods—or even a highest good. After all, he begins the *Nicomachean Ethics* by first identifying subordinate and superordinate activities and then saying, "in all of these the ends of the master arts are to be preferred to all the subordinate ends" [*EN* i,1,1094a14–15]. His point is rather that, despite such ordering, the good that is found in any one activity is unique to it. It has its own intelligibility (or *logos*). We cannot cross boundaries between types of goods and expect to find that the type of good pursued on the other side is basically the same as what we knew before the crossing. We cannot say, for instance, that philosophy contains the same type of good as bridle-making only more of it. We can, however, say that, as an activity, it is better—of a higher order. This approach leaves the way open for Aristotle, in the tenth book of the *Nicomachean Ethics*, to say that philosophical contemplation is the highest type of happiness, without falling into the Platonic conception that, *qua* highest, all other goods participate in it.[8]

Someone might well ask, however, what has this to do with commensurability? An answer to this question requires a bit more exposition and the identification of some more axioms. In *Metaph.* iii, having made the point we have just seen ("in the case of things in which the distinction of prior and posterior is present, that which is predicable of these things cannot be something apart from them"—iii,3,999a6–7), Aristotle adds: "but in the case of in-

---

mean by 'a thing itself,' if in man himself and in a particular man the account [*logos*] of man is one and the same. For *qua* man, they [i.e., man himself and a particular man] will in no respect differ; but if this is so, neither will they differ *qua* good. But neither will the one be more good for being eternal since that which lasts a long time is no more white than that which lasts for a day." It would seem that these Platonists wanted to be able to say both that "the thing itself" or "man himself" is in some sense higher than its quotidian counterparts and that the higher and the lower things share an account—i.e., a *logos*. But Aristotle objects that, if there is involved a common *logos*, this excludes such ordering, which is the only way of making "the thing itself" or "man himself" more important. "In brief," says Pakaluk, "Aristotle's point is that, if the possibility of making comparative claims of the form 'The Ideas are better than that of which they are ideas' implies that the Ideas and the things of which they are Ideas have one and the same λόγος, then it implies that the Ideas cannot be better—a contradiction" [Pakaluk (1992), p. 127]. Thomas says similarly, "considerandum est, quod illud bonum separatum, quod est causa omnium bonorum oportet ponere in altiori gradu bonitatis quam ea quae apud nos sunt eo quod est ultimus finis omnium, per hoc autem dictum videtur quod non sit altioris gradus in bonitate quam alia bona" [*in EN* lb.1 lect.7 ll.18–23 (§84)].

8. On this issue, see especially Cooper (1986 <1975>) and Kraut (1989).

divisibles [*atomoi*], one is not prior, another posterior" [iii,3,999a12–13].[9] The reason why ordering among indivisibles is impossible is their mutual indistinguishability.[10] Objects are ordered according to distinguishing characteristics. For instance, we can rank colors in an order of preference only if we can distinguish one from the other. This is not to say in any absolute sense, however, that indivisibles have no distinguishing characteristics. Aristotle speaks occasionally, for instance, of men as indivisible (and therefore mutually indistinguishable) although obviously men have individuating characteristics.[11] His point has to do rather with how they might be counted *as men*.[12] Suppose we are counting the number of men in a room. In doing so, we consider the objects counted as men; their individuating characteristics are irrelevant to the task at hand.[13]

In effect, then, at *EN* i,6 Aristotle is alluding to a number of interrelated principles. Besides the axiom that 'ordered series ⇒ no common idea,' he also holds, as we have just seen, that indivisibles (i.e., relative indistinguishables) do not admit of a before and after (i.e., of being put in an ordered series). But not admitting of a before and after is a consequence of falling under a common idea, since only relative indistinguishables can fall under a common idea. We might also derive from the remark about indivisibles the axiom that things can be counted if and only if they fall under a common idea and the

9. Thomas's commentary has both these elements: "Et hoc est quod dicit quod in quibus prius et posterius est, scilicet quando unum eorum de quibus aliquod commune praedicatur est altero prius, non est possibile in his aliquid esse separatum, praeter haec multa de quibus praedicatur" [*in Metaph.* §437]; "Sed manifestum est quod inter individua unius speciei, non est unum primum et aliud posterius secundum naturam, sed solum tempore" [*in Metaph.* §438].

10. See *Metaph.* xiii,6,1080a22–23; 7,1081a15–6 (εἰ μὲν οὖν πᾶσαι συμβληταὶ καὶ ἀδιάφοροι αἱ μονάδες). The word that Aristotle uses in *Metaph.* iii is not μονάς but ἄτομος; however, given the context (which in *Metaph.* xiii is mathematical), the idea is the same.

11. For instance, *Cat.* ii,1b4–9; see also *An.post.* ii,19,100b2 and *Metaph.* v,10,1018b5–6 (in which latter passage man and horse are said to be ἄτομα τῷ γένει, οἱ δὲ λόγοι ἕτεροι αὐτῶν). See Thomas, *in An.post.* lb.2 lect.20 ll.274–76 (§595): "anima stat per considerationem quousque inveniatur aliquid impartibile in eis, quod est universale"; see also lb.1 lect.36 ll.231–62 (§318).

12. See especially *Metaph.* xiv,1,1088a4–14. The standard Aristotelian definition of number is "a plurality of indivisibles." See *Metaph.* xiii,9,1085b22 and also *Metaph.* x,1,1053a30. According to Mignucci, this was the standard definition in Aristotle's time [Mignucci (1987), p. 197].

13. In order to keep this notion before us, in what follows, I shall often use the term 'relatively indistinguishable'—or simply 'indistinguishable'—when I might just as well use 'indivisible.' It should be understood as meaning 'indistinguishable relative to a particular procedure'—e.g., counting. To count men in a room is to regard them as indivisibles since, if each were to be regarded according to the number of his body parts, we would give the wrong number when asked, 'How many men are in the room?'

axiom that countable things *qua* countable cannot be put in an ordered series.

Here is a list of the pertinent axioms in abbreviated form.

[A]: 'ordered series $\Rightarrow$ no common idea'
[B]: 'indistinguishables $\Rightarrow$ no ordered series'
[C]: 'common idea $\Rightarrow$ indistinguishables'
[D]: '*sumblētos* $\Longleftrightarrow$ common idea'
[E]: '*sumblētos* $\Rightarrow$ no ordered series'

The word *sumblētos* obviously calls for comment. Depending on context, this can be rendered into English in a number of ways—as 'countable,' 'comparable,' 'combinable,' 'commensurable,' 'capable of combination,' 'addible,' etc. Because there is no one English term that corresponds to *sumblētos* and gives good English in the various contexts and because the word has for Aristotle nonetheless a particular meaning that is *involved* in each of the English terms although synonymous with none of them, in what follows I employ the transliterated Greek term. Or, more precisely, I employ both *sumblētos* and the word that signifies its contradictory, *asumblētos* (sometimes translated 'non-combinable' or 'non-comparable'). The basic idea behind the term *sumblētos* is that, if a number of units are *sumblētos,* they can be "thrown together" into a mathematical procedure of some sort and collectively—that is, by virtue of their mutual relationships—yield a product (as, for instance, 2 plus 3 yield 5). Needless to say, if a unit is *sumblētos,* it is also relatively indistinguishable in the sense identified above.[14]

The answer to the question posed above is now fairly apparent. The fact that things in an ordered series do not come under a common idea has a great deal to do with commensurability. By [D], if something is *sumblētos,* it must stand under a common idea; things in a series, therefore, are not *sumblētos*—at least *qua* being members of a series. They are, therefore, not commensurable.

Why would anyone maintain such a position? Well, I should think it quite

---

14. I shall use the words as English words—that is, without adjusting their endings according to number or gender. The once-classic work on *asumblētoi arithmoi* (uncombinable numbers) is Cook Wilson (1904); see also Cherniss (1944), Appendix VI. For a sharp criticism of Cook Wilson, see Burnyeat (1987); also Cleary (1995), p. 350.

reasonable, as long as one keeps in mind the contexts that the different procedures—counting and ordering—presume. Aristotle is not saying that the members of an ordered series cannot in any sense be counted but that *qua ordered* (and therefore differentiated) they cannot be, since the procedure counting involves relative indistinguishables (or indivisibles).

[2] Some more anti-Platonic arguments

In order to see how these concepts interact with one another, let us consider a number of related passages in *Metaph*. xiii. The point of this exercise has not so much to do with Aristotle's arguments—which are all aimed at Platonists of one sort or another, including Plato himself—but with his presuppositions, which, in fact, his opponents largely share. That is, all parties in the dispute(s) are agreed that counting and ordering are different procedures. It is that idea that I would like now to bring into relief.

In *Metaph*. xiii,6, Aristotle identifies the four positions he opposes: (1) the position maintaining that all units are *sumblētos*; (2) that maintaining that all units are *asumblētos*; (3) that maintaining that units within an Ideal number (e.g., "three itself") are *sumblētos,* although the units of one Ideal number, insofar as they hold together to form the Ideal number, are *asumblētos* with those of another; (4) that maintaining that some numbers are as in (1), some as in (2), some as in (3).[15] In *Metaph*. xiii, 7–8, he offers three series of counterarguments having to do with positions (1), (2), and (3), respectively. He never really considers position (4), probably because he thinks that refuting the first three takes care of the fourth also. I will look at one or two counterarguments from each of these three series. Only the third series is aimed at Plato himself, although the other two come out of a Platonic context.[16] Julia Annas says of the three series: "While the arguments are uneven, the organized ruthlessness of the whole polemic is impressive, and it is this that challenges comparison with Frege's *Foundations of Arithmetic*, chapters 2 and 3."[17]

15. This division presupposes Annas's emendation at 1080a18 (i.e., the elimination of ἤ). See Annas (1976), pp. 163–64. Also, I have reversed the order of the first two positions to correspond with the order of the answers Aristotle gives to them. Aristotle actually has in mind categories of position, but for simplicity's sake I speak simply of four positions.

16. It may be that position (1) had no serious proponents even within the Academy. See Annas (1976), p. 167; Ross (1953 <1924>), vol. 2, p. 435; and especially Reale (1993 <1968>), vol. 3, p. 644, who suggests that Aristotle is proceeding theoretically through the various possibilities that present themselves, given general Platonic presuppositions.

17. Annas (1976), p. 167.

Before going through Aristotle's counter-arguments, there is one preliminary point. It is important to realize that in none of what follows ought we to
have in mind the modern conception of the series of natural numbers '1, 2, 3,
4 . . . '. The basic notion is rather that of units; the numbers are made up of
groups of units. Thus, the number series would go:

● / ●● / ●●● / ●●●● / ●●●●● / . . .

Let us then consider position (1), according to which all units are
sumblētos. Aristotle points out that, if this were true, there would be no Ideal
numbers but only mathematical numbers [*Metaph*. xiii,7,1081a6–7]—i.e., we
could not speak of a unique 2 or 3, etc., but only of various 2s and 3s, etc.
Aristotle's is making an *ad hominem* metaphysical point here. If we cannot
identify such unique numbers, Platonic Ideas cannot be numbers (as at least
some Platonists claim), since Ideas are differentiated [1081a7]. But his argument points also to a mathematical problem, which he discusses more extensively in another place. If no units were differentiable, not only would it be
impossible to identify unique formal numbers, but it would also be impossible to count off the mathematical numbers 1, 2, 3, etc., by adding one unit to
the former number, since the former number would not be identifiable *as* a
certain number—i.e., as something distinct from the units themselves.[18]
Thus, since such counting off is quite basic to mathematics, arithmetic, etc.,
position (1) cannot be right.

Position (1), in fact, looks something like Aristotle's own, for he too is always inclined to reject the notion of something standing over and above the
things that we count. But it is not the same as his, for he does hold that there
is such a thing as the number 3 or the number 5, as I shall explain more fully
below. For the present, we are interested only in the fact that Aristotle recognizes two distinct procedures: that of assigning to a group of things a certain
number and that of putting distinguishable things in an order. We recognize
this especially in his insistence that, e.g., the number 3's coming after 2 is distinct from the fact that either contains (in some sense) indistinguishable
units.

Position (2) maintains that all units are *asumblētos*. This too would create
problems, says Aristotle. Consider the series of numbers

---

18. *Metaph*. xiii,7,1082b24–28. With Ross, I take ὥσπερ εἴρηται πρότερον [1082b26] to be referring to 1081a5–17 [Ross (1953 <1924>), vol. 2, p. 439].

$$\bullet \ / \ \bullet\bullet \ / \ \bullet\bullet\bullet \ / \ \bullet\bullet\bullet\bullet \ / \ \bullet\bullet\bullet\bullet\bullet \ / \ \ldots$$

Since the units are *all asumblētos*, they can all be put into an ordered series. In fact, they must be, which itself makes arithmetic impossible, since arithmetic presumes relative indistinguishables [*Metaph.* xiii,7,1081a19–20]. And there is another problem, as well. Let us distinguish the units by means of superscript numbers (which play no part in Aristotle's actual argument).

$$\bullet^1 \ / \ \bullet^2\bullet^3 \ / \ \bullet^4\bullet^5\bullet^6 \ / \ \ldots$$

Since the units in, for example, the sector $\bullet^2\bullet^3$ are not relatively indistinguishable, they cannot be lumped together. The result is that there must be two things going on in this "series" of numbers. Both $\bullet^2$ and $\bullet^3$ must be ordered and distinguished and so must the sector $\bullet^2\bullet^3$ (this is presupposed by the Platonic theory). But where in this series should sector $\bullet^2\bullet^3$ go? Between $\bullet^2$ and $\bullet^3$? It would seem that $\bullet^2$ should come before the compound $\bullet^2\bullet^3$; but then in what sense can $\bullet^2\bullet^3$ be said to be 2?[19]

Finally, there is the hybrid position (3). Let us take the Ideal numbers 2 ($\bullet\bullet$) and 3 ($\bullet\bullet\bullet$). The units in either, according to this approach, are indistinguishable among themselves, although $\bullet\bullet$ and $\bullet\bullet\bullet$ themselves, insofar as they are ideal numbers, are different one from the other. (If they were not, we could not distinguish two men from three men.) Obviously, however, nothing except Platonic scruples prevents us from simply taking one of the units in ideal 2 and considering it together with one of the units in ideal 3—adding them together, that is, and getting $\bullet\bullet$ (*Metaph.* xiii,7,1082b16–17). The resulting 2 must be distinguishable, since the one unit comes from ideal 2 and the other from ideal 3—and the Platonic theory says only that units are indistinguishable within ideal numbers, distinguishable elsewhere. But as distinguishable (i.e., orderable) where in the number series shall this new 2 be put (*Metaph.* xiii,7,1082b13–14)?

Now a Platonist will certainly respond that it has been stipulated that the units from 2, for example, are only indistinguishable among themselves and that therefore adding one of them to a unit of 3 is illicit. But Aristotle replies that one thing added to another come to two things, even if they are ulti-

19. See *Metaph.* xiii,7,1081a21–29 (especially 1081a25–29). The text is difficult and possibly corrupt, but Aristotle's point is fairly clear (see Reale (1993 <1968>), vol. 3, p. 645). See also the similar argument at 1081a29–35 where Aristotle argues that, according to position (2), "the units must be prior to the numbers by which they are named in counting."

mately distinguishable. "We, for our part, suppose that in general 1 and 1, whether the things are equal or unequal, is two, e.g., the good and the bad, or a man and a horse" [1082b16–19]. In other words, it is true that within the number series we must suppose distinguishability since the whole point is to put distinguishable things in order. But counting is quite a different procedure—and one we can hardly dispense with even for well-intended philosophical reasons.

[3] Aristotle's position

What then is Aristotle's own position? How does he escape the paradoxes that he himself identifies in Platonic number theory? At the end of this series of counter-arguments in *Metaph.* xiii,7,[20] he says that, in order to maintain consistency, the Platonists have to make radically implausible claims about arithmetic, abandoning, for instance, the idea that in counting we add a unit to the preceding number, since, as they see it, we cannot say whether counting involves adding (as when one adds a fourth apple to three) or dividing (as when one depicts the natural numbers by dividing a line into equal segments).[21] Aristotle regards this apparent dilemma as nonsense: "We do both. Thus, it is ridiculous to refer this to so great a difference of substance" [*Metaph.* xiii,7,1082b35–37].

Aristotle's ultimate complaint about Platonic philosophy of mathematics is, therefore, that it seeks an ontological basis for distinctions that are simply procedural. If sometimes we count by adding, sometimes by dividing, there is nothing to be puzzled about, since counting *itself* does not imply any special type of object.[22] That is, counting is not to be explained by pointing to objects that are unambiguously and inseparably one. We can count by dividing what in another context would be considered indivisible: a man can count, using, for instance, his fingers and then his toes, arms and legs, although *qua* man he is indivisible. Or, as Aristotle points out, we can also regard two men as

20. Annas, Ross, and Reale extend the list of counterarguments into chapter 8 of book xiii; but it is clear that chapter 8 (the first sentence of which reads, "First of all, it is well to determine . . .") marks a new beginning. Thus, the last remark in chapter 7 can be seen as a conclusion of some sort, even though Aristotle goes on to offer another counterargument to position (3).

21. *Metaph.* xiii,7,1082b28–36.

22. Aristotle complains often that Plato (and the Pythagoreans) make one and being substantial: see for instance *Metaph.* i,6,987b21–22; iii,1,996a5ff. and iii,4,1001a9ff. Aristotle's own position is that being and one are not substances but attributes.

one (pair) without also positing something beyond them that constitutes their unity [*Metaph.* xiii,7,1082a22–23]. "Some things are one by touching, some by mixing, some by position," he says [*Metaph.* xiii,7,1082a20–21]— which is to say that, at least in counting, it is up to us what we regard as one or not. Similar things can be said about the number series, as we have seen. It is not to be explained by pointing to objects that are necessarily distinguishable, one from the other. Anything that is distinguishable can also be regarded as indistinguishable, just as anything that is indivisible in one context can be divided in another (at least theoretically).

All this is not to say, however, that there is no difference between ordering and counting. The distinction, indeed, is fixed and inexorable. If one is counting, one is not ordering since counting, *qua* counting, is done with (relative) indistinguishables while ordering—again, by its very nature—involves distinguishing. The two procedures are irreducibly different. And that has important consequences, particularly in the field of ethics.

[4] Synonyms and homonyms

There is another very similar (although non-mathematical) line of argument in Aristotle which, because of its differences from the above, complicates matters for us considerably. The complications correspond, however, to genuine and important distinctions within the way things stand, so this line of argument is well worth investigating in some detail.

Consider the following quotation from Aristotle's *Categories:*

Substance, it seems, does not admit of a more and a less [*to mallon kai to hētton*]. I do not mean that one substance is not more a substance than another (we have said that it is), but that any given substance is not called more, or less, that which it is. For example, if this substance is a man, it will not be more a man or less a man either than itself or than another man. For one man is not more a man than another, as one pale thing is more pale than another and one beautiful thing more beautiful than another. Again, a thing is called more, or less, such-and-such than itself; for example, the body that is pale is called more pale now than before, and the one that is hot is called more, or less, hot. Substance, however, is not spoken of thus. For a man is not called more a man now than before, nor is anything else that is a substance. Thus substance does not admit of a more and a less. [*Cat.* v,3b33–4a9]

Although he ultimately denies here that substance itself admits of more and less, Aristotle also acknowledges that there is a sense in which it does; i.e., we can say that this substance is more a substance than that when the various types of substance are put in an ordered series and compared on that basis. A primary substance such as Socrates himself is more of a substance [*Cat.* v,2b17] than the species man and the genus animal (both secondary substances); and, "of the secondary substances, the species is more a substance than the genus, since it is nearer to the primary substance" [*Cat.* v,2b7–8]. Note, however, that this way of admitting of more and less is quite different from the way that an individual man might be more or less pale either than another man or than himself at another time.[23] As Michael Pakaluk has pointed out, what I will call 'position-more-and-less' (as when first substance is positioned higher than second) "seems to have its origins in theory"; 'intensity-more-and-less,' on the other hand, as when one man is said to be more or less pale than another, "is grounded in comparative predications concerning individuals."[24]

This interpretation requires some defense. Aristotle says that intensity-more-and-less can exist only if the predicate involved is not being used homonymously, as is the predicate 'sharp' when it said both of a flavor and of a note.[25] Thus, although we can certainly say that this flavor is more sharp than that one, we cannot say that this flavor is sharper than that note. Obviously Aristotle is making here a point similar to the one he makes in his philosophy of mathematics. Things are *sumblētos* (here—that is, at *Top.* i,15,107b13,17—one might want to use the translation 'comparable') if and only if they fall under something common (cf. axiom [D] above).

It is not absolutely clear in the above quotation that the ordering that, e.g., genus and species admit of does not correspond to a *sumblētos* quality; but other places in Aristotle make it clear that it does not. In the early work *Protrepticus,* for instance, Aristotle says that active knowledge is more knowledge than inactive (or "passive") knowledge and he explicitly excludes the notion that it might be such on account of intensity-more-and-less:

23. My interpretation of this passage differs considerably from that of Morrison. See especially Morrison (1987), p. 386.

24. Pakaluk (1992), p. 119. The rather ugly expressions 'position-more-and-less' and 'intensity-more-and-less' are not Pakaluk's but mine. Plato suggests at *Phlb.* 53ab that to speak of the "most white" is not to speak of something that is more of something (i.e., white) but to say that no other color is mixed in.

25. *Top.* i,15,107b13–18; *Phys.* vii,4,248b7–249a25. For homonymy, see especially *Cat.* i,1a1–6; also Flannery (1999).

When, therefore, each of two things is called by the same term, the one by being active the other by being passive, we shall say that the former possesses the property to a greater degree; e.g. we shall say that a man who uses knowledge knows to a greater degree than a man who possesses knowledge, and that a man who is looking at something sees to a greater degree than one who can do so. For we use 'to a greater degree' not only in virtue of an excess (in the case of things that share a single account [*logos*]) but also in virtue of priority and posteriority; e.g., we say that health is good to a greater degree than healthy things, and that what is by its own nature desirable is so to a greater degree than what is productive of this; yet we see that there is not a single account [*logos*] predicated of both when we say both of useful things and of excellence that each is good.[26]

Aristotle obviously wants here to contrast intensity-more-and-less and the type of ordering that pertains to active and passive potencies.[27] Moreover, in another work (*De interpretatione*), he explicitly says that active and passive "capabilities" are homonymous—precisely that which excludes intensity-more-and-less.[28]

But are ordered substances (or substance types) homonymous? There is one passage suggesting that they might not have to be: the opening words of the famous passage in the *Metaphysics* where Aristotle speaks about the relationships among the various types of being. "There are many senses in which a thing may be said to 'be,' but they are related to one central point, one definite kind of thing, and are not homonymous."[29] If the different senses of 'substance' mentioned in *Cat.* are of this type, they too might be non-homonymous and therefore possibly *sumblētos*. However, most commentators acknowledge that Aristotle means here that these senses are not *merely* homonymous or that they are not homonymous in the very obvious sense discussed at *Cat.* i,1a1–6.[30] Moreover, it is clear that substance ordering, like the ordering involved in active and passive potencies and types of being

---

26. *Protr.* B 81–82. ROT reads οὐχ εἰς instead of οὐχ ῇ in B 82.

27. Cp. Morrison (1987), pp. 386,399.

28. *Int.* xiii,23a6–11. Aristotle speaks here of walking and being capable of walking.

29. Τὸ δὲ ὂν λέγεται μὲν πολλαχῶς, ἀλλὰ πρὸς ἓν καὶ μίαν τινὰ φύσιν καὶ οὐχ ὁμωνύμως [*Metaph.* iv,2,1003a33–34].

30. See for instance Zanatta (1989), p. 395; Ross (1953), vol. 1, p. 256; Owens (1978), pp. 116–18. At *EN* i,6,1096b26–28, Aristotle suggests that among the alternatives to falling under a common idea is not only *pure* homonymy (i.e., homonymy that arises by chance) but also an analogous relationship which yet stops short of synonymy.

(*Metaph.* iv,2), is theory-dependent. Thus, it involves homonymy and position- rather than intensity-more-and-less.

[5] Common ideas and analogy

Having established, then, that in *Cat.* v,3b33–4a9 Aristotle is distinguishing intensity- and position-more-and-less, we can begin to discuss some of the complications this brings into our account of the commensurable, the incommensurable, and the orderable. The first of these has to do with axiom [A] of the list set out above: 'ordered series ⇒ no common idea.' Attending especially to its converse ([A'] 'common idea ⇒ no ordered series'), it is apparent that it cannot hold. In cases of intensity-more-and-less, we have a common idea but also an ordered series (for instance, a man might be extremely pale Sunday, less pale Monday, even less pale Tuesday, etc.). This means that we must alter axiom [A], turning it into {A} 'ordered series of positionables ⇒ no common idea' (and, of course, its converse {A'} 'common idea ⇒ no ordered series of positionables').

This means that, if we have a concept such as 'man,' by means of which we count men, or a concept such as 'pale,' by means of which we rank things according to degree of paleness, then we do not have the sort of ranking involved in the different types of substance or the different types of knowledge. This axiom is not as artificial as it might at first appear. Both 'man' and 'pale' hold immediately of the things they refer to; as we have seen, however, rankings such as first and second substance, first and second potential, etc., are second order or "meta-" rankings: they do not really pertain *to* the subjects of which they speak. So then, although a certain type of substance might be more substance than another, "any given substance is not called more, or less, that which it is" [*Cat.* v,3b34–6]. Also, as Aristotle notes at *EN* x,3,1173a24–25, health admits of more and less intensity; but, in another sense, 'healthy' as said of an animal can be ordered with respect to 'healthy' as said of urine or of medicine.

But is it so clear that second-order rankings do not involve a common idea? It is undeniable that, at least in certain instances, there is involved a common idea. So, although, for instance, if a man ranks the favorite days of his life there need not be some one thing that they all share and according to which they are ranked, when Aristotle says that active knowledge is more

knowledge than passive, clearly there is something common between the two
things ranked—and this common idea in some sense occasions the ranking.
That is, the two types of knowledge are ranked *as* types of knowledge—a nature they both share. But there is an important dissimilarity between this sort
of common idea and the sort involved when we say that this man is more
pale than that. The difference between active and passive knowledge is not
one of intensity. Knowledge is knowledge: in itself, it does not admit of degrees. Applying what Aristotle says of 'man,' it is nonsense to say of a given instance of knowledge that it is more or less that which it is. If active knowledge
is more knowledge than passive, this is not because *qua* knowledge it *glows*
more than passive knowledge. *Qua* knowledge, it is exactly the same thing
that was previously passive knowledge—only now it is active—and according
to that principle it is ranked higher (i.e., according to the principle that the
active is higher than that which is not).[31]

Aristotle connects this ranking of things according to principles with what
he calls *analogia*. The concept comes from geometry. The Pythagoreans had
made great strides in this field, investigating particularly the relationships
among commensurable lengths by means of the numerical theory of proportion.[32] Then, however, they discovered the incommensurability of the diago-
nal of a square with its side—that is, they discovered the "irrationality" of the
square root of 2.[33] This caused great consternation in the school, which led
to an attempt to keep the existence of the irrational a secret. It was only with
Eudoxus, a contemporary of Aristotle's, that things were once again put on a
solid footing, for Eudoxus invented a way of analyzing even "irrational"
relations in a second-order way. That is, instead of trying to grasp in a direct
and intuitive way the square root of 2 (or any other irrational), he showed
how any such concept could be understood by understanding the way it be-
haves mathematically with respect to other mathematical concepts. The resulting theory of proportion was eventually incorporated into Euclid's
Elements as its fifth book.[34] It involves such formulae as 'if $a:b = c:d$, then

31. On the common idea in such relationships, see especially McInerny (1968a); see also
McInerny (1961), pp. 141–52 and (1996), pp. 128–36. For a summary of McInerny (1996), see
Flannery (1998a).
32. Heath (1981 <1921>), vol. 1, pp. 155, 167, 190. For a summary of the progress in geometry
made up until Eudoxus, see pp. 216–17.
33. See Heath (1981 <1921>), vol. 1, pp. 90–93, 154–57.
34. Heath (1981 <1921>), vol. 1, p. 326–27.

ma:*nb* = *mc*:*nd*.'[35] Obviously, no attempt is made with this formula to inves-
tigate directly, for instance, the component '*ma*:*nb*' (although in certain instances it could certainly be done). Eudoxus investigates rather the "*logos* of
the two *logoi*," '*ma*:*nb*' and '*mc*:*nd*'—just as, in the ranking active and passive
knowledge, Aristotle is concerned not directly with the *logos* of either but
with the second-order question of what *logos* there is between the two *logoi*
(i.e., how they are ordered).

There is no doubt that Aristotle understands these geometrical ideas as
applying in ethics and in other fields (even biology).[36] In the *Rhetoric,* for instance, he says, "that which is produced by a greater good is itself a greater
good; thus, if what is wholesome is more desirable and a greater good than
what gives pleasure, health too must be a greater good than pleasure."[37] The
fact that we can say in a second-order way like this that one good is greater
than another does not mean that good is a common idea: quite to the contrary, it means (in accordance with {A}) that good is not a common idea.
This becomes most apparent a few lines later where Aristotle notes that one
thing may be greater (or more good) from opposite points of view. For instance, one thing "may appear the greater because it is an origin and the other
thing is not, and also because it is not an origin and the other thing is—on
the ground that the end is greater and is not an origin" [*Rhet.* i,7,1364a15–18].
He then uses the example of a rhetorician who says that the man who sets in
action a plot is worse since the crime would not have happened without him
and then (in another situation) that the man who actually perpetrates the
crime is worse since no crime occurs without such an agent. It is clear here
that good is not, according to Aristotle, a quality that admits of intensity-
more-and-less. Which of these two figures would be more *intensely* bad (or
less good)? To say that something is more, or less, good or bad is to establish a
second-order ranking. It is to relate *logoi* by means of another *logos*; in short,
it is to operate by analogy, or, at least, by some sort of second-order ranking.

35. Euclid, *Elem.* v,4 (14.10–16.19). The symbol ':' stands for a ratio or λόγος: see *Elem.* v,df.3
(2.6–7).

36. See for instance *PA* i,4,644a12ff. At 644a16–19 Aristotle says, "Groups [of animals] that only
differ in degree, and in the more or less of an identical element that they possess, are aggregated
under a single class; groups whose attributes are only analogous are separated" ['Όσα μὲν γὰρ
διαφέρει τῶν γενῶν καθ' ὑπεροχὴν καὶ τὸ μᾶλλον καὶ τὸ ἧττον, ταῦτα ὑπέζευκται ἑνὶ
γένει, ὅσα δ' ἔχει τὸ ἀνάλογον, χωρίς]. See also *An.post.* ii,14,98a20–23.

37. *Rhet.* i,7,1363b36–38; note also the word ἀνάλογον at 1363b26.

It is also clear here that orderings are "arbitrary" things in the sense that they are things that people choose to do. This is not to say that one ordering might not be better than another or that an ordering might not be true. But, in order to determine this, one must look beyond the ordering itself to the principles (or measure) on which it is based. We shall return to this important point below.

[6] Other complications

So, instead of [A] we have {A}, 'ordered series of positionables ⇒ no common idea.' What about [B]: 'indistinguishables ⇒ no ordered series' and its converse [B']: 'ordered series ⇒ no indistinguishables'? This axiom has held fast. A person might want to argue that, for instance, white things, which can be ranked according to brightness, can also be counted. If to each of ten slots on a color scale we assign a paint chip, we have ten white things. But we must recall that the notion of 'indistinguishable' (or 'indivisible') that we are operating with is a relative one. If we are counting white things, that is a different procedure from positioning them on a scale of brightness. We can maintain [B] as it stands. It is essential to Aristotle's philosophy of number and it is not inconsistent with the idea that some things that fall under common ideas also admit of ranking (i.e., intensity-more-and-less).

The latter idea, however, points to a problem with the next axiom [C] or 'common idea ⇒ indistinguishables' for, if it is true that some things that fall under common ideas admit of ranking, these things cannot be indistinguishables. It is precisely because they are distinguishable that they are orderable. I would propose that we simply change [C] to {C}: 'common idea ⇒ (indistinguishables or intensity stages).' If we were to suppose that the triad of (1) position ordering (including that involved in the series of natural numbers), (2) intensity ordering, and (3) adding of indistinguishables were exhaustive of the possible procedures in this particular area of concern, we could also state as an axiom that position ordering is equivalent to not-(counting or degree ordering). But I am not sure that the above triad is exhaustive—and, in any case, that would be going beyond anything Aristotle actually says.

Is the new axiom {C} an implausibly makeshift one? I do not think so. Indistinguishables and intensity stages are not unlikely bedfellows. Although it is true that, for instance, stages of paleness are distinguishable, they are not as essentially distinguishable as positionables. (Again, we must remember that positionables may in fact be indistinguishable, although *qua* positionable they are not.) Moreover, both indistinguishables and intensity stages fall under a single *logos* (although the *logos* sometimes admits of degrees). Positionables, on the other hand, each have their own *logos,* which is related to the others by means of a second-order *logos.*

Axiom [D] was '*sumblētos* ⟺ common idea.' In moving beyond Aristotle's mathematical ideas, we encountered a different way of being *sumblētos*—i.e., admitting of intensity-more-and-less. It is tempting therefore to revise [D] so as to mention what we might refer to as the addition-*sumblētos* and the intensity-*sumblētos.* But in fact we were careful from the beginning to say that the concept *sumblētos* is itself a broad one in Aristotle, more broad than any of the English words that are used to translate it. So, we can leave [D] as is. It is interesting to note that by combining axiom {A} and the proposition—easily derivable from [D]—'no common idea ⟹ not *sumblētos*,' we can get the point argued for at some length above: i.e., the proposition that an ordered series of positionables implies that the elements so ordered are not *sumblētos.*

Axiom [E], however, '*sumblētos* ⟹ no ordered series,' will have to be revised since the intensity-*sumblētos* do admit of an ordered series. That is, *sumblētos* in this case will have to be limited in scope, giving the revised axiom {E} 'addition-*sumblētos* ⟹ no ordered series.' Examining {A} and {E}, we see that together they capture what we have been saying about the two types of ordered series. Axiom {A} ('ordered series of positionables ⟹ no common idea') in effect tells us that if there is an ordered series of positionables, neither the addition- nor the intensity-*sumblētos* enters in (since they both involve a common idea); and the converse of {E} ({E′}): 'ordered series ⟹ no addition-*sumblētos*') tells us that an ordered series implies either the intensity-*sumblētos* or position ordering, presuming that these are the only remaining possibilities once the addition-*sumblētos* is excluded. Also, from {E} and {C′} plus the assumptions that there are present an ordered series and a common idea, one can conclude that there are present intensity stages, which would clearly be right.

I leave it to the interested reader to test the consistency of the revised axioms by further derivations. Here is the list:

{A}: 'ordered series of positionables ⇒ no common idea'

[B]: 'indistinguishables ⇒ no ordered series'

{C}: 'common idea ⇒ (indistinguishables or intensity stages)'

[D]: '*sumblētos* ⟺ common idea'

{E}: 'addition-*sumblētos* ⇒ no ordered series'

[7] Ethico-political applications

Let us return, however, to the question whether Aristotle's theory of before and after, more and less, etc., can be applied in the sphere of ethics. It was apparent above, when discussing *Rhet.* i,7, that Aristotle is not opposed to so applying these ideas. And there are a number of important passages in the *Eudemian* and the *Nicomachean Ethics,* some of which we have already seen, where they are employed in a specifically ethical context.[38] But the work in which Aristotle gets most involved in the practical application of his more theoretical ideas is certainly the *Politics.* There we find that the irreducible differences among adding, ordering according to intensity, and positioning are of decisive importance.

Although he introduces the work in a very promising tone of voice—saying, "if all communities aim at some good, then the state or political community that is the highest of all and that embraces all the rest, aims at good in a greater degree than any other, and at the highest good" (*Pol.* i,1,1252a3–7)—Aristotle's conclusions regarding the best political arrangement are notoriously indeterminate.[39] In books vii and viii, for instance, where he supposedly answers the question, which is the best constitution (see *Pol.* vii,1,1323a14; 4,1325b35–38), it would appear that the answer is kingship and aristocracy. But this does not really tell us which is the *best* constitution.[40] In a recent symposium on the *Politics,* one major scholar suggested that Aristotle "had a tendency toward totalitarianism";[41] another said that in *Pol.* vii,1–3 Aristotle proposes an egalitarian or "distributive" conception of the best political arrangement.[42]

38. See also *De an.* ii,3,414b20–22; also Thomas, *in De an.* lb.2 cap.5 ll.229–81 (§§295–98).

39. See Kahn (1990), pp. 370–71.

40. See Newman (1988 <1887–1902>), vol. 1, p. 291: "The answer is that the best constitution will assume the form of an Absolute Kingship or the more equal form of an Aristocracy of σπουδαῖοι, according to circumstances."

41. Barnes (1990a), p. 259; see also the response by Richard Sorabji, who argues that Aristotle was at least more inclined to democracy than Plato [Sorabji (1990a), p. 267].

42. Nussbaum (1990), p. 153; see also the response by David Charles [Charles (1990)].

This indeterminacy is apparent also in Aristotle's treatment of more particular issues. In *Pol.* iii,12, for instance, having again begun in an upbeat way—"Since in all sciences and arts the end is a good, and the greatest and most important is in the most authoritative of them all . . . , i.e., the common good . . ."—he almost immediately drops into talk of the difficulties of determining what is this common good. "For they say that what is just is just *for* someone and that it should be equal for equals. But there still remains a question: equality or inequality of what?"[43] And in *Pol.* iii,1, where his stated task is to give a definition of a citizen and where he actually does this ("the citizen strictly speaking is defined by nothing other than participation in judging and ruling"—1275a22–23), he also admits that, strictly speaking, this definition applies only to the citizen of a democracy (1275b5–6).

Certainly some of this indeterminacy is due to Aristotle's tendency to address any philosophical question by looking first at the puzzles or problems *(aporiai)* associated with it. But it is also apparent that in the *Politics* something else is going on. Aristotle identifies in a number of places the reason why such questions are *systematically* irresolvable. In *Pol.* iii,1, for instance, the reason why Aristotle's definition of a citizen does not apply across the board is that "things of which the basic subject matters differs in kind—one of them being first, another second, another third—have, *qua* being such, nothing, or hardly anything, in common."[44] And in *Pol.* i,13, having raised some puzzles about why if the natural ruler and the natural subject both require excellence of character they should not both be capable of ruling, he says that the explanation is not that they differ in degree of "more and less" but that they "differ in kind."[45]

Aristotle is clearly alluding in both these passages to the theory of commensurability and incommensurability that he works out in the *Categories,* the *Metaphysics,* and other places. The *Pol.* iii,1 passage is an invocation of ax-

43. *Pol.* iii,12,1282b20–22; see also *Pol.* iii,13.
44. *Pol.* iii,1,1275a34–38: δεῖ δὲ μὴ λανθάνειν ὅτι τῶν πραγμάτων ἐν οἷς τὰ ὑποκείμενα διαφέρει τῷ εἴδει, καὶ τὸ μὲν αὐτῶν ἐστι πρῶτον τὸ δὲ δεύτερον τὸ δ' ἐχόμενον, ἢ τὸ παράπαν οὐδὲν ἔστιν, ἢ τοιαῦτα, τὸ κοινόν, ἢ γλίσχρως. Thomas's commentary offers basically a paraphrase of this point: *in Pol.* lb.3 cap.1 ll.155–64 (§354).
45. 1259b34–38. Thomas remarks: "Nec potest dici quod virtus principantis et subiecti differant secundum magis et minus; magis enim et minus non variant speciem, sed principari et subiici differunt specie: unde non videtur sufficere ad differentiam principantis et subiecti quod unus habeat plus de virtute quam alius" [*in Pol.* lb.1 cap.10 ll.173–79 (§157)].

iom {A}: 'ordered series of positionables ⇒ no common idea.' Since by employing various principles having to do with autonomy, unity, the common
good, etc., it is possible to rank constitutions and also therefore their citizens,
these citizens, *qua* being ordered in this way (and *qua* receiving their individual *logoi* from the particular constitutions), are not *sumblētos* with respect to
intensity-more-and-less (each is citizen in his own way), nor are they even
countable as if they fell under a common idea of citizenship. The *Pol.* i,13,
passage, on the other hand, is alluding to the fact that intensity ordering is
quite a different thing from position ordering.

[8] Chancellors and slaves

It might be useful to consider for a moment how such an approach might
be applied. Let us think of an organizational chart, say, of a university. Employing certain principles—who gives orders to whom, on whom do more
people depend than he on them, etc.—the various positions and roles can be
ranked, as we choose.[46] At the top of the chart might stand the President or
the Chancellor. Which it is will depend on what sort of ordering the chart
represents—i.e., what principles are being used. If the governing principle is
'importance with regard to decision making,' the President will probably be at
the top (and the Chancellor perhaps off to one side); if, on the other hand,
ceremonial precedence is the principle, the Chancellor will be at the top. In
any case, below them will be ranked the various other people in the university, from vice-presidents and deans to full professors, assistants, janitors,
kitchen help, and students. How these are ranked will depend, again, on what
the principles of precedence are.

Now, according to Aristotle's theory, although each of the positions on
such an organizational chart is filled by men, it would be a mistake to make
any judgments about these men, *qua* men, basing one's judgments on the
ranking of the organizational chart. The chart is simply a ranking based on
certain principles or others; it represents a particular ordering of positionables. There is vast difference—in fact, a logical difference—between such an

46. Aristotle often uses as a criterion or measure of something's being prior, other things' depending on it but not it on them: see e.g. *Cat.* xii,14a29–35, *Metaph.* v,11,1019a1–4. For various
ways in which something might be prior, see in general *Metaph.* v,11. Another interesting passage
is *Cael.* ii,5,288a2–12: "If nature always follows the best course possible, and, just as upward movement is the superior form of upward movement," etc., etc.

analysis and the consideration of individuals as what they are essentially—i.e., human beings.[47]

This would also be the case if one should choose to rank *men*—i.e., different types of men. In fact, and as is well-known, Aristotle does just this. He holds that a master is higher than his slave, a man than his wife and children, a brother higher than his sister.[48] But he is also quite aware that such rankings do not say anything about these individuals *qua* men. As he states in the passage we examined above, "if this substance is a man, it will not be more a man or less a man either than itself or than another man. For one man is not more a man than another, as one pale thing is more pale than another and one beautiful thing more beautiful than another" [*Cat.* v,3b39–4a2]. He makes this point precisely of the very controversial slave-master relationship. A master stands toward his slave as an artificer toward a tool, says Aristotle; therefore, "there cannot exist on the master's part friendship [*philia*] toward the slave insofar as he is a slave—but it can exist insofar as he is a man."[49] It may be that Aristotle's principles of societal organization were wrong, but his logic was impeccable. Ordering is a different procedure from counting something as a certain thing; and it is only the latter that treats of an individual's essence.

[9] Thomas's hierarchy of precepts

We come back, finally, to the question with which we began this chapter, whether the hierarchy of precepts presented in *ST* I–II q.94 a.2 is an invitation to consequentialist commensuration. There are a number of passages in

47. For the idea that individuals as such do not come into orderings, see *Cat.* vi,5b16–17; vii,8a22–23; also, *Metaph.* vii,12,1038a33–34 (τάξις δ' οὐκ ἔστιν ἐν τῇ οὐσίᾳ· πῶς γὰρ δεῖ νοῆσαι τὸ μὲν ὕστερον τὸ δὲ πρότερον;). See also Thomas, *in Metaph.* §1563. Note too that Plato says at *Phd.* 102c1–5 that Simmias is large not by virtue of being Simmias but insofar as he can be compared to Socrates.

48. See, for instance, *Pol.* i,3–7,12–13. But note too that households are ordered according to disparate polar-pairs: slave-free; husband-wife; father-children. On the superiority of a father to a mother, see *EE* vii,11,1244a13–14; see also vii,2,1237a4–5.

49. *EN* viii,11,1161b5–6; in Thomas, see *in EN* lb.8 lect.11 ll.163–73 (§1700). Note that Aristotle also says that masters would not need slaves if they had machines that operate automatically [*Pol.* i,4,1253b32–1254a1]—which gives us some insight into what he means by saying that slaves are like tools. Aristotle says that slaves don't have a βουλευτικόν [*Pol.* i,13,1260a12], but he also insists at *Pol.* i,13,1260b5–7 that they do have reason—and therefore can be admonished. They must, therefore, lack a βουλευτικόν only *qua* slave (see *De an.* iii,11,434a7). On slavery in Aristotle, see Schofield (1990).

Aristotle in which he clearly rejects consequentialism; but there is one in which he seems to come out in its favor.[50] In fact, however, the passage provides us with a good insight into the issue before us now. The passage comes in chapter 11, book iii of *De anima*:

Sensitive imagination, as we have said, is found in other animals, deliberative imagination in those that are calculative: for whether this or that shall be enacted is already a task requiring calculation; and there must be a single standard to measure by, for that is pursued which is greater. It follows that what acts in this way must be able to make a unity out of several images.[51]

It is true that Aristotle says here that, by a process involving some sort of comparison, we can arrive at conclusions regarding the greater good. But he cannot mean that this "greater good" is quantitatively better in the sense that, having added up *sumblētos* units of good, we see that one sum is greater than another. This would run contrary to the idea that ordering is a procedure quite distinct from counting—an idea that, as we have seen, pervades Aristotle's entire treatment of such matters. Rather, the insight into the greater good spoken of in this passage has to do with ordering. Such ordering, he makes clear, is an active procedure—an activity of the "deliberative imagination," as opposed to the reception of "images" or sense data [*phantasmata*].[52]

50. For the rejection of commensuration, see especially *Pol.* iii,12,1283a3–11. Aristotle treats of incommensurability also in *Phys.* vii,4 (see especially 248b4–10). One finds incommensurability arguments also in Thomas. He writes, for instance, that "those things that are not of one genus are not comparable—as sweetness is inappropriately said to be more or less than a line" [*ST* I q.6 a.2 obj.3]. (Thomas's statement comes in an objection, but his response makes it apparent that he accepts the point.) See also *De pot.* q.7 a.8 obj.2 and ad 2.

51. ἡ μὲν οὖν αἰσθητικὴ φαντασία, ὥσπερ εἴρηται, καὶ ἐν τοῖς ἄλλοις ζῴοις ὑπάρχει, ἡ δὲ βουλευτικὴ ἐν τοῖς λογιστικοῖς (πότερον γὰρ πράξει τόδε ἢ τόδε, λογισμοῦ ἤδη ἐστὶν ἔργον· καὶ ἀνάγκη ἑνὶ μετρεῖν· τὸ μεῖζον γὰρ διώκει· ὥστε δύναται ἓν ἐκ πλειόνων φαντασμάτων ποιεῖν) [*De an.* iii,11,434a5–10]. Penner and Rowe cite this passage, claiming that Aristotle does not hold for incommensurability [Penner and Rowe (1994), p. 4, n. 6]. Thomas comments on *De an.* iii,11,434a7–10 as follows: "Dicit ergo primo quod 'phantasia sensibilis,' ut ex dictis patet, est etiam in 'aliis animalibus,' sed illa quae est per deliberationem est tantum in rationalibus, quia considerare utrum 'hoc' sit agendum 'aut hoc,' quod est deliberare, 'est opus rationis, et' in tali consideratione 'necesse' est accipere aliquam unam regulam vel finem, vel aliquid huiusmodi, ad quem mensuretur quid sit magis agendum; manifestum est enim quod homo 'imitatur,' idest desiderat, id quod est magis in bonitate, id est quod est melius; melius autem semper diiudicamus aliqua mensura, et ita oportet accipere aliquam mensuram in deliberando quid magis sit agendum et hoc est medium, ex quo ratio practica syllogizat quid sit eligendum; unde manifestum est quod ratio deliberans 'potest ex pluribus phantasmatibus unum facere,' scilicet ex tribus quorum unum praeeligitur alteri et tertium est quasi mensura qua praeelegit" [*in De an.* lb.3 cap.10 ll.69–87 (§§840–41).

52. As we shall see in chapter 5, Aristotle's design in this general section of *De an.* is to distin-

But, if this is true, i.e., that the ordering spoken of is contributed by the rational creature, the outcome of an ordering cannot already have been determined by the state of the objects of deliberation. No matter what the independent attraction of a certain good or prospect of good, if deliberation is a rational process, it must be possible for the deliberator to step back and ask *whether* to pursue that good. It is perfectly possible for a philosopher to say, for instance, that the precepts corresponding to the inclination to worship God are higher than all others, that the precepts corresponding to the inclination to preserve life are next in order, etc., without saying or suggesting in any way that the various levels might be played off against each other, since, for one thing, precepts are not goods but rather human artifacts aimed at preserving goods and, secondly, things put into an order do not count one against the other, as if a higher one contained more of that which a lower one contained. Ordering of the type performed in *ST* I–II q.94 a.2 <7>, <8>, <9> is, as Pakaluk suggests, theory-laden. It may very well be that there are real reasons (i.e., reasons pertaining to the way things stand in the world) why a certain order is posited; but the *ordering* is not something found in the world: it is something we do.[53] And this is enough to exclude most consequentialist theories, for they usually involve a confusion of two distinct procedures: counting and ordering.

It must be acknowledged, however, that there are some varieties of consequentialism that the considerations put forward in this chapter do not touch—or, at least, touch very directly. Suppose that someone accepts all we have said and yet still wants to maintain a certain type of "weighing." He is not interested in calculating the quantity of goods promised by a prospective course of action but sees in *ST* I–II q.94 a.2 a hierarchy of precepts and concludes that it is perfectly in accord with Thomas's philosophy to allow a higher precept (let us say, "one should preserve life") to override a lower (let us say, "one should tell the truth").[54] Here we must remind our interlocutor of what it means to set up a hierarchy of precepts—either as an individual or as

---

guish non-rational animals from rational—which he does by identifying rational animals' ability to realize a certain distance between themselves and the objects of their deliberations.

53. In taking this approach, I am much indebted to Ralph McInerny's writings on analogy and, in particular, to his insight that the analogy of names is a logical doctrine. See McInerny (1961), (1968b), and (1996), all *passim.*

54. This type of consequentialism is discernible, for instance, in the utilitarian J. C. C. Smart, who quite readily admits that "the utilitarian is reduced to an intuitive weighing of various conse-

a culture or as a political entity. As Thomas maintains, any such activity of practical reason depends upon ("is founded upon": *ST* I–II q.94 a.2 <5>) goods. Goods define the infrastructure of the system of precepts amid which such actions are contemplated—and it never makes sense within such a system to attack the infrastructure, just as it never makes sense within geometry to employ a definition incompatible with a definition set out among the original definitions.

Pursuing the good that is the object of any one precept is always a good thing, provided another good (protected by another precept or by other precepts) is not harmed. The crucial question becomes, then, not whether one precept has more value than another but whether a good is being attacked. If going to Church means for some reason directly taking a life, then one ought not to go to Church. If preserving a life means directly harming the truth, then one ought not to preserve the life—the presupposition being, of course, that one is not directly taking the life. The crucial question in such cases is, obviously, When is a person directly attacking a good? I take up this issue in chapter 7.

---

quences" [Smart (1967), p. 210]. Smart argues that for utilitarianism we do not need a quantitative judgment of utility but only an ordinal judgment. See also Donagan (1977), p. 200. For similar ideas, see Hare (1981), p. 121; see also Broome (1991), pp. 145–48. Broome acknowledges that we may not be able to put a number on goodness; but, he says, if we are capable of having preferences (i.e., preferring one thing over another), this can be represented by a pair of numbers.

Acts

CHAPTER 5

VOLUNTAS ARISTOTELIAN
AND THOMISTIC

ITH THE BEGINNING of this second part of the present work, our focus of attention shifts from precepts to acts. A central issue in the analysis of acts, especially within an Aristotelian or Thomistic context, is the relationship between intellect and will. This is no abstract, "metaphysical" issue; nor is it of merely historical interest, although the approach I take in this chapter is historical. If intellect's grasp of an act and will's providing motion are regarded as linked, it becomes impossible to argue, along paths not infrequently trod, that a person performed what he knew to be such-and-such an act but morally that was not his act since his will was not to do harm. I discuss this issue in a more philosophical way in chapter 6. My task here is to determine the character of the theory that Thomas brings to bear upon it.

[1] The claims of Dom Lottin

In the late 1920s the Benedictine scholar Odon Lottin brought into the world of Thomistic studies the notion that a change occurred in Thomas Aquinas's understanding of free will sometime around 1270, the year in which Étienne (Stephen) Tempier, bishop of Paris, issued a number of condemnations of propositions especially popular at that time among Aristotelians influenced by Arabic interpreters. They include the proposition (or propositions), "Free choice is a passive potency, not active, and it is necessitated by that which is desired."[1] Lottin claims, first, that Thomas's *De veritate* (years 1256 to 1259), *Summa contra gentiles* (years 1258 to 1261), and *Summa theologiae* I (years 1265 to 1268) all represent the intellect as that which initiates action, will responding to this initiative, whereas, in *De malo* q.6 (1270) and *Summa theologiae* I–II (1271), will becomes the active member of the pair.[2] Secondly, Lottin claims that in the same three earlier works (*De ver.*, *SCG*, and *ST* I), intellect is the final cause in human action, will the efficient cause, whereas in *De ma.* q.6 and *ST* I–II will takes over also the role of final cause, leaving intellect with only the role of formal cause. Thirdly, he claims that the distinction in the earlier works between free willing *(libera voluntas)* and free choice *(liberum arbitrium)* gives way to a new distinction between liberty of exercise ("liberté d'exercice") and of specification ("liberté de spécification").[3]

1. See Lottin (1928), pp. 373–80, (1929 <1927>) (especially pp. 129–59), (1956a), (1956b) and (1942–1960), vol. 1, pp. 221–62; see also San Cristóbal-Sebastián (1958). On the Paris condemnations, see Lottin (1942–1960), vol. 1, p. 252, (1956a), p. 329; Gallagher (1994b), pp. 249–51; San Cristóbal-Sebastián (1958), pp. 9–20; Van Steenberghen (1991), pp. 411ff.; Westberg (1994a); Wippel (1977). The proposition condemned by Étienne Tempier on December 10, 1270, which has attracted special attention is number 9 (of 13) in the list that appears in the *Chartularium Universitatis Parisiensis* [=Denifle and Chatelain (1889), vol. 1, p. 487]: "Quod liberum arbitrium est potentia passiva, non activa; et quod necessitate movetur ab appetibili." (In one manuscript the words "non activa" do not appear.) Other propositions in the list are also concerned with determinism—i.e., number 3 ("Quod voluntas hominis ex necessitate vult vel elegit") and number 4 ("Quod omnia, quae hic et in inferioribus aguntur, subsunt necessitati corporum celestium"). Three others have indirectly to do with determinism: number 10 ("Quod Deus non cognoscit singularia"), number 11 ("Quod Deus non cognoscit alia a se"), number 12 ("Quod humani actus non reguntur providentia Dei"). This is important, since part of my argument here is that Thomas's main preoccupation in *De ma.* q.6 is not the nature of *voluntas*; rather, he is primarily occupied in arguing against determinism. If this is correct, even if *De ma.* q.6 was written with the condemnations in mind, this itself does not say much in favor of a developed theory of *voluntas*. Few scholars would be prepared to sustain that Thomas's views on determinism (*qua* determinism) developed. (The propositions condemned by Tempier in 1270 and 1277 are also given and discussed in the third volume of the Marietti edition of *SCG*, pp. 491–504.)

2. Lottin (1928), p. 378. For the dating of *De veritate* and *Summa theologiae* I–II, see Lottin (1928), Torrell (1996 <1993>), pp. 63–64, 146–47, 333, Weisheipl (1983 <1974>), pp. 123–26, 362–63, and Tugwell (1988), pp. 249, 255–56 (and especially note 527, p. 336). In 1956, Lottin acknowledged the findings of F. Van Steenberghen to the effect that the list of condemned propositions was in circulation before they were officially issued, so that Thomas could have been prompted to write *De ma.* q.6 as early as 1269. In Appendix C, I dispute any dating of *De ma.* q.6 that puts it after *De ver.* q.24 a.1.

3. Lottin (1928), p. 379. Note that in *De ma.* q.6, Thomas never uses the expressions *libertas quantum ad exercitium* or *libertas quantum ad specificationem;* he does however use the phrases *quantum ad exercitium* and *quantum ad specificationem*—also, *quantum ad determinationem,* which in this context is equivalent to *quantum ad specificationem*.

Both Lottin and Thomas distinguish between *liberum arbitrium* and *libera voluntas;* but, since this distinction (*qua* verbal distinction) does not play a large part in the present discussion, I do not advert directly to it. The distinction itself, however, has much to do with the distinction

In Thomas's later writings, according to Lottin, free choice, which is to be associated with the freedom of the practical *intellect*, becomes less important.[4]

Lottin is restrained in making these claims. In an article that appeared in 1928, he speaks fairly straightforwardly of "development";[5] but even by 1929 he is issuing serious qualifications. Regarding the thesis that only later in Thomas do we find the distinction liberty of exercise/liberty of specification, he remarks (having first referred to *De ma.* q.6) that

[i]t is not necessary to emphasize [urger] the difference, manifest though it is, that exists between this treatment in *De malo* and that in *De veritate*. For the distinction between liberty of exercise and liberty of specification, which provides the frame for question 6 of *De malo*, is not unknown in *De veritate* (q.22 a.6), where St. Thomas speaks of the indeterminacy of the will [la volonté] with respect to the act of willing itself and the object of this act. On the other hand, the psychological law that refers action to the will and this to judgment is not in any sense repudiated in *De malo*, for it is repeated at the very beginning of the treatment.[6] One cannot therefore speak of opposition—nor of diversity of doctrine. The line of thought [tour de pensée], however, is different and the emphasis is shifted.[7]

---

between liberty of specification and liberty of exercise; so, in that sense, I do consider it fairly extensively. [Lottin discusses the difference between *libera voluntas* and *liberum arbitrium* at Lottin (1956a), pp. 326ff.]

In what follows, instead of the word 'will,' I use the Latin word *voluntas*. The reason for this is that the modern expression 'free will' has come to connote a sort of rival center of agency besides the intellect. I wish rather to encourage the idea (argued for later in this chapter) that this power, although separate, is not a rival to the intellect [see Allan (1962), p. 183; also Bourke (1964), pp. 30–33]. For similar reasons, I also translate the Latin expression *liberum arbitrium* as 'free decision' instead of the more usual 'free will.'

In this chapter, references to line numbers ('ll.*nnn*–*nnn*') are to line numbers of the text stabilized by the Leonine Commission. This text, with line numbers, is given in Appendix D, with a facing English translation.

4. Lottin (1942–1960), vol. 1, pp. 261–62.

5. Lottin (1928), p. 375.

6. Lottin is apparently referring to the words "Hoc autem activum sive motivum principium in hominibus proprie est intellectus et voluntas, ut dicitur in III De anima" [*De ma.* q.6 ll.272–75]. (See also, somewhat later, "Si ergo consideremus motum potentiarum animae ex parte obiecti specificantis actum, primum principium motionis est ex intellectu: hoc enim modo bonum intellectum movet etiam ipsam voluntatem" [*De ma.* q.6 ll.339–43].) Lottin regards this "psychological law" that in some sense *voluntas* also depends on intellect as connected with the intellectual determinism that existed within the tradition of Aristotelian interpretation in Thomas's time [Lottin (1942–1960), vol. 1, pp. 231, 256].

7. Lottin (1929 <1927–1929>), p. 153 n. 1. This section of Lottin (1929 <1927–1929>) first appeared in *Revue Thomiste*, vol. 34, 1929 (pp. 400–430). The same remark appears, nearly word-for-word, at Lottin (1942–1960), vol. 1, p. 258.

In a later work, written in reaction to R. Z. Lauer's objection that the intellect is regarded as formal and final cause both before and after *De ma.* q.6, Lottin writes, "We are bid, therefore, not to emphasize the change in formulation to the point of necessarily seeing here proof of a change of doctrine."[8]

But if Lottin is restrained, the same cannot be said of many who make use of his ideas in order to find in Thomas a turn toward their favorite strain of modern philosophy. George Klubertanz, for instance, writing in 1961, connects the supposed shift in Thomas toward considering the will as final cause with a parallel drawn by Thomas in *De ma.* q.6 between natural appetite (for the good) and "animal appetite," for which latter "the known object is like the substantial form"—that is, it has to do not just with acts but with the acting being itself.[9] Understanding man's natural appetite in this way, "the formal causality of the known form is thus not absolutely immediately upon the act of tending, but immediately upon the agent." Will, therefore, closely bound up, of course, with natural appetite, is also closely bound up with the agent *himself* as he experiences his existential condition, buffeted here and there by desires and limitations. "This analysis is more metaphysical than the earlier ones," writes Klubertanz, "since it works out from the relation of form to tendency in being. It is at the same time more existential and personal, since the being of the agent and the dynamism of his act of existing are involved directly."[10] More recently, James Keenan has seen in the later Thomas, as posited by Lottin, a turn toward a type of moral theory in which "goodness" takes precedence over "rightness"—i.e., a theory that, in the moral evaluation of persons, looks more toward the good they will than toward whether the objective acts they perform are the "right" ones.[11]

---

8. Lottin (1956a), p. 325; see also Lauer (1954) and Lottin (1956b). The quoted remark comes immediately after Lottin's consideration of a passage in the late work *De carit.* (q.un a.3) where Thomas, while speaking of charity, seems to identify formal and final cause with respect to actions. Writes Klubertanz: "One could question whether charity is 'form of the virtues' in the same sense as, for example, prudence is; if so, [Lottin's] concessions seem unnecessary" [Klubertanz (1961), p. 702, n. 6]. But Klubertanz is overlooking the passage from *ST* II–II (which comes, of course, after *ST* I–II) cited by Lottin in which Thomas says the same about moral acts in general and then moves on to speak about charity: "Respondeo dicendum quod in moralibus forma actus attenditur principaliter ex parte finis. . . . Manifestum est autem . . . quod per caritatem ordinantur actus omnium aliarum virtutum ad ultimum finem" [*ST* I–II q.23 a.8 c].

9. Klubertanz (1961), p. 711.

10. Klubertanz, citing Lottin (1942–1960), vol. 1, pp. 253, 258, goes on immediately to say, "Thus also the spontaneity of the acting subject is stressed, as Dom Lottin and others have pointed out" [Klubertanz (1961), p. 711]. Lottin discusses natural appetite at Lottin (1929 <1927–1929>), pp. 150–51.

11. Keenan (1992). On Keenan (1992), see Dewan (1995).

In the present chapter I confront none of these interpretations directly. I do not attempt to demonstrate that Lottin is wrong or that people like Klubertanz and Keenan are misapplying Thomas. The first task, refuting Lottin, has, in a sense, already been done; in another sense, it could never be done. Critics of Lottin's—and, in fact, Lottin himself—adduce numerous texts that are extremely difficult to reconcile with the notion of development in Thomas in the pertinent respects;[12] but Lottin's various disclaimers ensure that his position itself will always defy falsification, with the natural consequence that it also lacks a clear sense. The second task, demonstrating that Thomas is being misapplied, would be frustrating in a similar way. Often enough a scholar is willing to admit that Thomas wrote things that are impossible to reconcile with whatever more modern theory is being proposed;

12. See Lottin's discussion of *De carit.* q.un a.3 (note 8 above); see also his acknowledgment (in the paragraph translated just above) that one can find also in *De veritate* the distinction between liberty of exercise and liberty of specification. Although at Lottin (1928), p. 379, it is stated that the commentary on the *Sentences* "n'offre rien d'utile à notre dessein," in a subsequent writing [Lottin (1929 <1927–1929>), p. 140], Lottin acknowledges that, at *in Sent.* lb.2 d.7 q.1 a.1 ad 1 & 2, Thomas distinguishes liberty of exercise and of specification. (Lottin (1929 <1927–1929>), pp. 129–59 was published in 1929.) See also Lottin (1942–1960), vol. 1, p. 227; also Lottin (1956a), p. 328, n. 13, where he says, "Saint Thomas avait certes reconnu l'existence de cette double liberté" [he cites *in Sent.* lb.2 d.7 q.1 a.1 ad 1 & 2 and *De ver.* q.22 a.6]; "mais la formule est une création du *De malo*." Klubertanz too, although an advocate of the Lottin position, suggests some texts which he thinks go against some of Lottin's claims: see Klubertanz (1961), p. 707.

Lauer (1954) cites as problematic for Lottin's views on final and formal causality: *in Metaph.* §§766–70 (where formal is connected with efficient causality), *De ver.* q.22 a.14 (where the intellect is also formal cause), *De ver.* q.22 a.12 (where it is suggested that formal causality as well as final implies a passive *voluntas*), *SCG* lb.2 cap.48 (where it is suggested that not only final but also formal causality has "implications of efficiency"—p. 310, n. 21), *SCG* lb.3 cap.73 and cap.88 (where the formal causality of the intellect is emphasized), *ST* I q.82 a.4 (where the intellect's final causality is not detrimental to *voluntas*'s active nature), and *De ma.* q.6 ad 6 (where "the intellect is a final cause through the medium of the object inasmuch as it belongs to the intellect to perceive the *ratio* of good in the object"—p. 316). (One might also mention Thomas's *in Int.* lb.1 lect.14 ll.475–522 [§199], where, although apparently writing between 1270 and 1271 [Torrell (1996 <1993>), pp. 224–26, 342–43], he seems unconcerned about ruling out a possible intellectual-deterministic interpretation of his words.)

In his reply to Lauer, Lottin remarks, "Il n'était pas question de savoir si saint Thomas avait définitivement renoncé à voir dans la raison pratique la cause finale de l'acte libre; mais constatant que dans le *De malo* la raison était présentée comme cause formelle, je m'étais demandé, pourquoi, dans un exposé traitant exactement le même problème que dans le *De veritate*, saint Thomas avait jugé bon de modifier sa formule." One wonders, however, whether we have then even a different "tour de pensée," such as he speaks of at Lottin (1929 <1927–1929>), p. 153, n. 1. Lottin also says that Lauer fails to notice that he (Lottin) distinguishes between the situation presented by Étienne Tempier's condemnations regarding passive *voluntas* and the situation presented by the intellectual determinism in the universities of Thomas's time. Lottin says that he discusses the treatment of the intellect as the formal cause with respect to the latter situation only—i.e., not with respect to whether *voluntas* is passive. But this is hard to square with Lottin (1942–1960), vol. 1, pp. 252–54 and also the text cited by Lauer in her note 5, p. 301.

the claim is usually that, nonetheless, he was leaning in the preferred direction.

The whole business needs to be brought out onto a larger historical field. The issue is ultimately whether Thomas, given his basic principles, would have felt at all comfortable espousing the modern positions or whether his ethical thought was fundamentally ancient and Aristotelian. It is only in such a larger context that we can confront the issue of a "modern turn" in Thomas and have any purchase on the truth. Certainly, if it can be shown that his allegedly developed views are not only present in the tradition of which he is a part but are quite prominent there, it will have been shown that any formulaic changes, made because he happens to be thinking about the (perhaps impending) condemnations of Étienne Tempier, are only accidental to his thought as a whole. In this way, we also avoid getting bogged down in questions about whether, for instance, Thomas's position in *De ma.* q.6 is different from that in *ST* I q.82 *(De voluntate)*. These are interesting and important questions; but they are not the ones I am asking here.

Our first task is to determine what is Thomas's general position regarding free choice in *De ma.* q.6. Fortunately, his scholastic methodology enables us to locate this quite easily: it is set out in the article's body, which I examine here in sections [2] to [4]. In sections [5] to [9], I go about the task of showing that this general position is Aristotelian. Finally, in section [10], I discuss in a similar way a number of the article's many objections and corresponding responses.

[2] *De malo* q.6: the body (first section)

The title of *De ma.* q.6 is "About human choice" *(De electione humana)*, although immediately after the title Thomas gets more specific, saying, "And first it is asked whether man has the free choice of his acts or whether he chooses from necessity." The body of *De ma.* q.6 begins with the following remark:

[S]ome have assumed that man's *voluntas* is moved from necessity toward something which is to be chosen. But neither were they assuming that *voluntas* is coerced— for not every instance of necessity is an instance of being forced but only that one whose principle is outside. Whence also natural movements are, some of them, discovered to be necessary but not instances of being forced, for an instance of being forced is incompatible both with the natural and with the voluntary since the principle of both of these is inside; the principle in an instance of being forced, however, is outside.

This opinion, however, is heretical. It eliminates the reason for merit and demerit in human acts, for that seems not to be meritorious or demeritorious which someone does so much from necessity that he could not avoid it.

It is, furthermore, to be numbered among aberrant philosophical opinions since it not only is contrary to the Faith but also subverts every principle of moral philosophy [ll.238–56].

It is important that we understand just what is being criticized here, for this has a bearing on the question of the nature of the relationship between *De ma.* q.6 and Étienne Tempier's condemnations. It has appeared to at least one influential scholar that the object of criticism is "the idea of freedom as non-coercion."[13] Such an interpretation would favor those who sustain that there is a development in Thomas, since, of course, they wish to see this development in his conception of *voluntas* (or will), which is said to take on in *De ma.* q.6 a new positive character not captured by speaking of mere non-coercion. But, in fact, a comparison of the above passage with a parallel version in *De ver.* q.24 a.1 reveals that Thomas is vilifying not the point about non-coercion but determinism itself.[14]

Here is the first section of the body of *De ver.* q.24 a.1:

Without any doubt, it is necessary to suppose that man is free with respect to decision. For faith requires this since, without free decision, there cannot be merit or demerit, fitting punishment or reward. Clear indicators also suggest this, according to which man appears freely to choose one thing and reject another. Apparent reasoning also compels us to this conclusion—and, in conducting this investigation, pursuing the origin of free decision, we shall proceed in this way.

13. Lonergan (1942), p. 533. Lonergan, citing Lottin, says that in his earlier writings Thomas occasionally employs this idea that freedom equals non-coercion. (Lonergan refers to it as "this relic of the pre-philosophic [!] period of medieval thought.") Thomas, however, supposedly made up for this in his later writings: "This lapse in the teeth of contrary theory was repudiated with extreme vehemence in the later *De malo* as heretical, destructive of all merit and demerit, subversive of all morality, alien to all scientific and philosophic thought, and the product of either wantonness or incompetence" (p. 534). Lonergan cites at this point *De ma.* q.6 and suggests a contrast with *De ver.* q.22 a.7. The places in the earlier Thomas where Lonergan finds traces of the "heretical" idea include *in Sent.* lb.2 d.25 q.1 a.4; *De ver.* q.23 a.4; *De pot.* q.10 a.2 ad 5.

14. I argue more extensively in Appendix C that *De ver.* q.24 a.1 is a rewrite of *De ma.* q.6. Another problem with the position that Thomas in *De ma.* q.6 is opposing the definition of liberty as non-coercion is that at ad 23 [l.721] he employs that definition in a positive manner.

Among things that are moved or activate something else there is to be discerned this difference: that some have the principle of their movement or action in themselves, others have it outside themselves, as, for instance, those that are moved by force—"in which the principle is outside, that which is acted upon contributing no force," according to the Philosopher in the third book of the *Ethics*.[15]

The *De ma.* q.6 version is not as well written as this one, for in *De ma.* q.6 one might get the impression that the words "This opinion . . . is heretical" [l.248] refer to the remark that immediately precedes them—i.e., the remark that sets coercion off against both natural necessity and *voluntas*—rather than to the more general opening remark about those who hold that "man's *voluntas* is moved from necessity toward something which is to be chosen" [ll.238–40]. In this *(De veritate)* version, however, it is clear that the "heretical opinion" is not the opinion that freedom equals non-coercion; rather, it refers to any sort of theory entailing determinism, for Thomas's remark about what the faith requires comes immediately after one that speaks simply about free decision. That is, the opening remark, "it is necessary to suppose that man is free with respect to decision," is immediately followed by the sentence, "For faith requires this since, without free decision there cannot be merit or demerit, fitting punishment or reward." (Note that this is the same explanation offered in *De ma.* q.6 for the charge of heresy: "It takes away the significance of merit and demerit in human actions . . ." [ll.248–49].)

This all suggests that Thomas is not immediately interested in *De ma.* q.6 (or, for that matter, in *De ver.* q.24 a.1) in recasting or even clarifying his doctrine of *voluntas*—presumably, in order to remain outside the scope of Étienne Tempier's condemnations. He is interested rather in explaining how a truly Aristotelian approach to action does not entail determinism.[16]

---

15. *De ver.* q.24 a.1 ll.226–42: "Responsio. Dicendum quod absque omni dubitatione hominem arbitrio liberum ponere oportet. Ad hoc enim fides astringit cum sine libero arbitrio non possit esse meritum vel demeritum, iusta poena vel praemium; ad hoc etiam manifesta indicia inducunt, quibus apparet hominem libere unum eligere et aliud refutare; ad hoc etiam evidens ratio cogit: qua quidem ad investigationem, liberi arbitrii originem sequentes, hoc modo procedemus.

In rebus enim quae moventur vel aliquid agunt, haec invenitur differentia quod quaedam principium sui motus vel operationis in seipsis habent, quaedam vero extra se, sicut ea quae per violentiam moventur, 'in quibus principium est extra, nil conferente vim passo,' secundum philosophum in III Ethicorum . . .". The latter reference is to *EN* iii,1,1110a1–2. See *De ma.* q.6 obj.4.

16. That Thomas is putting forward what he regards as an Aristotelian position is strongly suggested by the explicit citations in the body of *De ma.* q.6, nine of which are to Aristotle, the other two being to Boethius's *Philosophiae consolatio* and Averroes's commentary on *De anima*

[3] The first consideration

Having denounced determinism as contrary to both faith and philosophy, Thomas, as his first consideration ("to be considered first"), sets out a number of distinctions [ll.269ff.]. Man, he says, is both like and unlike other natural things that have within themselves the principles of their own action or motion. Like them, his action involves both form and natural appetite; but unlike them, this form is intellectual. With man, but not with other natural things, action involves an apprehended intellectual form, which is a principle of action, and *voluntas,* which follows the form [ll.284–88].

An intellectual form is universal, says Thomas, in the sense that, with a single apprehended form before him, a man might go off in several directions. A builder, for instance, might think in a general way of building a house; once he begins building, however, that idea becomes more determinate: he might build a square house, a round house, etc. [ll.292–96]. Either moment, the general or the determinate, is part of the way he does things. The form of a mere natural thing, on the other hand, is determined from the outset toward a single thing. A tree does what trees do—grow—in a determinate way from the very beginning. There is never a moment when it pauses to think about growing, then proceeds to follow that idea in a more determinate way. Even though it is true that trees grow in spectacularly individual ways, they take no notice of this. We think about trees in general and how they differ. They just grow.

One might think at first that brute animals are in this respect exactly like men since, unlike trees, they do not always do the same thing. But they behave this way not because they are possessed of intellectual forms but because they have a more complex relationship with the world than trees do. They have senses that react to diverse objects, sometimes positively, sometimes negatively [ll.301–6], so that we can expect watching a dog to be more inter-

---

(i.e., a commentary on a work by Aristotle). Note also the reference to Aristotle in the *De ver.* q.24 a.1 quotation.

In this connection, it is worth comparing *De ma.* q.6 to Albert the Great's consideration of the proposition, "Quod liberum arbitrium est potentia passiva non activa," etc.: *Quin.prob.* IX (p. 41). Albert, while acknowledging that Aristotle speaks of passive potencies in *De an.* iii (apparently, 427b23–24), argues that *voluntas* is actually more active than passive. He says that the pseudophilosopher who propounds the idea that *voluntas* is wholly passive subverts the whole of book vii of Aristotle's *Nicomachean Ethics.*

esting than watching a tree. But however variegated the activity of a dog, neither does it ever sit back to consider in a general way what it will do, so that it might then proceed in a more determinate way, seeking out means of getting to where it wishes to go. When a dog receives the form of a singular, this elicits an inclination "toward one act, as in natural things" [l.301]. Like a tree, at that point it just does what it does.[17]

Thomas has made a number of points here which it would be well to identify clearly since, in what follows (i.e., in the "second consideration"), they are reworked in important ways. First, the intellect is, indeed, to be associated with form. Secondly, this intellectual form is universal in character, at least in the preliminary moment of action. Thirdly, intellect and *voluntas* are bound up with one another as the principle of human action: the "active or motivating principle in men properly," says Thomas, "is intellect and *voluntas*" [ll.272–74]. Fourthly, intellect can be said in a certain sense to have the lead in the initiation of action. If, for instance, a person decides to stay at home one evening to read a book, he must first understand (with his intellect) what reading a book is; this is a prerequisite to his wishing to do this.[18] It is this fourth idea which seems especially to lead in the direction of determinism, since, hearing this, we tend to think of the impulse for action as coming toward the subject in such a way that it is guaranteed that the subject will react.

[4] The second consideration

As part of his second consideration ("To be considered secondly") [ll.308ff.], Thomas distinguishes two perspectives upon any sort of action or motion: one is that of the thing moving or acting (Thomas speaks in this connection of the subject's exercise of an act), the other is that of the object toward which the thing moves (he speaks of the act's specification or determination). The exercise of the act has to do with whether to act or not; we might think of it as an on-off switch.[19] Specification has to do with what the

17. I do not mean to suggest that free choice necessarily involves "sitting back" and considering but only that a being possessed of free choice can do this. I discuss this issue in chapter 6, section [5].

18. This is not to say that he first has the thought and then adds to it the corresponding appetite. The dependence is a logical rather than a temporal one.

19. But note that exercise also has to do with how well a particular potency operates: ll.315–17. Gavin Colvert has pointed out to me very acutely that this on-off switch is also "a loaded switch," "since the will remains a rational appetite actualized with respect to its first object" [comments made in private correspondence].

act is and involves options: the person staying home might read a novel, a book of essays on modal logic, etc.

The distinction applies to merely natural things and also to creatures endowed with reason. With respect to merely natural things, the situation is quite simple. The specification of the act comes from the non-intellectual form (the object); the exercise comes from the agent (the subject). But even given this exercise of the act on the subject's part, "it remains that the first principle of motion as to the exercise of the act is from the end" [ll.324–25]. Thus, with natural things, there exists a certain separation of specification and exercise; but, in the end, even exercise is reduced to specification since it is a reaction to the end specified. (It is on account of this that merely natural things are subject to a high degree of necessity.)

With respect to rational creatures such as man, on the other hand, the situation is more complex. Since in a rational creature the activating principle is double, involving both intellect and *voluntas,* it involves also two objects—both of which are the highest in their genus. That is, the proper object of each in some way contains the other objects connected with it: the proper object of intellect is "being and the true," which contains all things that might be known; the proper object of *voluntas* is "the good" or happiness, which is the overall reason why a person seeks anything. In other (i.e., Thomas's) words, the object of intellect is "primary and principal within the genus of formal cause," the object of *voluntas* "primary and principal within the genus of final cause" [ll.326–33]. The result of this is that exercise and specification are not separate—at least, not in the way they are in merely natural things. Since each object is "primary and principal" within its respective genus (each genus being at the highest level of generality), each includes the other, although under a different aspect. The object of *voluntas,* the good, includes the object of intellect, being, but not as being, since being *as* being is primary and principal within its genus. And so also for the object of intellect, being. It includes the object of *voluntas,* good, but not *qua* good. The result is that, although *voluntas* and intellect are separate (i.e., insofar as they have separate objects), depending on the perspective from which the issue is approached, the one might be said to include the other—or even to be superior to it.[20]

---

20. On the inseparability of *voluntas* and intellect, see Gallagher (1994b). See also, Westberg (1994a) and (1994b), pp. 50–60, 130–35, 223–26; but also Flannery (1995b).

Thomas has this conception that liberty of exercise is to some extent involved in liberty of

Thomas next [ll.343ff.] considers how freedom is preserved in the exercise of the act of a rational being. This involves primarily *voluntas*, which, since its object is the good, includes anything a rational being might do, for doing is always for a good and the good is the object of *voluntas*. Thus, one wills to eat, to take exercise—even to think and to will [ll.360–63]. The last two objects of *voluntas* are, obviously, very important. Thomas says very clearly that intellect comes under the command of *voluntas*: "I understand," he says, "because I will" [l.351]. (He actually uses a military image in this regard: "as the soldier moves the maker of bridles into operation" [ll.348–49].) As to willing to will, this cannot go on forever, says Thomas. Ultimately, *voluntas* must be prompted into motion by something else. This something else, says Thomas, is God [ll.407–10]. But since God's influence on a creature is always proportionate to its nature, he acts in such a way as not to destroy the rational creature's freedom [ll.410–17].

As to how freedom is preserved in the specification of the act [ll.418ff.], the primary focus of Thomas's treatment is intellect. If an object apprehended by the intellect is good in every way conceivable, it is in fact the proper object of the intellect, happiness; there is no freedom of choice in this respect. But if the intellect can consider an object as not good in every way conceivable, freedom is thereby in that respect ensured: one can always look at a less

---

specification very early on in his philosophical career, i.e., as early as his commentary on Peter Lombard's *Sentences* (written and edited between 1252 and 1256). See, for instance, *in Sent.* lb.2 d.7 q.1 a.1 ad 1, where he argues that the angels are ordered toward the good as their end, and yet they are also possessed of a certain freedom: "[A]pud illos quorum est indeficienter recta aestimatio finis, sicut apud angelos, qui ipso fine perficiuntur, impossibile est esse voluntatem alicujus eorum quae a fine deordinant, cujusmodi est voluntas peccati. Sed tamen possunt velle hoc vel illud, quorum neutrum a fine deordinat; et sic salvatur proprietas rationalis potestatis, inquantum possunt hoc facere vel non facere; quamvis non possint in haec opposita, bonum et malum." Thomas uses the phrase "velle hoc vel illud" (or similar phrases) to signify liberty of specification [see e.g. *De ma.* q.6 ll.419–20]. Liberty of exercise is represented as *velle hoc et non velle* or *velle hoc vel non velle* (or similar phrases) [*De ver.* q.24 a.3 ad 3 l.107; see also e.g. *De ma.* q.6 l.316]. Note that here, in *in Sent.* lb.2 d.7 q.1 a.1 ad 1, angels "possunt velle hoc vel illud" and thus "possunt hoc facere vel non facere." The two types of liberty are also combined in ad 3 ("potestas Angeli . . . possit hoc facere vel non facere, aut hoc vel illud facere"); see also *in Sent.* lb.3 d.18 q.1 a.2 ad 5.

In these regards, therefore, I cannot go along with Lottin, who, having noted that in *in Sent.* lb.2 d.7 q.1 a.1 ad 1 Thomas speaks of the angels' liberty of specification, says: "Mais une question se pose: cette liberté de spécification est-elle essentielle au libre arbitre; ou au contraire ne faut-il pas maintenir que la liberté, d'exercice suffit pour sauvegarder la liberté et, dès lors, assurer le mérite? Il semble bien que saint Thomas ait admis cette suffisance, et pour les anges et pour le Christ" [Lottin (1942–1960), vol. 1, pp. 227–28]. (Lottin cites *in Sent.* lb.2 d.7 q.1 a.1 ad 4; d.25 q.1 a.1 ad 4; *in Sent.* lb.3 d.18 q.1 a.2 ad 5; d.12 q.2 a.1 ad 2 & 3.) One cannot have liberty of exercise without the specification of acts. This point becomes important in chapter 6.

pleasing or less suitable aspect of the object and, on that basis, not choose it. Even in the former case, however, i.e., the case in which the specification of the act allows no room for freedom, there remains, says Thomas, freedom of exercise: "[S]omeone is able not to will to think of happiness at a given time—for also the acts of *voluntas* and intellect are themselves particulars" [ll.438–40; see also ll.482–85]. We must assume, however, that, even in this case, the person would so choose for the sake of (presumed) happiness; otherwise his willing not to think of happiness at a given time would not fall under the proper object of *voluntas*—i.e., it would not be an act of *voluntas* at all. Moreover, when the man in question wills not to will happiness, although it is true that he is not specifying a certain aspect of happiness as not good, in taking advantage of his liberty of exercise he is specifying that particular action—since there is no such thing as an unspecified action. He is specifying it as a choice not to exercise his capacity to think of the goodness of goodness. This is to move from the universal intellectual form to the act—and acts exist "in singulars."[21] So again that which distinguishes man from brute animals comes to the fore: his ability, first, to understand what he is about to do, and then to do it—in a determinate way.[22]

It is clear then that, for Thomas, *voluntas* enjoys a certain predominance in human action. It is of primary importance in freedom of exercise. In freedom of specification, intellect enjoys some predominance, although, ultimately, even here *voluntas* is more important. It is through *voluntas* that we choose to see a good under one aspect or another, and, where intellect is unfree—i.e., with respect to the ultimate good—*voluntas* is still free "not to will to think of happiness at a given time."

[5] A list of major ideas

My next task is to determine whether the general position set out in the body of *De ma.* q.6 is Aristotelian. I do this by discussing what Aristotle says with respect to four ideas found in the body of *De ma.* q.6 and often associat-

---

21. *De ma.* q.6 ll.288–89; see also ll.425–26.
22. None of what Thomas says here contradicts what he says in *ST* I q.82 a.2 c about the state of a soul once it arrives at the beatific vision. At that point, although obviously the soul having the vision stands at a distance from its object, the connection between its own happiness and its object is so obvious (or "demonstrated") that it is impossible for it not to adhere to its object (God).

ed with the supposed development in Thomas's thinking with respect to the role and nature of *voluntas*. They are as follows:

[[1]] the idea that *voluntas* enjoys a certain predominance over intellect;

[[2]] the idea that freedom is directly due to rationality and our capacity to stand back from a particular course of action and consider whether to do it;

[[3]] the idea that in rational beings we can distinguish two types of liberty, liberty of specification and liberty of exercise;

[[4]] the idea that the principle of our actions is God.

I go through these ideas (which I refer to as 'major ideas') in order.

As explained above, my task here is not to determine whether the supposed development in Thomas did occur but whether, even if it did, it would have brought him closer to modern ideas about freedom. If these ideas are found in the works of Aristotle himself, it will be difficult to sustain that any formulaic changes represent a turn toward more modern ideas.

[6] The predominance of *voluntas*

Major idea [[1]], i.e., that *voluntas* enjoys a certain predominance over intellect, would seem to conflict with Aristotle's general approach to their relationship. In *De an.* iii,4, for instance, he says that intellect must be "unmixed" in its function of knowing "in order that it might dominate."[23] And in *De an.* iii,19, he writes:

[T]hat which is the object of appetite is the stimulant of practical thought; and that which is last in the process of thinking is the beginning of the action. It follows that there is a justification for regarding these two as the sources of movement, i.e., appetite and practical thought; for the object of appetite starts a movement and, as a result of that, thought gives rise to movement, the object of appetite being to it a source of stimulation [433a16–20].

Obviously, this is a very complex passage; but it is not unreasonably interpreted as maintaining that intellect, insofar as it originally introduces the object of movement, has the lead in human action, appetite or *orexis* (including

---

23. ἀνάγκη ἄρα, ἐπεὶ πάντα νοεῖ, ἀμιγῆ εἶναι, ὥσπερ φησὶν Ἀναξαγόρας, ἵνα κρατῇ, τοῦτο δ' ἐστὶν ἵνα γνωρίζῃ [*De an.* iii,4,429a18–20]. This remark appears to be connected with the Socratic doctrine that the mind cannot be "dragged about like a slave" by the lower powers. See Plato, *Prt.* 352b8–c2; see also Aristotle, *EN* vii,2,1145b23–24; 3,1147b15–17. [Cp. Penner (1992), p. 129–30.]

voluntas) passively receiving this information from the intellect and only then being put into action.[24]

We find Aristotle saying similar things about the relationship between theoretical reason (the proper realm of intellect) and practical reason (the proper realm of *voluntas*). At the end of *EN* vi,7, for instance, having explained that often the person who knows particular facts, such as that "chicken is wholesome," is the better healer, Aristotle insists that, nonetheless, one should prefer to have impractical theoretical knowledge or wisdom (1141b21–22). At the end of that book, he similarly insists that practical wisdom *(phronēsis)* "is not supreme over wisdom, i.e., over the superior part of us [i.e., the intellect], any more than the art of medicine is over health" (*EN* vi,13,1145a6–8). And in *Metaph.* i,2, while considering the relationship among the various disciplines, he says, "The wise man must not be ordered but must order, and he must not obey another, but the less wise must obey *him.*"[25]

Despite all this, however, we also find in Aristotle passages according to which intellect is under the control of *voluntas*. For instance, at *De an.* iii,10, he writes:

That which moves therefore is a single faculty, the faculty of appetite. For if there had been two sources of movement—thought and appetite—they would have produced movement in virtue of some common character. As it is, thought is never found producing movement without appetite (for *voluntas* is a type of appetite; and, when movement is produced according to calculation it is also according to *voluntas*), but appetite can originate movement *contrary* to calculation, for desire is a form of appetite.[26]

Thomas says in his commentary on this passage, "It is not to be said that appetite moves under the species of intellect but rather the converse, the intellect or the intelligible under the species of appetite, for intellect is not found moving without appetite, for *voluntas*, with respect to which intellect moves,

24. This is more or less the way that Thomas sums up the passage in his commentary: "Sic 'igitur' apparet quod 'unum est movens, 'quod' est 'appetibile'; hoc enim et appetitum movet et est principium intellectus, quae duo ponebantur moventia" [*in De an.* lb.3 cap.9 ll.75–78 (§823)].

25. *Metaph.* i,2,982a17–19; emphasis in ROT.

26. *De an.* iii,10,433a21–26 [emphasis in ROT]: ἓν δή τι τὸ κινοῦν, τὸ ὀρεκτικόν. εἰ γὰρ δύο, νοῦς καὶ ὄρεξις, ἐκίνουν, κατὰ κοινὸν ἄν τι ἐκίνουν εἶδος· νῦν δὲ ὁ μὲν νοῦς οὐ φαίνεται κινῶν ἄνευ ὀρέξεως (ἡ γὰρ βούλησις ὄρεξις, ὅταν δὲ κατὰ τὸν λογισμὸν κινῆται, καὶ κατὰ βούλησιν κινεῖται), ἡ δ' ὄρεξις κινεῖ καὶ παρὰ τὸν λογισμόν· ἡ γὰρ ἐπιθυμία ὄρεξίς τίς ἐστιν. See also *De an.* iii,9,432b26ff.; also *MA* vi,700b22–25.

is a sort of appetite."[27] Is Thomas over-interpreting Aristotle? I think not, for, given that the use of intellect is a movement, if without appetite there can be no movement, intellect cannot act except under the influence of appetite. When the act of intellect is a deliberate one (i.e., not simply a reaction to what the intellect "suffers" from the senses), intellect is under the control of *voluntas*.[28]

The same approach is also apparent a few lines later in *De anima*, where Aristotle remarks that movement involves three elements: "(1) that which originates the movement, (2) that by means of which it originates it, and (3) that which is moved. The expression 'that which originates the movement' is ambiguous: it may mean either something which itself is unmoved or that which at once moves and is moved."[29] Elements (2) and (3) do not interest us here, since they are not immediately about the origins of movement; but element (1) is important.[30] Aristotle says that 'that which originates the movement' has two possible meanings: one, that which is not moved but moves; the other, that which both moves and is moved—which would include things that move themselves. The first is the object as presented by the intellect; the second is the *orektikon*, whether it takes the form of *voluntas*, desire, or passion. According to this analysis, then, the only essentially *active* element in this type of movement is the *orektikon* (which includes *voluntas*), since "that which originates the movement" according to the first meaning of (1) is not, at least *qua* object of appetite, capable of moving itself: it is immobile.[31]

27. "[N]on autem dicendum quod appetitus moveat sub specie intellectus, sed magis e converso intellectus vel intelligibilis <sub specie appetitus>, quia 'intellectus non' invenitur 'movens sine appetitu,' quia 'voluntas,' secundum quam movet intellectus, est quidam 'appetitus'" [*in De an*. lb.3 cap.9 ll.84–89 (§824)]. (Thomas then cites *Metaph*. ix [4,1048a8–16].) See also *in De an*. lb.3 cap.9 ll.57–60 (§821) (on *De an*. iii,10,433a15), where Thomas puts the intellectual grasp of the end at the service of *voluntas*: "[C]um enim volumus aliquid deliberare de agendis, primo supponimus finem et deinde procedimus per ordinem ad inquirenda illa quae agenda sunt propter finem . . .".

28. As to the place of *phronēsis*, note that, at *EN* vi,10,1143a8–10, while discussing various functions of the intellect, Aristotle says that, by contrast with these, "practical wisdom issues commands": ἡ μὲν γὰρ φρόνησις ἐπιτακτική ἐστιν· τί γὰρ δεῖ πράττειν ἢ μή, τὸ τέλος αὐτῆς ἐστιν· ἡ δὲ σύνεσις κριτικὴ μόνον.

29. *De an*. iii,10,433b13–17: ἐπεὶ δ' ἔστι τρία, ἓν μὲν τὸ κινοῦν, δεύτερον δ' ᾧ κινεῖ, ἔτι τρίτον τὸ κινούμενον, τὸ δὲ κινοῦν διττόν, τὸ μὲν ἀκίνητον, τὸ δὲ κινοῦν καὶ κινούμενον, ἔστι δὴ τὸ μὲν ἀκίνητον τὸ πρακτὸν ἀγαθόν, τὸ δὲ κινοῦν καὶ κινούμενον τὸ ὀρεκτικόν . . .

30. (2) refers to the bodily aspect of appetite; (3) is the animal itself, which is moved [*De an*. iii,10,433b18–19].

31. Aristotle, in fact, calls attention to this essentially active character of the *orektikon* by interjecting the remark, "for that which is moved is moved insofar as it desires, and appetite in the

There is even a passage in Aristotle which suggests that *voluntas* might work against intellect. In the *Eudemian Ethics,* he says that *"voluntas* [*boulēsis*] is of the good naturally, but of the bad contrary to nature, and by nature one wills the good, but contrary to nature and through perversion the bad as well."[32] According to this conception, although it is certainly true that *voluntas* in its central and defining instance is to be associated with reason, it might also exist in a perverted form. And, in fact, in some sense this must be the case if *voluntas* is to be a rational potency at all, since rational potencies (including the various crafts and sciences) have as their objects opposites.[33] They are not like natural potencies such as fire's potency to produce heat and heat alone. A doctor, for instance, knows better than all others how to ruin health. Thus, *voluntas* is necessarily associated with options—which is simply for it to be a rational potency, i.e., a potency not determined to a single end, as Thomas too says in *De ma.* q.6.

Is Aristotle then, in saying both that intellect is predominant and that *voluntas* is, attempting to reconcile the irreconcilable? There is available one rather quick answer to this challenge—and that is that Aristotle is only saying that *voluntas* is predominant in the practical sphere. Since he regards the practical sphere itself as inferior to the theoretical, he can still maintain the overall superiority of intellect. But there is more yet to be said about the relationship of intellect and *voluntas* within the practical sphere. That is, even within the practical sphere (where *voluntas* certainly must enjoy a certain predominance over intellect), the two, in the final analysis, are seen to work in unison. In *De an.* iii,10 *voluntas* is *defined* by Aristotle as appetite in accordance with reason.[34] Thus, *voluntas* does not exist in the practical sphere ex-

---

sense of actual appetite *is* a kind of movement" [κινεῖται γὰρ τὸ κινούμενον ᾗ ὀρέγεται, καὶ ἡ ὄρεξις κίνησίς τίς ἐστιν, ἡ ἐνεργεία—*De an.* iii,10,433b17–18; emphasis in ROT].

Writes Alexander of Aphrodisias in his *De an.* 79.21–27: "Just because thought and *phantasia* come first before the movement, we needn't therefore say that *they* are the movers. Neither of them can move without impulse and desire; therefore the motion should be attributed to these. For it is not the case that, if there is a desire, one of those [thought or *phantasia*] having preceded, therefore one of those is the mover. Rather, since neither of those is sufficient to produce a movement if some impulse or desire is not present or ensues, *this* [impulse or desire] ought to be considered the moving <power>."

32. ὁμοίως δὲ καὶ ἡ βούλησις φύσει μὲν τοῦ ἀγαθοῦ ἐστί, παρὰ φύσιν δὲ καὶ τοῦ κακοῦ, καὶ βούλεται φύσει μὲν τὸ ἀγαθόν, παρὰ φύσιν δὲ καὶ διὰ στροφὴν καὶ τὸ κακόν [*EE* ii,10,1227a28–31]; see also *EN* iii,4,1113a15ff. and *Rhet.* i,10,1368b37–1369a4.

33. See *An.pr.* i,1,24a21; *Phys.* viii,1,251a30; *De an.* iii,3,427b6; *EN* v,1,1129a11–17; *Metaph.* ix,2,1046b4ff.; 5,1048a8–11.

34. The pertinent remark is at *De an.* iii,10,433a23–25: "wish [βούλησις] is a form of appetite;

cept insofar as it follows reason. This idea stands in apparent tension with the passage from *EE* which we examined just above, where Aristotle says that *voluntas* can be "of the bad." We must, therefore, regard the latter as a secondary usage of the term *voluntas* (or *boulēsis*). But this is to take up a perfectly Aristotelian position, since, although he too can speak of a doctor who causes ill health, his ultimate judgment is that, when the doctor acts in this way, he is not doing so *qua* doctor.[35]

Thus, just as in the body of *De ma.* q.6, where we find a certain predominance assigned to *voluntas* in the practical sphere but also the idea that the (single) motivating principle in men "*is* intellect and *voluntas*," so in Aristotle we discover that real initiative (which is the mark of the practical) belongs only to *voluntas* but also that the two potencies are mutually dependent on one another for their very existence within the practical sphere. This situation comes across in a particularly striking way at the end of *EN* vi where, as we have seen, Aristotle says that *phronēsis* "is not supreme over wisdom." In the same breath, he also says that *voluntas* does issue the orders; it does so for the sake of wisdom, he says, but not to it [*EN* vi,13,1145a9]. Presumably, then, even when it puts intellect into action pursuing wisdom, it does so for the sake of wisdom—since it is intellect which understands that wisdom is to be pursued.

This approach to *voluntas* (or "the will") does not correspond to the modern one. We tend to say that the will is what makes actions that are motivated solely by passion nonetheless "voluntary." Aristotle's *voluntas*, on the other hand, is deliberately separated off from the lower desires. He does says that when the *akratēs* follows a mere desire he does so *hekousiōs*—usually translated 'voluntarily.'[36] But he locates more deliberate actions—actions that con-

---

and when movement is produced according to calculation [κατὰ τὸν λογισμὸν] it is also according to wish [κατὰ βούλησιν]." One might also cite *De an.* iii,9,432b5–6: "wish is found in the calculative part, and desire and passion in the irrational." See also *EN* iii,2,1111b11; *MA* vi,700b22–24.

35. See especially *Metaph.* ix,2,1046a36–1046b20. See also chapter 7, section [3] of the present work. I have been much enlightened in these respects by what the late Michael Woods writes at Woods (1992), p. 149. "Capacities like knowledge, unlike certain others, involve reason *(logos)*, and reason reveals both a thing and its privation *(sterēsis)*: a *specification* or *determination* of what constitutes being φ determines at the same time what counts as being non-φ; hence, knowledge of (what is) φ is at the same time knowledge of (what is) not-φ, and knowledge of how to make something φ will, in general, include knowledge of how to make something non-φ" [emphasis mine]. Thomas connects this section of *Metaph.* with the rational soul's being "domina sui actus" [*in Metaph.* §1787].

36. *EN* iii,1,1109b30–1111b3. See also *EN* v,9,1136b6–7, where the *akratēs* is said to act contrary to his own *voluntas*. On *EN* v,9, see Flannery (1995e).

tribute to moral character, as opposed to those that are done more or less un-thinkingly—closer to the reasoning center of the soul, the intellect. In *EE* ii,7, he says that something done in accordance with *voluntas (boulēsis)* is "more voluntary" ("more *hekousion*") than something done in accordance with mere appetite or anger.[37] Thus, the voluntary (i.e., the *hekousion) is* linked to *voluntas* (boulēsis). But this link consists in the fact that an action becomes more voluntary *(hekousios)* the closer it gets to "desire in accordance with reason." We cannot be held responsible for that of which we have no knowl-edge, and, the more we are aware of something, the more we are responsible. Thus, the element that determines the voluntary is not whether we *do* some-thing with our will but whether we know what we are doing.

As we have seen, according to the body of *De ma.* q.6, we escape determin-ism precisely insofar as we are rational. In this respect, then, Thomas's under-standing of *voluntas* is essentially Aristotelian. In the case of *akrasia*, it is nev-er *voluntas* which works against reason; that role is taken by the non-rational appetites.[38] A will that is autonomous of intellect, such as Lottin and his fol-lowers seem to prefer, has more in common with what Thomas attributes to merely natural beings—for whom exercise and specification are quite sepa-rate [ll.320–23]—than with his conception of human freedom.

[7] Rationality and freedom

Major idea [[2]] is the idea, just mentioned, that freedom is linked to ration-ality—or to our ability to stand back from a particular course of action and consider whether to do it. To use Thomas's way of speaking in *De ma.* q.6, what distinguishes the action of rational animals is a universal intellectual form "under which many things can be comprehended," acts themselves ex-isting "in singulars, in which there is nothing that comes up to the potency of the universal," so that "the inclination of *voluntas* remains indeterminately open to many things" [ll.288–92].

37. *EE* ii,7,1223b26–27 [μᾶλλον ἑκούσιον τὸ κατὰ βούλησιν τοῦ κατ᾽ ἐπιθυμίαν καὶ θυμόν]; note, however, that he also says in this chapter that the voluntary is not equivalent to that which is in accordance with *boulēsis* [*EE* ii,7,1223b28ff.].

38. See *in Rom.* §§564–82, Thomas's exegesis of the classical description of *akrasia*, Romans 7.15–20. Although the Greek in verse 15 reads, οὐ γὰρ ὃ θέλω τοῦτο πράσσω, ἀλλ᾽ ὃ μισῶ τοῦτο ποιῶ . . . , the Vulgate text upon which he comments is, "Non enim quod volo bonum hoc ago, sed quod odi malum illud facio," which in a number of ways lends itself to an Aristotelian inter-pretation. See Kretzmann (1988). See also Thomas's *in Sent.* lb.2 d.7 q.1 a.1 ad 1.

There can be little doubt that Thomas takes this distinction between universal and particular—along with the idea that the acts are in the particular—from Aristotle. In discussing *akrasia* (within the context of a practical syllogism), Aristotle remarks: "Further, since there are two kinds of propositions, there is nothing to prevent a man's having both and acting against his knowledge, provided that he is using only the universal and not the particular; for it is particular acts that have to be done."[39] He also remarks in this same chapter of the *Nicomachean Ethics,* and following a more extensive discussion of rational creatures' use of the "two kinds of proposition"—i.e., universal and particular—that, "this is the reason why the lower animals are not incontinent, viz. because they have no universal beliefs but only imagination and memory of particulars."[40] Moreover, in *De an.* ii, Aristotle associates universals with that which is "up to us," as opposed to particulars which are not: ". . . what actual sensation apprehends is individuals, while what knowledge apprehends is universals, and these are in a sense within the soul itself. That is why a man can think when he wills to but his sensation does not depend upon himself—a sensible object must be there."[41] Thus, according to Aristotle too, rationality is tied to having not only particular knowledge but also—and more importantly—universal knowledge. And this itself is tied to the voluntary.

This is not to say, however, that the universal/particular relationship of which we are speaking here is the genus-species or even the species-particular relationship of theoretical reason. Thomas enunciates this for us quite clearly in an argument against the position that law cannot be ordered toward the common good since human acts are in particulars. "Actions are indeed in particulars, but these particulars can be referred to the common good—not,

---

39. *EN* vii,3,1146b35–1147a4 (also the entire chapter, *EN* vii,3); see also *EN* vi,11,1143a28–b17 and Thomas's *in EN* lb.6 lect.9 ll.152–86 (§§1247–49); see also *MM* ii,6,1201b21–39; ii,11,1211a16–25. On *EN* vii,3,1146b35ff., see Kenny (1966), pp. 166–73.

40. *EN* vii,3,1147b3–5. For Aristotle's ideas on non-rational animals' memory, see *Metaph.* i,1,980a27ff.

41. *De an.* ii,5,417b22–26: αἴτιον δ' ὅτι τῶν καθ' ἕκαστον ἡ κατ' ἐνέργειαν αἴσθησις, ἡ δ' ἐπιστήμη τῶν καθόλου· ταῦτα δ' ἐν αὐτῇ πώς ἐστι τῇ ψυχῇ. διὸ νοῆσαι μὲν ἐπ' αὐτῷ, ὁπόταν βούληται, αἰσθάνεσθαι δ' οὐκ ἐπ' αὐτῷ· ἀναγκαῖον γὰρ ὑπάρχειν τὸ αἰσθητόν. At *Metaph.* vii,8,1033b19–1034a8, Aristotle argues that, during the process of generation, the thing to be generated is still only the "such" [τὸ τοιόνδε] and not yet the determinate thing [τόδε . . . ὡρισμένον οὐκ ἔστιν—*Metaph.* vii,8,1033b22]. Among the examples that he uses is that of building a house—as in *De ma.* q.6 ll.292–96.

however, by virtue of a commonality of genus and species but by virtue of a commonality with the final cause, according to which the common good is said to be a common end."[42] This is consistent with what we saw in chapter 1 about the nature of the Aristotelian practical syllogism. The point of a practical syllogism is not to find out a truth but to get somewhere—and there are various ways of doing this, none of them, presumably, logically compelling.[43] Thus, there is a sort of practical distance between what one might think of doing in a general way and what one actually does. It is in this space between universal and particular that Thomas too locates free choice.

Does Aristotle actually make the point about voluntary action and the (practical) distance between universal and particular? Indirectly, certainly he does. Where the *akratēs* falls short, the man of practical wisdom is accomplished. That at which the latter aims (the universal) and that which he does (the particular) are habitually joined; and this is *achieved* by repeated free choices—i.e., he must go some distance. But a clearer statement of this idea comes in the Aristotelian commentator Alexander of Aphrodisias, in his *De fato*. Much of that work seeks to refute a version of determinism according to which we react automatically to the impressions that come to us through the senses from the external world. This supposedly Stoic position has affinities to some of the opposing positions mentioned in *De ma.* q.6.,[44] according to which *voluntas* is completely passive with respect to its object.[45] Alexander responds:

It is agreed by everyone that man has this advantage from nature over the other living creatures, that he does not follow appearances in the same way as them, but has reason from her as a judge of the appearances that impinge on him concerning certain things as deserving to be chosen. Using this, if, when they are examined, the things that appeared *are* indeed as they initially appeared, he assents to the appearance and so goes in pursuit of them; but if they appear different or something else appears more deserving to be chosen, he chooses that, leaving behind what initially appeared to him as deserving of choice.[46]

42. *ST* I–II q.90 a.2 ad 2.

43. See chapter 1, sections [2] and [3]; also chapter 8, section [1]. See also *De ver.* q.24 a.1 ad 18.

44. Whether Alexander is right to attribute such a theory to the Stoics is doubtful: see Sharples (1983), pp. 139–41.

45. See *De ma.* q.6 obj. 7 (summarized in section [10]); see also objection 11.

46. Alexander, *De fat.* 178.17–24. I make no claims that Thomas actually read Alexander's *De fato*, but simply that this idea is prominent in the tradition of Aristotelian interpretation before

In *De fato*, in his own *De anima*, and in other works, Alexander (or his school) makes many similar statements about the connection between rationality and free choice, about man's capacity to pass judgment on appearances, and so on.[47]

[8] Liberty of exercise and liberty of specification

Is the distinction liberty of specification/liberty of exercise (i.e., major idea [[3]]) found in Aristotle? That he recognizes liberty of exercise has already been shown—i.e., in section [6], where it was argued, using especially *De an.* iii,10, that for Aristotle *voluntas* falls under the dominion of itself. Liberty of specification is a more complicated matter.

To begin with, we note that the idea that the specification of actions belongs to intellect is put forward in *De an.* iii,7. There Aristotle conducts a comparison and contrast between sense and the intellect. In several respects the two are the same. They have, for instance, the same objects—in practical matters, the pleasant and the painful. Their "being," however, says Aristotle, "is different" [431a8–14]. "To the thinking soul, images [*phantasmata*] serve as if they were the contents of perception (and when it asserts or denies them to be good or bad it avoids or pursues them)" [431a14–15]. Thus, intellect does consider the pleasant and the painful, at a certain remove.

---

him. Grabmann searched in vain for references to *De fato* in Thomas [Grabmann (1929), p. 14, n. 3; pp. 60–61]. See also Thillet (1963), p. 22. It is certainly possible, of course, that Thomas was influenced by the work through others, such as Proclus. See Sharples (1983), pp. 28–29 (who cites *ST* I q.14 a.13 in this respect). On the influence of *De fato* on Boethius and Nemesius (and others), see Sharples (1978), *passim*; on Alexander's influence in general see also Théry (1926), pp. 13ff.

47. *De fat.* 183.34ff.; 205.20–21. At *De an.* 71.22–24, Alexander says that animals receive φαντασίαι and act upon the συγκαταθέσεις that come from them since they do not have reason. On the other hand, at *De an.* 72.13ff., he says that in us a συγκατάθεσις does not always follow a φαντασία, nor a ὁρμὴ a συγκατάθεσις, nor a πρᾶξις a ὁρμὴ. That which ensures that we act, says Alexander, is βούλησις (i.e., *voluntas*) [Alexander of Aphrodisias, *De an.* 73.2]. (He defines βούλησις in an Aristotelian way at *De an.* 74.8–9.) See also *De an.* 79.21ff. Similar ideas turn up in *Mantissa*, which is probably not by Alexander, although it comes out of his school. See, for instance, *Mant.* 172.30–31: "[A]lone of all the animals [man] is responsible for his own action since he has also the capability of not doing that very thing." See also pseudo-Alexander, *Quaest.* 107.19ff. At *De fat.* 179.3–8;179.20–1, Alexander remarks that deliberation is not for its own sake—i.e., it is an instrumental good; but he also says at *De fat.* 180.8 that choice is the characterizing function of men. Sharples says in this regard: "Alexander indeed probably wishes to argue, not that responsibility is confined to cases where we do in fact deliberate, but rather that the fact that we are rational and can deliberate shows that we are responsible for all our actions, whether or not we actually deliberate on any particular occasion" [Sharples (1983), p. 145]. This understanding is supported by *De fat.* 184.27–185.1.

The faculty of thinking then thinks the *forms* in the images, and as in the former case [i.e., where there is sensation] what is to be pursued or avoided is marked out for it, so where there is no sensation and it is engaged upon images it is moved to pursuit or avoidance. E.g. perceiving by sense that the beacon is fire, it recognizes in virtue of the general faculty of sense that it signifies an enemy, because it sees it moving; but sometimes by means of the images or thoughts which are within the soul, just as if it were seeing, it calculates and deliberates what is to come by reference to what is present; and when it makes a pronouncement, as in the case of sensation it pronounces the object to be pleasant or painful, in this case it avoids or pursues; and so generally in cases of action.[48]

Aristotle is maintaining here that specification of that which is eventually to be done is provided by the intellect, which stands toward "images" as the senses stand toward "the contents of perception." Intellect regards images— wherein it thinks "the forms"—"just as if it were seeing."

We should be surprised to learn that Thomas did *not* have in mind this very central passage, with its mention of "the forms in the images," when saying, in *De ma.* q.6, that specification pertains to the intellect which has as its object the apprehensible form. Thomas's association, in *De ma.* q.6, of *voluntas* with final, intellect with formal cause cannot therefore be, as Lottin and his followers contend, a turn toward a more modern, less Aristotelian analysis. The ideas are taken from Aristotle, although Thomas uses them very ingeniously to demonstrate the difference between the actions of merely natural things and those of rational beings, and also the mutual interaction, in rational beings, between intellect and *voluntas*.[49]

---

48. τὰ μὲν οὖν εἴδη τὸ νοητικὸν ἐν τοῖς φαντάσμασι νοεῖ, καὶ ὡς ἐν ἐκείνοις ὥρισται αὐτῷ τὸ διωκτὸν καὶ φευκτόν, καὶ ἐκτὸς τῆς αἰσθήσεως, ὅταν ἐπὶ τῶν φαντασμάτων ᾖ, κινεῖται· οἷον, αἰσθανόμενος τὸν φρυκτὸν ὅτι πῦρ, τῇ κοινῇ γνωρίζει, ὁρῶν κινούμενον, ὅτι πολέμιος· ὁτὲ δὲ τοῖς ἐν τῇ ψυχῇ φαντάσμασιν ἢ νοήμασιν, ὥσπερ ὁρῶν, λογίζεται καὶ βουλεύεται τὰ μέλλοντα πρὸς τὰ παρόντα· καὶ ὅταν εἴπῃ ὡς ἐκεῖ τὸ ἡδὺ ἢ λυπηρόν, ἐνταῦθα φεύγει ἢ διώκει—καὶ ὅλως ἐν πράξει [*De an.* iii,7,431b2–10; translation and emendation from ROT, emphasis mine].

49. If it is apparent that Aristotle in *De an.* iii,7 associates intellect with form, it is even more apparent that he associates *voluntas* with final cause. At *EN* iii,2,1111b26, for instance, he notes that *boulēsis* "relates rather to the end," an idea he repeats in the opening sentence of his more formal treatment of boulēsis: "That wish is for the end has already been stated . . ." [*EN* iii,4,1113a15]. In book 6, he remarks: "The origin of action—its efficient not its final cause—is choice, and that of choice is desire and reasoning with a view to the end" [πράξεως μὲν οὖν ἀρχὴ προαίρεσις— ὅθεν ἡ κίνησις ἀλλ᾽ οὐχ οὗ ἕνεκα—προαιρέσεως δὲ ὄρεξις καὶ λόγος ὁ ἕνεκά τινος— *EN* vi,2,1139a31–33]. The combination of desire and intellect being equivalent to *voluntas*, it is legitimate to interpret Aristotle as here associating *voluntas* with the final cause. (See

In his remarks on this same section of *De anima,* Thomas explains how intellect goes beyond the mere operation of the senses:

[J]ust as sense does not apprehend the universal good, so the appetite of the sensitive part is not moved by universal good or evil but by a determinate good that is pleasurable with respect to sense and by a determinate evil that gives pain to sense. In the intellectual part, however, there is the apprehension of universal good and evil; whence also the appetite of the intellectual part is moved immediately by virtue of the apprehended good or evil.[50]

Thomas is speaking of much the same thing in the body of *De ma.* q.6 when he identifies the object of *voluntas* as "the good, under which are comprehended all ends" [ll.331–32]. It is true that here in the commentary on *De anima* he speaks of intellect apprehending the universal good; but the whole point of the *De ma.* q.6 passage is, as we have seen, to argue that, insofar as the good is being, it also comes under the intellect: "the good itself, insofar as it is an apprehensible form, is contained under the true as something true" [ll.333–36].

So, it is clear that for Aristotle specification of actions belongs to intellect in much the same way as Thomas describes in *De ma.* q.6. But can we also attribute *liberty* of specification to Aristotle—i.e., the idea that a certain amount of liberty is assured by virtue of our capacity to specify an act in different ways? There are a number of places in his works where this idea too is

---

{Heliodorus}, *in EN* 115.32, where the author identifies Aristotle's ὄρεξις καὶ λόγος as ἡ βούλευσις—i.e., as deliberation.) There are also a number of other places in the *Nicomachean Ethics* where Aristotle uses the word βούλησις or one of its derivatives in conjunction with the expression 'for the sake of . . .'—i.e., with *heneka* plus the genitive, which is also the expression he uses to refer to final causality. Many of these have to do with love of friends. In book 8, for instance, he writes, "Now those who wish [βουλόμενοι] good for their friends for their sake [ἐκείνων ἕνεκα] are most truly friends" [*EN* viii,3,1156b9–10]; and in book 9, "For men think a friend is one who wishes [βουλόμενον] and does what is good, or seems so, for the sake of his frend [ἐκείνου ἕνεκα], or who wishes his friend to exist and live, for *his* sake" [*EN* ix,4,1166a2–5—my emphasis]. See also *EN* viii,5,1157b31–32; 7,1159a8–11; ix,8,1168b1–3. See also *Rhet.* ii,4,1380b36–1381a1; iii,15,1416a17–18. At *EN* ix,7,1167b30–31, Aristotle speaks of creditors who "have no friendly feeling for their debtors, but only a wish [βούλησις] that they may be kept safe with a view to what is to be got from them [τῆς κομιδῆς ἕνεκα]. See also *Phys.* ii,5,197a15–18 and *Top.* i,11,104b10–12.

50. *in De an.* lb.3 cap.6 ll.118–26 (§771). "[S]icut sensus non apprehendit bonum universale, ita appetitus sensitivae partis non movetur a bono vel malo universali, sed a quodam determinato bono quod est delectabile secundum sensum et a quodam determinato malo quod est contristans sensum, in parte autem intellectiva est apprehensio boni et mali universalis; unde et appetitus intellectivae partis movetur statim ex bono vel malo apprehenso . . ." [ll.111–26].

found, but perhaps the most striking is his discussion of weakness of will, in which the *akratēs* is portrayed as wavering between two practical syllogisms: "When, then, the universal opinion is present in us restraining us from tasting, and there is also the opinion that everything sweet is pleasant, and that this is sweet (now this is the opinion that is active), and when appetite happens to be present in us, the one opinion bids us avoid the object, but appetite leads us towards it (for it can move each of our bodily parts) . . ." [*EN* vii,3,1147a31–35]. Although the right action, not tasting, is good, it is not good under every aspect.[51] As Thomas says in the body of *De ma.* q.6, "someone can will its opposite, even while thinking of it, because, as might happen, it is good or suitable with respect to some other particular that is considered—as, for instance, what is good for the health is not good to the taste, and so also with other things" [ll.444–49]. It is true that in pointing to the fact that the *akratēs* goes back and forth between different aspects of a prospective choice we have not proved but only asserted that his action is free; this is true, however, also in both Thomas and Aristotle, where the proof properly speaking pertains to the analysis of *voluntas,* under whose universal object the use of intellect falls. We are free so to shift aspects by virtue of the fact that a use of the intellect is a particular way of determining a universal intellectual form. To recall a remark we have already seen—and which occurs a few lines after the Aristolelian passage just quoted—"this is the reason why the lower animals are not incontinent, viz. because they have no universal beliefs but only imagination and memory of particulars."[52]

---

51. Penner offers an analysis of *akrasia* that exploits the idea that, at the moment of *akrasia*, the *akratēs* switches aspects, seeing the bad choice as good. See Penner (1990), p. 46 and also p. 69, where he speaks of "a kind of flip-flopping of gestalts." Such an approach is also put forward in the present book, chapter 6, section [3].

52. *EN* vii,3,1147b3–5. There is a very pertinent passage in Thomas where he explicitly attributes the approach found in *De ma.* q.6 to Aristotle. In *De Interpretatione,* Aristotle makes the following remark: "[W]e see that what will be has an origin both in deliberation and in action, and that, in general, in things that are not always in act, there is the possibility of being and of not being . . ." [*Int.* ix,19a7–9]. Thomas writes at *in Int.* lb.1 lect.14 ll.493–519 (§199): "Ita etiam est quoddam bonum quod est propter se appetibile, sicut felicitas, quae habet rationem ultimi finis, et huiusmodi bono ex necessitate inhaeret voluntas: naturali enim quadam necessitate omnes appetunt esse felices. Quaedam vero sunt bona quae sunt appetibilia propter finem, quae comparantur ad finem sicut conclusiones ad principium, ut patet per philosophum in II Physicorum. Si igitur essent aliqua bona quibus non existentibus non posset aliquis esse felix, haec etiam essent ex necessitate appetibilia, et maxime apud eum qui talem ordinem perciperet; et forte talia sunt esse, vivere et intelligere, et si qua alia sunt similia. Sed particularia bona, in quibus humani actus consistunt, non sunt talia, nec sub ea ratione apprehenduntur ut sine quibus felicitas esse non

[9] God's influence on human action

That brings us to the final "major idea," the idea that the principle of our actions is in some sense God. In a way, this idea is not strictly relevant to the present concern, which is to show that *De ma.* q.6 does not offer evidence of a change in Thomas's thought regarding *voluntas* itself, since no modern scholar claims (as far as I know) that Thomas's thinking with respect to God's role in human action changes or develops at this point in his career. Nonetheless, it is striking—and relevant to the present concern—that even this more properly theological idea can be traced to Aristotle, lending further credence to the thesis that *De ma.* q.6 is basically Aristotelian in inspiration. And, in any case, as we shall see shortly, God's influence on human action is integral to Thomas's understanding of *voluntas* and its freedom.

In the second last chapter of the *Eudemian Ethics* (i.e., *EE* viii,2), Aristotle discusses different ways in which chance or good fortune [*tuchē*] has a bearing on human character and actions. The first part of the chapter [1246b37–1247b38] makes the point that often good fortune is due to a person's having well-ordered appetites, so that, not reasoning his way to the good result, he appears to stumble his way there by chance, although his rightly ordered appetites are the true cause. Aristotle then says, "Someone might, however, ask this: whether fortune is therefore the cause of just this, of desiring what one ought when one ought, or whether even so it will be rather the cause of everything, even of thinking and deliberating?" [*EE* viii,2,1248a16–18].

---

possit, puta comedere hunc cibum vel illum, aut abstinere ab eo, habent tamen in se unde moveant appetitum, secundum aliquod bonum consideratum in eis; et ideo voluntas non ex necessitate inducitur ad haec eligenda. Et propter hoc Philosophus signanter radicem contingentiae in his quae fiunt a nobis assignavit ex parte consilii [*Int.* ix,19a8], quod est eorum quae sunt ad finem et tamen non sunt determinata; in his enim in quibus media sunt determinata, non est opus consilio, ut dicitur in III Ethicorum." At this point the Leonine edition cites *EN* iii,7,1112a34–b9. The words "in his enim in quibus media sunt determinata, non est opus consilio" probably refer, however, to *EN* iii,3,1112b17–18, where Aristotle suggests that during the deliberative process it may turn out that just one means is available or useful for arriving at a certain end. (But even in this case, one needs to consider "how it will be achieved by this and by what means *this* will be achieved" [i.e., using the one means in a certain manner—emphasis in ROT]. The idea is that, in moral matters, there will always be something to deliberate about—i.e., something indeterminate, determination coming in the act itself. In this respect, Thomas remarks [*in EN* lb.3 lect.8 ll.52–53 (§475)] that determining how the end will be achieved by way of the single means requires "constantia et solicitudo." Thus, it is clear that, for him, the mode of using the single means might become quite set—a doctor, for instance, might always wield a scalpel in a certain manner—and still the action would be freely chosen.)

At this point, Aristotle is moving beyond the natural [1248a14, 1248b3–7] account of some instances of good fortune to an account that looks beyond the nature of the acting thing to the context within which that nature exists. For he continues:

For one does not deliberate having previously deliberated and having previously deliberated about this, but there is some principle [or starting point: *archē*]; nor does one think having previous to thinking thought, and so on to infinity. Thought, then, is not the principle of thinking, nor deliberation of deliberating. What, therefore, is the principle except fortune [*tuchē*]? Thus, everything will come from fortune. Or is there some principle outside of which there is no other, this one being capable of acting in this way by being such as it is?[53]

There can be no doubt that, although he does not acknowledge it, Thomas has this passage in mind when, in the body of *De ma.* q.6, he writes,[54]

But since *voluntas* does not always will to take counsel, it is necessary that it be moved by something else so that it wills to take counsel; and if, indeed, by itself <it is so moved>, it is necessary again that a movement of *voluntas* precede counsel and counsel precede the act of *voluntas*. And, since this cannot go on to infinity, it is necessary to suppose that, as to the first movement of *voluntas,* the *voluntas* (of whoever is not forever actively willing) is moved by something external, by the prompting of which *voluntas* begins to will. [ll.381–91]

Returning to *EE,* Aristotle goes on to argue that this "principle outside of which there is no other" is God: "That which we are seeking is this: what is the principle of motion in the soul? It is apparent therefore that, as in the universe, so also in this case: it is God. For the divine in us somehow moves everything. The principle of reason is not reason, but something greater.

---

53. οὐ γὰρ δὴ ἐβουλεύσατο βουλευσάμενος, καὶ τοῦτ᾽ <αὖ> ἐβουλεύσατο, ἀλλ᾽ ἔστιν ἀρχή τις, οὐδ᾽ ἐνόησε νοήσας πρότερον <ἢ> νοῆσαι, καὶ τοῦτο εἰς ἄπειρον. οὐκ ἄρα τοῦ νοῆσαι ὁ νοῦς ἀρχή, οὐδὲ τοῦ βουλεύσασθαι βουλή. τί οὖν ἄλλο πλὴν τύχη; ὥστ᾽ ἀπὸ τύχης ἄπαντα ἔσται. ἢ ἔστι τις ἀρχὴ ἧς οὐκ ἔστιν ἄλλη ἔξω, αὕτη δὲ διὰ τὸ τοιαύτη {τῷ} εἶναι {τὸ} τοιοῦτο δύναται ποιεῖν; [*EE* viii,2,1248a18–24].

54. The proof is at *De ma.* q.3 a.3 obj.11 ll.71–89 (§20): "Praeterea, Philosophus in . . . Ethicae Eudimicae, inquirit quid sit principium operationis in anima, et ostendit quod oportet esse aliquid extrinsecum. Omne enim quod incipit de novo, habet aliquam causam: incipit enim homo operari, quia vult; incipit autem velle, quia praeconsiliatur. Si autem praeconsilietur propter aliquod consilium praecedens, aut est procedere in infinitum, aut oportet ponere aliquod principium extrinsecum quod primo movet hominem ad consiliandum; nisi forte aliquis dicat quod hoc est a fortuna, ex quo sequeretur omnes actus humanos esse fortuitos. Hoc autem principium in bonis quidem dicit esse Deum . . .". For Thomas's use of the *Eudemonian Ethics* and also for the phrase *in . . . Ethicae Eudimicae,* see the preface to the Leonine edition of *De ma.,* p. 42*.

What therefore could be greater than knowledge and intellect except God?"[55]
Thomas does acknowledge in *De ma.* q.6 *this* Aristotelian contribution to his
understanding of how God's influence is present in human actions, citing *EE*
viii,2 as "the chapter *De bona fortuna*" [l.408], and writing:

that which first moves *voluntas* and intellect is something above *voluntas* and intellect—that is to say, God, who, since he moves everything according to the *ratio* of
movable things (e.g., light things upwards, heavy things downwards), also moves *voluntas* according to its condition: not from necessity but as something indeterminately
open to many things. [ll.408–15]

One might wish to argue that, although the idea of God's being a cause of action is to be found here in Aristotle, Thomas's point that such divine action
does not lead to determinism is not. But Aristotle says in this section of *EE*
that "if it *is* through chance [*tuchē*] that one is fortunate, the cause of his fortune is not the sort of cause that produces always or usually the same result."[56] Also, it is clear in *Metaph.* vi,3 that Aristotle is eager to exclude a deter-
ministic universe (see 1027a29–32). As we shall see in the next section, in his
commentary on this section of the *Metaphysics,* Thomas argues that divine
providence, such as Aristotle posits in both the *Eudemian Ethics* and *Metaph.*
vi,3, does not interfere with human action.[57]

[10] The objections and their responses

We come now to the objections and their responses, which are twenty-
four in number—i.e., a great many, even for the *Quaestiones disputatae.* I do
not deal with all of them nor, with respect to those with which I do deal, each
of these equally extensively, since (a) some make points that are not especially
relevant to whether Thomas's approach is Aristotelian, (b) some make points
already shown to be Aristotelian, and (c) some make points only a slightly
different from those made by other objections or responses. Since we are interested in general orientations, we can ignore such minor variations.

55. τό δὲ ζητούμενον τοῦτ' ἐστί, τίς ἡ τῆς κινήσεως ἀρχὴ ἐν τῇ ψυχῇ. δῆλον δὴ· ὥσπερ
ἐν τῷ ὅλῳ θεός, {καὶ} κἀν ἐκείνῳ. κινεῖ γάρ πως πάντα τὸ ἐν ἡμῖν θεῖον· λόγου δ' ἀρχὴ οὐ
λόγος, ἀλλά τι κρεῖττον· τί οὖν ἂν κρεῖττον καὶ ἐπιστήμης εἴη <καὶ νοῦ> πλὴν θεός; [*EE*
viii,2,1248a24–29]. See also *EN* x,9,1179b20–23. On this general passage (i.e., *EE* viii,2 [=vii,14])
and its connection with the Thomistic doctrine of grace, see Kenny (1992), pp. 80–82. Kenny cites
Thomas's *SCG* lb.3 cap.89 (§2651) and *ST* I–II q.9 a.4.
56. *EE* viii,2,1247a33–35 [emphasis in ROT].
57. *in Metaph.* §§1216–22.

Objections 3 to 5 (and also, to some extent, objections 17 and 21) deal with the influence of God on human action. They argue that, since "the *voluntas* of man is immovably moved by God," it is not free but necessitated or "forced." Thomas responds that, since God is creator, he can create man as he wills—and he willed to create him with freedom of choice. His influence cannot be such, therefore, that it overrides that which he wills for man's *voluntas*. Nonetheless, what ultimately comes about on account of the operation of human *voluntas* is according to God's will.

In the previous section, we saw that Thomas derives many of his ideas about God's role in human action from Aristotle, and particularly from the *Eudemian Ethics*. The place, however, where he most clearly attributes to Aristotle the idea that God's influence does no damage to human freedom comes in his commentary on the *Metaphysics*. In *Metaph.* vi,3, Aristotle discusses the "fortuitous"—which, he says, does not occur "of necessity" (see 1027a29–32)—as when a man suffers a violent death because he went out, went out because he was thirsty, was thirsty because he ate pungent food, etc. Such strings of fortuitous causes must come to an end, says Aristotle. "This then will be the starting-point for the fortuitous, and will have nothing else as cause of its coming to be" [*Metaph.* vi,3,1027b12–14]. At *Phys.* ii,6,198a9–13, Aristotle says the "prior causes" of the universe, which includes fortune [*hē tuchē*] and chance [*to automaton*], are (divine) intelligence [*nous*] and nature [*physis*]; and, as we have seen, in *EE* viii he refers everything having to do with human fortune to God.

This presents a problem, notes Thomas in his commentary on *Metaph.* vi. It is impossible "that something be foreseen by God and that it not come about," although that which comes about must be non-necessary [*in Metaph.* §1218]. The solution to this puzzle, he says, is to realize that God can create things not to be subject to necessity. "Thus it is clear that, when we speak of divine providence, we ought to say not only that 'it is foreseen by God that this should be' but that 'it is foreseen by God that this should be contingently' or that 'this should be necessarily.'"[58] It is true that Aristotle himself does not make precisely this point, but surely Thomas is correct in believing that

---

58. *in Metaph.* §1222: "Sic ergo patet, quod cum de divina providentia loquimur, non est dicendum solum, hoc est provisum a Deo ut sit, sed hoc est provisum a Deo, ut contingenter sit, vel ut necessario sit."

something like it must be put forward if Aristotle's position is to be maintained.[59] Moreover, Thomas's approach to the issue is consistent with the Aristotelian idea that things that stand in an ordered relationship maintain their own, independent intelligibility. If we think of the universe as a whole, ordered in terms of necessity and contingency, with God at the top, the stars which guide the workings of nature coming next, and contingent events below, there is not only no problem in saying that the bottom tier maintains its own special nature (i.e., contingency) but it is essential that it do so.[60]

Objections 6 and 7 (and, to some extent, 8, 9, 11, and 14) raise the issue, how *voluntas* can be a passive potency without leading to determinism. Objection 7, probably the most important of this group, compares *voluntas* to the sense faculties, which are passive with respect to their objects. Just as a sense organ when presented with an appropriate object, provided there is no impediment, necessarily sees it, so also with *voluntas*. With respect to its objects, man is, therefore, not free "to will or not to will"—ll.64–65]. The objection cites as support two Aristotelian passages: *De an.* iii,10 and *Metaph.* xii,7, in each of which we find the idea that *voluntas* is, in some sense, a passive potency.[61]

As noted above, those who follow Lottin are inclined to say that, in *De ma.* q.6, Thomas is primarily interested in disassociating himself from the idea that *voluntas* is a passive potency, an idea correctly regarded as Aristotelian. But Thomas in his reply to objection 7 does anything but disassociate himself from the idea. In fact, he reiterates it when he says that "the active factor does not move from necessity except when it overcomes the power of the passive" [ll.541–43]. He does not challenge the idea that *voluntas* is a passive potency; he says rather that, given a passive potency, it reacts in a necessary way only when it is overcome by the active factor, as happens, for instance, when heat is presented to our senses and we have no option but to feel it. There is an in-

---

59. Another pertinent passage is *in Int.* lb.1 lect.14 ll.321–461 (§§191–97), in which Thomas, commenting on Aristotle's *Int.* ix, treats of God's efficacious foreknowledge of human actions: "voluntas enim Dei inefficax esse non potest" [l.362 (§192)].

60. See the present work, chapter 4, section [1].

61. Thomas often uses the phrase 'passive potency' (or something similar) of *voluntas* or appetite. See, for instance, *in Sent.* lb.3 d.27 q.1 a.1 c ("appetitus autem est virtus passiva; unde in III De Anima, dicit Philosophus, quod appetibile movet sicut movens motum" [see *De an.* iii,10,433b16–18]) and *ST* I–II q.18 a.2 ad 3. On passive potencies, see *Metaph.* v,15,1021a14–26; ix,7,1048b37–1049a18. On v,15,1201a14–26, see Thomas's *in Metaph.* §§1023–25.

stance in which such necessity does overcome *voluntas,* says Thomas: i.e., when it is presented with that good that "is good with respect to every consideration" [ll.546–47]. But *voluntas* is capable of not willing even this good "actively," for *voluntas* "can divert the thought of happiness since it moves the intellect toward its act" [ll.550–52].[62] We have already seen these ideas. The last mentioned is treated just above, in section [8]; the idea that *voluntas* is in some sense also active, in section [6] (i.e., in the exegesis of *De an.* iii,10). Both are clearly Aristotelian.

Objections 15, 16, 18, and 19 are all concerned with the idea that *voluntas* is "open to opposites" *(se habet ad opposita).*[63] Objection 15, for instance, sets out a proof, based on Avicenna's understanding of causation,[64] that the will is necessitated. The objection notes that, according to Aristotle, since a rational potency is open to opposites, in order for it to be put into action in a determinate way for one or the other, a cause is required. But (the objection continues) a cause necessarily issues in its effect for, as Avicenna argues, if it doesn't, it is not really the sufficient cause.[65] Thomas replies that a cause—even a sufficient cause—need not produce its effect necessarily. Indeed, in his commentary on the *Metaphysics,* Thomas argues that Avicenna should not be interpreted as denying this but that, in any case, the position that everything is caused necessarily is irreconcilable with what Aristotle says in *Metaph.* vi,3.[66]

Objection 16, misusing Aristotle's *Metaph.* ix,5,1048a9–10, argues that *voluntas,* an active potency, must be necessitated because that with respect to which it is active must be possible: it is impossible, however, for opposites to come about at the same time; therefore, *voluntas* must be open toward just

---

62. This point must be understood in the way in which his remarks at ll.438–40 must be understood: i.e., so as not to be inconsistent with the idea that the choice to "divert the thought of happiness" is a specified act, for this is required by what he says about the objects of *voluntas* and intellect.

63. Note that objection 17 is out of place. See Appendix C.

64. See Avicenna, *Phil.pr.* I.6 (pp. 43–48). See also Thomas, *De ver.* q.23 a.5 obj.1 ll.3–17 (§194) and *ST* I q.14 a.8. See also Aristotle, *Metaph.* ix,5 (and Thomas, *in Metaph.* §§1820–21).

65. Avicenna reduces all causation to sufficient causation. See Avicenna, *Phil.pr.* I.6.52–55 (p. 45).

66. *in Metaph.* §§1192–93. Thomas does often himself invoke Avicenna's principle, "Once the cause is posited, it is necessary that the effect be posited" ["causa autem posita necesse est effectum poni"]. But he says (at *in Metaph.* §1193) that this must be understood "supposing that no impediment to the cause comes about." See also *in Sent.* lb.2 d.36 q.1 a.1 ad 2; *ST* I q.115 a.6; *ST* I–II q.75 a.1; *in Int.* lb.1 lect.14 ll.231–36 (§186). Note that, in *De ma.* q.6 ad 21, Thomas says that even sufficient causes do not always produce their effect. He refers again to *Metaph.* vi,3.

one thing and is, therefore, necessitated. Thomas points out that the Aristotelian passage maintains not that a potency would not be active were it truly
open to opposites but that such a potency does not produce its effect necessarily. We note that, although elsewhere both objections and responses speak
of *voluntas* as passive and of this being an Aristotelian idea, Thomas here goes
along with the idea, attributed to Aristotle, that *voluntas* is an active potency.

Objection 18 argues that, since we have sensible experience of only one of
two opposites at a time, we in fact have no evidence, when one of them is
present, that the other is possible—i.e., that there exists a potency, *voluntas*,
which is open to opposites; therefore, as far as we know from examining the
evidence, *voluntas* is determined. Thomas replies that not all knowledge
comes directly from the senses, for (1) *voluntas* is known in its operation, and
(2), as in the case of primary matter, we can reason to the existence of *volun-*
tas as a power open to opposites by considering the succession of singular
acts issuing from it. Both these arguments are Aristotelian-inspired.[67]

Objections 20 and 21 both have to do with how we account for the movement of *voluntas*. The first sustains that *voluntas* cannot move itself. Thomas
replies, in good Aristotelian fashion, that, although it is true that one thing
cannot move itself in the same respect, in a different respect it can do so.[68]
Objection 21 argues that the multiform movement of *voluntas* must be reduced to the uniform, necessary movement of the heavens. Thomas says,
first, that the movement of *voluntas* is reduced in a direct manner not to the
movement of the heavens but to the influence of God—who, as we have seen,
created *voluntas* as something free. He then argues that what influence the
heavens do bring to bear on *voluntas* is not necessary since not everything in
nature follows from necessity. He cites and uses in this respect Aristotle's
Metaph. vi,3.

---

67. *De an.* iii,4,429b26–430a9. See also *in De an.* lb.3 cap.3 ll.61–106 (§§724–26) (§725 being especially pertinent): "Accidit autem hoc intellectui possibili, quod non intelligatur per essentiam
suam sed per speciem intelligibilem, ex hoc quod est potentia tantum in ordine intelligibilium:
ostendit enim Philosophus, in IX Metaphysicae [10,1051a29–33], quod nihil intelligitur nisi secundum quod est in actu. Et potest accipi simile in rebus sensibilibus: nam id quod est in potentia
tantum in eis, scilicet materia prima, non habet aliquam actionem per essentiam suam, sed solum
per formam ei adiunctam; substantiae autem sensibiles, quae sunt secundum aliquid in potentia
et secundum aliquid in actu, secundum se ipsas habent aliquam actionem. Similiter et intellectus
possibilis, qui est tantum in potentia in ordine intelligibilium, nec intelligit nec intelligitur nisi
per speciem in eo susceptam . . ." [ll.87–102].

68. See, for instance, *Metaph.* ix,1,1046a10–11; also 1046a28–29.

I conclude then that, whether or not it was written in response to or even in anticipation of Étienne Tempier's condemnations of propositions having to do with intellectual determinism, the theory presented in Thomas's *De ma.* q.6 is basically Aristotelian. We have little reason to find in that article an historical development toward a more modern conception of *voluntas* (or the will). What we find, rather, is a conception of *voluntas* according to which liberty of both exercise and specification are closely linked to our nature as rational, intellectual creatures. *Voluntas* does not work against intellect, nor intellect against *voluntas,* for the one allows the other to exist within the practical sphere.

CHAPTER 6

PRACTICAL REASON AND
CONCRETE ACTS

A S WE HAVE SEEN, in *ST* I–II q.94 a.2, Thomas draws a parallel be
tween "the first principle in practical reason" [FPPR] and the first
principle in theoretical reason or the principle of non-contradiction
[PNC]. The difference between the two depends on their diverse objects: being (and not-being) for PNC, good (and not-good) for FPPR, although, as
Thomas asserts in many places (including *De ma.* q.6), just as every being is
good, so every good has being.[1] The intellect itself, Thomas says, is a single
"power" which might "accidentally" be directed to one or the other object,
being or good, thus putting into operation either PNC or FPPR.[2]

This close relationship between PNC and FPPR is very important espe-

---

1. See, for instance, *ST* I q.5 a.1 c: "[B]onum et ens sunt idem secundum rem, sed differunt secundum rationem tantum. Quod sic patet. Ratio enim boni in hoc consistit, quod aliquid sit appetibile, unde Philosophus, in I Ethic., dicit quod bonum est quod omnia appetunt." See also *ST* I
q.17 a.4 ad 2; I–II q.18 a.1 ("sic igitur dicendum est quod omnis actio, inquantum habet aliquid de
esse, intantum habet de bonitate"); *De ver.* q.21 aa.1&2.

2. *ST* I q.79 a.11. In the *sed contra* he says that Aristotle says in *De an.* iii (9,433a1) that "intellectus speculativus per extensionem fit practicus." Thomas apparently did not read these words
when he wrote his commentary on this section of *De anima*: see *in De an.* lb.3 cap.8 ll.237–98
(§§812–17). He repeats or alludes to them, however, in a number of other places: *ST* II–II q.4 a.2
ad 3; *in Sent.* lb.3 d.23 q.2 a.3 sol.2 c; *De ver.* q.2 a.8 c ll.52–55; q.14 a.4 c ll.102–3 ["unde sola exten-
sio ad opus facit aliquem intellectum esse practicum"]; qu.22 a.10 obj.4 ll.26–27. The words apparently go back to the *vetus translatio* of *De anima*: see the Leonine Commission edition of *De
veritate, apparatus criticus* for p. 69 (ad q.2 a.8 l.55). On the relationship between practical and
theoretical reason, see McInerny (1998); on the remark "intellectus speculativus per extensionem
fit practicus" in particular, see McInerny (1998), p. 84, and Kluxen (1964), pp. 24-25. See also chapter 8, section [2].

cially for the earlier sections of the present chapter, for what I hope to do is to "prove" FPPR by employing an elenchic demonstration modelled upon the elenchic demonstration of PNC in Aristotle's *Metaph.* iv,4.[3] I place the word 'prove' in scare quotes since, as Aristotle himself points out, one cannot really prove a first principle. But one can show "elenchically"—that is, "for the sake of the argument"—that the person who denies PNC in fact asserts it. Since Aristotle's demonstration points to some very basic metaphysical notions,[4] applying his method to FPPR should reveal to us some very basic ethical notions, which we shall be able to employ in the analysis of action or of "concrete acts."

There is evidence that Thomas would not resist such an effort to demonstrate FPPR. First, in *Metaph.* iv,4, which Thomas cites in *ST* I-II q.94 a.2, Aristotle, as part of an argument that even those who deny PNC implicitly hold it, employs as evidence an exercise of practical reason.[5] Secondly, Thomas also says there that PNC is "founded upon the intelligibility of being and not-being" and that FPPR is "founded upon the intelligibility of good." The remark about PNC is an allusion to the way in which Aristotle in *Metaph.* iv,4 goes below PNC to "significations" that something "is or is not this" [1006a30] in order to prove (elenchically) that PNC is true and necessary. By making a parallel remark about FPPR, identifying its foundation as the intelligibility of good, Thomas appears to be deliberately allowing scope for an elenchic demonstration of FPPR.

I begin by setting out (in sections [1] and [2]) Aristotle's demonstration of

---

3. The expression 'elenchic demonstration' refers to *Metaph.* iv,4,1006a5ff., where Aristotle acknowledges that, since PNC is a first principle [ἀρχή], it cannot be demonstrated. It can however, he says, be "demonstrated by elenchus" [ἔστι δ' ἀποδεῖξαι ἐλεγκτικῶς—1006a11–12]. For the sake of brevity, in what follows I shall sometimes drop the qualifier 'elenchic.' Aristotle actually proposes in *Metaph.* iv,4 a series of arguments for PNC; I shall be concerned, however, almost solely with the first in this series (i.e., 1005b35–1007b18). Accordingly, I shall speak in the singular of Aristotle's "elenchic demonstration."

4. Inciarte argues very convincingly that the kernel of Aristotle's *Metaphysics* (or, at least, of books iv, vii–ix, and xii) is to be found in the elenchic demonstration of PNC [Inciarte (1994b)].

5. *Metaph.* iv,4,1008b14ff.; see also Thomas, *in Metaph.* §658. Can we be sure that Thomas was immediately aware of *Metaph.* iv,4,1008b14ff. when he wrote *ST* I-II q.94 a.2? The various books of the commentary on the *Metaphysics* are difficult to date, but Weisheipl claims that the one on *Metaph.* iv was probably written at roughly the same time as *ST* I-II [Weisheipl (1983 <1974>), pp. 361, 379]. Indeed, Thomas's *in Metaph.* §595 (on *Metaph.* iv,3,1005b5–8, i.e., Aristotle's remarks immediately prior to his elenchic demonstration of PNC) is so close to what is said in *ST* I-II q.94 a.2 about the things that are *per se nota* that it is difficult to believe that he did not have the demonstration in mind as he was writing *ST* I-II q.94 a.2.

PNC in *Metaph.* iv,4, along with my own running commentary. In section [3], I apply the same proof method to FPPR. In section [4], I discuss some of the implications of the former demonstration for our understanding of practical reason. In particular, I speak of the matter and form of human action— i.e., of the necessity of conceiving of human action in terms of concrete acts. Finally, in section [5], I discuss what all this says about the role of options in free choice, connecting this with Thomas's understanding of the stages of human action.

[1] Aristotle's elenchic demonstration of PNC

Before beginning his elenchic demonstration of PNC, Aristotle says that PNC, "the most certain principle of all," is not an hypothesis.[6] "For a principle that every one must have who knows anything about being, is not an hypothesis; and that which every one must know who knows anything, he must already have when he comes to a special study" [*Metaph.* iv,3,1005b14–17].

This non-hypothetical nature of the demonstration is not always appreciated. R. M. Dancy, for instance, regards Aristotle's approach in *Metaph.* iv,4 as a pragmatic one. "One way of summing up the effect of the argument might be this," writes Dancy: "if you accept a contradiction, you will not be able to give a sense to it."[7] But Fernando Inciarte has shown that this is a misinterpretation of Aristotle.[8] Aristotle holds not that *if* we are to talk sense, *then* we must assume PNC but that PNC is true and the basis of all communication— therefore, it makes no sense to deny it.

It is no argument against Aristotle to point out that people (or, at least, philosophers) sometimes do say that PNC does not hold.[9] Aristotle does not deny that—in fact, he assumes it; but he does deny that anyone can actually believe that PNC does not hold. "For it is impossible for anyone to believe [*hupolambanein*] the same thing to be and not to be, as some think Heraclitus says; for what a man says he does not necessarily believe" [*Metaph.* iv,3,1005b23–26]. As we shall see more clearly below, Aristotle is employing

---

6. *Metaph.* iv,3,1005b14. At *Metaph.* iv,4,1006a3 Aristotle says that he has previously "assumed" [εἰλήφαμεν] that the same thing cannot be and not be. But this must be interpreted (as both Alexander of Aphrodisias [*in Metaph.* 272.6] and Thomas [*in Metaph.* §606] do) in terms of the previous passage, which denies that PNC is an hypothesis.

7. Dancy (1975), p. 34.

8. See especially Inciarte (1994a), p. 135, n. 11.

9. Dancy (1975), pp. 35–36; Łukasiewicz (1910), p. 21.

here a particular sense of 'believe.' To *believe* that PNC is false, one would have to be able to conceive of a world in which the same attribute might "at the same time belong and not belong to the same subject in the same respect" [*Metaph.* iv,3,1005b19–20]. But this is impossible; therefore one cannot believe that PNC is not valid.

Aristotle has been criticized for not clearly distinguishing "the ontological formulation" of PNC ("the same attribute cannot at the same time belong and not belong to the same subject in the same respect"—*Metaph.* iv,3,1005ba19–20) and "the psychological formulation" ("it is impossible for anyone to believe the same thing to be and not to be"—*Metaph.* iv,3,1005b23–24).[10] But his insistence that one cannot believe PNC invalid makes it clear that this is no slip. Moreover, as we shall see below, the close relationship between the psychological and the ontological formulation is of key importance to the elenchic demonstration itself. This does not necessarily imply psychologism on Aristotle's part.[11] He does not hold that logical laws are just the laws of human thought, which in other creatures might be quite different; he holds rather that the world (in the sense of "all there is") is not and cannot be illogical—and that our minds *share* in this characteristic.

[2] *Metaphysics* iv,4

Aristotle begins the demonstration of PNC proper by identifying his opponents as those who "say" that it is possible that something might be and not be, etc., and who also say that it is possible to "believe" this [*Metaph.* iv,4,1006a1–2]. Following Dancy, I shall refer to the holder of this position as "Antiphasis" (from the Greek *antiphasis,* 'contradiction').

Antiphasis need only "say something that is significant both for himself and another" and we have him [1006a21]. (If Antiphasis refuses to signify anything, says Aristotle, he is no better than a plant and we can ignore him [1006a14–15].) Although the example that Aristotle uses is an essence— Antiphasis is supposed to select as his signification 'man'—it does not much

---

10. These phrases, "the ontological formulation" and "the psychological formulation," come from Łukasiewicz (1910), p. 16. Łukasiewicz also speaks of the "logical formulation" ("the most indisputable of all beliefs is that contradictory statements are not at the same time true" [*Metaph.* iv,6,1011b13–14]). On Łukasiewicz's understanding of PNC, see Flannery (1996), pp. 712–19.

11. For a good exposition of the history of psychologism and (especially Fregean) antipsychologism, see Baker and Hacker (1984), pp. 33–62.

matter what Antiphasis signifies. Signification, however, as opposed to assertion, must be the basis of the demonstration, otherwise it would beg the
question—which is whether a thing must definitely be something to the ex-
clusion of its opposite.[12] As I suggested just above, Aristotle here moves down
a level from asserted propositions to the "significations" upon which they depend. He knows that he cannot ask Antiphasis to admit that, for instance, 'all
men are mortal' has a single, definite sense; but Antiphasis, in order even to
say 'all men are mortal' (which he presumably regards as not having a definite
sense), must assume that 'man' is doing its proper work as a signifying expression.[13]

What does it mean for a signifying expression to do its proper work? It
must mark out a definite thing, but a definite thing that is recognized as such
not only by Antiphasis but also by those with whom he speaks. "This is necessary," says Aristotle, "if [Antiphasis] really is to say anything. For if he does
not, such a man will not be capable of reasoning, either with himself or with
another" [1006a22–24]. So, reasoning itself, even reasoning that is done pri-
vately, depends on the sort of concepts whose meanings are fixed in conversation with others [1006a21]. This is not to say that Antiphasis, having, for instance, identified a previously unknown subatomic particle, might not coin a
word for it which he might use in wholly private research; the expression,
however, would have to be such that in principle others might be able by
means of it to pick out the same thing that Antiphasis picks out.

Aristotle does not believe that a sly Antiphasis might be tempted to signify

12. "I don't think it matters a *lot* what he says. . . . All that matters is that he utter a word, and
one that signifies something, to himself and to others; and his uttering of any such word is also
not a matter of saying that anything is so, or that it is not so" [Dancy (1975), p. 31, omitting references and footnotes]. The range of possible significations must be very wide in order for Aristotle
to be demonstrating PNC—whose application, of course, is as wide as being itself.

13. Aristotle makes a similar move to a lower level in several places in the *Prior Analytics*, particularly when he employs the proof method known as *ekthesis* (on which see chapter 8, sections
[2] and [8]). For instance, when early in the *Prior Analytics* he proves that universal negative
propositions convert (i.e., that, if A holds of no B, then B holds of no A), because he cannot rely
on the logical apparatus that he is yet to construct, which itself depends on the conversion of universal negatives, he argues in this fashion: "Now if A holds of no B, B will not belong to any A; for
if it does belong to some (say to C), it will not be true that A belongs to no B—for C is one of the
Bs [*An.pr.* i,2,25a15–17]." "C" belongs not to the syllogistic (i.e., to the theory set out in *An.pr.*); it
constitutes rather Aristotle's recourse to something more basic than the syllogistic in order to
avoid begging the question. This is Alexander of Aphrodisias's interpretation and I believe it is the
correct one. See Flannery (1995d), pp. 16–19, 38–45. On "levels of discourse" in Aristotle, see
Flannery (2000).

something that does not have a fixed signification. "Not to signify one thing," says Aristotle, "is not to signify at all" [1006b7]. Just as no one is told to *follow* FPPR (one cannot help but follow it), so Antiphasis is not being *instructed* by Aristotle to signify something definite. The point is, rather, that Antiphasis cannot speak unless he signifies something definite. "The person responsible for the demonstration," says Aristotle, is Antiphasis [1006a25–26]. Thus, there is no begging of the question.

Moreover, although Aristotle quite naturally speaks of Antiphasis's saying something to an interlocutor that is significant in a language, the point is not a linguistic one. "For it is impossible to think if we do not think of one thing; but if it is possible, one name might be assigned to this thing."[14] One cannot even reason, says Aristotle, unless the concepts with which one reasons exclude the sense of their opposites—which is to say that one can reason (and also converse), since concepts do exclude their opposites. We see in all this, again and again, the absolute inevitability of the "basis" of PNC—and also the central role of belief within Aristotle's demonstration.

In one section of *Metaph.* iv, 4 (1006b11ff.), Aristotle also says that, when he speaks of signifying one thing, he does not mean that Antiphasis might simply "signify" predicates that hold of nothing else. Suppose that the expression is 'man.' This might be construed as not incompatible with 'not-man' if it were possible to limit its use to "saying things of" (something) and never to bring in that of which it is said [1006b14–15].[15] For predicates can in a sense blend together ('white' and 'musical' and even 'man' might all apply to *a* man, the former three thus "sharing the same space"); but that which constitutes the basis of the reference—let us say, Socrates, that essence—cannot blend with any other reference, if he is to be referred to at all.

Aristotle is in effect admitting here that mere "saying things of" would not constitute the sort of signifying expression he needs for an elenchic demonstration, for no one thing would be signified that need exclude not being that one thing. But this admission is no great sacrifice: "[T]he point in question is not this, whether the same thing can at the same time be and not be a man in name, but whether it can in fact" [1006b20–22]. Were Antiphasis only to "say

---

14. 1006b10–11. I follow Jaeger (and Alexander) in reading οὐδὲ in line 10. Cp. Ross (1953 <1924>) and Reale (1993 <1968>).

15. See *Cat.* v,2a14–17.

things of" and never "say things of something" (if this can even be imagined), his conversation would never succeed in signifying anything, which is the point from which the elenchic demonstration takes off. Not that Aristotle's demonstration depends on signifying things that actually exist; he means rather that the things to which Antiphasis might refer must at least be capable of existing—as man or Socrates or even sitting-Socrates are capable of existing.

But how, once Antiphasis has signified something in the appropriate way, can PNC be said to be demonstrated? Throughout *Metaph.* iv,4 Aristotle simply assumes that this is obvious; but, as so often in Aristotle, what he proclaims to be obvious is far from obvious to us. The key to understanding the force of the argument is the original formulation of the problem. Aristotle's opponents, as we saw, are those who not only say that PNC is not true but who also say that it is possible to believe that it is not true [1006a1–2]. His repeated use, especially in the various formulations of PNC, of the expression 'at the same time,'[16] makes it clear that the believing involved is a single act of believing that something is and is not—or could both be and not be—a certain thing. We may indeed be capable of believing, in a way that does not force us to bring our theory to bear upon a particular instance, that PNC is not always valid; but if we try to think of a particular instance in which it does not hold, we shall not succeed. We cannot have before our mind's eye the man Socrates and believe that he is at the same time both standing and not standing (in the same sense of standing). Or to use Aristotle's own example, we cannot have before our mind's eye 'man' and believe that man is both what he is (two-footed animal) and what he is not (not a two-footed animal) [1006b28–34].

This is not a physical or psychological incapacity—although the physical and the psychological are intimately bound up in it. When we try to think of Socrates as both standing and not standing, we realize that the difficulty in doing so has to do in the first place not with Socrates or with posture, nor with an incapacity of ours that another person or type of creature might not share. In fact, incapacity is not at issue at all but rather an impossibility that is quite general. It is incorrect to speak of Socrates's standing and not standing

16. The Greek word is ἅμα; it appears at *Metaph.* iv,3,1005b19,27,29,30; *Metaph.* iv,4,1006b21,33, 1007a18, 1007b13,18,19. On this point, see Schiaparelli (1994), p. 51.

precisely because it is impossible *logically* for him to be such. Logical positivism bequeathed to the modern world the idea that contradiction is solely a matter of propositions that exclude one another's truth. But Aristotle holds that the impossibility of contradictory propositions being true together is only a manifestation of a deeper and more pervasive "law."[17] According to this law, not only does it make no sense for the propositions 'Socrates is standing' and 'Socrates is not standing' to be true together but neither does it make sense for *Socrates* to be that way (which, of course, is not "a way" at all, for it is utter nonsense).

As elsewhere in Aristotle's philosophy, so in this instance too, the general becomes manifest in the particular: PNC is proved in considering the signifying of Socrates. Or, more precisely, the acknowledgment of PNC in a particular instance *is* the acknowledgment of the general principle. Attending to particular significations is the way we get at PNC in order to see it in action. PNC has to do not just with language or even just with thoughts (or beliefs) but with the most general structure of reality: the "rationem entis et non entis," as Thomas puts it. Or, as I might put it rather more germanically, there are logico-psychologico-ontological truths, the most basic of which is PNC.

[3] An elenchic demonstration of FPPR

The person who denies FPPR—let us call him Antipraxis—denies that the good is to be pursued (in the sense identified above). There are two ways in which he might deny this. He might hold that some people (himself, for example) actually choose bad things *qua* being bad things or he might hold that at least some of the things that a person might choose are morally indifferent, so that it is false to say that everyone seeks good. But if it can be demonstrated that every action is pursued as good, both these positions will have been refuted, for together they constitute the contradictory of FPPR. Thus, in what follows, Antipraxis represents the thesis that every action is not pursued as good—that is, he represents the person who asserts the contradictory of FPPR.

As we have seen, practical reason's object—good, instead of mere being—

---

17. I put the word 'law' in scare quotes because (at least in a certain sense) PNC is not a rule that a person might choose to violate. For the sense I have in mind, see Wittgenstein (1981 <1921>), 5.4731.

determines its differences from theoretical reason. The elenchic demonstration of FPPR must therefore be different from its counterpart in theoretical reason in any respect that involves good as opposed to being. I shall identify three such respects, while making no claims to exhaustiveness.

First of all, although the denial of FPPR is certainly illogical, it is *practically* illogical. The problem is not in the first place that the denial of FPPR cannot be true (although it cannot be) but that one cannot *do* what it suggests one can do: i.e., pursue what one does not consider good. The demonstration of FPPR seeks therefore to show not that FPPR is true but that, without it, there would be no intelligible human action.

This is not to say that practical reason lacks definiteness. Practical reasoning is practical *discourse* in the sense that it leads to things that people do (or might do) and that are (or might be) recognized by others as things that a person does voluntarily.[18] Just as the denier of PNC who refuses to "say something that is significant both for himself and for another" [*Metaph.* iv,4, 1006a21] is no better than a plant, so he who refuses even to consider doing anything that might be recognized by others as an intelligible action is beyond refutation but also beyond bothering about. We presuppose that one cannot consider doing something unless one considers doing *something*; and what might count as doing something is in principle recognizable by others as a definite (intelligible) human action. The definiteness of a "theoretical" signifying consists in the fact that being the opposite of what is signified is excluded by being what is signified. Similarly, in the practical sphere, definiteness consists in the fact that pursuing the opposite of what is signified is excluded by pursuing what is signified. It is because practical significations are this way that they can be part of a shared community of practices, judgments about those practices, etc.

Secondly, the "signifying" that Antipraxis will be asked to do is not the signifying of a definite thing *as* a being; it is rather the "practical signifying" of a definite thing as a good possibly to be sought.[19] If I signify Socrates, my act is in some sense a signifying of his being. When a person thinks to himself, for

---

18. Note, however, that the class of voluntary acts is larger than the class of acts done by choice: see *EN* iii,1–2.

19. For the sake of simplicity and where I can do so without causing confusion, in what follows I shall sometimes drop from 'practical signification' (and similar phrases) the qualifier 'practical.'

instance, 'I will pursue the right theory' (about practical reason), his signifying is a signifying not merely of being but of being-a-good-thing (a thing to
be pursued). This means that a practical signifying, instead of being in principle an element of an assertion, is in principle an element of a choice to do
something. In theoretical reason, the basic elements are terms ('white' and
'Socrates') which might be brought together into assertions ('Socrates is
white'). In practical reason the basic elements are, like terms, delimited ('the
right theory' regarded as to be pursued is incompatible with its not being
such); but the point is not to combine one element with another in order to
assert something but to pursue something as part of a project. For instance, a
person might believe that happiness is to be found in having a reputation.
Believing that he will gain a reputation if he attains the right theory, he pursues the right theory. The point of associating reputation and the right theory
is not to make a claim about the world ("that's the way to gain a reputation")
but to get to happiness—or, at least, to apparent happiness.

So then, since we are now dealing with practical (not theoretical) reason,
we ask Antipraxis to signify something that might be an object of practical
reason: a *"prosequendum."* This means that he identifies something that
makes sense to pursue, although he need not have committed himself to pursuing it.[20] Let us say again that he picks 'the right theory.' We do not want to
beg the question by asking him to *decide* to pursue the right theory (which he
might argue would be to proclaim that that thing is definitely good, which is
precisely what he is contesting);[21] but he has agreed to reason practically, so
we can ask that he at least signify in a practical way the type of thing that
might result in a decision to do that thing. Let us say again that Antipraxis is
interested in making a reputation for himself. He considers two ways in
which he might do this: by pursuing the right theory about practical reason

20. So, in order to signify practically, Antipraxis must consider the thing signified as a single
thing possibly to be pursued (as a *prosequendum*), just as, in order to signifying theoretically,
Antiphasis must consider something as if it were one existent thing. If Antipraxis somehow man-
ages to limit himself to act descriptions (the practical equivalent of only "saying things of"), he
would not succeed in signifying practically. Also, even a *prosequendum* that involves a not-doing-
something (i.e., an avoiding of it) is a positive *prosequendum* (i.e., *something* one might do) since,
its avoidance would involve a definite course of action. Similarly, according to Thomas, negation
is always "reducible to the genus of affirmation" [*in Int.* lb.1 lect.5 ll.164–65 (§61); see also lect.1
ll.153–68 (§10), lect.8 ll.388–439 (§108)]. Pure not-doing cannot be the object of practical reason
any more than pure not-being can be the object of theoretical reason. Thus, a *prosequendum* that
is a something-not-to-be-done is a practical signifying.

21. Cp.*Metaph.* iv,4,1006a18–21.

or by striking his interlocutor. We do not ask him to choose to do one or the other (which would be the practical equivalent of asserting a proposition); the elenchic demonstration of FPPR begins rather from a stage prior to such a choice.

Antipraxis might argue that it is possible to regard pursuing the right theory as being either good *or* bad since it might involve leaving his wife and children destitute or it might mean bringing great happiness to a large number of people. We can point out that he is making the same type of mistake that people often make with respect to Aristotle's elenchic demonstration of PNC. That is, they think that he is concerned in the first instance with what a person might believe in general. But, as we have seen, that argument is concerned not with general but with particular beliefs. So also here. We would be foolish to deny that Antipraxis can at 10 A.M. consider the pursuit of the right theory in a positive light and at 3 P.M. as something to be avoided. What is impossible on the present account is that he might (in a practical way) at any *one* time consider having the right theory both to be pursued and not to be pursued. If he is thinking, 'I'll pursue the theory and thereby bring great happiness to others,' he cannot at the same time be thinking, 'I'll not pursue the theory since doing so would hurt the family.'

Antipraxis might reply: "Look, Mr. A, who has no family, can come along and see the right theory as a good; and at the same time Mr. B (who has a family) can come along and see *the same thing* as something bad. Therefore, the act itself is morally indifferent; and it can be so at one particular time." We however have an answer for him: "But you agreed to make a practical signification, didn't you? What Mr. A and Mr. B think about having the right theory does not enter into your signification, which is the basis of the present demonstration. We are saying that *you* cannot both pursue and not pursue the same thing at the same time in the same respect. And that is the basis of our demonstration."[22]

We are focussing right now upon the practical equivalent of what, in the theoretical sphere, is trying to see a particular signification under contradictory aspects (Socrates sitting and standing at the same time). What occurs in either practical or theoretical reason is "a kind of flip-flopping of ge-

---

22. This argument is related to Thomas's position that an act might be morally indifferent *secundum speciem* but not *in individuo consideratus: ST* I–II q.18 a.9 (see also q.18 a.8).

stalts."[23] Antipraxis might be said to be in doubt at a particular time, but necessarily this involves flipping from one way of seeing the pursuit of the right theory to another way of seeing it. His doubting might consist, for instance, in thinking of the prospect at one moment as a thing to be avoided ("how could I ever support the family?"), at another as a thing to be pursued ("it could make me famous"). But a doubt as such could not subsist in just *one* of these moments, except insofar as it is conjoined with the other.

Why is this necessarily the case? Why, that is, can pursuing a particular thing not "get into" the same moment as avoiding it? Because practical significations exclude their practical contradictories just as theoretical significations exclude their theoretical contradictories. We tend to think that there is a lack of parallel between practical and theoretical reason in this regard: in theoretical reason, a sort of picture of Socrates standing excludes a similar picture of Socrates not-standing; but the practically contradictory pair 'pursuing the right theory'/'not-pursuing the right theory' is just a matter of different attitudes cast upon the prospect 'pursuing the right theory.' But there is a closer parallel than this unconsidered reaction allows.

Consider again the *prosequendum* 'the right theory.' Its practical contradictory is a wholly different, *positive* prospect. At first it might indeed be specified by no more than the element 'the right theory' plus a negative practical operator—just as a person might learn *just* that Socrates is not standing. But 'not-pursue-(the right theory)' must have a positive aspect, if it is to enter into practical reason at all.[24] That which is pursued must be pursued under the aspect of good. In this sense then it is like 'Socrates not standing.' This, the negation of 'Socrates is standing,' does not represent absolute not-being, for it has definite and positive content: Socrates doing *something* (i.e., not standing). Similarly, not pursuing the right theory cannot exist as a pure practical negation: that would be for it to be evil and no one can pursue that. One does-not-pursue the right theory by doing something else—including, perhaps, doing nothing. Even such inactivity can be considered intelligible only to the extent that it is considered under a positive aspect.

23. These words (quoted also in chapter 5, note 51) come from Penner (1990), p. 69. Penner is speaking, however, solely of practical reason.

24. I understand 'not-pursue-(the right theory)' not as the *mere* not pursuing of the right theory—a person who has never thought of pursuing any theories is not pursuing a particular right theory when, for instance, he is playing golf—but as a positive prospect having to do with the possible pursuing of the right theory.

How then is Antipraxis refuted? We have asked him to signify something in a practical way—e.g., the right theory (as something to be pursued). As with PNC, the claim is that at this point he has refuted himself: the elenchic demonstration is immediate. Just as insisting that Antiphasis attend not to general beliefs but to significations forces him to concentrate on an indivisible portion of his world and acknowledge in *its* respect that the world cannot be contradictory (since one cannot get an attribute and its contrary into the same "picture"), so also our insistence that Antipraxis attend not to general indecision but rather to practical significations forces him to acknowledge that, if he were to decide to do something, he would have to decide upon it as good and not bad or indifferent. Just as in theoretical signification Antiphasis comes face-to-face with the truth, so in practical signification Antipraxis comes face-to-face with the good (which excludes its contrary). If a practical signification is a possible object of practical reason, it has to be regarded as good. And we know that it *is* a possible object of practical reason since that is a presupposition of the entire enterprise: Antipraxis has agreed to enter into practical discourse.

Someone might object: "But the only reason why Antipraxis is forced to acknowledge definite goods is that you have insisted that he buy into your conception of practical reason, according to which we always choose goods." We can reply: "We have only insisted that he signify something that might be an intelligible action. It is true that the notion of an intelligible action bears with it the idea that something is pursued (for the action is not yet completed); and this in turn implies that the thing pursued is at least viewed as good (since nothing is sought if it is not considered good). But insisting on this is just to insist that Antipraxis live in the same practical world with us, where we are able to recognize one another's actions as actions that make sense. If he refuses even this, as we admit, we cannot refute him."

So, to conclude this demonstration, apparent *in* practical signification is FPPR: that everyone pursues good things in such a way that pursuing them excludes not pursuing them (i.e., avoiding them). 'The right theory' is a particular good thing, but the impossibility of its including 'not–the right theory' is quite general. The fact that we cannot conceive of what it would be like to both pursue and avoid the right theory at the same time in the same respect shows that the practical world cannot be like that. That is, it shows that "good is to be done and pursued and evil avoided" or that "good is that which all de-sire."[25]

[4] Practical matter, practical form

All this has implications for our understanding of practical reasoning. I shall discuss two such implications, the first (treated here in this section) having to do with the material and formal aspects of human action, the second (treated in section [5]) with free choice.

At *Metaph.* iv,4,1006a22, just after saying that for the elenchic demonstration of PNC to get underway Antiphasis must say something significant for himself and for another, Aristotle remarks that "this is necessary, if he really is to say anything." And, as we have seen, at *Metaph.* iv,4,1006b7, Aristotle says, "Not to signify one thing is not to signify at all." Thomas makes a related point with respect to practical reason in his commentary on Aristotle's *De anima*. He insists that every appetite is for the sake of something: "It is nonsense," he asserts, "to say that someone wants in order to want, since to want is a sort of motion tending toward something."[26] As seen in chapter 5 and as I discuss again below, Thomas insists that an interior act of *voluntas* is always attached to an exterior "something" which it wills. Much of this doctrine derives from Aristotle's *De an.* iii,10.

This idea has important consequences for our conception of practical reason especially. It means that practical reason involves, at every step of the way, what we might call "practical matter," since there cannot be individuation without matter of some type (which is always, of course, tied to the appropriate type of form).[27] This is not to say, however, that the matter in practical reason is physical matter. I am not espousing "physicalism," such as various authors of the Roman Catholic "manualist tradition" are accused of doing. Practical matter is more like logical matter, according to which conception

25. Many of the ideas put forward in this section are discernible also in Plato: see Flannery (1996).

26. "Et manifestum est etiam quod 'omnis appetitus est propter aliquid' (stultum enim esset dicere quod aliquis appetat propter appetere; nam appetere est quidam motus in aliud tendens) . . ." [*In De an.* lb.3 cap.9 ll.50–53 (§821); comment on Aristotle's *De an.* iii,10,433a15–17: "Every desire is for the sake of something since that for which there is a desire, this is the beginning of practical intelligence. For the ultimate thing is the beginning of action"].

27. For matter as the principle of individuation in Thomas, see for instance *ST* I q.3 a.3 c; q.39 a.1 ad 3; q.39 a.2 c; I–II q.63 a.1 c.

one can say that 'the table is blue' and 'the stove is hot' are of the same form but of different matter.[28] The matter here is neither a blue table nor a hot stove but that which differentiates the one proposition from the other—i.e., the fact that the one *speaks* about the table's being blue, the other about the stove's being hot, although they are of the same "shape" (or form).

In an article in the *Summa theologiae* devoted to the question whether a human action receives its goodness or badness from its object, the following objection is raised: "the object is compared to the action as its matter. The goodness of a thing, however, is not from its matter, but rather from its form, which is the act. Therefore, the good or bad in acts is not on account of the object."[29] The object spoken of here is not what Thomas calls "the object of the interior act of the *voluntas*" or *finis;* rather, it is the object of the exterior act.[30] Since the object in this sense is part of the exterior act, there is a temptation to associate it with physical matter. But Thomas, in his reply to the objection, excludes this notion: "the object is not matter *ex qua* but matter *circa quam* and it has, in a way, the intelligibility of form insofar as it provides the species."[31] It is clear here that Thomas is no physicalist. This matter is the individuating principle in Thomas's metaphysics—"that which contracts," allowing one to speak, for instance, not of murder in general but of one particular murder.[32] This is what allows this type of matter to have also a formal as-

28. On logical matter, see Barnes (1990b) and also Flannery (1995d), chapter 3. At *in An.post.* lb.1 lect.1 ll.28–29 (§2), Thomas says that the *materia circa quam* of logic is the act of reason.

29. "Praeterea, obiectum comparatur ad actionem ut materia. Bonitas autem rei non est ex materia, sed magis ex forma, quae est actus. Ergo bonum et malum non est in actibus ex obiecto" [*ST* I–II q.18 a.2 obj.2].

30. *ST* I–II q.18 a.6: "In actu autem voluntario invenitur duplex actus, scilicet actus interior voluntatis, et actus exterior, et uterque horum actuum habet suum obiectum. Finis autem proprie est obiectum interioris actus voluntarii, id autem circa quod est actio exterior, est obiectum eius. Sicut igitur actus exterior accipit speciem ab obiecto circa quod est; ita actus interior voluntatis accipit speciem a fine, sicut a proprio obiecto. Ita autem quod est ex parte voluntatis, se habet ut formale ad id quod est ex parte exterioris actus, quia voluntas utitur membris ad agendum, sicut instrumentis; neque actus exteriores habent rationem moralitatis, nisi inquantum sunt voluntarii."

31. *ST* I–II q.18 a.2 ad 2: "Dicendum quod obiectum non est materia ex qua, sed materia circa quam, et habet quodammodo rationem formae, inquantum dat speciem." See also ad 3. For more on the notion of *materia circa quam*, see *ST* I–II q.55 a.4 c; q.60 a.2 c; q.65 a.2 c; q.72 a.3 ad 2; q.73 a.3 ad 1; q.75 a.4 ad 1; also *in Sent.* lb.1 d.48 q.1 a.2 c; *in Sent.* lb.2 d.36 q.1 a.5 ad 4. The expression *materia circa quam* comes originally from Aristotle's περὶ τί at *EN* iii,1,1111a4: see *in EN* lb.3 lect.3 ll.140–42 (§415) and *ST* I–II q.7 a.3.

32. See *ST* I–II q.18 a.7 ad 3. See also *ST* I–II q.75 a.4 obj.1 and ad 1 and *De ma.* q.2 a.4 c ll.228–29: "nondum habet rationem boni vel mali moralis, nisi aliquid addatur ad speciem contrahens."

pect: it *specifies* the act, just as the specific form of Socrates specifies him as distinct from man in general.[33]

It also becomes clear, however, in this question of the *Summa* that an action's object is connected with the interior act of the *voluntas* in such a way that only given *it* (that is, the interior act) can we speak about an exterior moral act at all: "Now that which is on the part of the *voluntas* is formal in regard to that which is on the part of the external action: because the *voluntas* uses the limbs to act as instruments; nor have external actions any measure of morality, save insofar as they are voluntary."[34] These two—the interior and the exterior acts—are not separate *things*, so that an act of adultery, for instance, without an act of the *voluntas* is still an act of adultery but not a morally relevant one. If the corresponding act of *voluntas* is not present, neither is there an exterior act of adultery. The two come into existence together, as matter and form.[35]

This close association, however, between the interior and the exterior act ought not blind us to the fact that the exterior has its own intelligibility and even (in a certain respect) primacy. Even if it is true that an act of adultery is dependent on an interior act of *voluntas* for its very existence, the exterior act of *voluntas* is for *something*—i.e., for something that might be signified in human moral discourse and as such excludes not being that thing. Writes Thomas:

We may consider a twofold goodness or malice in the external action: one in respect of due matter and circumstances; the other in respect of the order to the end. And that which is in respect of the order to the end depends entirely on *voluntas*, while that which is in respect of due matter or circumstances depends on the reason; *and on this goodness depends the goodness of voluntas*, insofar as *voluntas* tends toward it.[36]

Perhaps I can make all this talk of objects, internal acts, and matter more intuitively apparent by employing a rather unconventional image. We might imagine that the practical (as opposed to the theoretical) life is like a penny arcade video game in which a person drives along a simulated road. But in-

---

33. See *De ma.* q.2 a.5 c; also q.9 a.2 ad 10.
34. *ST* I–II q.18 a.6 c.
35. In fact, at *ST* I–II q.20 a.3 c, Thomas says that "actus interior voluntatis et actus exterior, prout considerantur in genere moris, sunt unus actus" (see also ad 3; see also q.17 a.4 c).
36. *ST* I–II q.20 a.2 c (my emphasis). I am much indebted in this section to William May's brilliant article on this topic. See, especially, May (1984), pp. 580–85.

stead of his driving along a preset road, the road is extemporaneously constructed in front of him as he considers things to do *(prosequenda)*. He can never drive where there is no road, which is to say that practical reasoning is about definite, concrete things (it involves matter); but it is also true that in order to have road to drive on, he need only consider the possibility of his taking that road.[37] In practical reason, one cannot fly over a stretch of road, any more than one can in an automobile, since progressing along the road of practical reason just *is* having road onto which to drive and so doing. On the other hand, one's practical reasoning is completely free since, given that one can drive only on road, one can take any road one wants. Moreover, even staying by choice on a single road is free since it involves projection of the road and driving down it. Not driving down that road would be another road, a free alternative to driving down the first.

Louis Janssens fails to understand at least a part of this story when, in a recent article, wishing to justify certain types of lying by an appeal to Thomas, he writes: "The end of the person, the protection of the professional secret, is the formal element of the object of the action that justifies what is done, even when, of necessity, telling a *falsiloquium* constitutes the material object of the act."[38] Janssens means that the internal object (or *finis*) determines the goodness of the act regardless of the character of the exterior object. But the two elements cannot be in tension in this way, for the one comes with the other. It is true that the road comes up only if one projects it, but one has to project something and then take that road projected. Practical reason proceeds along *prosequenda*.

Janssens's misconception is reflected in a misinterpretation he makes earlier in the same article. He writes, "[T]he object is not only the material in which the act consists *(non est materia ex qua)*, but the material with which one actively works *(materia circa quam)*."[39] But Thomas does not say in the relevant place that "the object is *not only* the material in which the act consists"; he says precisely what Janssens gives in the Latin: "non est materia ex qua." The matter of an action is *not* like bricks and stones, matter *from* which

---

37. In accordance with the above elenchic demonstration, perhaps we would have to say also that as the driver posits one possible turning, any other possible turning that he may be considering necessarily disappears from vision. But we should not, I think, make this analogy do more work than it is capable of.

38. Janssens (1994), p. 111. The word *falsiloquium* is normally translated 'falsehood.'

39. Janssens (1994), p. 105. He cites *ST* I–II q.18 a.2 ad 2 (see above, note 31).

we might produce a house. In human action, the material is bound up with the object. It is the thing at which we aim, not that from which we produce what we will.[40]

It is true, of course, that what Janssens calls "the end of the person, the protection of the professional secret," might be the object of that person's intention; but there is no jumping over the stretch of road that leads there— nor does the matter 'protection of the professional secret' (which, of course, must go along with its corresponding form) ever replace the matter 'tell a falsehood.' Both *prosequenda,* each composed of form and matter, are objects of the person's intentions.

Thomas makes this point in a comment on Aristotle's *Metaphysics* iii,2,1013a35-b3: "Not only the ultimate thing, for the sake of which the agent acts, is called an end in relation to the things that precede; but also all of the intermediate things, which are between the first agent and the ultimate end, are called end in relation to the things that precede [them]."[41] There is no doubt that in Thomas (and in Aristotle) the "end specifies the act," so that telling a falsehood may indeed be "protecting a professional secret."[42] But it is also telling a falsehood. The form "protecting a professional secret" does not obliterate that. And, since telling a falsehood is something that the person protecting the professional secret deliberately *does,* it needs to be assessed on its own merits, since everyone is responsible for what he deliberately does. Accordingly, Thomas, by constant repetition, makes his own the saying of pseudo-Dionysius: "Good comes of a single and perfect cause, evil from

40. Janssens also writes: "[I]t appears that the end toward which the subject strives in each case is not merely an element of the object of the action but the formal element that is so important that it determines whether the material element is *materia debito modo disposita*" [p. 111]. (The phrase "materia debito modo disposita" is a reference to Thomas's remark at *ST* I–II q.4 a.4: "just as matter cannot receive a form, unless it be duly disposed thereto [*debito modo disposita ad ipsam*], so nothing gains an end, except it be duly ordained thereto." Thomas's point is that in the practical sphere, just as for example a saw cannot be made of wax, so a good act cannot be a good act unless the material of which it is "composed" is also good.) But the "formal element" cannot "determine" anything about the "material element," in the way that Janssens suggests. Travelling along the strange road of practical reason where options suddenly appear as we deliberate, we might choose not to turn onto a particular stretch of road that we regard as immoral; but certainly our choosing it cannot make it moral.

41. *in Metaph.* §771: "Non solum autem ultimum, propter quod efficiens operatur, dicitur finis respectu praecedentium; sed etiam omnia intermedia quae sunt inter primum agens et ultimum finem, dicuntur finis respectu praecedentium . . .". See also *in Phys.* lb.2 lect.5 n.6 (§181); also Finnis (1992 <1991>), pp. 134–37.

42. See for instance *in De an.* lb.2 cap.6 ll.131–90 (§§305–8) (ad *De an.* ii,4,415a17–22); also Finnis (1983), pp. 20–21, 25 and Finnis (1992 <1991>), p. 138, n. 33.

many and particular defects."[43] *Any* action in a chain of actions might be deemed wrong.

There are a number of places where Thomas seems to speak of the true intention of an act as the ultimate as opposed to the proximate end(s) of an action—as if the individual acts along the way to the goal were the matter, the goal itself the form. Such remarks are easily reconciled, however, with those that speak of the intimate bond between practical form and matter once we take account of the nature of practical matter. Practical matter is practical insofar as it is aimed at good; as such, it necessarily contains the ultimate object within itself. Telling a falsehood, as we are considering it here, is not just telling a falsehood (considered in a non-practical way) but it is telling a falsehood with the aim of protecting a professional secret. Otherwise, i.e., if it did not have an ultimate object, it would not be practical matter. Thus, to speak of an action along the way to a goal as matter and the goal as form (to say, e.g., as in Thomas's example, that, if a person robs in order to commit adultery, the matter is robbery, the form adultery),[44] is Thomas's way of excluding neither the idea that the adultery give species (form) *to* the robbery nor the idea that the matter *circa quam* one commits adultery is, at one stage in the process, an act of robbery. We have to be able to say these things (i.e., that sometimes someone committing a robbery *is* going about committing adultery) if it is to be accurate to say that the form gives species to the act. Of course, the person will not have *committed* adultery until he engages in sexual intercourse with the spouse of another.

[5] Free choice and the stages of action

All this has a bearing upon how we understand free choice. I have discussed this issue extensively, of course, in chapter 5; but to conclude the present chapter I would like to approach it from a slightly different perspective.

---

43. "Bonum procedit ex una et perfecta causa, malum autem procedit ex multis particularibus defectibus" [*De div.nom.* §572]. See ps.-Dionysius, *Div.nom.* iv,30 (*Pat.Gr.* 729C): Τὸ ἀγαθὸν ἐκ μιᾶς καὶ τῆς ὅλης αἰτίας, τὸ δὲ κακὸν ἐκ πολλῶν καὶ μερικῶν ἐλλείψεων. As I have said, Thomas quotes or cites this remark often: *ST* I–II q.18 a.4 ad 3; q.18 a.11 obj.3; q.19 a.6 ad 1; q.19 a.7 ad 3; q.71 a.5 ad 1; q.72 a.9 obj.1; in *De malo* q.2 a.4 ad 2; q.2 a.7 obj.3; q.2 a.9 obj. 12; q.4 a.1 ad 13; q.8 a.1 obj.12 et c; q.10 a.1 c; q.16 a.6 ad 11; *in EN* lb.2 lect.7 ll.9–12 (§320) (ad *EN* ii,6,1106b29–30).

44. See the end of *ST* I–II q.18 a.6 c (the first portion of which is given in note 30 above): "Et ideo actus humani species formaliter consideratur secundum finem, materialiter autem secundum obiectum exterioris actus. Unde Philosophus dicit, in V [cap.2] Ethic., quod ille qui furatur ut committat adulterium, est, per se loquendo, magis adulter quam fur."

Thomas identifies a number of stages that correspond to what we would find an agent doing if we were to stop the process leading up to the action at various points. The stages are *apprehensio, intentio, consilium, iudicium, consensus, electio, imperium, usus* (although in certain instances some stages might not exist independently of others). Various neo-scholastic schemes, by adding stages and particularly by putting *iudicium* after *consensus*, attained for the Thomistic theory a certain symmetry between the role of intellect and the role of will: the intellect apprehends [*apprehensio*], giving rise to simple volition [*simplex voluntas*]; the intellect settles on the end [*iudicium circa finem*], the will intends [*intentio*]; the intellect deliberates [*consilium*], the will gives its *consensus*; the intellect makes a judgment about the means [*iudicium*], the will chooses [*electio*]; finally, the intellect issues an *imperium*, the will puts the *imperium* into active use.[45]

Such schemes, however, besides putting intellect and will *(voluntas)* in separate and sequestered compartments and also ignoring what Thomas says about the place of *consensus*,[46] obscure the fact that even after the agent makes a judgment [*iudicium*] about the means he will use, he still has a choice to make. If the process of practical reasoning truly leads to choice [*electio*], at the threshold of choice, there must yet exist options among which the agent chooses.[47] The scholastic ordered pairings *consilium-consensus/iudicium-electio* suggests that the job of the *voluntas* is to deliver propulsion (by *consensus* and *electio*) to what is decided only in the intellect *(consilium* and *iudicium)*. The genuinely Thomistic order, on the other hand—*consilium, iudicium, consensus, electio*—makes it apparent that the entire moral agent is present right at the very threshold of going into action. Intellect and *voluntas*, matter and form are never entirely independent of one another. Or, to employ the above simile, *electio* is a sort of intellectual steering into a particular *prosequendum*. "Choice is either desiderative thought or intellectual desire" [*EN* vi,2,1139b4–5]; it involves both intellect and *voluntas* since steering is choosing a road and there is no choosing that is not the choosing of a road.[48]

45. See Finnis (1992 <1991>), pp. 129ff.; also Westberg (1994b), pp. 119–35, 168; also McInerny (1998), pp. 88–91.
46. See ST I–II q.15 a.3 c; q.74 a.7 ad 1.
47. See *in Sent.* lb.2 d.24 q.1 a.2 c; ST I–II q.13 a.4 ad 3; q.15 a.3 ad 3; *De ver.* q.22 a.15 c l.59.
48. At ST I–II q.15 a.3 ad 3, Thomas writes as follows: "Choice [*electio*] includes something that consent [*consensus*] has not, namely, a certain relation to something to which something else is preferred: and therefore after consent there still remains a choice. For it may happen that by aid

One of the advantages of this approach is that it provides an account of choice even when the options are not what we might call "lively options." Essential for any valid system of ethics is the idea that what counts are those things that are "up to us"—the things that we *do* in the sense that we could have done otherwise.[49] By making such things basic, we account for the fact that ethics is necessarily about personal moral character, praise and blame, virtues, etc. This essential aspect of ethics finds exaggerated expression in ethical theories that place emphasis on the instances in which a person stands at the "Moment of Decision"—i.e., the moment when, for instance, the person hesitates before his options, thinks, then chooses to lie or not, to become a Mafia hitman or not, etc., etc. Certainly such Moments of Decision are character-determining in a strong sense, so that they might even serve as paradigm examples of free choice; but Thomas's scheme, according to which *every* human act remains undecided right up to the last moment, gives a better account of the blame we heap upon the Mafia hitman precisely *for* his umpteenth murder, even though it has not been preceded by a Moment of Decision.[50]

Provided a person is not out-of-control when he acts (due, for instance, to use of drugs or alcohol) and that he is not ignorant of any crucial circumstance of his own action (e.g., that the gun is loaded), if he commits a blam-

---

of counsel [*consilium*] several means have been found conducive to the end, and through each of these meeting with approval, consent has been given to each: but after approving of many, we have given our preference to one by choosing it. But if only one meets with approval, then consent and choice do not differ in reality, but only in our way of looking at them; so that we call it consent, according as we approve of doing that thing; but choice according as we prefer it to those that do not meet with our approval." Even if *consensus* does not present multiple options of the sort that belong to its domain, there is still a choice [*electio*] to be made, since the person can always choose not to effect the one option.

49. See *EN* iii,5,1113b6; also iii,1,1110a15–18, iii,5,1113b21–1114a7,1114a21–31.

50. I understand some of the things that Germain Grisez and Joseph Boyle have written as propounding a "Moment of Decision" approach to the analysis of actions. See Boyle, Grisez, and Tollefsen (1976), p. 164, and Boyle (1994). On Boyle (1994), see Flannery (1995c), pp. 498–500. In a version of the present argument that appeared in George (1998), the capital letters in 'Moment of Decision' were inadvertently eliminated during the editorial process. This unfortunately affected the sense of the argument, for I do not deny that, for instance, the Mafia hitman decides to do that which he does, and obviously such a decision occurs at a moment. I do deny, however, that this event has to be one in which "the person hesitates before his options, thinks, then chooses to lie or not, to become a Mafia hit-man or not, etc., etc."—i.e., that there is a grand "Moment of Decision." If one understands my 'Moment of Decision' as a (mere) moment of decision, the point made by Germain Grisez and Joseph Boyle later in the same volume (pp. 217–18) in response to my contribution appears more compelling than in fact it is.

able deed, he is to be blamed for *that act,* since anything one so does involves projecting (as a good thing) a stretch of road ahead and taking it. If the person is an habitual killer, for instance, so that he never thinks of *not* taking that road when the possibility presents itself, this does not lessen the blame attached to his latest murder. In fact, his not thinking of alternatives is reason for greater blame. Killing has become quite "natural" for him; it is part of his character. And, as we have seen, character is what ethics is all about.[51]

This all holds also on the positive side—i.e., with respect to the virtuous person. Even though the good man may be habituated to doing the right thing so that, for example, he never hesitates about whether or not to be faithful to his wife nor about whether to go about his daily work helping the poor, his individual actions are part of him—his character—and they are good. Even in such cases, there is still a choice—a choice to go ahead along the same path that looks so attractive. As Thomas says in *De ma.* q.6, even when face-to-face with perfect happiness in this life, a person *can* turn away from it.[52] He can do so insofar as he has the liberty of the exercise of his *voluntas.* Of course, such an act of turning away from the perfect good found in

51. See Thomas's *De ma.* q.3 a.13 ad 5, where he discusses the bearing of passion on culpability. He says that if the impulse to sin comes from without, it decreases culpability; if, however, it comes from within—that is, from *voluntas*—it increases culpability and, the more vehement *voluntas,* the greater the sin. Then Thomas says that habit makes the will to sin more vehement; thus, he who sins from habit, sins more gravely—and more vehemently! The murderer need not furrow his brow or slap his thigh with a determined exclamation, "I'll do it." Although such behavior might be good indication of a committed *voluntas,* better indication (as the *De ma.* passage would suggest) is the fact that the murderer *does not* give external expression to his consent but simply goes ahead and kills.

52. The philosophical problem regarding the freedom of the good man (also of angels) is treated fairly extensively also among the Aristotelian commentators (and others) before Thomas. See Alexander, *De fat.* 196.24–29; 200.2ff. (note especially 204.7–8 and 204.22); 205.20–21. See also {Alexander}, *Mant.* 174.27–35. See also Nemesius, *De nat.hom.* c.40, especially ll.48ff. [Burgundio of Pisa translation = Verbeke & Moncho (1975)] (cited as Gregory of Nyssa in Thomas's *De ver.* q.24 a.1 ad 16 l.457). See also Maximus Confessor, *Opus.th.polem.* 32AB, 48AB, 81CD, 137A (all having to do with whether Christ had free will). Sharples argues that Aristotle raised this question and answered it inadequately [Sharples (1983), pp. 6, 159, 163–64]. See also D. Frede (1970), p. 119.

In Aristotle, see *Top.* iv,5,126a34–126b1: "[E]ven God and the good man are capable of doing bad things, but that is not their character; for it is always in respect of their choice [κατὰ προαίρεσιν] that bad men are so called. Moreover, a capacity is always a desirable thing; for even the capacities for doing bad things are desirable, and that is why we say that even God and the good man possess them; for they are capable (we say) of doing evil." Thomas says of this passage, "[V]erbum Philosophi intelligendum est cum conditione, quia scilicet posset, si vellet" [*in Sent.* lb.3 d.12 q.2 a.1 ad 4]. With respect to this passage in Aristotle, Alexander says that, although they have the capacity, the good do not do evil things "because they do not choose" [τῷ μὴ προαιρεῖσθαι] to do them [*in Top.* 348.32].

virtue would have to be specified since, as we have seen especially in this chapter, there is no such thing as an unspecified choice.[53]

In short, the Moments of Decision approach puts undue emphasis on options as an element of free choice. It is true that free choice is and must be among options, but it is not the options *qua* options that makes free choice morally essential. Rather, the essential thing is that free choice is an opportunity to go toward or away from the good and thus to become either virtuous or not. One cannot go in the direction of the good if there are no options; but one's character is formed in the doing, not by virtue of having had—and mulled over—various options.

Approaches, such as the neo-scholastic approach discussed above, which locate the decisive ethical factor elsewhere than in the actualization of a *prosequendum* composed of practical form and matter, tend to present intention "as if it were a distinct content of consciousness," as John Finnis puts it.[54] They must do this since, if the decisive factor does not subsist in the matter of the act itself, other matter must be pressed into service in order to be able to talk about one's "intentions." This allows scope for claims along the following lines: "I performed the murder, that is true; but I regretted performing it. The act itself is a horrible one, but my intention was right." The intention, however, with which one does something is not located in the emotions that precede (or, obviously, follow) an act. One intends in and by means of *significations*—which are active, free positings of *prosequenda*. Emotions, by contrast, are passive things—things we suffer rather than do—and we may well intend something without feeling any emotion at all. Or, what comes to much the same thing, one may choose something without ever adverting to the fact that it is a choice. No trumpets sound, no cymbals clash. One simply moves ahead.

53. See chapter 5, section [4]; compare also the view of Lottin, chapter 5, note 20.
54. Finnis (1992 <1991>), p. 127; see also pp. 146–48.

CHAPTER 7

THE PRINCIPLE OF DOUBLE EFFECT
AND FIXED PATHS

AN IMPORTANT principle within the tradition of Thomistic ethical theory is the so-called principle of double effect (henceforward PDE),
according to which a person might knowingly bring about an effect
which would be immoral if brought about directly but which is permitted insofar as it is a side effect of an action that is moral. PDE is, however, a much
controverted principle, not only among moralists coming from other philosophical directions, but also among those belonging to the Thomistic tradition itself. In particular, there is disagreement, even among the latter scholars,
regarding what types of actions PDE allows and prohibits. The present chapter is an attempt to help remedy this situation by introducing—or, rather, as I
believe, by re-introducing—a factor essential for the effective use of the principle in the analysis of actions.

I begin (in section [1]) with an exegesis of the body of Thomas's *ST* II–II
q.64 a.7, which is the *locus classicus* for PDE. In section [2], I identify a number of cases left indeterminate by the standard understandings of PDE. In
section [3], I introduce the missing factor just spoken of, arguing that it plays
an important part in the ethical theories of both Plato and Aristotle. In sections [4] and [5], I show how this factor helps to resolve the indeterminacies
introduced in section [2]. In section [6], I defend the introduction of this
"new" element from the possible objection that it entails "legalism." In section [7], I discuss the relationship between PDE and the idea that goods are
to be pursued.

[1] *Summa theologiae* II–II q.64 a.7

PDE can be traced back to Thomas's *ST* II–II q.64 a.7, which asks, "Whether it is lawful to kill a man in self-defense."[1] I quote the body of the article in full, since I shall be discussing it in some detail.

[N]othing hinders one act from having two effects, only one of which is intended, while the other is beside the intention. Now moral acts take their species according to what is intended, and not according to what is beside the intention, since this is accidental as explained above.[2] Accordingly, the act of self-defense may have two effects: one is the saving of one's life, the other is the slaying of the aggressor. Therefore this act, since one's intention is to save one's own life, is not unlawful, seeing that it is natural to everything to keep itself in being, as far as possible. And yet, though proceeding from a good intention, an act may be rendered unlawful, if it be out of proportion to the end. Wherefore if a man, in self-defense, uses more than necessary violence, it will be unlawful: whereas if he repel force with moderation his defense will be lawful, because according to the jurists, "it is lawful to repel force by force, provided one does not exceed the limits of a blameless defense."[3] Nor is it necessary for salvation that a

1. See especially Mangan (1949). Also on PDE (and related topics), see Grisez (1970); Boyle (1977), (1978), (1991a), (1991b); Anscombe (1981 <1961>), (1982); Belmans (1982); Cavanaugh (1997); Daniel (1979); Finnis (1991a), (1992 <1991>), (1998), pp. 275–93; Flannery (1993b), (1995a), especially pp. 392–99; Foot (1978 <1967>); Hart (1968 <1967>); Lee (1996), chapter 4.

2. I.e., at *ST* II–II q.43 a.3; pertinent also is *ST* I–II q.72 a.1.

3. Friedberg (1881), cols. 800–801 [*Decretalium Gregorii IX* lb.5 tit.12 ("De homicidio voluntario vel casuali") cap.18 ("Significasti . . .")]. I quote this chapter (largely concerned with how a priest who kills in self-defense is to be treated) at some length, for it tells us much about how Thomas understands the case of legitimate personal self-defense. My own explanation of what Thomas means by legitimate self-defense is much dependent on it. "Nos in praemisso casu credimus distinguendum, utrum constare possit, quod praefatus sacerdos non inflixit percussionem letalem, de qua vidilicet, si aliorum non fuissent vulnera subsecuta, percussus minime interiisset, et si percussor voluntatem non habueret occidendi, neque ipsius studio, consilio vel mandato processerint alii contra illum. Et quidem, si hoc ita se habet, quod forsan ex eo posset ostendi, si certa apparuisset percussio ab eodem inflicta tam modica et tam levis, in ea parte corporis, in qua quis de levi percuti non solet ad mortem, ut peritorum iudicio medicorum talis percussio assereretur non fuisse letalis, quum de ceteris credendum sit ipsi sacerdoti, qui non accusatur vel denunciatur ab aliquo, sed per se ipsum, de sua salute sollicitus, consilium appetit salutare, post poenitentiam ad cautelam iniunctam in sacerdotali poterit officio ministrare, maxime religionis accedente favore, quum sit canonicus regularis, et sine omni scandolo possit sacerdotale officium celebrare. Quodsi discerni non possit, ex cuius ictu percussus interiit: in hoc dubio tanquam homicida debet haberi sacerdos, etsi forte homicida non sit, a sacerdotali officio abstinere debet, quum in hoc casu cessare sit tutius quam temere celebrare, pro eo, quod in altero nullum, in reliquo vero magnum periculum timeatur. [Utrum autem de illis sit simile sentiendum, quorum unus, sed quis omnino nescitur, homicidium perpetravit, si forsan ad recipiendos sacros ordines praesententur, utrum omnes sint pariter repellendi, quum discerni non possit, qui debeant culpabiles iudicari, diligens investigator advertat, quamvis hic casus sit ab illo valde diversus.] Si vero,

man omit the act of moderate self-defense in order to avoid killing the other man, since one is bound to take more care of one's own life than of another's.

But as it is unlawful to take a man's life, except for the public authority acting for the common good, as stated above,[4] it is not lawful for a man to intend killing a man in self-defense, except for such as have public authority, who while intending to kill a man in self-defense, refer this to the public good, as in the case of a soldier fighting against the foe, and in the minister of the judge struggling with robbers,[5] although even these sin if they be moved by private animosity.[6]

This passage raises a host of issues, both exegetical and philosophical, all of which, obviously, cannot be addressed here. There are, however, a couple of issues that need to be addressed here in order to lay the philosophical

---

quemadmodum perhibetur, sacerdos iste prius ab illo percussus sacrilego, mox eum cum ligone in capite repercussit, quamvis vim vi repellere omnes leges et omnia iura permittant; quia tamen id debet fieri cum moderamine inculpatae tutelae, non ad sumendum vindictam, sed ad iniuriam propulsandum: non videtur idem sacerdos a poena homicidii penitus excusari, tum ratione instrumenti, cum quo ipse percussit, quod, quum grave sit, non solet levem plagam inferre, tum ratione partis, in qua fuit ille percussus, in qua de modico ictu quis letaliter solet laedi, maxime quum secundum vulgare proverbium asseratur, quod, qui ferit primo, ferit tangendo, qui ferit secundo, ferit dolendo. Unde, pensatis omnibus, ei creditur expedire, ut cum humilitate abstineat a sacerdotali officio exsequendo." What is placed in square brackets, Thomas probably would not have read. (I owe this information to Clarence Gallagher.) This title also contains the famous canon "Si aliquis causa explendae libidinis vel odii meditatione homini aut mulieri aliquid feceret, vel ad potandum dederit, ut non possit generare, aut concipere, vel nasci soboles, ut homicida teneatur" [cap.5].

4. *ST* II–II q.64 a.3.

5. The list of characters comes from Augustine, *De lib.arb.* lb.1 cap.4 n.25: "Si homicidium est hominem occidere, potest accidere aliquando sine peccato. Nam et miles hostem et iudex vel minister eius nocentem, et cui forte invito atque imprudenti telum manu fugit, non mihi videntur peccare, cum hominem occidunt."

6. "Respondeo dicendum quod nihil prohibet unius actus esse duos effectus, quorum alter solum sit in intentione, alius vero sit praeter intentionem. Morales autem actus recipiunt speciem secundum id quod intenditur, non autem ab eo quod est praeter intentionem, cum sit per accidens, ut ex supradictis patet. Ex actu igitur alicuius seipsum defendentis duplex effectus sequi potest, unus quidem conservatio propriae vitae; alius autem occisio invadentis. Actus igitur huiusmodi ex hoc quod intenditur conservatio propriae vitae, non habet rationem illiciti, cum hoc sit cuilibet naturale quod se conservet in esse quantum potest. Potest tamen aliquis actus ex bona intentione proveniens illicitus reddi si non sit proportionatus fini. Et ideo si aliquis ad defendendum propriam vitam utatur maiori violentia quam oporteat, erit illicitum. Si vero moderate quam oporteat, erit illicitum. Si vero moderate violentiam repellat, erit licita defensio, nam secundum iura, vim vi repellere licet cum moderamine inculpatae tutelae. Nec est necessarium ad salutem ut homo actum moderatae tutelae praetermittat ad evitandum occisionem alterius, quia plus tenetur homo vitae suae providere quam vitae alienae. Sed quia occidere hominem non licet nisi publica auctoritate propter bonum commune, ut ex supradictis patet; illicitum est quod homo intendat occidere hominem ut seipsum defendat, nisi ei qui habet publicam auctoritatem, qui, intendens hominem occidere ad sui defensionem, refert hoc ad publicum bonum, ut patet in milite pugnante contra hostes, et in ministro iudicis pugnante contra latrones. Quamvis et isti etiam peccent si privata libidine moveantur."

foundations for what follows. The first is whether, in saying that an act of killing in personal self-defense is permitted if and only if the killing is not intended, Thomas would allow as non-intended more than just those killings that happen, as Italian expresses it so well, *all'improvviso*—i.e., those that are required "of a sudden," where the person has time to think of just one thing, the preservation of his life.

Most pertinent in this regard is Thomas's remark that a person is not obliged to "omit the act of moderate self-defense in order to avoid killing the other man." This remark would be unnecessary unless it meant that, even knowing that an act will quite likely kill, one might perform it without that knowledge or thought bringing the death of the assailant within one's intention. But if this is the case, one can actually be thinking that a particular act will kill and yet perform it morally. Thus, Thomas would allow a case in which, for instance, a man deliberately loads a weapon, takes aim and shoots, knowing full well that his action will most likely kill his opponent, provided he believes that this action, performed in the way he is performing it, is the only way he can preserve his own life.[7] What counts, however, in determining intention is not so much the thoughts that go through the agent's mind regarding the possibility of killing ("what he had time to *think* of") but rather the whole analysis of the situation within which he acts, as we shall see more clearly in a moment. An action need not be so much *all'improvviso* that knowledge and even deliberation and setting of oneself are excluded.

That said, however, there is a sense in which the death of possible assailants cannot be premeditated. One finds this latter point in Thomas's stipulation that the man not use "more than necessary violence" or that the means adopted not be "out of proportion to the end." If a person who might keep a weapon sufficient to incapacitate but not certain to kill purchases instead a large-caliber gun and loads it with "dumdum bullets" (such as tear up a large radius of flesh upon leaving a body), this is enough to determine in almost all cases that the second effect is not "beside his intention"—or *praeter intentionem* (I shall use the Latin expression). If a man keeps such a disproportionately damaging weapon for self-defense, knowing its character and knowing too that other means are available, and does nothing further about this, then when he kills he kills with the intention to kill, no matter what sto-

7. Cp. Anscombe (1981 <1961>), p. 54.

ry he might tell himself about performing *simply* an act of self-defense. Elsewhere Thomas defines intention in terms of its etymology: "Intention, as the very word denotes, signifies 'to tend toward something.'"[8] The agent imagined is clearly "tending toward" killing rather than, or perhaps in addition to, the preservation of life. The secondary effect of the death of the intruder cannot be considered *praeter intentionem.*

If, however, on Saturday evening the man comes to see the wrongness of his having selected that means of defense and on Sunday (i.e., before he has a chance to get a new weapon) he is attacked, he might kill the attacker with the lethal weapon without that being within his intention, since he is using the only means available to him and one is not obliged to omit an act of "moderate self-defense in order to avoid killing the other man." Here the act of "moderate self-defense" would be the use of the minimally damaging but effective means available. Although the means used are identical to those in the previous case, the man is not "tending toward" the death of his assailant but rather, and only, toward the preservation of life.

Suppose that a man, well used to firearms, keeps what would normally be called a moderate means of self-defense at his bedside—e.g., a pistol that could be used merely to incapacitate an intruder—but intends to shoot lethally whoever might break into the house. Knowing, as he does, that in many circumstances he could merely shoot to wound, his setting himself in this way would be immoral. If, on the other hand, a man believes that almost all circumstances where he might need to defend his life would exclude the possibility of taking aim less than lethally and for this reason is quite sure that in the pertinent situation he would have to shoot lethally, he might set himself to do something that the former man cannot: to shoot in a way that he knows will kill, just in order to preserve his life, the second effect being *praeter intentionem.* In order for this to be so, obviously he would have to truly believe that no other means (for instance, the purchase of a stun gun or a lower-caliber weapon) would preserve his life. It is presumed too that, if he has the opportunity just to wound and still save his life, he would take that opportunity.

That Thomas holds this general position is evident from what he says in *ST* II–II q.64 a.7 about acts of killing performed by public officials. Such acts

---

8. *ST* I–II q.12 a.1: "intentio, sicut ipsum nomen sonat, significat in aliquid tendere."

are acts of self-defense, he says, and they are intended: "[I]t is not lawful for a man to intend killing a man in self-defense, except for such as have public authority, who while intending to kill a man in self-defense, refer this to the public good." Note that the immoral (i.e., the intending) self-defender is said here to do that which the public authority does, although the latter does it morally. The public official, precisely because he wants to kill, prepares means that he knows will kill. That is his job: to make sure that the malefactor is dead. If he, let us say, in order to save money, reduces the strength of a dose of poison and the malefactor does not die, he has not done his job. The immoral self-defender must do something similar—i.e., he must in some way be preferring lethal means—for Thomas associates him with the public defender. So, it is the preference for what is least likely to kill (and yet be effective) that makes it moral for the private person to kill in self-defense.

One final remark, before moving on, about Thomas's position that the public official intends to kill and yet does so morally. It appears to conflict with the approach, maintained in a number of places in the present work, according to which attacks on the basic human goods are immoral because the basic goods are at the basis of the principles of practical reason (and, therefore, of the ethical life). One way of getting past this problem would exploit Thomas's remark that the public authority intends to kill but refers this to the public good. Here, it might be argued, the intention to kill has been re-routed into the other intention (promoting the public good) in such a way that it is no longer really an intention to kill. But one might have doubts about this solution, for Thomas says quite explicitly that the public official does intend to kill. We shall return to this problem below (i.e., in section [7]), once we have a few more ideas on the table.

[2] Indeterminacies

What Thomas says in *ST* II–II q.64 a.7 is fairly apparent. How it is to be applied, however, is considerably less so, as is evident, for example, in the fate of the famous fat potholer of modern analytic philosophical literature. The case is set out by Philippa Foot in the following manner.

A party of potholers have imprudently allowed [a] fat man to lead them as they make their way out of the cave, and he gets stuck, trapping the others behind him. Obviously, the right thing to do is to sit down and wait until the fat man grows thin; but philosophers have arranged that flood waters should be rising within the cave.

Luckily (luckily?) the trapped party have with them a stick of dynamite with which they can blast the fat man out of the mouth of the cave. Either they use the dynamite or they drown.[9]

Foot uses this example, she says, as "light relief" but also in order to show "how ridiculous one version of the doctrine of double effect would be."

For suppose that the trapped explorers were to argue that the death of the fat man might be taken as a merely foreseen consequence of the act of blowing him up. ('We didn't want to kill him . . . only to blow him into small pieces' or even '. . . only to blast him out of the cave.') I believe that those who use the doctrine of double effect would rightly reject such a suggestion, though they will, of course, have considerable difficulty in explaining where the line is to be drawn. What is the criterion of 'closeness' if we say that anything very close to what we are literally aiming at counts as if part of our aim?[10]

Foot obviously believes that defenders of PDE will be especially inclined to say that blowing the fat potholer out of the way would be direct killing.[11] It is an indication of the indeterminacy of PDE, at least as formulated in the modern literature, that in fact a number of defenders of the principle think that doing this would not be direct killing. Joseph Boyle, for example, writes as follows. "Foot's colorful description of the explorers' deliberation notwithstanding, the double effect theorist can admit that the killing of the hapless fat man is not direct; his *death* is not what opens the cave but rather his being removed from the entrance."[12]

Another example of PDE's indeterminacy involves what I shall refer to as the craniotomy and hysterectomy cases. Roman Catholic ethicians employing PDE at the end of the last century held that it is immoral for a surgeon to crush the cranium of a fetus, even if doing so would save the life of its mother by, for instance, allowing the fetus to pass through the pelvic cavity, since such an act would be a direct attack on the fetus's life.[13] In the case, however,

---

9. Foot (1978 <1967>), p. 21.

10. Foot (1978 <1967>), pp. 21–22.

11. See also Anscombe (1982), p. 21: "The example of the stuck pot-holer was invented (without the choice of ways of escape) to illustrate the iniquity of abortion: you wouldn't say you could kill the pot-holer to get out—it was argued. But people did say just that—at least if the posture of the pot-holer was so described that he was going to get drowned too!" Anscombe also assumes that PDE dictates that the people behind "must *not,* not on any account, blow up the pot-holer" [Anscombe (1982), p. 22; her emphasis].

12. Boyle (1977), p. 307 [emphasis Boyle's]. Boyle believes, however, that the killing might be disallowed on grounds other than its being a direct killing.

13. See Connery (1977), pp. 225–303. On May 31, 1884, after more than a decade of controversy,

of a pregnant woman who is suffering from cancer of the uterus that, even if she were not pregnant, would require immediate surgical removal (i.e., an hysterectomy), this latter operation would be permitted, since the death of the fetus would be an unwanted side effect of an action whose intention is the saving of the mother's life. In other words, the hysterectomy would be allowed but the craniotomy would not since the latter does not fall under PDE. As with the fat potholer, the claim is often made that in the craniotomy case the death of the fetus is simply "too close" to what one is doing (i.e., crushing the cranium) to be considered *praeter intentionem*. In a somewhat similar manner, it is sometimes claimed that the hysterectomy involves a single action from which the good effect follows immediately, whereas the craniotomy is concerned with an intermediate step, i.e., the dismantling of the cranium, and is therefore immoral.[14]

Again, however, Boyle is one of a number of scholars who, on the basis of PDE, say that the craniotomy might be allowed. His argument is conducted to some extent in response to H. L. A. Hart's rejection of the idea that there is a morally significant distinction between the craniotomy and hysterectomy cases. Writes Hart,

If the craniotomy is contrasted with the removal [hysterectomy] of the womb containing the foetus as a case of "direct" killing, it must be on the basis that the death of the foetus is not merely contingently connected with the craniotomy as it is with the removal of the womb containing it. But it is not clear that the supposition of the survival of the foetus makes better sense in the one case than the other.[15]

---

the Holy See issued a decision on the question of craniotomy. A question had been posed to the Holy Office by D. Caverot, Cardinal Archbishop of Lyons. It read as follows: "May it safely be taught in Catholic schools that the surgical procedure known as 'craniotomy' is permissible when clearly, if the procedure is omitted, both mother and fetus will perish but, if it is allowed, the child perishing, the mother's life would be saved?" The response was: "This cannot safely be taught" ("Tuto doceri non posse") [*Acta Sanctae Sedis* 17 (1884), p. 556]. See Flannery (1993b), pp. 508–10.

14. J. P. Gury [Gury (1890), vol. 1, p. 98] formulates PDE in this fashion: "It is licit to posit a cause that is either good or indifferent and from which follows immediately a twofold effect, one good and one evil, provided that there is present a proportionately grave reason [*causa proportionate gravis*] and that the end of the agent is good [*honestus*]—that is to say, if he does not intend the evil effect." Gury also formulates conditions for restricting employment of the principle: (1) the agent's end must be good [*honestus*]; (2) the cause to be posited must be good [*bona*]—or, at least, indifferent; (3) the good effect must be immediate; (4) there must be present a grave reason for positing the good cause and the agent not be bound either by justice or office or charity to omit the act. Condition (3) might be interpreted as requiring a single action. See also Grisez (1970), pp. 87–90; Boyle (1977), p. 307; cp. Bennett (1995), pp. 196–200.

15. Hart (1968 <1967>), p. 123–24.

Boyle makes some minor criticisms of the last sentence ("In late pregnancies fetuses have survived hysterectomies"), but in general he agrees with Hart. He writes: "It seems to be *logically* possible that the craniotomy be performed and the fetus not be killed."[16] And a bit later: "Thus, in the case under consideration the craniotomy is not essentially destructive; it is essentially an act of changing the shape of the fetus' dimensions."[17]

It is not entirely without reason that Boyle (and others) feel that they are justified in regarding both the killing of the potholer and that of the fetus in the craniotomy as indirect. To return to Thomas's remarks, how does the *ST* II–II q.64 a.7 act of personal self-defense differ from using dynamite on the potholer? A person might argue that the potholer is innocent of any wrongdoing whereas an attacker is not; but it could be that the attacker is out of his mind or is a public official acting in good faith, believing that you are an enemy of the state. Thomas does not insist that you ascertain true culpability before using force; in fact, the scenario he has in mind seems to exclude such verification since, if you had time to perform it, you would probably not need to employ lethal force in order to preserve your life. And, in any case, he gives no indication that the philosophical basis of his position has to do with the moral status of the attacker; all indications are that it has to do rather with the obligation to "take more care of one's own life than of another's."

What of the traditional condition that the considered act not be a separate step on the way to the desired effect? Well, it is not so clear that blowing up the fat potholer is—or need be—a separate step. He is done away with as if he were any other obstacle, such as a large rock. Once the obstacle is cleared away, that is achieved which was desired: a clear passage. But even supposing that the potholer must be cleared away first so that then a passage might be cleared, what is so important about the number of steps involved? When Thomas says that an act of personal self-defense might be justified, he does not, as we have seen, require that it be so *all'improvviso* that the act of personal self-defense would be a sort of surprised grasping at self-preservation which happens to be accompanied by a death. The attacked person might have to load a pistol, steady his shaking hand, take aim, and fire. Only after having performed that act, does he walk away free. This would seem also to

16. Boyle (1977), p. 308 (emphasis Boyle's).
17. Boyle (1977), pp. 310.

render useless the argument that the craniotomy or the use of dynamite on the potholer are immoral because they are "just too close in" to be considered not what the agent is doing. What could be "closer in" than aiming and firing? And, as Boyle argues with respect to the craniotomy, if a defender of PDE tries to argue that the use of dynamite on the potholer is conceptually too closely connected to his death, we can certainly imagine a possible world in which the bits of his body might be put back together and he might live happily ever after.

One might also bring into the argument Thomas's position on communal self-defense. There it makes no difference that the act is intentional and direct. How could that then be the determinative moral factor? An objector, again, might argue that the public official is permitted to kill only non-innocents; but Thomas also mentions in *ST* II–II q.64 a.7 "the case of a soldier fighting against the foe"—which foe may be innocent of any wrongdoing and be simply doing what soldiers do, arguably not unlike the fetus who is simply doing what fetuses do. And if a soldier can kill those who threaten the state, why not also depute surgeons as functionaries of the state with similar protective duties, so that they might bear the same mantle of legitimacy when they directly bring about a death in order to save the life of a citizen? The objector might argue that such actions are simply individual lethal encounters in the just war against ill health.

Obviously, some of these points are stronger than others, and it would be possible to continue to argue about any of them, as the sizable modern literature on PDE shows. I believe, however, that such debates are inherently interminable, given what are regarded as the basic factors involved in analysis in terms of PDE. I would like, therefore, as I have said, to introduce a new factor into the debate: the idea that at the base of ethics are not so much goods simply considered, nor even goods as desired by human beings, but rather goods as ends of human practices. By practices I mean fixed and recognizable patterns (or types) of behavior such as one looks about in the world and sees people doing. One looks about and sees, for instance, a teacher teaching philosophy, a doctor performing an hysterectomy, a soldier defending his country. I shall be more specific about practices, as I continue.[18]

---

18. See note 44, in chapter 1 above. For my understanding of practices, I am much indebted to MacIntyre (1981) (especially pp. 175–89), although my understanding of them is somewhat different from his. See also MacIntyre (1990b), pp. 60–68.

[3] Goods in ancient practices

In order to make plausible the idea that practices are an essential factor in the understanding of PDE, it will help to show that they play a very important role in ancient ethical theories, and particularly in the theories of Plato and Aristotle.

Very often in Plato's dialogues the phrase "practicing one's own business"—meaning to do those things proper to one's calling—plays a decisive role.[19] A good example occurs in *Charmides,* where the youthful character after whom the dialogue is named suggests that *sōphrosunē* (which denotes in this dialogue the virtue resulting in morally correct behavior) might be "doing everything in an orderly and quiet manner" [*Chrm.* 159b2–3] and then that it might be "modesty" [*Chrm.* 160e4–5]. Socrates has little trouble knocking down these definitions ("Which is most honorable when at the schoolmaster's, to write the same sort of letters quickly or slowly?" [*Chrm.* 159c3–4]), so Charmides offers another: "I remembered just now what I once heard someone say, that goodness [*sōphrosunē*] might be practicing one's own business" [*Chrm.* 161b5–6]. Socrates has some fun also with this definition, which Charmides has apparently learned from Critias, for he asks whether the schoolmaster teaches only when writing or reading his own name.[20] But it is clear that this time his jesting has a point. His intention is not to reject the idea that goodness might consist in practicing one's own business but to become clearer about what the end of such a practice might be.[21] As always, he is circling around, attempting to lay hold of the definition of the Good, the ultimate object of all human pursuit. The phrase 'practicing one's own business' is in fact a traditional one, and Plato has the greatest respect for it. In the *Timaeus,* for example, having said some positive things about mysticism, he says that mystics are not the best judges of what they themselves have experienced: "[I]t was well said of old that practicing and knowing one's own busi-

19. τὸ τὰ ἑαυτοῦ πράττειν. The translation is an ugly one; my excuse is that I am interested in establishing a connection with the English word 'practice.'

20. *Chrm.* 161d6–9. Diels and Kranz (1951) say the phrase appeared in Critias's *Conversations* (see Diels and Kranz 88 B 41a). A contemporary of Socrates and a character in *Charmides,* Critias was a politician and associate of the Sophists.

21. In *Chrm.* 162a10–b11 Socrates leaves open the possibility that the "selfish" understanding of τὸ τὰ ἑαυτοῦ πράττειν is not the only one, for he suggests that the problem is that Critias does not understand his own definition—not that it is wrong.

ness and oneself is fitting to the wise man alone."[22] Here, knowing one's own business is linked to one of the most august sayings of ancient Greece, "Know thyself."

That Plato thought 'practicing one's own business' pertinent in understanding moral issues is also apparent in the first book of the *Republic*, in an exchange that introduces a number of other ideas that will be useful in coming to understand the structure and character of the basic elements of Thomas's moral universe. The exchange is between Socrates and the violent Thrasymachus, who argues that justice simply means "the advantage of the stronger" [*R.* i,338c1–2] and that obedience to these leaders is just [*R.* i,339b7–8]. Socrates gets Thrasymachus to admit that rulers, even according to his own definition of the just, sometimes enact unjust laws (i.e., laws that are not to their own best advantage) [*R.* 339b7–c12]. Socrates is not here simply setting Thrasymachus up: the idea that unjust laws are those that do not correspond to the Good is an important one in his overall theory. In any case, Thrasymachus's admission leads him into contradiction, since it means that obeying the leaders might in fact not be just, for justice is, by the definition stipulated, to the leaders' advantage.

Thrasymachus is, therefore, forced to state a doctrine that Socrates eventually also makes his own.[23]

Why, to take the nearest example, do you call one who is mistaken about the sick a physician in respect of his mistake or one who goes wrong in a calculation a calculator when he goes wrong and in respect of this error? Yet that is what we say literally—we say that the physician erred and the calculator and the schoolmaster. But the truth, I take it, is, that each of these insofar as he is that which we entitle him never errs; so that, speaking precisely, since you are such a stickler for precision, no craftsman errs. For it is when his knowledge abandons him that he who goes wrong goes wrong— when he is not a craftsman. So that no craftsman, wise man, or ruler makes a mistake then when he is ruler, though everybody would use the expression that the physician made a mistake and the ruler erred. [*R.* i,340d1–e6]

---

22. *Ti.* 72a4–6: ἀλλ᾿ εὖ καὶ πάλαι λέγεται τὸ πράττειν καὶ γνῶναι τά τε αὑτοῦ καὶ ἑαυτὸν σώφρονι μόνῳ προσήκειν. See also *R.* iv,433a8–b1: Καὶ μὴν ὅτι γε τὸ τὰ αὑτοῦ πράττειν καὶ μὴ πολυπραγμονεῖν δικαιοσύνη ἐστί, καὶ τοῦτο ἄλλων τε πολλῶν ἀκηκόαμεν καὶ αὐτοὶ πολλάκις εἰρήκαμεν.

23. See *R.* i,341c4–342e11.

Presupposed by this discourse is a conception of how society—and, in fact, morality itself—is structured. There are things that people do right, and doing right means practicing a business. If one is not doing right, in a sense one is not doing anything at all. One is doing something that merely appears to be intelligible, i.e., that merely appears to be a practice defined by a particular end—the overall result being that, e.g., what appears to be a doctor is often not a doctor at all, just as what appears to be a calculation, is not a calculation at all. Such a practice, lacking as it does intelligibility, is a sort of monster or freak of nature: a non-being, if one considers being to consist in participation in the Ideas of Good or Justice or Truth.[24]

We can see emerging, even in this overture to the *Republic* which is book 1, the conception (which appears more explicitly later) of an Ideal City in which each goes about his own business—and goes about it, obviously, in the correct manner.[25] By way of contrast, one thinks of Socrates's constantly recurring criticism of the Sophists, that they appear to be practicing philosophy but are not really doing so since they do not know what the Good is.[26] Or one thinks of the dismissive treatment in *Laches* of "fighting in armor," the staging of mock battles for show, looked askance upon by the true soldiers of Sparta.[27] It would seem that, according to Plato, there are practices and there are practices—i.e., some are truly practices and some not, depending upon

24. *Sph.* 254a4–b1 (and *Sph.* generally); see also Flannery (1996), pp. 721–22. See also *ST* I–II q.18 a.1: "Sic igitur dicendum est quod omnis actio, inquantum habet aliquid de esse, intantum habet de bonitate: inquantum vero deficit ei aliquid de plenitudine essendi quae debetur actioni humanae, intantum deficit a bonitate, et sic dicitur mala, puta si deficiat ei vel determinata quantitas secundum rationem, vel debitus locus, vel aliquid huiusmodi"; see q.18 a.2. See also q.7 a.2 obj.2: "ut dicitur in VI Metaph., nulla ars vel scientia est circa ens per accidens, nisi sola sophistica." Thomas's reference is to Aristotle's *Metaph.* vi,2,1026b14–15: διὸ Πλάτων τρόπον τινὰ οὐ κακῶς τὴν σοφιστικὴν περὶ τὸ μὴ ὂν ἔταξεν. Aristotle, in turn, is citing Plato's *Sophist*; the Jaeger (Oxford Classical Texts) edition suggests *Sph.* 237ff. See also *ST* I–II q.18 a.3 obj.2; also *in Metaph.* §1177.

25. See, for instance, *R.* ii,370a4; iii,400e5–6; iv,433b3–5; 443c4–7, etc.

26. See, for instance, *Prt.* 311a8ff. (and, in fact, the whole dialogue). See also *Grg.* 519c3–d7; *Sph.* 233c10–11,254a4–b1; and *Lg.* xi,937e3ff. (at 938a3–4 Plato suggests that what the Sophists do is not really a craft but a knack; cf.*Grg.* 462d5–466a3). See also Aristotle's *Metaph.* iv,2,1004b25–26. See also Irwin (1977), pp. 180–81. Irwin is much concerned throughout this book with what he calls the "craft analogy." See also his newer version of the same (or, at least, similar) arguments: Irwin (1995), especially pp. 65–77.

27. See *La.* 182d6–184c8 (cp. *Lg.* viii,830a3ff.), *La.* 186b8–c5. See also *La.* 185b9ff., where Socrates contrasts fighting in armor [μάχεσθαι ἐν ὅπλοις] with medicine and bridle-making, the difference being that the latter two aim at concrete goods external to themselves, fighting in armor at display of itself.

whether they bring us toward the Good. That 'practicing one's own business' may even have played a role in Plato's time in the analysis of actions is suggested in *Euthydemus* by the confused eristic argument of the character Dionysodorus, who proposes that, since a caterer is in the business of cutting up flesh, if someone flays the caterer, he will being doing nothing immoral [*Euthd.* 301d2–6].

The idea of 'practicing one's own business' also comes into Aristotle but in a more global way. Like Plato, he assumes that human goods always come as part of a package (i.e., a practice), there being no such thing as a good that is not so embodied; but he expands this notion to encompass change in general. A good example of this occurs in *EN* vii, where he considers a list of arguments to the effect that pleasure is not good, among which is the evidently Platonic argument that "there is no craft [*technē*] of pleasure, but every good is the product of some craft."[28] His response is: "The fact that no pleasure is the product of any craft arises naturally enough; there is no craft of any other activity either, but only of the capacity; though for that matter the crafts of the perfumer and the cook *are* thought to be crafts of pleasure."[29]

This remark is interesting because it shows that Aristotle has at least some inclination to assign intelligibility even to actions that Plato dismisses as dealing in non-being or mere opinion, thereby suggesting that every act of man has intelligibility although not necessarily an intelligibility of the highest order. But it also shows that Aristotle accepts the idea that a good sought needs to be attached to an intelligible structure that precedes it (at least logically). He says that there is no craft precisely *of* pleasure since crafts are not about the activities they lead to but about that which leads to the activities; but this leaves the general approach of the objection not only standing but confirmed.[30] Aristotle also places this approach within a more general setting. Crafts, he says, have to do not with activities but with capacities. The struc-

---

28. *EN* vii,11,1152b18–19. Gauthier and Jolif connect this with *Grg.* 462a–465e [Gauthier and Jolif (1958–1959), vol. 2, p. 790].

29. *EN* vii,12,1153a23–27 [emphasis in ROT]: τὸ δὲ τέχνης μὴ εἶναι ἔργον ἡδονὴν μηδεμίαν εὐλόγως συμβέβηκεν· οὐδὲ γὰρ ἄλλης ἐνεργείας οὐδεμιᾶς τέχνη ἐστίν, ἀλλὰ τῆς δυνάμεως· καίτοι καὶ ἡ μυρεψικὴ τέχνη καὶ ἡ ὀψοποιητικὴ δοκεῖ ἡδονῆς εἶναι. See also Thomas, *in EN* lb.7 lect.12 ll.182–93 (§1496), where he explains that what a cook produces is not the *delectatio* but the *delectabilia*.

30. Gauthier and Jolif write: "L'art du sculpteur fait qu'il est *capable* de sculpter une belle statue, ce qui n'est qu'une puissance et n'entraîne aucun plaisir; il ne fait pas que le sculpteur sculpte

ture that he tacitly acknowledges in his response to Plato is, therefore, not specific to crafts or even to human action in general but is bound up with his metaphysical understanding of change as such: i.e., with his theory of act and potency.

This is confirmed by turning to what Aristotle says in the *Physics*. As has been noted often, his conception of physical change is modelled on his understanding of a craft, rather than vice-versa. In *Phys.* ii,8, having first argued that the phenomena of nature cannot be explained as due to mere chance, he writes:

> Further, where there is an end, all the preceding steps are for the sake of that. Now surely as in action, so in nature; and as in nature, so it is in each action, if nothing interferes. Now action is for the sake of an end; therefore the nature of things also is so. Thus if a house, e.g., had been a thing made by nature, it would have been made in the same way as it is now by a craft; and if things made by nature were made not only by nature but also by a craft, they would come to be in the same way as by nature. The one, then, is for the sake of the other; and generally craft in some cases completes what nature cannot bring to a finish, and in others imitates nature. If, therefore, artificial products are for the sake of an end, so clearly also are natural products. The relation of the later to the earlier items is the same in both.[31]

The point of the last sentence, and indeed of this entire passage, is that natural motion, like human-initiated action when it is not just random, has an intelligible structure: it goes toward an end that matches the capacity whence it originates.[32]

---

effectivement une belle statue, ce qui est une activité, et un plaisir: ce passage de la puissance à l'acte relève de la sagesse pratique, qui dit qu'en telles circonstances l'exercice de l'art contribue au bonheur . . ." [Gauthier and Jolif (1958), vol. 2, p. 799].

Elsewhere (i.e., *Metaph.* vi,2,1026b6–10) Aristotle provides an example. One who produces a house does not produce those things that happen to come with the house, e.g., whether it brings pleasure or not. See Charles (1984), p. 47: "[I]f the house is a source of joy to Z, 'a source of joy to Z being built' describes the effect accidentally, because when described thus (and not as 'this house being built') the effect is not appropriately related to the cause: the builder's building." See also *Phys.* ii,3,195b21–25; also *Pol.* vii,8,1328a32–33: "[T]he house and the builder have nothing in common, but the art of the builder is for the sake of the house."

31. *Phys.* ii,8,199a8–20: the Greek of the sentence translated, "Now surely as in action, so in nature; and as in nature, so it is in each action, if nothing interferes" (ROT) is: οὐκοῦν ὡς πράττεται, οὕτω πέφυκε, καὶ ὡς πέφυκεν, οὕτω πράττεται ἕκαστον, ἂν μή τι ἐμποδίζῃ [199a9–11].

32. As Aristotle says, somewhat paradoxically, "motion is in the movable" [ἡ κίνησις ἐν τῷ κινητῷ] [*Phys.* iii,3,202a13–14]. He goes on to explain: "It is the fulfillment of this potentiality by the action of that which has the power of causing motion; and the actuality of that which has the power of causing motion is not other than the actuality of the movable; for it must be the

In modern times the standard objection to this approach has been that, in effect, it reads psychological concepts such as choice, intention, and purpose into natural events. But at least some recent scholarship has argued that this is not a telling objection, for Aristotle's conception of a craft excludes the psychological. A craft *qua* craft has to do not so much with what a craftsman wants or chooses but with the intelligible structure of which his action and its product give indication. One of the key texts in this interpretation comes shortly after the one just quoted. Again Aristotle makes the point that natural events do not come about by chance but have a purpose. And then he says, "It is absurd to suppose that purpose is not present because we do not observe the agent deliberating. Neither does craft deliberate."[33]

Sarah Broadie has an austere reading of Aristotle's doctrine in this regard, based not only on this latter passage (and especially the last sentence) but also on his understanding of what it means to act *qua* a certain function or role. Unlike ordinary human purpose, a craft is not essentially "animated by desire or reasoned concern for the end," she says. "The builder as such cannot want to build houses in any sense in which wanting to build houses could explain building by *the builder*."[34] A less austere approach is taken by Stephen Brock, according to whom the intending—or "tending toward"—that we find in Aristotle's physics might be analogically related to the intending in human action, thereby leaving open the possibility that, e.g., crafts are essentially within the realm of the voluntary, without it ceasing to be the case that they contain fixed patterns of behavior existing quite independently of what the craftsman wants or chooses or intends *qua* anything else than *qua* that type of craftsman.[35]

As we shall see below, whichever of these two readings is correct, Aristo-

fulfillment of *both*" [202a14–16; emphasis in ROT]. See also *Phys.* iii,2,202a7–12; also very pertinent are Aristotle's remarks in *Phys.* v,4 about the unity of motion (he speaks in this context of motions that are essentially [τῇ οὐσίᾳ—227b21] one). See Steven Brock's very acute treatment of Aristotle's doctrine of physical motion as it applies to human action: Brock (1998), *passim*, but especially pp. 53–61. See also Brock (1991), *passim*. See also Dewan (1985), *passim*, but especially p. 64: "It is only insofar as one grasps a thing *as source of form for another thing* that one grasps it *as efficient cause*. And this is actually to see *the depending of the thing on its form* 'stretched out,' as it were, beyond the confines of the thing to another thing" [emphasis his].

33. *Phys.* ii,8,199b26–28: ἄτοπον δὲ τὸ μὴ οἴεσθαι ἕνεκά του γίγνεσθαι, ἐὰν μὴ ἴδωσι τὸ κινοῦν βουλευσάμενον. καίτοι καὶ ἡ τέχνη οὐ βουλεύεται. . . .

34. Broadie (1990), p. 397 (emphasis hers); see also Cooper (1982).

35. Brock (1998), chapter 1. Regarding *Phys.* ii,8,199b26–28, Thomas writes: "[M]anifestum est quod ars non deliberat. Nec artifex deliberat inquantum habet artem, sed inquantum deficit a

tle's non-deliberative understanding of crafts is useful in resolving the type of problems that plague the interpretation of PDE, for it establishes within the realm of human mores itself precisely what is needed in order to overcome the indeterminacies noted above: a relatively stabile element, an element not immediately dependent upon decision. For the moment, however, we note simply that in Aristotle, as well as in Plato, fixed paths or practices are basic. For Aristotle this idea extends well beyond the ethical to the most general characterization of reality itself; but, clearly, he does not reject the idea that craft-like structures play their part in the makeup of human society as well.

[4] Resolving indeterminacies: hysterectomy and craniotomy

How, then, does the idea of practices bring us closer to a resolution of the indeterminacies set out in section [2]? Let us consider first the hysterectomy and craniotomy cases. The interminability of arguments about, for instance, what is unacceptably "close in" to what an agent is doing should be enough to convince us that such is not the route to determinate answers. If one philosopher might argue that the death of the fetus in the hysterectomy case is sufficiently "distant" from what the medical doctor is doing to be moral, since an hysterectomy is a morally neutral act that merely results in—but is not constituted by—the death of the fetus, another philosopher might put a similar construction upon the craniotomy case. To quote Boyle, the craniotomy might be merely "an act of changing the shape of the fetus's dimensions." Similar difficulties arise, as we have seen, with other attempts to account for the difference between the two procedures. But a morally significant distinction between the two can be drawn if we first identify medicine as a discipline that excludes the craniotomy procedure but includes the hysterectomy procedure, and then say that the true procedures (or practices) of medicine are by nature just and moral. Thus, a craniotomy cannot be justified by arguing that it is a medical procedure, but an hysterectomy can be.

The question immediately arises, of course, whether a correct characterization of medicine would exclude the craniotomy procedure. I have already mentioned the idea, found in both Plato and Aristotle, that a craftsman func-

certitudine artis: unde artes certissimae non deliberant, sicut scriptor non deliberat quomodo debeat formare litteras. Et illi etiam artifices qui deliberant, postquam invenerunt certum principium artis, in exequendo non deliberant: unde citharaedus, si in tangendo quamlibet chordam deliberaret, imperitissimus videretur" [in Phys. lb.2 lect.14 n.8 (§268)].

tions *qua* the type of craftsman he is only insofar as he aims at the good that defines his craft. The good that defines the craft (or profession) of medicine is the health of the patient. But who is the patient? Aristotle provides an answer to this question, an answer much tied up with the parallel between physical motion and the structure of crafts.[36] A motion originates in a mover and is completed in the thing moved, whose action complements the mover's action. For a pool cue to have the capacity to put the cue ball into motion is for the cue ball to have the corresponding capacity to be put into motion; and for the action to occur is for these matching capacities to be put in act with respect to one another. There may be further motions in other balls after the striking of the cue ball, but these actions too correspond in intelligibility to the actions to which they respond. There is no jumping over steps in the causal chain.[37] Applying these ideas within the realm of crafts and other such disciplines, we can say that the object is that which immediately corresponds to the action of the agent understood in a particular way. The object of the building craft is the house being built; the object of a particular nailing of a plank is the plank; the object of a particular driving of a nail is the nail. In medicine, the object of a medical procedure—also, and very appropriately, called the patient—is the person "under the knife" (or scalpel), the person given a prescription and instructed to take it, the person whose limbs are rubbed in order to improve circulation.[38]

36. See references in note 32.

37. In other words, there is no action at a distance [*Phys.* iii,2,202a6; the principle is argued for in *Phys.* vii,2]. See also S. Brock (1998), pp. 49–53. Vlastos claims that Plato also holds the principle: Vlastos (1975), p. 77 (citing in n. 19 *Ti.* 56d–57a). See also here, chapter 6, section [4]: ". . . one cannot fly over a stretch of road . . .".

38. See *De ma.* q.2 a.4 ad 5 ll.278–86: "Actus autem moralis . . . recipit speciem ab obiecto secundum quod comparatur ad rationem. Et ideo dicitur communiter quod actus quidam sunt boni vel mali ex genere, et quod actus bonus ex genere est actus cadens supra debitam materiam, *sicut pascere esurientem*, actus autem malus ex genere est qui cadit supra indebitam materiam, sicut subtrahere aliena: materia enim actus dicitur obiectum ipsius." See also *in Metaph.* §21: "Unde medicus non sanat hominem nisi per accidens; sed per se sanat Platonem aut Socratem, aut aliquem hominem singulariter dictum, cui convenit esse hominem, vel accidit inquantum est curatus"; the corresponding passage in Aristotle is *Metaph.* i,1,981a18–20. The idea also shows up in the *Peri Ideōn*: see Alexander, *in Metaph.* 79.24–80.6. See also Thomas's *in Sent.* lb.2 d.36 q.1 a.5; lb.4 d.28 q.1 a.4; d.31 q.1 a.2. See also Aristotle's *Metaph.* ix,8,1050a28–29 ("the art of building is in the thing built"); also *Phys.* iii,3,202b5–8 ("teaching is the activity of a person who can teach, yet the operation is performed in something—it is not cut adrift from a subject but is of one thing in another" [i.e., teaching is in the person taught]. At *Pol.* iii,6,1278b37–1279a7, Aristotle says that arts such as medicine and gymnastics are only incidentally for the "artists" (i.e., the gymnast and the doctor) and are more properly for the sake of their objects (i.e., the men trained and the patients

Now, if this is correct, i.e., that the good that defines medicine is the health of the patient so identified, craniotomy does not fall under the intelligibility of medicine, for the patient, the object that comes under the knife or forceps or whatever, is the fetus, and a craniotomy does a fetus no good. The action engaged in by the doctor who performs a craniotomy may indeed be defined by a good—in fact, it *has* to be defined by some good, otherwise it would be unintelligible as a human act—but a craniotomy is not part of the medical profession whose practices are, by definition, aimed at the good of the patient.

Given this framework of suppositions, the medical doctor who performs an hysterectomy upon a pregnant woman can truthfully say that he is doing something good and that that is all he is doing, since he *need* say nothing more. The phrase 'performing an hysterectomy' describes essentially what he is doing and it describes something good.[39] On the other hand, the "medical doctor" who performs a craniotomy cannot truthfully say that he is just doing something good, for unlike the doctor who performs the hysterectomy, he cannot speak of a practice that "leads right up to" a patient for whom he hopes to do some good. What he does has as an object, a patient, for whom it does no good. He may indeed insist that he is doing something to promote the health of the mother, but this is not a claim to be performing a medical procedure (i.e., a practice). He has only succeeded in putting his action within a general context that makes it intelligible as an action. He has not succeeded in identifying what he is doing *as* a medical practice; and it is that which is needed if the death of the fetus is to be regarded morally as a side-effect of that which he is really doing.[40]

[5] Resolving indeterminacies: the fat potholer

Let us move on to the potholer case. How do practices help us to understand this case? We have already seen that difficulties arise when attempting

---

healed). See also Plato, *La.* 185c5–9: the object of medicine for the eyes is the eyes; also *Chrm.* 168b2–168e7. See also Kenny (1963), pp. 187–202.

39. It is assumed that what the doctor does is necessary and proportionate to the problem, and that the other conditions of a moral action (e.g., that the operation be consented to) are met. I am ignoring such considerations for the moment, although obviously they do have a bearing on the morality of the doctor's action.

40. The present approach is consonant with Kass (1980). See also Kass (1992). Kass's position has to do, however, solely with what medical doctors should and should not do—not with the ultimate moral questions I am discussing here.

to distinguish this case from that of personal self-defense as described in *ST* II–II q.64 a.7. It does not work, for instance, to let the difference between the two cases depend on the suddenness of the action, for not only might personal self-defense involve some very careful, deliberate actions, but the decision to blow away the fat potholer might conceivably be taken in a split second and the deed accomplished in the next. On the other hand, it does not appear that an act of personal self-defense represents a practice such as we find, for instance, in the medical profession.

Or does Thomas not say otherwise? If one looks closely at *ST* II–II q.64 a.7, one perceives a strong concern to show that the act of self-defense is *lawful*. As a conclusion to the opening section—i.e., the section in which he says that the death of the attacker is *praeter intentionem*—he remarks, "this act, since one's intention is to save one's own life, is not unlawful [*non habet rationem illiciti*]." A few phrases later, with respect to the point about proportionate means, he says: "Wherefore, if a man in self-defense uses more than necessary violence, it will be unlawful: whereas if he repel force with moderation his defense will be lawful, because according to the jurists, 'it is lawful to repel force by force, provided one does not exceed the limits of a blameless defense.'"[41] The final section of the body, in which he discusses the actions of public officials, is also about what is lawful:

But as it is unlawful to take a man's life, except for the public authority acting for the common good, as stated above, it is not lawful for a man to intend killing a man in self-defense, except for such as have public authority, who while intending to kill a man in self-defense, refer this to the public good, as in the case of a soldier fighting against the foe, and in the minister of the judge struggling with robbers, although even these sin if they be moved by private animosity.

The aim of *ST* II–II q.64 a.7 is not the moral analysis of actions in terms of intention but rather to shed light upon what qualifies as lawful and why—which involves a fairly detailed account, in terms of intention, of what might count as an act of personal self-defense. We tend to read *ST* II–II q.64 a.7 as a tract on intention and side effects ("De his quae praeter intentionem sunt"?), for we read it as part of the subsequent tradition of PDE; but, in fact, intention and side-effects come into it only as necessary conditions of licit kill-

41. See above, note 3.

ing—and the article's actual title is "Utrum alicui liceat occidere se defenden-do."[42] But, if this is the case, Thomas's basic point in *ST* II–II q.64 a.7 would be that personal self-defense also qualifies as a fixed path of behavior. If the various criteria mentioned in the law (e.g., "does not exceed the limits of a blameless defense") are met, the man who kills an attacker in self-defense can truthfully say that he was just seeking to preserve his life. The man who dyna-mites the potholer cannot say the same.

In the case of self-defense, there exists a fixed path, established not by any conceptual or temporal relationships but by law, leading directly to the preservation of life, which allows the man who defends his life to claim that that was all he was doing. It is true that personal self-defense is not part of a discipline or profession of the same order as that of the public official, the soldier, or the police officer ("the minister of the judge struggling with rob-bers"), which practices establish the broader outlines of the law. But the law also has the capacity of reaching down into the more particular details of hu-man life that escape its more general precepts.

[6] Law

There is one fairly obvious possible objection to the present approach to PDE, and that is that it is too legalistic. How can the merely lawful have such an effect on the morality of an act and, ultimately, on whether a person is characterized as good or bad? But such an objection fails to appreciate that neither Plato, nor Aristotle, nor Thomas makes the type of distinction we tend to make between the lawful and the moral. For Thomas, at least when he is referring to the focal meaning of 'law,' positive law is very intimately tied up with natural law or morality.[43] "Every humanly posited law," he says, "to the extent that it has the intelligibility of law, is derived from the law of nature. If, however, in anything it is inconsistent with natural law, then it will not be law

---

42. It is to be recalled that the killing carried out by the public official is also described as self-defense, referred to the common good: "illicitum est quod homo intendat occidere hominem ut seipsum defendat, nisi ei qui habet publicam auctoritatem, qui, intendens hominem occidere ad sui defensionem, refert hoc ad publicum bonum . . .".

43. See the present work, chapter 3, sections [6] and [7]. On the focal meaning of 'law' as in-tended here, see Finnis (1980), pp. 9–11, 276–81. Says Finnis (p. 277): "[T]he meaning [of 'law'] has been constructed as a *focal* meaning, not as an appropriation of the term 'law' in a univocal sense that would exclude from the reference of the term anything that failed to have all the characteris-tics (and to their full extent) of the central case." On Thomas's use of a focal meaning of law, see especially pp. 363–66.

but the corruption of law."[44] This is why in *ST* II–II q.64 a.7, he can switch so easily back and forth between, for instance, citing "the jurists" on repelling "force by force" and the precept of the natural law according to which "it is natural to everything to keep itself in being." He does not regard the latter as necessarily standing outside and separate from the positive law.

'Legalism' signifies a conforming of oneself to the legal, whether doing so leads to human fulfillment or not; it is also, according to a related sense, connected with the habitual tendency to try to "get around" laws, regarding them as mere conventions, necessarily inadequate attempts to specify just behavior.[45] Neither of these significations applies to what Thomas promotes in saying that morality and law are bound up with each other. If a law does not conform to the natural law, which is by definition the way to human fulfillment, it is not a law (in its focal meaning). In this, Thomas is at one with Augustine, citing often the famous Augustinian dictum "Lex injusta non est lex."[46] He is also at one with Plato of the *Republic*, whose understanding of justice as paths of intelligible behavior ("practicing one's own business") pertains not to any city but only to the Ideal City.[47] It clearly entails no minimalist attitude toward the law. On the contrary, if a law is just, that law bears with it all the moral weight of the natural law.[48] As we have seen (see especially chapter 3, section [8]), the first principle of practical reason reaches down in

44. *ST* I–II q.95 a.2: "[O]mnis lex humanitus posita intantum habet de ratione legis, inquantum a lege naturae derivatur. Si vero in aliquo, a lege naturali discordet, iam non erit lex sed legis corruptio."

45. On legalism, Finnis (1983), pp. 77–78, 93–94, and Grisez (1983), pp. 13, 105–6 (see also the many other references in Grisez's index under 'legalism').

46. See *ST* I–II q.96 a.4; also q.95 a.2 and q.95 a.4: "Aliud [regimen] autem est tyrannicum, quod est omnino corruptum: unde ex hoc non sumitur aliqua lex." Augustine's actual expression is as follows: "lex esse mihi non videtur, quae justa non fuerit" [*De lib.arb.* lb.1 cap.5 §33]. H. L. A. Hart, much of whose academic career was spent opposing natural law interpretations of positive law, often cited against natural lawyers the Augustinian tag "lex injusta non est lex." See, for instance, Hart (1994 <1961>), p. 8: "[T]he assertion that 'an unjust law is not law' has the same ring of exaggeration and paradox, if not falsity, as 'statutes are not laws' or 'constitutional law is not law.'" Nonetheless, near the end of his career, Hart was able to say of "Finnis's flexible interpretation of natural law" (employing as it does a "focal meaning" of law: see above, note 43) that it "is in many respects complementary to rather than a rival of positivist legal theory" [Hart (1983), p. 10]. On unjust laws, see Finnis (1980), pp. 351–68, and (1998), pp. 266–74. See also Weinreb (1987), pp. 60, 97–126.

47. *R.* ii,369b5–372c1. The idea survives into the *Laws*, but in appropriately different form. At *Lg.* iv,715b2–4, the Athenian Stranger asserts that an unjust polity is no polity, unjust laws no laws; a true law has to be for the common good (see also *Lg.* ix,875a5–b1).

48. *ST* I–II q.96 a.4.

all its bindingness to the lowest precepts of morality. It is as irrational to say that a particular minor traffic law is, at the same time and in the same respect, to be followed and not to be followed as it is to say that the common precept 'one should act rationally' (chapter 2, section [7]) admits of such contradictory application.

Thomas gets this general association of the moral and the lawful more directly from Aristotle. In the first book of the *Nicomachean Ethics*, Aristotle remarks that "the end of political science [*politikē*]" is "the best end, and political science spends most of its pains on making the citizens to be of a certain character, viz. good and capable of noble acts" [*EN* i,9,1099b28–32]. Later in the same book, he says, "The true student of politics, too, is thought to have studied virtue above all things; for he wishes to make his fellow citizens good and obedient to the laws" [*EN* i,13,1102a7–10].[49] And in book 5 he says, "[T]he things that tend to produce virtue taken as a whole are those of the acts prescribed by the law that have been prescribed with a view to education for the common good" [*EN* v,2,1130b25–26].

This Aristotelian approach might be thought to represent state positivistic totalitarianism but it does not do so, since Aristotle has also his version of the Platonic "Ideal City" doctrine. Indeed, he has to have some such a doctrine, since he too holds that politicians and legislators, when they truly function *qua* politician and legislator, cannot enact an unjust law. But his doctrine is more subtle than Plato's—or, at least, than what we find in the *Republic*. On the one hand, in wondering indignantly at the audacity of statesmen who would dominate and tyrannize over others, he says, "How can that which is not even lawful be the business of the statesman or the legislator? Unlawful it certainly is to rule without regard for justice, for there may be might where there is no right."[50] Thus, like Plato, Aristotle does not think that a law gains

---

49. See also *Rhet.* i,2,1356a26–27; 4,1359b2–18; *Pol.* iii,9,1280a25–b12. By 'political science' and related expressions Aristotle means, at least in *EN* i, that science which rules other sciences such as "strategy, economics, and rhetoric" and which "*legislates* as to what we are to do and what we are to abstain from" [*EN* i,2,1094b2–7 (emphasis mine): ὁρῶμεν δὲ καὶ τὰς ἐντιμοτάτας τῶν δυνάμεων ὑπὸ ταύτην [= πολιτικὴν] οὔσας, οἶον στρατηγικὴν οἰκονομικὴν ῥητορικήν· χρωμένης δὲ ταύτης ταῖς λοιπαῖς τῶν ἐπιστημῶν, ἔτι δὲ νομοθετούσης τί δεῖ πράττειν καὶ τίνων ἀπέχεσθαι, τὸ ταύτης τέλος περιέχοι ἂν τὰ τῶν ἄλλων, ὥστε τοῦτ' ἂν εἴη τἀνθρώπινον ἀγαθόν]. Note, however, that at *EN* vi,8,1141b23–29 Aristotle distinguishes ἡ πολιτική and ἡ νομοθετική.

50. *Pol.* vii,2,1324b26–28. A few lines later, he draws a contrast between unjust political regimes and the crafts, where such arbitrariness would not be tolerated [1324b29ff.].

legitimacy simply by virtue of having been enacted *as* law. On the other hand, he recognizes a range of constitutions, each with its proper justice, thereby ensuring that justice exist not in a Platonic ideal realm but within the concrete world where people actually attempt to govern and to pursue justice. His is a sort of threshold theory of what constitutes a just regime with just laws: he holds that, given particular circumstances—its geographical location, the character of its people, its history, and so on—a regime that has as its goal the good of the citizens should be obeyed as just. Nor would this be mere playacting—even if, for instance, a law in Sparta is the contradictory of one in Athens—since justice derives its sense from the particular political entity within which it is sought.

Aristotle also sees advantages in allowing laws to change.

Such changes in the other sciences have certainly been beneficial [he says]; medicine, for example, and gymnastics, and in general all crafts and capacities have departed from traditional usage. And, if politics be a craft, change must be necessary in this as in any other craft. Someone might say that a proof of this is in what they produced: the old customs are exceedingly simple and barbarous. For the ancient Hellenes went about armed and bought their brides from each other. The remains of ancient laws which have come down to us are quite absurd; for example, at Cumae there is a law about murder, to the effect that if the accuser produce a certain number of witnesses from among his own kinsmen, the accused shall be held guilty. Again, men in general desire the good, and not merely what their fathers had.[51]

But this does not mean that *any* law might change. Aristotle says a few lines later (*Pol.* ii,8,1269a19–24) that we ought to be more willing to change the "laws" of a craft than the laws of a society, since the latter type of change risks weakening the social fabric.

The law reflects the contours of human nature, and there are certain aspects of the latter that do not change. Someone might ask, Why do we not simply pass a law saying that medical doctors can intentionally kill? Why go through the rigamorole of arguing that craniotomy but not hysterectomy is direct killing, when direct killing is allowed in another social role (that of the public official) and we could just as easily pass a law allowing direct killing also in medicine? The reason is that it is part of human nature that doctors

51. *Pol.* ii,8,1268b34–1269a4.

do not take lives. By definition—that is, by a definition which captures the essence of the medical practice in general—doctors seek the health of their patients. To allow as part of medicine a procedure whose end is the death of the patient would not promote the common good.

[7] Promoting and protecting goods

This general approach helps us to toward a solution of the problem mentioned above, at the end of section [1]. The problem is how to understand Thomas's statement that the public official, the soldier, and the minister of the judge intend to kill but "refer this to the public good." If the most serious offenses against the moral law are those that involve attacks on the infrastructure of morality (including the good of human life), it would seem that Thomas could not allow the intentional killing of a human being as moral. Given this, the suggestion was that perhaps the intention to kill is re-routed into the other intention in such a way that it is no longer really an intention to kill. On the other hand, Thomas does say, and quite clearly, that the public official intends to kill.

We can now see that the problem arises because of certain presuppositions about what are the components of the moral analysis of human action. Obviously, intention is extremely important. We have to know what act the agent is performing, and intention specifies the act. It is apparent that, for Thomas, intention to take a person's life is good indication that the basic good of human life is being attacked, for his initial point in the body of *ST* II–II q.64 a.7 is that "the slaying of the aggressor" can sometimes be considered *beside* the intention (i.e., *praeter intentionem*). If intention to kill had nothing to do with whether such an act is an attack on human life, there would be no need to say this. Moral action, however, occurs within a context, within the system of laws of a particular society, which laws or fixed paths are the basic elements of the ethical life and are therefore essential for making judgments about the moral character of particular actions. In other words, *all* the components of the moral analysis of human action must be taken into consideration.

Although the presence of an intention to kill is certainly *prima facie* evidence that a basic human good is being attacked, following a particular fixed path (e.g., that of a public official, a soldier, etc.) allows the intention to kill to be referred—i.e., re-directed into a path defining an intelligible practice which is part of ethical behavior in general—since fixed paths are among the basic components of moral analysis. This does not mean that the intention to kill becomes a different intention. It is still an intention to kill, but it does not constitute an attack on the good of human life, because it is referred along a path that does not attack that good. One can intend to kill without attacking the basic good of human life if the intention is in accordance with law. Someone might object: Why doesn't Thomas just say that also the private self-defender intends to slay his aggressor but that this is not contrary to the law? The ultimate answer is that law is simply basic here; but neither is this law without sense. There is good reason in a society not to allow private, intentional killing. If such intentional personal self-defense were licit, how could private executions for defensive purposes be prohibited?

This, of course, is not to say that everything might be determined just by looking to see whether everyone is doing his job ("practicing his own business") or is obeying the law. As Thomas says in *ST* II–II q.64 a.7, even the public official's act of killing is immoral if he is "moved by private animosity." Such an act takes on an immoral aspect because of the damage it does do to the fabric of the moral life, which includes the heart of the public official. But, absent such animosity, the public official can truthfully claim that he does not cause any such damage. Indeed, he does something that, according to the law, *preserves* the fabric of the moral life.

In saying that the analysis of actions includes consideration of practices and law, I do not claim to have provided the formula that will allow a person always to determine immediately whether a particular action is or is not moral, is or is not damaging of, or dangerous for, the infrastructure of morality (i.e., the basic human goods). But neither are we without tools of analysis. Call to mind again Aristotle's remarks on motion. He recognizes a certain intelligible structure in any physical motion, including, for instance, a cue ball's striking other billiard balls, a scalpel's dismantling a cranium, etc. It is here that any analysis of human action must begin: i.e., by attending to the intelligible structure of the physical motion. One must ask, for instance, Is this act aimed at—intended for—the death of a human person? But the intelligible structure of a human act simply *qua* movement is just one factor in its analysis. The removal of a gravid cancerous uterus appears, because of its physical structure, to be a direct attack on human life; on further analysis, we discover that it is not, for hysterectomy is a part of (a practice within) medicine. If we cannot find such a true description of the act and if we cannot discover any other exonerating factor (such as that the agent did not know what he was doing, what instrument he was using, etc.), we must conclude that the act is immoral.

The difficulty, of course, will always be in determining which type of acts constitute fixed paths: which acts are included among the legitimate practices of a craft or among the acts permitted by good law. Determining such issues requires analysis, in the technical sense already discussed in chapter 3 and to be discussed further in chapter 8. For millennia, human beings—philosophers, moralists, legislators, politicians, and so on—have been considering and reconsidering issues having to do with justice and beneficial action. Setting up sound systems of laws and practices has never been a matter of consulting the highest principles of natural law and deriving directly from them the rules of right behavior. It is always a matter of sifting through opinions and considerations posed by circumstances in order to *devise* laws and practices that lead up to the principles that constitute human happiness. Records of such deliberations and the systems of law they have produced are valuable resources in determining the morality of types of actions—and usually, in a basically just society, it is sound policy simply to follow what is decreed and established.

But even within basically just societies situations sometimes arise in which it is necessary to pass new laws and to prescribe new practices. The modern field of bioethics is rife with examples. Here again the process of establishing precepts and principles is not a "top-down" deductive one. Theses are assumed without proof. If political and professional discourse is free and honest, an attempt is made to connect these theses up with the relevant first principles. If the attempt is successful, something like a synthetic, deductive phase follows: judges, lawyers, administrators, etc., derive judgments about legal behavior from the law as established; doctors, technicians, etc., do something similar. In geometry, a proof can often be accomplished in a single sitting; with laws and practices, the process is longer and more complicated. But the logical structure of either process is the same.

In short, there is not always a quick and easy way of verifying the truth or validity of moral precepts and laws. Although it is true that those actions and laws that attack basic human goods are unjust, this truth cannot function as an immediately applicable criterion of good actions and laws since, for instance, even an intention to kill might not be an attack on the basic good of human life. We cannot use standard modern action theory—or, more precisely, the analysis of discrete actions—as our means of determining what is good behavior, since such analysis prescinds from an essential factor in the analysis of action: the place that the discrete act occupies in the complex system of laws and practices within which it is performed.[52]

52. Allow me to quote at some length some relevant remarks by John Finnis: "Natural law is not a doctrine. It is one's permanent dynamic orientation toward an understanding grasp of the goods that can be realized by free choice, together with a bias (like the bias in one's 'speculation' towards raising questions that will lead one on from data to insight and from insight to judgment) towards actually making choices that are intelligibly (because intelligently) related to the goods which are understood to be attainable, or at stake, in one's situation" [Finnis (1970), p. 366]. "There is no mechanical or speculative solution to the problems of indirect voluntariness, double effect and the like: the human mind is capable of indefinitely revising the meanings it attributes to acts in order to escape the characterization of its acts and choices as directly opposed to a basic value. Concentrate on any given action and you can dissolve it into acceptable meanings; but when one raises one's eyes to other actions one may find that the principles of one's solution have tripped one up; or one may find that one has no principles but only a desire to avoid discomfort, or that one was banking on an arbitrarily adopted belief in some imagined future totality of best consequences (the supremacy of the West, the Marxian realm of freedom, the rule of the Saints, the Advent of the Omega Point . . .)" [Finnis (1970), pp. 378–79]. Along similar lines, see also Finnis (1968), especially pp. 469–70.

CHAPTER 8

ACTS AMID PRECEPTS—II

THE PURPOSE of this final chapter is to show in a more logically precise way than has been attempted in previous chapters how particular acts fit into the larger structure of practical reason. It also serves as a sort of summary of the book, epitomizing many of the themes we have already seen: the nature of the practical syllogism, the relationship between theoretical and practical reason (and thus the relationship between intellect and *voluntas*), the role and nature of moral precepts, the various levels of moral precepts, and the function of the principle of double effect. Most of the fundamental logical concepts are taken from Aristotle's logical writings since, although Thomas employs Aristotelian logical ideas constantly, he rarely discusses them in a direct manner. Some of the applications I make of Aristotelian logical ideas are not found in either Aristotle or Thomas, although neither are they inconsistent with their ethical theories. I also employ a number of more modern logical ideas—making a connection, in particular, between the traditional method of analysis and modern natural deduction methods.

[1] More marks of the practical

In chapter 1, I discussed some of the characteristics of practical syllogisms, noting especially that they proceed in a "direction" quite different from standard (i.e., theoretical) syllogisms and that they are defeasible. That is, the movement of the practical syllogism proceeds from its minor term, up through its middle term, to the major term; and it does so in such a way that the various connections are not necessary: even if a cloak might lead to warmth insofar as it is a covering, if every available cloak is infested by insects, "get a cloak" is not something we need do.

In the following, syllogism [A] is a theoretical syllogism; syllogism [B], the corresponding practical syllogism:

[A]   Warm holds of every CoveRing
      CoveRing holds of every cloaK
      Thus, Warm holds of every cloaK

[B]   CoveRing leads to Warmth
      CloaK leads to coveRing
      Thus, cloaK leads to Warmth

To represent the relation "holds of" in [A], we might use an arrow ($\rightarrow$), calling it a "holding arrow" (not to be confused with the implication arrow $\Rightarrow$, which has quite another significance). Replacing the terms with the bold-faced letters as already indicated in [A], we get:

[A]′ **W** $\rightarrow$ every **R**
      R $\rightarrow$ every **K**
      $\overline{}$
      W $\rightarrow$ every **K**

Here it is apparent that the direction of the syllogism is downward. For the practical syllogism, we reverse the direction of the holding arrow (calling it the "conducting arrow"):

[B]′ **W** $\leftarrow$ **R**
      R $\leftarrow$ **K**
      $\overline{}$
      W $\leftarrow$ **K**

I understand the conducting arrow as conveying not only the idea that a piece of practical reasoning proceeds in the opposite direction to theoretical reasoning but also that the link represented is defeasible. Furthermore, as is evident from the absence of the word 'every' in [B]′, in a practical syllogism it is not specified whether the relationship among the terms is universal or particular—whether, for instance, we are talking about *every* covering leading to warmth. Aristotle calls such propositions, when they appear in the syllogistic of *An.pr.*, "indefinite propositions."[1]

---

1. "I call universal the holding of every or the holding of none; particular, the holding of some

Indefinites play a part in practical reasoning even more clearly than in the-oretical reason, where Aristotle, once he has introduced them into the syllo-gistic, tends to ignore them. When a man exercises the practical reasoning represented in [B]′, he may know or think that every covering leads to warmth and that every cloak is a covering—in other words, that may indeed be the basis of his reasoning; but as he is thinking about how to get to warmth, he does not think about getting every cloak, nor about getting every covering. He just thinks 'cloak leads to covering, covering to warmth.'

It might be suggested against this position, that the propositions involved are not indefinites at all but rather particulars, the practical equivalents of 'covering holds of some cloaks.'[2] But if it is some cloaks that are coverings, the practical reasoner is going to have to determine which cloaks these are—even if it turns out that 'some cloaks' comprises all cloaks. He cannot just figure, 'coverings lead to warmth; a cloak is a covering; I'll get a cloak.' But this *is* the piece of reasoning about which we are talking. Again, however, this is not to say that either 'R ← K' or 'W ← R' is a universal. If the practical reasoner in question somehow acquires all the coverings and all the cloaks, he will doubt-less get warm. But the whole class of coverings or the whole class of cloaks do not enter into the practical reasoning represented in [B]′.

The presence of indefinites in practical reasoning is then another charac-teristic distinguishing it from theoretical reasoning, for in the latter a syllo-gism of the first figure containing an indefinite major premiss is invalid—as Aristotle notes.[3] A first-figure syllogism must always have a universal major

---

or the holding not of some (or not of every); indefinite, the holding or not holding, without the <designation> universal or particular—as in, for instance, 'opposites are of the same science' or 'pleasure is not a good'" [λέγω δὲ καθόλου μὲν τὸ παντὶ ἢ μηδενὶ ὑπάρχειν, ἐν μέρει δὲ τὸ τινὶ ἢ μὴ τινὶ ἢ μὴ παντὶ ὑπάρχειν, ἀδιόριστον δὲ τὸ ὑπάρχειν ἢ μὴ ὑπάρχειν ἄνευ τοῦ καθόλου ἢ κατὰ μέρος, οἷον τὸ τῶν ἐναντίων εἶναι τὴν αὐτὴν ἐπιστήμην ἢ τὸ τὴν ἡδονὴν μὴ εἶναι ἀγαθόν—*An.pr.* i,1,24a18–22]. On the articles τῶν and τὴν in τῶν ἐναντίων and τὴν ἡδονὴν, see Mignucci (1969), p. 186. Mignucci calls attention to the very interesting remarks at Philoponus, *in An.pr.* 20.23–21.20.

When I speak of the "syllogistic" in this chapter, I mean the syllogistic of the *Prior Analytics*. For reasons that will become apparent shortly, I do not speak of the "practical syllogistic" but rather of the "practical extension."

2. Bonitz holds that indefinites *are* just particulars [Bonitz (1961 <1870>) 9b53]; but Maier takes issue with him, saying that, although indefinites have many of the same logical properties as particulars, they are different from them [Maier (1936 <1896–1900>), vol. 1, pp. 160–61]. See also Mignucci (1969), p. 186. Maier (p. 161) sees indefinites as equivalent to the propositions of *Int.* vii that state things of universals but not universally [*Int.* vii,17b7]; and, indeed, *An.pr.* i,1,24a19–22 does seem to regard them as, in some sense, unexpressed universals (see note 1).

3. *An.pr.* i,4,26a30–39. For the syllogistic figures, major terms, etc., see below, p. 200.

premiss. In this respect, indefinites function logically like particulars. Were the major premiss of a syllogism a particular proposition, the syllogism would be invalid. Even if we know that greedy holds of some scholars and that scholar holds of some philosophers (or even all philosophers), we do not yet know whether greedy holds of any philosophers. The reason is that the major term does not encompass the middle term in such a way that nothing can escape its influence (its "holding"), as it would in the valid first-figure syllogism: "greedy holds of every scholar; scholar holds of every philosopher; greedy holds of every philosopher." Similar things can be said of combinations of premisses in which the major is an indefinite: they do not manage— or, perhaps better, they do not even attempt—"to nail down" the truth.

We might think of a standard syllogism as an effort to mark out an area in logical space from which, given the premisses that mark out the space, no escape is possible: all philosophers *must* be greedy, given that they are all scholars and all scholars are greedy. In practical reasoning, the effort is quite different, for, as Kenny puts it, the point is not to "preserve truth" but to get to a perceived good.[4] In order to do this one need not ensure that nothing escapes but only that at least some means leads to the end sought.

The presence of indefinites in practical syllogisms confirms both Aristotle's and Thomas's observation that practical reasoning—or, more precisely, deliberation—proceeds by way of the traditional method of analysis. As we saw in chapter 3, section [4], the analysis phase of the analysis/synthesis method proceeds from the proposition to be proved, "against the flow," toward the principles, in seemingly reckless disregard of whether the propositions above the desired conclusion imply it or not. The only requisite of an *akolouthon* (a "concomitant") is that it not be inconsistent with the previous step. In traditional logic, if the middle term is not "distributed" at least once, there cannot be a valid syllogism.[5] Analysis ignores such issues and seeks only "concomitants" on its way to the principles. It is solely in the (deductive) synthetic phase, if it occurs, that one shows that the conclusion follows from the propositions above it.

---

4. See chapter 1, note 27.

5. Universal propositions distribute their subject terms; negative propositions distribute their predicate terms; a particular proposition has no distributed term.

[2] A base in theoretical reason

Given, then, that practical reasoning has characteristics logically so much at variance with theoretical reasoning, does this not raise a problem for anyone who would try (as we are trying here) to systematize practical reason? If practical syllogisms are invalid forms, is this not a threat to the consistency of the theory? Yes and no. Obviously, if we were to add to the syllogistic invalid syllogisms, the result would be a disaster. But if we take seriously and put into effect the idea that "intellectus speculativus per extensionem fit practicus,"[6] no such result need be forthcoming. The syllogistic is, of course, consistent. If syllogisms containing, for instance, indefinite majors in the first figure are inserted into it, the syllogistic forfeits consistency; but if the set of practical syllogisms is kept out of the syllogistic, although mapped onto it, the consistency of the syllogistic is not affected.

What then about the practical extension? Would it be consistent? The various steps in a piece of practical reasoning must be concomitant one with the other, but consistency is not the primary issue here since, in the practical extension, one's immediate concern is how to get to (or remain with) goods. Rather than consistency, practical reason seeks what I shall call "rationality."[7] It is my task now to explain what this is and to show that the practical syllogisms as proposed here preserve it.

In the syllogistic, there are fourteen recognized valid syllogisms, divided into three groups depending on where in the syllogism the middle term (i.e., the term that occurs twice in the premises) appears. The fourteen, assigned to their respective figures and given their traditional names, are given in Table 1. The major term is represented as L ("large"), the middle as M, the minor term as S ("small"). Holding is represented by the holding arrow ($\rightarrow$), not holding by a "not-holding arrow" ($\nrightarrow$).

The syllogisms of the first figure are "perfect." "I call perfect," says Aristotle, "a syllogism which needs nothing other than what has been stated to make the necessity evident . . .".[8] I have argued elsewhere that Aristotle means

---

6. See chapter 6, note 2. At *ST* I q.79 a.11 Thomas says that the intellect is a single "power" which might "accidentally" be directed to one or the other object, being or good, thus putting into operation either PNC or FPPR.

7. I shall use this as a technical term. It would be more accurate to speak always of the "practically rational," but that becomes rather a mouthful.

8. *An.pr.* i,1,24b22–24: τέλειον μὲν οὖν καλῶ συλλογισμὸν τὸν μηδενὸς ἄλλου προσδεό-

TABLE 1

FIRST FIGURE		SECOND FIGURE	
Barbara	*Darii*	*Cesare*	*Festino*
L→ every M	L→ every M	M↛ any L	M↛ any L
M→ every S	M→ some S	M→ every S	M→ some S
L→ every S	L→ some S	L↛ any S	L↛ some S
Celarent	*Ferio*	*Camestres*	*Baroco*
L↛ any M	L↛ any M	M→ every L	M→ every L
M→ every S	M→ some S	M↛ any S	M↛ some S
L↛ any S	L↛ some S	L↛ any S	L↛ some S

THIRD FIGURE		
Darapti	*Disamis*	*Bocardo*
L→ every M	L→ some M	L↛ some M
S→ every M	S→ every M	S→ every M
L→ some S	L→ some S	L↛ some S
Felapton	*Datisi*	*Ferison*
L↛ any M	L→ every M	L↛ any M
S→ every M	S→ some M	S→ some M
L↛ some S	L→ some S	L↛some S

by perfection that, in looking at a syllogism and without having to perform any additional operations, we can see immediately (it is "evident") that the

μενον παρὰ τὰ εἰλημμένα πρὸς τὸ φανῆναι τό ἀναγκαῖον. . . . I translate συλλογισμὸς as 'syllogism' here, although many modern scholars (with reason) prefer 'deduction.' 'Syllogism' is to be understood as having a wider extension than the traditional syllogisms *Barbara, Celarent,* etc., but a smaller one than 'valid argument.' At *An.pr.* i,32,47a33–35, Aristotle says, "[T]he necessary is wider than the syllogism; for every syllogism is something necessary, but not everything which is necessary is a syllogism" [ἐπὶ πλέον δὲ τὸ ἀναγκαῖον ἢ ὁ συλλογισμός· ὁ μὲν γὰρ συλλογισμὸς πᾶς ἀναγκαῖον, τὸ δ' ἀναγκαῖον οὐ πᾶν συλλογισμός]. See Smith (1989), p. 110; see also Flannery (1991), p. 188, and Barnes, Bobzien, Flannery, and Ierodiakonou (1991), p. 21.

major term is connected to the minor term.[9] This has a good deal to do with the way in which Aristotle typically states first-figure syllogism, saying not (as we tend to say) that, for instance, 'all animals are physical objects; all men are animals; therefore, all men are physical objects' but rather "'physical object" holds of "animal"; "animal" holds of "man"; therefore, "physical object" holds of "man."' In the latter arrangement, we can make a "clean sweep" through the syllogism, seeing at a glance that the major term holds of the minor by way of the middle: 'physical object' → 'animal'; 'animal' → 'man'; therefore (allowing 'animal' to drop out) 'physical object' → 'man.' There is a sort of straight conduit, without twists or turns, between the major and the minor terms.[10] It is for this reason, I believe, that Aristotle says, "[o]f the figures, the first is especially scientific" [An.post. i,14,79a17–18].[11] The validity of such syllogisms is especially perspicuous.

The rest of the syllogisms—i.e., those of the second and third figures—can be "perfected." A "perfected" syllogism is a syllogism in which the necessity has been made evident by means of other operations.[12] Aristotle often speaks of a perfected syllogism *becoming* a first-figure syllogism.[13] This appears to

9. Flannery (1987); see also Mignucci (1969), pp. 191–92; Patzig (1968 <1963>), pp. 43–87; Barnes, Bobzien, Flannery, and Ierodiakonou (1991), p. 75, n. 141.

10. With the negative first-figure syllogisms, things are not quite as smooth, but smooth enough for them to qualify as perfect. For instance, with *Celarent* (L $\rightarrow$ M, M → S, therefore L $\rightarrow$ S), we have to think of L as *not* holding of M (and therefore as not holding of S). Aristotle is aware that there is an extra move involved here (see *Metaph.* vi,4,1027b20–25) but still insists that the relation between L and M (or perhaps not-L and M) and therefore between L (not-L) and S is immediate. As Ross points out, Aristotle deals with this problem in *De an.* iii, chapters 2, 6, and 7 [Ross (1953 <1924>), vol. 1, p. 365].

11. At *An.post.* i,21,82b21–23, Aristotle appears to employ a syllogism in *Bocardo* even in a (strictly) scientific context; but see Barnes (1994 <1975>), p. 173.

12. *An.pr.* i,1,24b22–26: τέλειον μὲν οὖν καλῶ συλλογισμὸν τὸν μηδενὸς ἄλλου προσδεό-μενον παρὰ τὰ εἰλημμένα πρὸς τὸ φανῆναι τὸ ἀναγκαῖον, ἀτελῆ δὲ τὸν προσδεόμενον ἢ ἑνὸς ἢ πλειόνων, ἃ ἔστι μὲν ἀναγκαῖα διὰ τῶν ὑποκειμένων ὅρων, οὐ μὴν εἴληπται διὰ προ-τάσεων. That a syllogism not clearly valid from the beginning can be "perfected" is stated at, for instance, i,5,27a15–18: ὅτι μὲν οὖν γίνεται συλλογισμὸς οὕτως ἐχόντων τῶν ὅρων, φανερόν, ἀλλ᾽ οὐ τέλειος· οὐ γὰρ μόνον ἐκ τῶν ἐξ ἀρχῆς ἀλλὰ καὶ ἐξ ἄλλων ἐπιτελεῖται τὸ ἀναγκαῖον. For the distinction, perfect/perfected syllogisms, see Smith (1989), p. xx.

13. *An.pr.* i,7,29a31–36 (ἢ γὰρ δεικτικῶς ἢ διὰ τοῦ ἀδυνάτου περαίνονται πάντες· ἀμ-φοτέρως δὲ γίνεται τὸ πρῶτον σχῆμα, δεικτικῶς μὲν τελειουμένων, ὅτι διὰ τῆς ἀντι-στροφῆς ἐπεραίνοντο πάντες, ἡ δ᾽ ἀντιστροφὴ τὸ πρῶτον ἐποίει σχῆμα, διὰ δὲ τοῦ ἀδυνά-του δεικνυμένων, ὅτι τεθέντος τοῦ ψεύδους ὁ συλλογισμὸς γίνεται διὰ τοῦ πρώτου σχήμα-τος . . .). At i,5,28a3–7, Aristotle says that imperfect syllogisms, insofar as they are perfected not by reductio arguments but by conversions, contain that which is required for their perfection within themselves (i.e., implicit in their terms, of necessity): δῆλον δὲ καὶ ὅτι πάντες ἀτελεῖς εἰσιν οἱ ἐν τούτῳ τῷ σχήματι συλλογισμοί (πάντες γὰρ ἐπιτελοῦνται προσλαμβανομένων τινῶν, ἃ ἢ ἐνυπάρχει τοῖς ὅροις ἐξ ἀνάγκης ἢ τίθενται ὡς ὑποθέσεις, οἷον ὅταν διὰ τοῦ

mean that they too can be shown to depend on there being a conduit between the major and the minor term (in such a way that nothing of the minor term escapes the influence of the major). Take, for instance, *Cesare:* 'M ↛ any L, M → every S, therefore L ↛ any S.' This syllogism is imperfect since we cannot look from the major, through the middle, immediately to the minor and thereby be assured that the conclusion follows. But if we convert 'M ↛ any L,' as is logically permissible in the syllogistic, *Cesare* becomes *Celarent*, which is a first-figure (perfect) syllogism. That is, since from the proposition that 'M does not hold of any L' it follows that 'L does not hold of any M,' we can show that *Cesare* really does contain a conduit leading from the major term to the minor, although this conduit is obscured by the state of the major premiss.

The reduction of a syllogism such as *Bocardo* is a bit more complicated. Aristotle first uses a reduction *ad impossibile:* ". . . if S holds of every M and L does not hold of some, it is necessary that L not hold of some S. For if it held of every and S is predicated of every M, also L will hold of every M; but it was supposed not to hold" [*An.pr.* i,6,28b17–20].[14] Then he adds an interesting remark: "This [i.e., *Bocardo*] is proved also," he says, "without reduction *ad impossibile* if something from among the Ms is taken of which L does not hold" [*An.pr.* i,6,28b20–21]. In fact, if *Bocardo* is reduced to the first figure by reduction *ad impossibile* we do not see that *Bocardo* really contains within itself a conduit from the major to the minor term. We see only that a denial of the conclusion involves us also in a denial of the major premiss. But if we take "something from among the Ms . . . of which L does not hold," a perfect syllogism does come into view.

ἀδυνάτου δεικνύωμεν). . . . See also *An.pr.* i,23, in particular 41b3–5: τούτου δὲ δειχθέντος δῆλον ὡς ἅπας τε συλλογισμὸς ἐπιτελεῖται διὰ τοῦ πρώτου σχήματος καὶ ἀνάγεται εἰς τοὺς ἐν τούτῳ καθόλου συλλογισμούς.

The approach I take here is somewhat different from John Corcoran's, although it owes much to it. According to Corcoran, "[a]n imperfect syllogism is 'potentially perfect' and it is made perfect by *adding* more propositions which express a chain of reasoning from the premisses to the conclusion" [Corcoran (1973), p. 195 (my emphasis); see also p. 205; see also Smiley (1973), p. 137]. I agree that, according to Aristotle, a syllogism is perfected by performing additional operations; but the perfected syllogism does not seem to be this augmented chain of reasoning. As the above texts show, the perfected syllogism, for Aristotle, becomes a perfect (i.e., first figure) syllogism in the process of being perfected.

14. For no apparent reason, Aristotle reverses here the standard order of the premisses, stating in his initial description of *Bocardo* that 'S → every M and L ↛ some M' instead of 'L ↛ some M and S → every M'; but this makes no difference. (I have changed the letters that Aristotle uses so as to make them consistent with the letters used here in setting out the syllogistic figures.)

This proof method is known as ecthesis or "taking out."[15] Suppose that we take the "some M" of which L does not hold and consider it (or them) as a single class: call it M′. Then we have a negative universal major rather than a negative singular. Next we convert the minor premiss 'S → every M' to an affirmative singular proposition whose predicate term is M′ and whose subject term is S: 'M′ → some S.' We can do this since, if S holds of every M, it holds also of M′; but since M′ is S, some S must be M′. We end up with the following two premisses: 'L ↛ any M″' and 'M′ → some S.' From these it follows that 'L ↛ some S,' for 'L ↛ any M″' and 'M′ → some S' are the type of premisses belonging to the first figure inference scheme *Ferio* whose conclusion is 'L ↛ some S.' *Ferio* being of the first figure, there is a conduit of the required sort between its major and its minor term. But if this conduit exists in *Bocardo* without changing anything essential—we have only chosen to look at the "some M" of *Bocardo*'s major under a certain aspect of which it certainly admits and then to convert the minor with this same aspect in mind—*Bocardo* too must be valid, since one demonstrates the validity of a syllogism by showing that there is such a conduit between the major and the minor terms, i.e., by reducing it to the first figure.

[3] Mapping on

It is not necessary here to go through the entire syllogistic reducing syllogisms to the first figure. This has been done many times before, not least clearly by Aristotle himself in *An.pr.*, chapters 4 to 6. Our interest rather is in mapping the practical extension onto the syllogistic. And this is not a very difficult thing to do. Consider again the "cloak" syllogisms mentioned above.

[A]   **W**arm holds of every Cove**R**ing
      Cove**R**ing holds of every cloa**K**
      Thus, **W**arm holds of every cloa**K**

[B]   Cove**R**ing leads to **W**armth
      Cloa**K** leads to cove**R**ing
      Thus, cloa**K** leads to **W**armth

15. Beth associates this method (and this very passage) with natural deduction [Beth (1955), p. 335]. On the syllogistic in general as natural deduction, see especially Corcoran (1973), (1974), Smiley (1973); also Smith (1989), pp. xv–xxviii. On ecthesis, see Smith (1982), (1983), Mignucci (1991), Flannery (1995d), pp. 1–52, Thom (1996), pp. 25–26 (plus the many entries in the index).

The first is an instance of the first-figure syllogism *Barbara*. There is clearly a conduit going from the major term **Warm**, through every CoveRing, to every cloaK: **W** → every **R** → every **K**. Mapping the corresponding practical syllogism onto [A] is simply a matter of pointing out that every move in [B] is matched by a move in [A]. Whereas in [A] we have **W** → every **R** → every **K**, in [B] we have **W** ← **R** ← **K**, where the conducting arrow (←) signifies not only that the direction of the process is reversed but that the connection is defeasible and that the "propositions" involved are indefinite. As already explained, these are important differences between the syllogistic and the practical extension and, were the inference scheme corresponding to [B] introduced into the syllogistic itself, the result would be disastrous. Standing, however, as it does outside of the syllogistic, there is no such threat.

Does it make sense to do such mapping? For, given the strange logical properties of practical syllogisms, it is unlikely that we will ever be able to prove that the whole system is consistent. Yes, it does make sense since we are interested not in consistency but in saying what it means to pursue goods rationally. The mapping on shows that there is a conduit between the major and minor terms, for there is such a conduit in the theoretical syllogism onto which any practical syllogism maps. The practical extension ensures, therefore, that the action contemplated leads (defeasibly) to goods, given the truth of the premises of the corresponding theoretical syllogism. In other words, if the corresponding theoretical syllogism(s) is (are) valid, the practical syllogism is "rational" (understood as above).

What about a syllogism in *Bocardo?* Let us first invent one in the theoretical sector which looks like it could be the basis of a practical syllogism. Imagine a particular medical situation in which there is at least one operation possible that does not threaten to cause depletion of strength—every operation, however, being invasive.

[C] **Depletion**↛ some **Operation(s)**

Invasion→ every **Operation**

Depletion↛ some **Invasion(s)**

It is difficult to see any conduit between the major and minor terms (**Depletion** and **Invasion**), so we reduce it to the first-figure syllogism *Ferio* by ecthesis. That is, we take the some operation(s) that do not cause depletion, call it (them) **O**peration(s)[b] and consider them as a class, and convert the minor premiss:

[D]   **D**epletion⇢̸ any **O**peration[b]

Operation[b]→ some **I**nvasion(s)
_____

Depletion⇢̸ some **I**nvasion(s)

In [D] the conduit between **D**epletion and **I**nvasion(s) is apparent:

D⇢̸ any **O**[b]→ some **I**.

It does not make a great deal of sense to set out practical syllogisms corresponding to all of the standard syllogisms. Practical reason is, in certain respects, quite simple. It is unlikely that in considering what to do a doctor's thought patterns would look like this:

D ⇠̸ **O, I**← **O, D** ⇠̸ **I**

rather than this:

D ⇠̸ **O**[b] ← **I**.

And the latter is not a pattern of thought proper to *Bocardo*. Practical reason involves, in fact, only the practical analogues of the syllogistic's first figure. The reason for this is that practical reason is essentially interested in conduits: i.e., ways of getting to goods (principles).

Aristotle himself comes quite close to making this connection between practical reasoning and the first figure. In *An.post.* i,14, he says (as we have already seen), "Of the figures, the first is especially scientific." He adds immediately after: "For the mathematical sciences carry out their demonstrations through it—e.g. arithmetic and geometry and optics—and so do almost all those that make inquiry after the reason why; for the deduction of the reason why occurs, either in general or for the most part and in most cases, through this figure" [79a17–22]. In *Phys.* ii,3, in considering the way that men seek to grasp the "why" of something [194b19], Aristotle uses an example from medicine, in effect a practical syllogism: "Again, in the sense of end or that for the sake of which a thing is done, e.g. health is the cause of walking about. ('Why is he walking about?' We say, 'To be healthy,' and, having said that, we think we have assigned a cause.)"[16]

16. ἔτι ὡς τὸ τέλος· τοῦτο δ᾽ ἐστὶν τὸ οὗ ἕνεκα, οἷον τοῦ περιπατεῖν ἡ ὑγίεια· διὰ τί γὰρ

Indeed, in a sense, there are in the practical extension only two basic syllogisms, both perfect. Consider again syllogism [D]. The conclusion there was that 'Depletion ⤳ some Invasion(s).' This conclusion is true, given the premisses—i.e., given that members of the class Operation(s)^b do not deplete strength and some invasive procedures are of this type. It is a syllogism in *Ferio*. But if we could look at the major premiss of [C] ('Depletion ⤳ some Operation') as a universal, i.e., as the major premiss in [D] ('Depletion ⤳ any Operation^b'), we can do the same for 'Operation^b → some Invasion(s),' i.e., for the minor in [D]. The conclusion would then just be the similar transformation of 'Depletion ⤳ some Invasion(s).' In other words, [D] can be seen as:

[D]′ Depletion ⤳ any Operation^b

Operation^b → every Invasion^b

Depletion ⤳ any Invasion^b

where the superscript 'b' limits **I** to precisely those invasions that fall under 'Operation^b'—i.e., the non-depleting ones. [D]′ is an instance of *Celarent*.

Should we then say that the practical extension maps onto just *Barbara* and *Celarent*? We could, certainly, since a syllogism in *Ferio* can be looked at as an instance of *Celarent* and a syllogism in *Darii* as an instance of *Barbara*. But it is important to remind ourselves also that the corresponding practical syllogism contains indefinite propositions. They are neither universal nor particular and they map onto either.

Practical syllogisms, like their theoretical counterparts, can be arranged in "chains."[17] Thomas gives an example of a practical chain within the craft of medicine in his commentary on Aristotle's *Physics*. Having spoken of health as a final cause, Aristotle writes: "The same is true also of all the intermediate steps that are brought about through the action of something else as a means toward the end, e.g. reduction of flesh, purging, drugs, or surgical instruments are means toward health" [194b35-195a1]. Thomas understands the ele-

---

περιπατεῖ; φαμέν "ἵνα ὑγιαίνῃ", καὶ εἰπόντες οὕτως οἰόμεθα ἀποδεδωκέναι τὸ αἴτιον [194b32–35].

17. See Bonitz (1961 <1870>) 736b33–737a19. Bonitz's initial definition of συστοιχία is, "series notionum, quae eodem genere continentur, sive ita ut altera earum notionum alteri subiecta sit." See *An.pr.* ii,21,66b26–30.

TABLE 2

[E]	health→ every thinning	[G]	*health → every potion*
	thinning→ every purgation		potion→ every tool
	health→ every purgation		health→ every tool

[F]	*health→ every purgation*
	purgation→ every potion
	health→ every potion

ments in Aristotle's list ("reduction of flesh, purging, drugs, or surgical instruments") as related to one another:

[A]s a doctor thins the body in order to promote health, so also health is the end of thinning. Thinning, however, is brought about by purgation, and purgation by means of a potion; the potion, however, is prepared by certain instruments. Thus, all these things are, in a certain sense, ends: for thinning is the end of purgation, purgation of the potion, potion of the tools—and the tools are ends in the production of or searching for tools.[18]

It may indeed be the case that the doctor believes that every thinning in such circumstances will produce health and that every potion of certain type will produce purgation, etc. But the practical reasoning simply goes 'health ← thinning ← purgation ← potion ← tools.'

This chain might be mapped onto a chain of standard syllogisms, somewhat along the lines found in Table 2 (bearing in mind that most of the terms need to be understood as containing an implicit "of a certain type" clause). The transitional propositions (in italics) might then be eliminated, producing a chain of essentially the same structure as the piece of practical reasoning we have just seen ('health ← thinning ← purgation ← potion ← tools').[19] The latter, therefore, maps onto [E]–[G] in such a way that we can say that, since

18. ". . . sicut medicus ad sanitatem inducendam extenuat corpus, et sic sanitas est finis maciei; maciem autem operatur per purgationem; purgationem autem per potionem; potionem autem praeparat per aliqua instrumenta. Unde omnia haec sunt quodammodo finis: nam macies est finis purgationis, et purgatio potionis, et potio organorum, et organa sunt fines in operatione vel inquisitione organorum" [*in Phys.* lb.2 lect.5 n.6 (§181)].

19. Aristotle uses such chains (in sciences) at *An.post.* i,15,79b5–12. See Thomas, *in An.post.* lb.1 lect.26 ll.141–62 (§219), where a chain is called a *coordinatio*.

[E]–[G] is valid, 'health ← thinning ← purgation ← potion ← tools' is rational.

[4] The necessary and the contingent

We have now a fairly clear idea of how a particular act connects up with a more distant goal. Our next task is to obtain some clarity regarding how such acts and series of acts are situated within practical reason as a whole. In order to achieve this, we must first (in this section) say something about Aristotle's modal syllogistic and then (in the next section) describe the logical structure of an Aristotelian craft. At that point we shall be in position to describe the general structure of practical reason and to say something about how particular acts relate to this structure.

Aristotle's syllogistic, besides syllogisms made up of (apparently) assertoric propositions such as 'warm holds of every covering,' 'covering holds of every cloak, etc.,' contains also syllogisms including propositions that "wear their modes upon their sleeve," as it were. It contains syllogisms incorporating necessary propositions ("necessarily animal holds of every man"), possible propositions ("possibly man holds of every man"), and contingent propositions ("it is contingent that Socrates is white").[20] Sometimes a syllogism will contain premisses of two different modal types and sometimes the conclusion to a syllogism will be different in mode from either of its premisses. There are also some variations of necessary, possible and contingent propositions having to do with whether the modal indicator does its work only on the predicate term or also on the subject term. Thus, it is one thing to say that 'necessarily man holds of every upright biped,' quite another to say 'necessarily man holds of everything that is necessarily an upright biped.'[21]

Not everything that Aristotle says about modal syllogisms is correct—that is, he makes errors in attempting to determine which are valid modal syllogisms and which are not. Most of the problems occur in reducing syllogisms *to* perfect first-figure syllogisms, which is convenient for us since we are interested only (or at least primarily) in those modal syllogisms onto which we might map syllogisms of the practical extension, i.e., the perfect syllogisms.

20. On these different types of proposition, see Mignucci (1969), pp. 62ff., Thom (1996), pp. 7–18.
21. See Thom (1996), pp. 7–11, 36–37, 212–14, 220–24. See also Alexander of Aphrodisias, *in An.pr.* 166.19–25; also Flannery (1995d), p. 89.

In order to make the points we need to make, it is sufficient to set out two sets of inference schemes: those corresponding to the perfect syllogisms containing all necessary propositions (Table 3) and those corresponding to the perfect syllogisms containing all contingent propositions (Table 4). Both groups are of the first figure. Here the symbols **N** and **C** are modal indicators standing for "it is necessary that" and "it is contingent that." Although it is controversial, we can assume that these modal indicators have as their scope not the propositions themselves (as in 'the proposition "L → every M" is a necessary one') but rather the terms to which they are attached.[22]

The first group of inference schemes, i.e., the first-figure apodeictic syllogisms, are important for understanding the basic structure of an Aristotelian science. Aristotle says in the *Posterior Analytics* that scientific knowledge is of that which cannot be otherwise and that (as we have seen), "[o]f the figures, the first is especially scientific."[23] Moreover, in acquiring a science one comes to know what something is and why it is such. To understand what something is, is to understand something positive. Thus, says Aristotle, the second figure, which proves only negative conclusions, is not especially suited to science [79a25-27]. Also, understanding what something is, is a matter of knowing universals: one knows what Socrates is if one knows that he is a man or an animal. Thus, the third figure, which proves only particular conclusions, is ill-suited for Aristotelian science [79a27-29]. These ideas entail that, within the first group of inference

TABLE 3

Barbara	Darii
NL→ every M	NL→ every M
NM→ every S	NM→ some S
NL→ every S	NL→ some S

Celarent	Ferio
NL↛ any M	NL↛ any M
NM→ every S	NM→ some S
NL↛ any S	NL↛ some S

TABLE 4

Barbara	Darii
CL→ every M	CL→every M
CM→ every S	CM→ some S
CL→ every S	CL→ some S

Celarent	Ferio
CL↛ any M	CL↛ any M
CM→ every S	CM→ some S
CL↛ any S	CL↛ some S

22. On the controversy, see Becker (1933), pp. 37–42; Mignucci (1969), pp. 70–72; Patterson (1989); Patterson (1995), pp. 6–7, 16–17, 33–37, 47–48, 52–53, 77–80, etc.; Brennan (1997).

23. *An.post.* i,2,71b12; i,14,79a17–18.

schemes, *Barbara* occupies a special position since, of the syllogisms in the first figure, it alone has a conclusion which is neither negative nor particular.

The second group of inference schemes, i.e., the first-figure contingent syllogisms, are the theoretical counterparts of many practical syllogisms. In expounding above the practical syllogism, when talking about the corresponding theoretical syllogisms, we used for the sake of simplicity assertoric syllogisms. Such an approach is accurate as far as it goes. The theoretical syllogism corresponding to 'covering leads to warmth, cloak leads to covering, cloak leads to warmth' plausibly does contain three assertoric propositions: 'warm holds of every covering,' 'covering holds of every cloak,' and 'warm holds of every cloak.' A good deal of our practical reasoning, however, involves no such plain assertions. Suppose I have to get to the doctor's office by 4 P.M. I know that the 46 bus will probably get me there in twenty minutes and I estimate that a 46 bus will arrive at the stop near my home if I wait there for fifteen minutes. So, I decide to be at the stop at 3:25. Living as I do in Rome, the propositions in the syllogistic corresponding to my practical reasoning are by no means confident assertions. But my reasoning is reasoning nonetheless, and the argument is valid. The theoretical syllogism corresponding to my practical reasoning is a contingent syllogism in *Barbara* and would run something like the following: "'me getting to the doctor's on time' is likely to hold of 'me taking the 46 bus'; 'me taking the 46 bus' is likely to hold of 'me waiting at the stop between 3:25 and 3:40'; therefore, 'me getting to the doctor's on time' is likely to hold of 'me waiting at the stop between 3:25 and 3:40.'"

[5] An Aristotelian craft

Our next task is to describe the lineaments of an Aristotelian craft.[24] When Aristotle speaks in the *Analytics* of necessary propositions, he does not just mean propositions that are logically necessary. They include also propositions that are true "for the most part."[25] This fact allows us to describe the structure of an Aristotelian craft in the same language we use in speaking of a

24. As in the previous chapter, I will use 'craft' as a translation of τέχνη, although in standard English we do not normally speak of medicine (my primary example of a τέχνη) as a craft. The advantage of 'craft' is that it makes it apparent that we are dealing with a "productive science" (see Bonitz [1961 <1870>] 759a28) rather than a science in the strict Aristotelian sense.

25. The phrase is ὡς ἐπὶ τὸ πολύ; the topic is not without controversy. See especially Mignucci (1981) and Barnes (1982); see also Sorabji (1980), pp. 222–24, Barnes (1994 <1975>), pp. 92, 192–93, and Judson (1991).

science, such as geometry. Even among the sciences, there are some, such as biology, some of whose necessary propositions are not true without exception; there is, therefore, no insuperable difficulty in speaking of a proposition within a craft as necessary, even though it is not necessary in the strongest sense.

I will use as an example the craft of medicine, not only because Aristotle and Thomas often use medicine as an example, but because so many ethical issues have to do with medicine. Medicine, being a craft, is not a science like mathematics; but that does not mean that there is nothing stable in medicine or that it is without fixed principles or starting points.[26] What we find in a craft such as medicine, rather, is a structure in all essentials identical to that of an Aristotelian science. This means, first of all, that the craft of medicine contains definitions of terms (and the corresponding realities) such as 'doctor,' 'patient,' 'heart,' 'respiratory system,' etc.[27] It contains also *per se* propositions of various sorts. It is within, or against the background of, this structure that most of the particular medical decisions and acts take place. These latter are the matters that Aristotle describes as having "no fixity."[28]

Among the *per se* propositions of medicine are the common axioms—or, at least, their analogues. Aristotle says that these are common only "by analogy—since things are *useful* insofar as they bear on the genus under the science" (or discipline).[29] The first among the common axioms is the principle

26. See *Pol.* i,9,1257b25–26, where medicine is identified as a τέχνη (see also *EN* i,1,1094a8). At *Pol.* ii,8,1268b35–36, Aristotle notes that medicine, like politics, changes with time: it "has moved beyond its patrimony." At *Metaph.* xii,9,1075a1, Aristotle speaks of ποιητικαὶ ἐπιστῆμαι (i.e., τέχναι) (see also Bonitz [1961 <1870>] 759a28); and at *An.post.* i,1,71a3–4, even mathematics is included among the τέχναι (see also *Metaph.* i,1,981b24 and ii,2,997a5). (See Bonitz [1961 <1870>] 759a32–38.)

27. *An.post.* ii,17,99a22–23; also ii,2–6. On "the ingredients of an Aristotelian science," see Hintikka (1972); see also D. Frede (1974), which criticizes Hintikka (1972), and Hintikka (1974), a reply to D. Frede (1974). Hintikka identifies the said "ingredients" as (1) common axioms, (2) generic premisses, (3) premisses about atomic connections (immediate propositions), (4) nominal definitions. At Hintikka (1974), pp. 95–96, he explains that in Hintikka (1972) he employed the term 'ingredient' in order to include nominal definitions, which are not among the first principles of an Aristotelian science.

28. *EN* ii,2,1104a3–5: "[M]atters concerned with conduct and questions of what is good for us have no fixity, any more than matters of health." See above, chapter 1, note 33. The characteristic propositions of a craft such as medicine would be *per se* in way {4}, according to which the predicate represents an effect that is contained in the subject on account of itself, the subject being the corresponding cause, as when 'has perished' is said of 'the slain.' See Appendix B.

29. *An.pr.* i,10,76a38–40; emphasis in ROT. See also *Metaph.* ii,2,996b26–997a15 as well as xi,4,1061b18; see also Mignucci (1975), pp. 191–95.

of non-contradiction (PNC). It is difficult to imagine how PNC might assume a particular character within medicine; but perhaps it is sufficient simply to note that there it manifests itself only in propositions having to do with
medicine. It is easier to conceive of FPPR as taking on a specifically medical
character. The doctor *qua* doctor pursues not good in general but "medical
good." Let us call this good G^m and the corresponding principle FPPR^m. Since
medicine is a craft—that is, since it is a *poiētikē epistēmē*, oriented toward
action—PNC as applying in medicine ("PNC^m") would also be concerned
with G^m.

Like the more universal FPPR, there are two faces to FPPR^m. The one
would be 'medical good is to be done and pursued'; the other, the traditional
first principle of medicine, "primum non nocere," or "first, do no harm."
When I speak of the medical good, I do not mean health in general.
Legislators sitting on a nation's health committee, politicians responsible for
the allocation of medical resources and also their delegates—all these have as
their object health in general. The medical good is, rather, the health of the
individual patients whom a doctor treats. When a doctor makes a decision
about the allocation of medical resources, say as a member of a hospital's
medical board, he does so not *qua* doctor but *qua* representative of the proper authority. He is acting *qua* doctor when his attention (and intentions) are
directed toward the health of individual patients.[30]

Among the common axioms are also principles such as the "equals axiom"
('those things that are equal to one and the same thing are equal to each other') and the "part-whole axiom" ('every whole is greater than its part').[31]
According to Aristotle, such principles also find their way into medicine. In
An.post. i,13, he says that there is a certain relationship between geometry and
medicine: "for it is for the doctor to know that circular wounds heal more
slowly, and for the geometer to know the reason why" [79a14–16]. The commentators are not agreed about just what geometrical principles are involved
in the slower healing of circular wounds;[32] but, whatever knowledge of such

---

30. "For a doctor seems not even to study health in this way [i.e., by studying the Idea of
health], but the health of man, or perhaps the health of a particular man; for it is individuals that
he is healing" [*EN* i,6,1097a11–14].

31. Euclid, *Elem.* i (10.1–12). See chapter 2, note 34.

32. The doctor knows only "the that" (*quia*, τὸ ὅτι), the geometer knows the why (*propter quid*,
τὸ διότι). According to Thomas, the *propter quid* is that a circle is a figure without angles [*in*

principles there is in medicine, it would seem also to presuppose the part-whole axiom.

When medicine takes a practical turn—that is, when it is explicitly directed at the medical good—does it involve common precepts, such as exist in practical reason itself?[33] There is danger here of becoming too insistent on the discovery of parallels. The common precepts of practical reason include especially extremely general, almost truistic principles, such as 'ill is to be done to no one' and 'one should act rationally.' Perhaps "primum non nocere" ought to be counted among these common precepts of medicine; or perhaps 'act as a doctor should' or 'act in accordance with medicine's principles' is a common medical precept. I do not think we should press this issue too far.

Two precepts located just below FPPR^m and whatever common precepts there are would be 'keep blood circulation going,' and 'maintain oxygen flow to the brain.' In years past, just below these two would have been found precepts like 'keep the patient's heart beating' and 'keep the patient breathing.' Medicine changes, however, and so do its principles—or at least some of them do. It is now possible to keep someone's blood circulation going without keeping his heart beating. Thus, the very same physical act which a century ago would have constituted murder—i.e., cutting the attaching veins and arteries and lifting the patient's heart out of his body—is now a part of medicine, as when, following the removal, another heart is put in its place.

Kenny remarks that, according to Aristotle, a doctor who deliberates whether or not to heal is deliberating "not *qua* doctor, but *qua* moral agent."[34] This is right, I believe; but I should wish to add that a doctor's action *qua* doctor is always, in some sense, physical. He is the practitioner of a craft and, even if much of his work involves study, that study is oriented toward the

---

An.post. lb.1 lect.25 ll.161–82 (§212); see also lb.1 lect.41 ll.13–30 (§357)]. Barnes gives a different explanation having to do with the greater area of circular wounds [Barnes (1994 <1975>), p. 160]; Philoponus has both these explanations [*in An.post.* 182.13–27]. See also Mignucci (1975), pp. 323–24. It is interesting that Alexander, in explaining the logical concept of being "in as in a whole" uses the example of a face wound [*in An.pr.* 50.2–7].

33. For the idea of practical intellect being "directed toward" good, see above, note 6 and further references there. On the common precepts, see chapter 2, section [7].

34. Kenny (1979), p. 147. Kenny actually hedges a bit, saying that the doctor deliberates either *qua* moral agent and not *qua* doctor, "or if deliberating *qua* doctor, then *qua* subscriber to the Hippocratic Oath rather than *qua* possessor of a certain technical skill." The hedge is a wise one, for the doctor who deliberates about whether to heal stands beyond medicine and its principles but is also concerned with it—and even perhaps with particular procedures. See *EN* iii,3,1112b12–16; v,9,1137a21–26.

cure of bodies. This essentially physical character of medicine is discernible also in the idea that the principles of medicine change as its techniques develop. If a century ago a doctor decided to lift a patient's heart out of his chest and in that way *not* to pursue the patient's health (let us say, as an act of "mercy killing"), he would not have been performing a medical act. As physical as the act might have seemed, he would have been acting *qua* ethician or perhaps *qua* philosopher, and his object would have been something quite abstract: what he—or even the patient—considered the "greater good." A medical act *qua* medical act is always directed toward a patient—and, in particular, toward his physical health. The radically physical character of medicine also becomes apparent when we advert to the fact that the identical act has moved from a necessarily non-medical act to being part of medicine. It has "moved into" the medical manuals because of changes in what doctors can do for the human body.[35]

Just as practical reason in general includes, besides the common precepts, also more distant ones, so also, among the precepts of medicine, but not located so close to FPPR^m (or PNC^m), are found various precepts corresponding to medical procedures: the things that doctors, *qua* doctors, do. Among such procedures are heart transplants, the hysterectomy procedure (or perhaps procedures), drug therapy for cancer, the surgical removal of cancerous tumors, and so on. The precepts corresponding to such procedures would be of the form, "In such-and-such circumstances, perform such-and-such procedure."

The relationships among some terms of medicine are "necessary" and are, therefore, best depicted by means of apodeictic syllogisms; the relationships among others are looser and best depicted by means of contingent syllogisms. Let us say, then, that a doctor is deliberating about whether to attempt to deal with a patient's cancer by means of drug therapy or surgery. Neither procedure is infallible—drug therapy, if begun too late, cannot reverse massive metastasis and surgery might miss some cancer or possibly so weaken the patient that death results. So, in making this deliberation, the doctor is not directly concerned with the higher, necessary precepts of medicine, although they are in the background and could be made explicit.

---

35. For the application of similar ideas to the problem of craniotomy, see Flannery (1993b), *passim,* but especially p. 513.

In other words, we can construct a sorites (i.e., a chain) along the following lines, in which 'O' = 'act that maintains oxygen flow to the brain,' L = 'act that maintains normal lung functions,' R = 'act that retards cancer from spreading through the lung,' D = 'drug therapy,' and S = 'surgery (on the lung).' ('G^m' represents, of course, medical good.) Let us also suppose that due to the weakness of a patient's lungs, either procedure could have the effect of halting the lungs' normal function. The doctor in question would, therefore, be deliberating with respect to the two syllogisms found in Table 5. [D*] and [S*] then might both be broken up into two syllogisms (found in Table 6), the one specified as apodeictic, the other contingent. And both [D*] and [S*] (not to mention their component syllogisms, found in Table 7) have their counterparts in the practical extension.

TABLE 5

[D*]		[S*]	
G^m→ every O		G^m→ every O	
O→ every L		O→ every L	
L→ every R		L→ every R	
R→ every D		R→ every S	
G^m→ every D		G^m→ every S	

TABLE 6

$[D*]^1$	NG^m→ every O	$[D*]^2$	CL→ every R
	NO→ every L		CR→ every D
	NG^m→ L		CL→ every D
$[S*]^1$	NG^m→ every O	$[S*]^2$	CL→ every R
	NO→ every L		CR→ every S
	NG^m→ every L		CL→ every S

TABLE 7

$[D*]^p$	G^m ←O	$[S*]^p$	G^m ←O
	O ←L		O ←L
	L ←R		L ←R
	R ←D		R ←S
	G^m ←D		G^m ←S

With these syllogisms (i.e., the variations on [D*] and [S*]), we have a fairly complete view of the structure of the craft of medicine. There are still, however, some things to be said about how individual pieces of (medical) reasoning fit into medicine. We can, however, see at this point that medicine contains apodeictic syllogisms and also contingent ones. These may or may not be expressly linked up with each other, although any contingent syllogism that is part of medicine will presuppose some sort of link with higher precepts and, ultimately, with G^m. It will be possible to fill in the gaps leading up to G^m in a more or less complete fashion, although medicine makes no pretensions that the gaps can be filled entirely with *per se* propositions.

Corresponding to the "theory" of medicine is a practical extension. The syllogisms of this extension map onto the perfect syllogisms of medical theory. As we have seen, Aristotle favors *Barbara* as the bearer of scientific knowledge; but, since the practical extension employs indefinite propositions, syllogisms in *Darii* might just as well provide the reference points for such mapping.

[6] Acts amid precepts

Let us take a step back now and consider practical reason in general. We have spoken of it as an extension of theoretical reason, involving both necessary and contingent elements that map onto their counterparts in theoretical reason. As we saw in chapter 2, natural law, which is parallel to the first principles of theoretical reason, contains a number of tiers:

$[\delta^3]$ = natural law precepts pertaining to rationality <9>

$[\delta^2]$ = natural law precepts pertaining to life <8>

$[\delta^1]$ = natural law precepts pertaining to being <7>

$[\gamma]$ = common precepts

$[\beta]$ = FPPR (first principle of practical reason)

$[\alpha]$ = good

Thomas suggests that the precepts of tier $[\delta]$ (subtiers $[\delta^1]$, $[\delta^2]$, and $[\delta^3]$) are also common precepts, although they are less general than those of tier $[\gamma]$. The precepts of $[\gamma]$ and $[\delta]$ are very closely bound up with the goods that constitute the base of practical reason and, as such, are *per se notum quoad nos*.

Besides, however, tiers $[\beta]$ through $[\delta]$, which in the strictest sense are the precepts of natural law, there are precepts that are merely "of the natural law."[36] These would be precepts and laws not *per se notum quoad nos;* they would also include the practically reasonable (rational) practices of crafts

---

36. See, for instance, *in Sent.* lb.4 d.26 q.2 a.2 ad 1: "[I]lla quae in communi sunt *de jure naturali,* indigent institutione quantum ad eorum determinationem, quae diversimode competit secundum diversos status"; *in Sent.* lb.4 d.33 q.1 a.1 c: "Si autem sit incompetens fini secundario quocumque modo, aut etiam principali, ut faciens difficilem vel minus congruam perventionem ad ipsum; prohibetur non quidem primis praeceptis legis naturae, sed secundis, quae ex primis derivantur; sicut conclusiones in speculativis ex principiis per se notis fidem habent; et *sic* dicta actio contra legem naturae esse dicitur"; see also, *ST* II–II q.85 a.1 ad 1: "Similiter etiam oblatio sacrificii in communi est *de lege naturae,* et ideo in hoc omnes conveniunt. Sed determinatio sacrificiorum est ex institutione humana vel divina, et ideo in hoc differunt."

such as medicine. Thus, if the acts of the practitioner of a craft take place against a background of necessary precepts, so also crafts, law, etc., are situated within the structure of natural law depicted just above. We might think of a large space, delimited by an infrastructure of girders, within which are supported a number of other smaller infrastructures. There is fixedness here but also a goodly amount of free space both within the smaller infrastructures and outside of them, although within the purview of the larger one.

A piece of practical reasoning is not well understood unless we know where within the complex structure of practical reason it takes place. This structure is ordered not as the streets of central Paris are ordered but as an organism is ordered. Practical reason's order cannot be discovered by looking just at its principles, as if it were a form imposed upon recalcitrant material, whatever it may be; it is discovered, rather, within the organism itself, which gives every appearance of having developed along principles of its own.[37]

If we wish to evaluate the morality of a particular act, we cannot look just at it, nor even can we just take into consideration the act and the goods at which it aims; we must, rather, understand where in the structure of practical reason it fits. It is true that the goods that constitute the basis and, in a certain sense, the principles of practical reason are enormously important, especially when one considers the system as a whole: they define the system in such a way that an attack on one of them is necessarily an attack on practical reason itself. But also important are the concrete cultural contexts within which we pursue these goods and avoid that which is incompatible with their pursuit, for it is in such contexts that the order (the "lawlikeness") of practical reason is found. Such pursuit and avoidance occurs in arguments or reasonings of small compass, employing a limited number of terms, often (but not always) taken from a particular craft or segment of the law. In other words, such thinking is "localized"—which means not only that it has a location within the structure but that it is local: it does not concern the whole of the structure but a perspicuous part of it.

[7] Analysis and natural deduction

This more localized type of reasoning is recognizable also in the analysis/synthesis geometrical method discussed in chapter 3. Taking a more

37. See chapter 6, section [4].

global view of what occurs even in a proof employing this method—the analysis phase leading from the desired conclusion up to the principles, the synthesis phase reversing the process—one is in danger of not seeing the distinctive characteristic of the analysis phase. As Hintikka and Remes point out, this distinctive characteristic is not so much the direction of activity but the fact that analysis employs its energies upon a particular construction, positing also auxiliary constructions. This has enormous methodological and philosophical significance. Adverting to what happens in the analysis phase, one descries that in terms of which the geometrical system grows: the system's material.

These ideas are applicable not only to geometry but also to logic; they are, therefore, relevant to what we are doing in the present chapter. Hintikka and Remes draw, as they say,

a comparison between the old method of analysis and certain relatively new techniques in symbolic logic which may be called natural deduction methods. In fact, more than a mere comparison is involved here, for the thesis put forward here [i.e., in Hintikka and Remes (1976)] is that the method of analysis is almost a special case of these natural deduction methods. Perhaps the most profound link between the two is a direct corollary to our interpretation of the ancient method as an analysis of a definite figure (i.e., configuration of geometrical objects). This implies . . . that the logic of the method satisfies the so-called subformula property, which is the characteristic feature of natural deduction methods.[38]

The "subformula property" was formulated by Gerhard Gentzen, the discoverer of modern natural deduction methods. Put simply, an argument characterized by the subformula property contains no element that is not a "subformula" of the final formula of the argument (which is the formula to be proved).[39] This ensures that the argument involves a limited number of terms, all related to the desired outcome, as in ancient geometrical analysis.[40]

38. Hintikka and Remes (1976), p. 253.
39. Gentzen (1955 <1934>), pp. 4–5, 49–51 (in particular 2.513). See also Gabbay and Guenthner (1994), vol. 1, p. 177. For formulas and subformulas, see Gabbay and Guenthner (1994), vol. 1, p. 50. If '$\phi \, \nu \, \psi$ 'is a formula, its subformulas are itself plus the subformulas of ϕ and the subformulas of ψ. See also Gentzen (1955 <1934>), pp. 9–11.
40. Gentzen introduced the subformula property by eliminating the so-called "cut-rule," an inference scheme that allows some information appearing elsewhere in an argument not to appear in its final formula. Gentzen (1955 <1934>), p. 45 (1.21); also pp. 93–97 (commentary by Ladrière). For some comments on the cut-rule in relation to Aristotle's syllogistic, see Lear (1980), pp. 90–97. For the cut-rule with respect to the syllogistic, see Thom (1981), pp. 36–41.

Indeed, one of the great strides forward in the modern study of Aristotle's syllogistic was the realization that it is a system of natural deduction. It is notable, says John Corcoran, that Aristotle does not use as his starting points simple propositions *(per se notum quoad nos)* like 'everything is predicated of all of itself' and 'everything is predicated of some of itself.' This is the sort of thing done in an axiomatic system, such as Russell and Whitehead's *Principia Mathematica*, and favored by interpreters of the syllogistic writing in the 1950s and 60s, such as Łukasiewicz and Bochenski.[41] Aristotle certainly knew that such truths—of which the common axioms are instances—were important; but he deliberately passed them over as the basis of his logic, employing instead the (more complicated) perfect syllogisms, which make conspicuous the conduits among terms, as explained above.[42] He did this because it better represents the way we think—to wit, in systems smaller in scope than reason in general. This is not to say that, once a particular problem is reasoned out, its reasonability (or, in practical reason, its "rationality") might not be demonstrated by showing how it fits into the larger system; but it is to say that the real "stuff" of reasoning—its material—is found on a more local level.

[8] The logic of localized analysis

In order to understand this, it will be useful to go through a particular piece of theoretical reasoning as represented in a modern system of natural deduction. The following proof is taken from a 1955 monograph by E. W. Beth, one of the most successful developments of Gentzen's methods. I choose this proof because it deals with a purportedly syllogistic figure and because it makes use of moves not unlike those found in Aristotle's method of ecthesis, as Beth acknowledges.[43]

Let us say that someone maintains that the following is a valid syllogism:

41. Łukasiewicz (1957); Bochenski (1951), pp. 42–54; (1961), pp. 72–81 (§14) [=Bochenski (1956), pp. 84–93]; Patzig (1968 <1963>), especially pp. 132–37. See also Corcoran (1973), p. 200, (1974), pp. 85–98, also Kneale and Kneale (1962), pp. 80–81.

42. Aristotle was aware that his approach does limit the terms that might appear in an argument: "a deduction referring *this* to *that* proceeds through the propositions that relate this to that" [*An.Pr.*i,23,41a6–7; see Smiley (1973), pp. 139–40].

43. Beth (1955), p. 316. Beth also acknowledges that his approach "realizes to a considerable extent the conception of a purely analytical method, which has played such an important role in the history of logic and philosophy" [Beth then cites Plato, *Phlb.*18BD, Aristotle *Metaph.*iv,3,1005b2, and Leibniz (1966 <1903>), *passim*] [Beth (1955), pp. 318–19].

M ⇸ some L

S ⇸ some M

S ⇸ some L

Instead of the above symbols, we must employ a more modern notation. In this notation, 'M ⇸ some L' (i.e., 'M does not hold of L') becomes '(Ex)[L(x) & –M(x)]' (i.e., 'there exists an x such that x is L and x is not M'). The propositions 'S ⇸ some M' and 'S ⇸ some L' are abbreviated similarly.

In order to show that (Ex)[L(x) & –M(x)] and (Ey)[M(y) & –S(y)] does not imply (Ez)[L(z) & –S(z)], we construct what Beth calls a "semantic tableau" (see p. 221)—which is, in effect, to construct a counter-example to the formula '(Ex)[L(x) & –M(x)] & (Ey)[M(y) & –S(y)] ⇒ (Ez)[L(z) & –S(z)].' The left column of the tableau is marked 'valid' and there we put (Ex)[L(x) & –M(x)] and (Ey)[M(y) & –S(y)]; the right column is marked 'invalid' and there we put (Ez)[L(z) & –S(z)]. If, using valid rules of transformation, we can analyze (i.e., break up into parts) each side of the tableau, testing out the various possibilities thereby revealed, and thus find a combination of possibilities that does not involve any inconsistencies, we shall have constructed a counter-example demonstrating that, when (Ex)[L(x) & –M(x)] and (Ey)[M(y) & –S(y)] are true, (Ez)[L(z) & –S(z)] might be false.

The relevant rules of transformation are:

[i] If –X appears in one column, insert X in the other.

[ii] If 'X & Y' appears in a left column, insert X and Y in the same column.

[iii] If 'X & Y' appears in a right column, make two subcolumns and place X in one and Y in the other.

[iv] If (Ex)X(x) appears in a left column, insert X(a) in the same column; if (Ey)X(y) appears, insert X(b), and so on. (The alphabetically early letters, 'a', 'b', 'c', etc., represent individuals.)

[v] If in a left column are found X(a), X(b), etc., if in the right column is found (Ex)X(x), in the right column insert X(a), X(b), etc.[44]

These rules are complex, but the idea behind them is fairly simple. We are seeking a counter-example—i.e., a model satisfying both the premises and

---

44. Beth (1955), pp. 320–21; or see Hintikka and Remes (1976), p. 258. The rules that Beth gives are formulated slightly differently and he has more than the five I have given—which are the only ones needed for the tableau presented below.

TABLE 8

Valid		Invalid	
(1) (Ex)[L(x) & –M(x)]		(3) (Ez)[L(z) & –S(z)]	
(2) (Ey)[M(y) & –S(y)]		(7) M(a)	
(4) L(a) & –M(a)	{1}	(8) L(a) & –S(a)	
(5) L(a)		(9) –S(a)	{5},{8}
(6) –M(a)		(14) S(b)	{13}
(10) S(a)	{9}	(15) L(b) & –S(b)	{3}
(11) M(b) & –S(b)	{2}	(16) L(b)	{13},{15}
(12) M(b)			
(13) –S(b)			

the negation of the conclusion. That is the reason for putting the premises in the left column, the conclusion in the right ("invalid") column. Having done that, we want to test out all the possibilities residing in the terms as set out, to see whether the premises and the negation of the conclusion can be maintained in the presence of some model of the way things might stand in the world.

Thus, according to rule [i], if –X appears in one column, X appears in the other, for the columns assign opposite truth values. The sense of rule [ii] is obvious; that of rule [iii] is less so. The reason why 'X & Y' in a right column go into two subcolumns is that, in order to test out 'X & Y' in the invalid column, we must deal with both X *and* Y, which opens up two sets of possibilities which must be tested out.[45] Rule [iv] takes seriously the sense of a formula like (Ex)X(x) ('there exists an x such that x is X') by positing just such an x. (This is similar to what Aristotle does in ecthesis.) Rule [v] makes sure that the model posited for the left column is the same one tested out in the right. There is also a more general rule for interpreting the meaning of such a tableau: if we exhaust the possible uses of rules [i] to [v] without putting the same formula in two conjugate columns ('valid' and 'invalid'), then we have the counter-example sought.

The tableau for a counter-example to (Ex)[L(x) & –M(x)] & (Ey)[M(y) & –S(y)] ⟹ (Ez)[L(z) & –S(z)] is shown in Table 8. The numbers in round

45. If we are seeking a counter-example to the formula 'if x then y and z,' if it is demonstrated that 'if x then y,' we might still have a counter-example if 'if x then not z.'

DIAGRAM 1

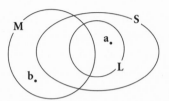

brackets in either column indicate the progress of the argument; the numbers in curly brackets indicate the lines upon which an operation depends. Thus, having set out the assumptions (1), (2), and (3), and then, employing rule [ii], having gone through steps (4) through (6) in the "valid" column, we jump over to the "invalid" column, employing rule [i]. Line (8) is in accordance with rule [v], etc., etc. It will be noticed that in line (8) rule [iii] is not followed through with respect to both conjuncts; this is because, in effect, L(a) appears in both the left and the right columns, thereby closing off that possibility. Following through, however, with the other conjunct, –S(a), is sufficient to produce the counter-example. A similar thing happens at lines (15)–(16). The jumping back and forth between the right and left columns is reminiscent of what happens in geometrical analysis. The proof does not proceed in linear fashion from the principles (i.e., the premises) down; it is a matter rather of, by means of an hypothesis, finding a way to bridge the gap between principles and conclusion. In this case, the effort is successful. The counter-example is a model in which b is not-L (16), M (12) and not-S (14), while a is L (5), not-M (6), S (10). Diagram 1 makes it apparent that the model is a possible one. The two objects demanded by the presuppositions, (1) through (3), have been brought into relation with each of the predicates (L, M, and S), in a way consistent with the two sides of the tableau and without contradiction.

A similar thing occurs in a typical piece of practical reasoning. The overall structure is not often that of constructing a counter-example—we recall that the point of the above tableau is to demonstrate that $(Ez)[L(z) \ \& \ –S(z)]$ does *not* follow from $(Ex)[L(x) \ \& \ –M(x)]$ and $(Ey)[M(y) \ \& \ –S(y)]$—but the principle is the same. The reasoning process makes use of a limited number of terms, by means of which it constructs a model—i.e., a way up to the principles which are the goods sought. In the example of natural deduction just given, it is also apparent why this method is called "analysis" or the breaking up of a larger unit into its smallest parts.[46] One constructs the counter-example by working toward simple formulas like L(a), S(b), etc. A good piece of practical reasoning does much the same: it goes from step to step until it arrives—or clearly fails to arrive—at the good sought. It is this correspondence between what happens in theoretical and in practical reason that allows the mapping on of which I spoke above.

A large number of important discoveries in both logic and mathematics have been made employing natural deduction methods. There can be little doubt that this usefulness arises from the fact that these methods approximate more closely the way we think naturally—that is to say, in smaller systems that can be "gathered together," so to speak, before the mind's eye. (The Greek word *syllogismos* means 'a gathering together.') We do sometimes set out whole systems so as to show how particular propositions are derived from the starting points or axioms; but this is a final, retrospective sort of task.[47] The growth of such systems occurs more locally.

[9] The principle of double effect, again

Let us take, then, a final look at the logic of moral prohibitions and the principle of double effect. To use the example discussed in the previous chapter, suppose there is a doctor whose patient is pregnant and would be more likely to survive if the cranium of the fetus she carries is crushed. Using the notation introduced earlier, we might say that the doctor reasons as follows:

medical-good ← craniotomy
craniotomy ← narrowing of skull
medical-good ← narrowing of skull

The procedure the doctor is contemplating would be allowable if he could show that this piece of reasoning is in accord with natural law, i.e., if he could show that it constitutes an accepted human practice. But it does not. In fact, it is false that 'medical-good ← craniotomy,' since only those things that lead to medical good (i.e., that fulfill FPPR[m]) are accepted medical practices. It is false to say that the practical reasoning going from 'craniotomy' to 'medical-

46. See chapter 3, note 47.
47. See Barnes (1969), (1981), MacIntyre (1990a), pp. 23–33.

good' is "rational," in the sense identified above. Or, as we might put this alternatively:

medical-good $\nrightarrow$ any craniotomy

craniotomy $\rightarrow$ any narrowing of skull

medical-good $\nrightarrow$ any narrowing of skull

The major premiss here corresponds to the negative side of FPPR$^{m\cdot}$ It is not required that we supply a series of steps between the concrete act of narrowing the skull and the highest medical principle, as we would in a positive chain of practical reasoning.

This assessment of the morality of the act of craniotomy depends on placing it within a particular context, medicine. We cannot go immediately to the principles (the goods) in order to determine the morality of an act; we must understand where within practical reason it fits. But could craniotomy be allowed under the aegis of some other craft or analogous manual of practices? Might it be justified somehow as an act of self-defense? In order to determine whether this is a legitimate interpretation of the act, a moralist would have to show that craniotomy belongs to some legitimate manual of practices in which self-defense plays a part. It seems unlikely that he will find craniotomy among the procedures listed in a military manual, so he will probably turn simply to the law and the accepted practice of personal self-defense. But a good system of law includes no provision for directly depriving an innocent person of life, so there is no avenue here. Obviously, I have made no effort here to demonstrate that no good system of law allows direct killing of the innocent; but I believe that this can be done by employing other well-known methods of investigation: testing for consistency of argumentation, for correspondence to common sense and to general principles of sound jurisprudence, etc.

Human nature includes a limited number of professions and crafts, so it will eventually be possible to say whether a procedure is moral or not. Why it is immoral is a more straightforward affair. Craniotomy is immoral because it is an attack upon human life—and life is "to be pursued." But in order to show that it is an attack upon human life, we have to show first that the intention to kill involved in craniotomy is not re-directed along a path defining an intelligible practice that is part of ethical behavior in general.

What about the hysterectomy case, i.e., the case where a woman requires an operation to remove a cancerous uterus which also happens to contain a live fetus? As explained in the previous chapter, in order to perform the hysterectomy morally, the doctor and the woman have to have been forced into the situation in which they find themselves. They cannot be using the presence of cancer on the uterus as a legalistic excuse for abortion, as they would be if the operation for cancer could just as well wait until after the birth of the fetus. Similarly, the person who deliberately keeps in his house only an assault weapon that cannot but kill when fired at an intruder cannot claim that he did not intend to kill the intruder he kills if he had the opportunity to exchange the weapon for a less damaging one but declined to make the exchange.

Such considerations make determining the morality of a prospective hysterectomy in such circumstances a difficult matter and one involving, as an indispensable element, prudential judgment. In order to decide whether he should perform the operation, the doctor must take into consideration things like how likely it is that the woman can wait for the operation until after giving birth. If it is apparent to him that she could wait, the piece of practical reasoning 'medical good ← hysterectomy ← removal of womb' would be defeated.

But it is to such type of judgment that the practical extension is exactly suited. Whether a hysterectomy is necessary in certain circumstances is not the sort of thing one determines by subsuming a case under a rule and making a deduction. In appropriate circumstances, the following is a sound (theoretical) syllogism: 'medical good → every hysterectomy; hysterectomy → every removal of womb; therefore, medical good → every removal of womb—i.e., in circumstances in which a woman requires an hysterectomy. But although the piece of the reasoning that goes into deciding whether or not to perform an hysterectomy might map onto that syllogism, as we have seen, practical reasoning is a looser affair. Prudential judgment in the light of circumstances may very well bring a doctor to the judgment that there is a true connection between the act of performing a hysterectomy and the medical good of his patient. But he is not obliged to draw the conclusion 'remove the womb,' as he is obliged to draw the conclusion (in certain circumstances) that 'medical good → every removal of the womb.'

Given, then, this caveat, i.e., that in order to perform a hysterectomy morally a doctor must be forced by circumstances into the act, it is apparent how the hysterectomy even of a gravid uterus could be judged the morally right thing to do. The doctor reasons as follows:

medical-good ← hysterectomy
hysterectomy ← remove the womb
medical-good ← remove the womb

Since there is an accepted medical procedure known as hysterectomy, unlike the craniotomy practical syllogism above, this one is true (or, rather, rational), presuming, of course, that the doctor is not deceiving himself about whether the hysterectomy is necessary. *Were* the doctor deceiving himself, there would be present in his soul a practical contradiction. He would be both pursuing and not pursuing the good of human life. He would be generally oriented, as we all are, toward pursuing and protecting human life, even while being prepared to attack it directly.

Appendices

SUMMA THEOLOGIAE I–II Q.94 A.2

Utrum lex naturalis contineat plura praecepta vel unum tantum

Videtur quod lex naturalis non contineat plura praecepta, sed unum tantum. Lex enim continetur in genere praecepti, ut supra habitum est. Si igitur essent multa praecepta legis naturalis, sequeretur quod etiam essent multae leges naturales.

Praeterea, lex naturalis consequitur hominis naturam. Sed humana natura est una secundum totum, licet sit multiplex secundum partes. Aut ergo est unum praeceptum tantum legis naturae, propter unitatem totius, aut sunt multa, secundum multitudinem partium humanae naturae. Et sic oportebit quod etiam ea quae sunt de inclinatione concupiscibilis, pertineant ad legem naturalem.

Praeterea, lex est aliquid ad rationem pertinens, ut supra dictum est. Sed ratio in homine est una tantum. Ergo solum unum praeceptum est legis naturalis.

Sed contra est quia sic se habent praecepta legis naturalis in homine quantum ad operabilia, sicut se habent prima principia in demonstrativis. Sed prima principia indemonstrabilia sunt plura. Ergo etiam praecepta legis naturae sunt plura.

<1> Respondeo dicendum quod sicut supra dictum est, praecepta legis naturae hoc modo se habent ad rationem practicam, sicut principia prima

SUMMA THEOLOGIAE I–II Q.94 A.2

Whether Natural Law Contains Many Precepts or One Only[1]

Objection 1: It seems that natural law does not contain many precepts but one only. For law is contained in the genus of precept, as stated above [*ST* I–II q.92 a.2]. If then there were many precepts of natural law, it would follow that there would also be many natural laws.

Objection 2: Moreover, natural law follows upon human nature. But human nature with respect to the whole is one, even though with respect to its parts it is many. So, either there is just one precept of the law of nature because of the unity of the whole, or there are many because of the variety of the parts of human nature. And in this way it will follow that even those things that are of the concupiscible inclination pertain to natural law.

Objection 3: Moreover, law is something that pertains to reason, as was said above [*ST* I–II q.90 a.1]. But reason in man is just one. Thus there is just one precept of natural law.

On the other hand, the precepts of natural law in man stand with respect to things to be performed as the first principles in demonstrative things. But the first indemonstrable principles are many. So also the precepts of the law of nature are many.

I respond that <1>, as was said above [*ST* I–II q.91 a.3], the precepts of the law of nature stand with respect to practical reason as the first principles of

---

1. I have inserted numbers in pointed brackets into the *corpus.* These are for easier reference. They also correspond to the numbers that Grisez uses in his translation of the *corpus* [Grisez (1965), pp. 170–71], although I have broken his <7> into three parts: <7>, <8>, and <9>. The Latin which has been translated appears on facing pages.

demonstrationum se habent ad rationem speculativam, utraque enim sunt quaedam principia per se nota.

<2> Dicitur autem aliquid per se notum dupliciter, uno modo, secundum se; alio modo, quoad nos. Secundum se quidem quaelibet propositio dicitur per se nota, cuius praedicatum est de ratione subiecti, contingit tamen quod ignoranti definitionem subiecti, talis propositio non erit per se nota. Sicut ista propositio, homo est rationale, est per se nota secundum sui naturam, quia qui dicit hominem, dicit rationale, et tamen ignoranti quid sit homo, haec propositio non est per se nota. Et inde est quod, sicut dicit Boetius, in libro De hebdomad., quaedam sunt dignitates vel propositiones per se notae communiter omnibus, et huiusmodi sunt illae propositiones quarum termini sunt omnibus noti, ut, omne totum est maius sua parte, et, quae uni et eidem sunt aequalia, sibi invicem sunt aequalia. Quaedam vero propositiones sunt per se notae solis sapientibus, qui terminos propositionum intelligunt quid significent, sicut intelligenti quod angelus non est corpus, per se notum est quod non est circumscriptive in loco, quod non est manifestum rudibus, qui hoc non capiunt.

<3> In his autem quae in apprehensione omnium cadunt, quidam ordo invenitur. Nam illud quod primo cadit in apprehensione, est ens, cuius intellectus includitur in omnibus quaecumque quis apprehendit. Et ideo primum principium indemonstrabile est quod non est simul affirmare et negare, quod fundatur supra rationem entis et non entis, et super hoc principio omnia alia fundantur, ut dicitur in IV Metaph.

<4> Sicut autem ens est primum quod cadit in apprehensione simpliciter, ita bonum est primum quod cadit in apprehensione practicae rationis, quae

demonstrations stand with respect to theoretical reason, for both are *per se* known principles of some sort.

<2> Something is said to be 'known *per se*' in two ways: either *secundum se* ["in consideration of itself"] or *quoad nos* ["with regard to us"]. Thus, a proposition whose predicate is part of the intelligibility of the subject is said to be *secundum se* known *per se,* although it can happen that, to one who does not know the definition of the subject, such a proposition will not be known *per se.* For instance, the proposition 'man is rational' is known *per se* with respect to its nature since whoever says 'man' says 'rational'; to one who does not know what man is, however, this proposition is not known *per se.* Whence it is that, as Boethius says in the book *De hebdomadibus,* there are certain axioms or propositions that are known *per se* commonly to all and of this sort are those propositions whose terms are known to all, such as 'every whole is greater than its part' and 'those things that are equal to one and the same thing are equal to each other.' Certain propositions, however, are known *per se* only to the wise, who understand what the terms of the propositions signify: as, for instance, to one who knows that an angel is not a body, it is known *per se* that an angel is not circumscriptively in a place—something that is not apparent to the uneducated, who do not understand this.

<3> Among those things, however, that fall within the apprehension of all,[2] a certain order is discovered. For that which falls first within apprehension is being, the comprehension of which is included in whatever a person apprehends. And therefore the first indemonstrable principle is that 'to affirm and simultaneously to deny is not [to be done],' which is founded upon the intelligibility of being and not-being; and on this principle all others[3] are founded, as is said in the fourth book of the *Metaphysics.*[4]

<4> Just as, however, being is the first thing that falls within apprehension *simpliciter,* so good is the first thing that falls within the apprehension of

2. Many modern editions read *hominum* ("of men") here instead of omnium ("of all"), but the Leonine edition's *omnium* is better attested.
3. Some few manuscripts read "super hoc principio omnia alia principia fundantur" instead of the Leonine edition's "super hoc principio omnia alia fundantur."
4. The Leonine edition makes reference to Thomas's *in Metaph.* §603 (ad *Metaph.* iv,3,1005b18). There Thomas says that every demonstration "reduces its propositions to this proposition" (i.e., to PNC). "Et propter hoc omnes demonstrationes reducunt suas propositiones in hanc propositionem, sicut in ultimam opinionem omnibus communem: ipsa enim est naturaliter principium et dignitas omnium dignitatum."

ordinatur ad opus, omne enim agens agit propter finem, qui habet rationem boni.

<5> Et ideo primum principium in ratione practica est quod fundatur supra rationem boni, quae est, bonum est quod omnia appetunt. Hoc est ergo primum praeceptum legis, quod bonum est faciendum et prosequendum, et malum vitandum. Et super hoc fundantur omnia alia praecepta legis naturae, ut scilicet omnia illa facienda vel vitanda pertineant ad praecepta legis naturae, quae ratio practica naturaliter apprehendit esse bona humana.

<6> Quia vero bonum habet rationem finis, malum autem rationem contrarii, inde est quod omnia illa ad quae homo habet naturalem inclinationem, ratio naturaliter apprehendit ut bona, et per consequens ut opere prosequenda, et contraria eorum ut mala et vitanda. Secundum igitur ordinem inclinationum naturalium, est ordo praeceptorum legis naturae.

<7> Inest enim primo inclinatio homini ad bonum secundum naturam in qua communicat cum omnibus substantiis, prout scilicet quaelibet substantia appetit conservationem sui esse secundum suam naturam. Et secundum hanc inclinationem, pertinent ad legem naturalem ea per quae vita hominis conservatur, et contrarium impeditur.

<8> Secundo inest homini inclinatio ad aliqua magis specialia, secundum naturam in qua communicat cum ceteris animalibus. Et secundum hoc, dicuntur ea esse de lege naturali quae natura omnia animalia docuit, ut est coniunctio maris et feminae, et educatio liberorum, et similia.

practical reason, which is ordered toward action; for every agent acts for an end, which has the intelligibility of a good.

<5> And therefore the first principle in practical reason is that which is founded upon the intelligibility of good, which is that 'good is that which all desire.' This is therefore the first precept of law: that good is to be done and pursued and evil avoided.[5] And on this are founded all the other precepts of the law of nature—so that clearly all those things that are to be done and avoided, which practical reason apprehends naturally to be human goods, pertain to the precepts of the law of nature.

<6> Because however the good has the intelligibility of an end, evil the intelligibility of the contrary, thus it is that all those things for which man has a natural inclination reason naturally apprehends as good and thus as actively to be pursued, and their contraries as evil and to be avoided.[6] Consequently, with respect to the order of natural inclinations, there is an order of the precepts of the law of nature.

<7> First of all, there is in man the inclination to good according to the nature that he shares with other substances—just as, that is, any substance desires the conservation of its own being in accordance with its nature. And in accordance with this inclination, those things by means of which the life of a man is conserved (and the contrary impeded) pertain to natural law.

<8> Secondly, there is in man the inclination to certain things more specific, according to the nature that he shares with other animals. And according to this, those things are said to be of natural law which nature teaches all animals[7]—as, for instance, the union of male and female, the raising of offspring, and similar things.

5. Of these two expressions—"is to be done" [*faciendum*] and "is to be pursued" [*prosequendum*]—the latter represents Thomas's central concern [see Finnis (1998), pp. 86, 99].

6. The expression 'to be pursued' *(prosequendum)* can be misleading. Thomas does not mean that a particular good ought always, all things considered, to be pursued. His point is that each good has its intelligibility as a good insofar as it is something to be pursued. If men did not regard it as to be pursued, it would not be a good. He takes the concept from Aristotle, for whom to perceive something as pleasant or painful is as if to pursue or avoid it (*De an.* iii,7,431a8–10; *EN* ii,3,1104b22; *EE* ii,4,1221b33). John Damascene associates pursuing and avoiding with the Stoic terms ὁρμή and ἀφορμή [*De fide orth.* bk.2 c.19]. See also Gauthier (1954), p. 66, especially n. 54. See also von Arnim (1964), vol. 3, §§169,175.

7. The Leonine edition cites here Justinian's *Digest*, the first book, first chapter ("De iustitia et iure") [P. Krueger and T. Mommsen (1900–1905), vol. 1, p. 1 (second series of page numbers)], where we find the words, "Ius naturale est, quod natura omnia animalia docuit . . .". Finnis points out that Thomas's words "the union of male and female" ["coniunctio maris et feminae"] also appear with minor changes within the same sentence of the *Digest*: "Hinc descendit maris atque

<9> Tertio modo inest homini inclinatio ad bonum secundum naturam rationis, quae est sibi propria, sicut homo habet naturalem inclinationem ad hoc quod veritatem cognoscat de deo, et ad hoc quod in societate vivat. Et secundum hoc, ad legem naturalem pertinent ea quae ad huiusmodi inclinationem spectant, utpote quod homo ignorantiam vitet, quod alios non offendat cum quibus debet conversari, et cetera huiusmodi quae ad hoc spectant.

Ad primum ergo dicendum quod omnia ista praecepta legis naturae, inquantum referuntur ad unum primum praeceptum, habent rationem unius legis naturalis.

Ad secundum dicendum quod omnes inclinationes quarumcumque partium humanae naturae, puta concupiscibilis et irascibilis, secundum quod regulantur ratione, pertinent ad legem naturalem, et reducuntur ad unum primum praeceptum, ut dictum est. Et secundum hoc, sunt multa praecepta legis naturae in seipsis, quae tamen communicant in una radice.

Ad tertium dicendum quod ratio, etsi in se una sit, tamen est ordinativa omnium quae ad homines spectant. Et secundum hoc, sub lege rationis continentur omnia ea quae ratione regulari possunt.

<9> Thirdly, there is in man the inclination to good according to the nature of reason, which is proper to him: man has, for instance, a natural inclination to know the truth about God, and to live in society. And in this respect, those things that concern an inclination of this sort pertain to natural law, with the result that man ought to avoid ignorance, ought not to offend those with whom he must deal, and others of this sort concerning the same.

Response 1: All those precepts of the law of nature, insofar as they are referred to a single first precept, have the intelligibility of a single natural law.

Response 2: Every inclination of whichever parts of human nature—for instance, the concupiscible part or the spirited part—to the extent that they are regulated by reason pertain to natural law and are reduced to the single first precept, as has been said. And in this respect, there are many precepts of the law of nature in themselves, which share however a single common source.

Response 3: Reason, although in itself one, directs all that concerns man. And in this respect, under the law of reason is contained everything that is capable of being regulated by reason.

---

feminae coniunctio, quam nos matrimonium appellamus, hinc liberorum procreatio, hinc educatio . . ." [Finnis (1998), pp. 97–98]. This lends credence to the Leonine edition's reading *coniunctio* instead of *commixtio*. (The reading is in any case well attested.) The difference is significant. The word *commixtio* tends to refer narrowly to sexual intercourse; *coniunctio* connotes also the common life that a couple enjoys together. See also *in Sent.* lb.4 d.26 q.1 a.1 c; *in EN* lb.5 lect.12 ll.57–75 (§1019). On the place of natural inclinations in Thomas's natural law theory, see Composta (1975).

THE *PER SE* IN THOMAS AQUINAS

Thomas explicitly recognizes in his commentary on the *Posterior Analytics* §§84–88 four ways of being *per se:* {1} when the predicate represents something that belongs to the essence of the subject; {2} when the subject represents something that contributes to the definition of the predicate; {3} when there is no question of a predicate holding of a subject; {4} when the predicate represents an effect that is contained in the subject on account of itself [*inest unicuique propter seipsum*], the subject being the corresponding cause, as when 'has perished' is said of 'the slain.'[1]

In *in An.post.* §83, he associates the *per se* with the various sorts of Aristotelian causation:

This preposition *per* designates the presence of a cause [*habitudinem causae*]; and it designates also sometimes a situation, as when someone is said to be *per se* when alone. Sometimes it designates the presence of a formal cause, as when it is said that a body lives *per* a soul; sometimes it designates the presence of a material cause, as when it is said that a body is colored *per* its surface—because, that is, the proper subject of color is a surface. It designates also the presence of an extrinsic cause—principally an efficient cause—as when it is said that water grows warm *per* fire. Just as this preposi-

---

1. John Philoponus is certainly right to say that we must understand at *An.post.* i,4,73b14 κατὰ σφαγήν (roughly, "on account of the slaying") [Philoponus, *in An.post.* 64.27–29]—and Thomas interprets Aristotle this way. The words *propter se ipsum* at *in An.post.* lb.1 lect.10 l.126 (§88) refer therefore to the subject (or cause): the slain thing has perished on account of being slain (i.e., the slaying). The expression translated here 'the slain has perished' is *interfectum interiit* [*in An.post.* lb.1 lect.10 ll.132–33 (§88)]. This corresponds to Aristotle's οἷον εἴ τι σφαττόμενον ἀπέθανε [*An.post.* i,4,73b14]. The word σφάζω has connotations related to ritual sacrificial killing and is probably best translated into English as sacrifice. See also *in An.post.* lb.1 lect.26 ll.31–38 (§214).

tion *per* designates the presence of a cause when something extrinsic is the cause of that which is attributed to the subject, so also, when the subject or some part of it is the cause of that which is attributed to it, *per se* signifies also this.[2]

The first sentence in this quotation refers to *per se* predications of type {3}. For Thomas, in any case, {3} does not play a large part in the account of the structure of sciences that Aristotle puts forward in *An.post.* i, for that account is tied up with the way terms are related to each other causally, whereas {3} involves a single term. It is very much like the English expression 'by oneself' which, if it might sometimes take on a causal sense ("he did it by himself"), is non-causal in most of its uses.[3]

The rest of the quotation refers to types {1}, {2}, and {4}, in that order. It is apparent that Thomas wishes to associate {1} and {2} with formal and material causation, respectively; but by distinguishing {1} and {2} from {4} is Thomas suggesting that category {4} excludes formal and material causation?[4] There is some reason to think that Thomas does mean to suggest this. In the passage just quoted, immediately after discussing {1} and {2}, Thomas says with reference to {4} that *per se* "designates also the presence of an extrinsic cause—principally an efficient cause—as when it is said that water grows warm *per* fire." Since only efficient and final causes are extrinsic,[5] he

---

2. "Circa primum sciendum est quod haec praepositio 'per' designat habitudinem causae, designat etiam interdum et situm, sicut cum dicitur aliquis esse 'per se,' quando solitarius. Causae autem habitudinem designat aliquando quidem formalis, sicut cum dicitur quod corpus vivit per animam; quandoque autem habitudinem causae materialis, sicut cum dicitur quod corpus est coloratum per superficiem, quia scilicet proprium subiectum coloris superficies est; designat etiam habitudinem causae extrinsecae, et praecipue efficientis, sicut cum dicitur quod aqua calescit per ignem. Sicut autem haec praepositio 'per' designat habitudinem causae quando aliquid extrinsecum est causa eius quod attribuitur subiecto, ita quando subiectum vel aliquid eius est causa eius quod attribuitur ei, et hoc significat 'per se'" [*in An.post.* lb.1 lect.10 ll.8–24 (§83)].

3. At *in Metaph.* §1057, Thomas remarks with respect to {3}: "Hic autem secundum se dicitur ratione solitudinis." I do not mean to suggest that {3} is entirely alien to theoretical and practical reason (see the summary of Albert the Great's analysis in note 17, below) but that more important for understanding the structure of theoretical and practical reason are the other three ways of being *per se*. Also, {3} might be said to play a role in *An.post.* ii, where Aristotle speaks a great deal about definitions; there is, however, no attempt either in Aristotle or in Thomas's commentary to link these *An.post.* ii discussions to type {3} *per se* predication.

4. The designations 'formal causation' and 'material causation' have more to do with the particular subject-predicate structure of a proposition which is part of a science than with causality properly considered. See, for example, *ST* III q.16 a.7 ad 4; also, Hoenen (1952), pp. 81–84 and Walton (1952), p. 294.

5. Thomas does not make this explicit in his commentary on the *Posterior Analytics*, but he discusses the issue frequently elsewhere. See, for instance, *SCG* lb.2 cap.31 (§1081), cap.81 (§1620); lb.3 cap.13 (§1966); *ST* I–II q.1 a.3 obj.1 (and ad 1); *De ver.* q.14 a.5 obj.2 ll.7–18; *in Phys.* lb.3 lect.5 n.15

would seem to be saying that {4} can represent neither formal nor material cause. Even though perishing (the example used for {4} above) clings very closely to 'being slain,' the relationship is still (shall we say) "linear." One thing *leads* to the other, even if there is no temporal distance. The situation is similar with final cause. Even though man seeks happiness by nature, happiness is something he needs to attain: it is not something he has, although he does have both matter and form.

There are, however, indications, even in this *lectio* of the commentary on the *Posterior Analytics,* that {4} might extend more widely than this. Thomas says in connection with way {4} that "haec praepositio 'per' designat habitudinem causae efficientis vel cuiuscunque alterius" ("this preposition *per* designates the presence of an efficient or of whatever other cause"—*in An.post.* §88).[6] The Leonine edition inserts in pointed brackets after *alterius* the word *extrinsicae,* which appears nowhere is the manuscript tradition, citing as reason *in An.post.* §83 (i.e., the passage given just above).[7] Textually, however, this clearly cannot stand; moreover, such an emendation would misrepresent Aristotle's meaning. First of all, the phrase *cuiuscunque alterius* is correlative with a type of cause, as the Commission acknowledges by supplying the specification "extrinsic"—and by not suggesting, for instance, that "whatever other" refers to possible instances or tokens of a type (or types). Besides efficient cause, however, there is only one other type of extrinsic cause, so the expression "*whatever* other" would be quite inappropriate did it refer to that. So, contrary to what the Leonine Commission suggests, way {4} must be capable of pertaining not only to extrinsic but also to intrinsic causes.

Is there then a contradiction between *in An.post.* §88 and §83, given that

---

(§322); *in Metaph.* §§833–35,899,1542,2464, 2468–70. In a short work entitled *De principiis naturae ad Fr. Sylvestrum,* he writes: "Causas autem accipit tam pro extrinsecis quam pro intrinsecis: materia et forma dicuntur intrinsecae rei eo quod sunt partes constituentes rem, efficiens et finalis dicuntur extrinsecae quia sunt extra rem . . ." [*De princ.nat.* cap.3 ll.47–51 (§352)].

6. *in An.post.* lb.1 lect.10 ll.123–25 (§88).

7. The Leonine edition cites with respect to *in An.post.* lb.1 lect.10 l.18 (§83) the words of Robert Grosseteste, "a sua causa vel efficiente vel formale vel materiale vel finale" [Grosseteste, *in An.post.* 111.56]. These words of Grosseteste refer, however, to {1}. Grosseteste thinks that {3} and {4} are added to the more important {1} and {2} in order to fill out the picture [Grosseteste, *in An.post.* 114.111–19]. The idea of extrinsic causes is quite strong in the Arabic Aristotelian tradition. See, for instance, Averroes, *in An.post.* 138b, who cites al-Fārābī in this connection. The idea that efficient cause is an external cause occurs perhaps also in a germane passage in Alexander: see his *in Metaph.* 416.24–25. See also Thomas's *in Metaph.* §764.

§83 speaks of "the presence of an extrinsic cause"? Closer study of the latter paragraph suggests no. Recall the final sentence of §83 (which comes just after the introduction of extrinsic causality): "Just as this preposition *per* designates the presence of a cause when something extrinsic is the cause of that which is attributed to the subject, so also, when the subject or some part of it is the cause of that which is attributed to it, *per se* signifies also this."[8] The first and second clauses of this "just as . . . so also" construction refer to different expressions: *per* and *per se*, respectively. Thomas is saying that, just as *per* signals an extrinsic cause, so *per se* signals the presence of a subject that is "the cause" of that which is attributed to it. In this second clause, just as in the expression *cuiuscunque alterius*, no mention is made of extrinsic causality. The mention of extrinsic causality in the remarks that immediately precede this sentence also refers to the word *per*, not to *per se*.

So, way {4} should not be separated off in any absolute fashion from predications of intrinsic cause. Its purpose, at least in certain contexts, seems rather to be to indicate the causal aspect of a predication within a demonstration, as opposed to the "directional-definitional aspect" indicated by {1} and {2}. That is, as opposed to {4}, ways {1} and {2} call attention to whether the subject is said to be part of the definition of the predicate or rather vice-versa.[9] But even this distinction is put forward fairly ambivalently, for Thomas is also quite willing to speak of {1} and {2} as involving causality. Way {1} does seem to be excluded from {4}—not, however, because it is intrinsic but because the direction of its (formal) causality goes from the predicate to-

---

8. *in An.post.* lb.1 lect.10 ll.19–24 (§83).

9. This is more or less the approach taken by Cajetan: "Circa quartum modum perseitatis diligenter adverte subtilissimam S. Thomae expositionem, secundum quam iste quartus modus distinguitur a secundo formaliter (ut dictum est) quia perseitas secundi est perseitas praedicationis, quarti vero causalitatis" [Cajetan, *in An.post.* lb.1 cap.4, p. 45]. It finds confirmation in Thomas's *in An.post.* lb.1 lect.10 ll.136–46 (§89): "Deinde cum dicit: 'Quae ergo dicuntur,' etc., ostendit qualiter utatur praedictis modis [i.e., ways {1}, {2}, {3}, and {4}] demonstrator. Ubi notandum est quod cum scientia proprie sit conclusionum, intellectus autem principiorum, proprie scibilia dicuntur conclusiones demonstrationis, in quibus passiones praedicantur de propriis subiectis; propria autem subiecta non solum ponuntur in definitione accidentium, sed etiam sunt causae eorum; unde conclusiones demonstrationum includunt duplicem modum dicendi per se, scilicet secundum et quartum." The second to last phrase here ("propria autem . . . causae eorum") seems to be the reason why ("*unde* . . ."), in the last phrase, he brings in type {4} predications as well as type {2}. I discuss this latter point below. Hoenan, referring to *ST* I q.77 a.6 ad 2 ["subiectum est causa proprii accidentis et finalis, et quodammodo activa; et etiam ut materialis, in quantum est susceptivum accidentis"], suggests that {4} "refers . . . to a cause that is in some way active" [Hoenan (1952), p. 98]. See also *ST* I–II q.54 a.2 ad 2: "diversa media sunt sicut diversa principia activa."

ward the subject. By contrast, we have a case of {4} "when the subject or some part of it is the cause of that which is attributed to it."[10]

Some other aspects of way {4} become evident in Thomas's commentary on *Metaphysics*, book v, chapter 18, in which latter place Aristotle again discusses the *per se*. Commenting in *in Metaph.* §1056 on the words at *Metaph.* v,18,1022a32–35 ("that which has no other cause other than itself; man has more than one cause—animal, two-footed—but man is man in virtue of himself"), Thomas says that Aristotle is there talking about "that of which there is no other cause, such as all immediate propositions—which, of course, are not proved by means of any middle term." He then identifies 'animal' and 'two-footed' as causes (in fact, formal causes) that might serve as middle terms in demonstrations, and he notes that no such demonstration is possible with the immediate predication 'man is man.'[11] He then says that "to this way is reduced the fourth way of saying *per se* posited in the *Posterior Analytics,* when an effect is predicated of its cause, as when it is said that the slain perishes on account of the slaying, or that that which is cold has become cold or becomes cool on account of the cooling."[12]

We have here more evidence that {4} pertains not just to extrinsic causes. The relationship between a cold thing and a cooling or between a slain thing and its slaying might be conceived as extrinsic, but it is very difficult to regard 'man is man' in this fashion. Indeed, one would think that 'man is man' involved formal causation.[13] But if we are being asked by Thomas, as seems to be the case, to assimilate these remarks to *in An.post.* §82–89, we should prob-

---

10. *in An.post.* lb.1 lect.10 ll.22–23 (§83); see also ll.131–35,147–54 (§§88–89).

11. Thomas's interpretation is also Ross's: "There are causes of man; his genus, his differentiae are formal causes of him. But there is no cause of man's being man; man is man καθ' αὑτό" [Ross (1953 <1924>), vol. 1, p. 334]. Cp. Kirwan (1993 <1971>), p. 170.

12. "Tertius modus est prout secundum se esse dicitur illud, cuius non est aliqua alia causa; sicut omnes propositiones immediatae, quae scilicet per aliquod medium non probantur. Nam medium in demonstrationibus propter quid est causa, quod praedicatum insit subiecto. Unde, licet homo habeat multas causas, sicut animal et bipes, quae sunt causae formales eius; tamen huius propositionis, homo est homo, cum sit immediata, nihil est causa; et propter hoc homo est homo secundum se. Et ad hunc modum reducitur quartus modus dicendi per se in posterioribus positus, quando effectus praedicatur de causa; ut cum dicitur interfectus interiit propter interfectionem, vel infrigidatum infriguit vel refriguit propter refrigerium" [*in Metaph.* §1056]. Among modern scholars, Kirwan, for instance, also says that the sense of *secundum se* explained at Metaph. v,18,1022a32–35 "reappears at *Posterior Analytics* i,4,73b10–16" [Kirwan (1993 <1971>), p. 170].

13. It might be argued that by saying "to this way is *reduced* the fourth way" Thomas means that {4} is not identical to the type of *per se* involved in 'man is man.' But he uses the word *reducitur* also at *in Metaph.* §1057, remarking that {3} is reduced to the fourth way of *Metaph.* v, and he

ably say that it involves material cause, the idea being presumably that the term 'man' can be predicated of 'man' because 'man' (the subject) necessarily is required by 'man' (the predicate). 'Man' the subject with respect to 'man' the predicate would then represent the limit-cases of proper subjects and predicates.[14] But perhaps we should not push Thomas's words too far in this instance: he is more interested in making sense of Aristotle's words in *Metaph.* v,18 than in reconciling them with what he says elsewhere.

Thomas's remarks at *in Metaph.* §1056 reveal also another, very important aspect of way {4}: that it involves immediate predications. He speaks, that is, of "that of which there is no other cause, such as all immediate propositions—which, of course, are not proved by means of any middle term." This idea also comes into the *Posterior Analytics* commentary. At *in An.post.* §88, for instance, he speaks of the slain who has perished—the two terms clearly being immediately related. There is also in the commentary on the *Posterior Analytics* an important passage in which he explains where in a demonstration immediate propositions might appear.

[S]ince in a demonstration the passion is proved to hold of the subject by way of a middle which is a definition, it is necessary that the first proposition, whose predicate is the passion and whose subject is the definition that contains the principles of the passion, be *per se* in the fourth way. <On the other hand, it is also necessary> that the

---

gives no indication of there existing a substantial difference between the two Aristotelian passages. This is not to say, however, that the concept 'to reduce' cannot be used to signify something less than identity.

At *in An.post.* lb.1 lect.35 ll.53–60 (§301) Thomas says that {3} and {4} can be "reduced" to {1} and {2} ["Nam 'impar' praedicatur de 'numero' per se secundo modo, quia numerus ponitur in definitione ipsius imparis: est enim impar numerus medio carens. 'Multitudo' autem vel 'divisibile' praedicatur de numero et ponitur in definitione eius, unde huiusmodi praedicantur per se de numero primo modo. Alii autem modi quos supra posuit reducuntur ad hos"]. On the basis of this passage, one might be tempted to take the opposite tack, discounting the differences among the ways of being *per se* identified by Thomas elsewhere (see, for instance, McInerny (1986), p. 192; also Schultz (1988a), pp. 168–69). But, although in Aristotelian contexts reduction does sometimes imply identity (this seems to be the case with the syllogistic reductions of the *Prior Analytics:* see *An.pr.* i,6,28b21; i,7,29a30–29b25), often it refers simply to a way of preventing infinite regresses. For instance, an efficient or final cause can always be led back to something's matter and/or form; but this does not mean that such causes are the intrinsic causes or principles of the things to which they are reduced. For Thomas, formal and material cause are reduced ultimately to God's final (and perhaps also efficient) causality (see *in Sent.* lb.1 d.19 q.5 a.1 c ["utraque autem veritas, scilicet intellectus et rei, reducitur sicut in primum principium, in ipsum Deum; quia suum esse est causa omnis esse, et suum intelligere est causa omnis cognitionis"] and lb.1 d.45 q.1 a.3 ad 5; also *in Metaph.* §70 and §840); but they are quite distinct from it.

14. On propositions "in quibus idem praedicatur de seipso," see *ST* I q.13 a.12 c. Here Thomas acknowledges that one element (the subject) functions as "material," the other (the predicate) as "form." See above, note 4.

second proposition, whose subject is the subject itself and whose predicate is the definition, be <*per se* in> the first way. The conclusion, however, in which the passion is predicated of the subject, is *per se* in the second way.[15]

What Thomas does here is, in effect, to put forward a model for all demonstrations of the *propter quid*—i.e., demonstrations of the reason why the predicate of a conclusion holds of the subject, which is the primary type of demonstration.[16] The conclusion, he says, must be of type {2}, the minor premiss of type {1}, and the major of type {4}.[17] Thomas says that the predicate of the minor "contains the principles of the passion," so the major premiss is clearly an immediate predication. A demonstration may actually involve a series of middle terms (or immediate definitions) by means of which the subject of the conclusion is connected with the predicate in a compact fashion.[18] The conclusion must be a proposition of type {2}, for it is not immediate and the minor term is proper to the major term (i.e., the "direction" is from bot-

15. "Sciendum autem est quod, cum in demonstratione probetur passio de subiecto per medium, quod est definitio, oportet quod prima propositio, cuius praedicatum est passio et subiectum definitio quae continet principia passionis, sit per se in quarto modo; secunda autem, cuius subiectum est ipsum subiectum et praedicatum ipsa definitio, <in> primo modo; conclusio vero, in qua praedicatur passio de subiecto, est per se in secundo modo" [*in An.post.* lb.1 lect.13 ll.60–69 (§111)].

16. On demonstrations of the *propter quid,* see Thomas's *in An.post.* lb.1 lect.13 ll.1–34 (§109), lb.1 lect.23 (§§192–200). At *in An.post.* lb.1 lect.26 ll.31–35 (§214), he remarks, "oportet autem in demonstratione 'propter quid' medium esse causam passionis quae praedicatur in conclusione de subiecto, et unus modus dicendi per se est quando subiectum est causa praedicati, ut: 'Interfectum interiit' . . .". Thomas is clearly referring here to way {4}. Hoenan notes that, although at *in An.post.* lb.1 lect.35 ll.46–60 (§301) Thomas suggests that {3} and {4} are reduced to {1} and {2}, here "the fourth <way> is considered the principle one" [Hoenen (1952), p. 321, n. 1; see also p. 98]. On *in An.post.* §301, see note 13.

17. Albert the Great gives a more complete scheme at his *in An.post.* 44–45. He first distinguishes demonstrations in which the "passion" (i.e., the predicate of the conclusion) is demonstrated of the minor term from those in which a material definition is demonstrated by means of a formal definition. The former have a type {4} major premiss and a type {2} conclusion; the latter have a {4}-{3}-{1} structure. In the former—let us call them "subject-predicate demonstrations"—if the middle term (which is expressed as a cause of the passion) is a definition of the passion, (a) it might be an essential part of the minor term or (b) it might be a consequence of the minor term. In case (a), the minor premiss is of type {1}; in case (b), it is of type {2}. Albert mentions also another type of subject-predicate demonstration in which the middle term is a formal definition of the minor term. Here, obviously, the minor premiss would be of type {1}. Both the major premiss and the conclusion would be of type {2}, "since the passion is predicated of the definition of the subject [i.e., it is predicated of the middle term, which is the definition of the minor term or subject] and the relation of the passion with respect to the subject is the same as toward its definition" [*quia praedicatur passio de definitione subiecti, et eadem est comparatio passionis ad subiectum et ad suam definitionem*—p. 45, col. a]. Cp. Tuninetti (1996), pp. 88–89.

18. *in An.post.* lb.1 lect.26 ll.54–83 (§216); lect.31 ll.34–78 (§§257–58).

tom to top). I refer to this model as the "{4}-{1}-{2} structure." One of the most important characteristics of these demonstrations is their compactness. There are no gaps within the string of middle terms connecting the subject and predicate of the conclusion.[19] How, or even whether, this structure comes into practical reason is an interesting question.

A passage cited above seems to go against the present interpretation.[20] In the passage (*in An.post.* §89), Thomas is dealing with *An.post.* i,4,73b16–18. The translation of the latter Aristotelian passage by James of Venice reads as follows: "Quae ergo dicuntur in simpliciter scibilibus per se sic sunt, sicut inesse praedicantibus aut inesse propter ipsa." Thomas associated these two ways of "existing in" something (i.e., "inesse praedicantibus" and "inesse propter ipsa") with ways {2} and {4} respectively. (Aristotle actually has in mind, however, not the difference between {2} and {4} but between that which is said *per se* in the sense of "inhering in what is predicated" and that which is said *per se* in the sense of "*being inhered in*": *An.post.*i,4,73b17–18: ὡς ἐνυπάρχειν τοῖς κατηγορουμένοις ἢ ἐνυπάρχεσθαι. This remark is difficult to interpret: see Barnes [1994 <1975>], p. 117.) In any case, Thomas says of 73b16–18:

Thus, when he says "Quae ergo dicuntur," etc., he shows how the demonstrator uses the aforesaid ways. Here it is to be noted that, since science is properly of conclusions and intellect is of principles, those conclusions of a demonstration are said to be properly knowable in which passions are predicated of their proper subjects. Proper subjects, however, are not only placed in the definitions of their accidents but also are their causes. Thus, the conclusions of demonstrations include a double way of saying *per se*—that is to say, the second and the fourth.

Thomas was criticized early on for interpreting Aristotle as saying that the conclusions to demonstrations are of type {2} or type {4}—or, more precisely,

---

19. For compactness in Aristotle, see Lear (1980), pp. 15–33. There are also a number of places in *in An.post.* where Thomas suggests that the connections among terms in *propter quid* demonstrations are necessary in either direction: see *in An.post.* lb.1 lect.11 ll.73–86 (§97); lb.2 lect.19 ll.85–136 (§578), ll.183–209 (§580). The idea of such mutual necessitation plays a part also in Euclid's geometry [Heath (1956 <1925>), vol. 1, p. 139], suggesting that the idea originates in that field of study. It seems to be present at *An.post.* i,4,74a3, ii,17,99a16–29, and also ii,18. On such "commensurate universals" see Barnes (1994 <1975>), pp. 258–59, who finds in Aristotle only the "rather humdrum thesis" that "some demonstrations will deal with commensurate universals." McKirahan offers a plausible way of understanding Aristotle's (and therefore also Thomas's) remarks in this regard [McKirahan (1992), pp. 95–98, 101–2 and especially 171–76].

20. The passage, *in An.post.* lb.1 lect.10 ll.136–46 (§89), is quoted and discussed in note 9.

for interpreting Aristotle as talking about conclusions rather than types of propositions used in demonstrations.[21] But, in fact, when Thomas says "conclusiones demonstrationum includunt duplicem modum dicendi per se, scilicet secundum et quartum," he does not mean that a conclusion might *be* of type {2} or type {4} but that conclusions "take in" propositions of type {2} and type {4}—i.e., they comprehend them insofar as the capability of deriving conclusions involves also the principles from which they arise. This idea turns up at a number of other places in Thomas. For instance, at *De pot.* q.1 a.3 obj.2, he says "in omni conclusione demonstrationis includuntur demonstrationis principia"; and, at *in Sent.* lb.3 d.30 q.1 a.4 c, he says, "alius est motus dilectionis qui terminatur in proximum et qui sistit in Deo, sicut alius actus est quo considerantur principia et conclusiones, quamvis praedicto modo mutuo se includant."[22]

To conclude, then, a passage in which Thomas actually discusses these matters will serve as an illustration of many of these ideas and also as an occasion to summarize what I have argued concerning Thomas's conception of *per se* predications. The discussion comes in *in De.an.* lb.2, cap.14 and concerns the syllogism "'visible' holds of 'moving the diaphanous'; 'moving the diaphanous' holds of 'color'; therefore, 'visible' holds of 'color.'" This latter is of the standard {4}-{1}-{2} structure: the motion of the diaphanous (i.e., the medium of light) is the immediate cause of visibility; 'moving the diaphanous' is bound up in the definition of color; color causes the visible as a proper passion.

---

21. See Zabarella, *in An.post.* 708DF; see also his *De prop.nec.* lb.2 cap.14–17 (400F–412C). See also Cajetan, who defends Thomas on the grounds that, as he interprets Thomas, "secundus modus et quartus modus coincidunt in unam propositionem secundum diversas conditiones" [*in An.post.* 45B].

22. The latter reference ("praedicto modo") is to the previous sentence: "[D]ilectio Dei est causa et ratio dilectionis proximi; unde dilectio Dei includitur virtute in dilectione proximi sicut causa in effectu, et dilectio proximi includitur in dilectione Dei sicut effectus in causa potestate." I understand Thomas, in the passage at *in Sent.* lb.3 d.30 q.1 a.4 c, to be presuming that, just as love of God and love of neighbor *can* be considered one, so also can a conclusion be considered as including its principles. See also *ST* I–II q.57 a.2 ad 2: "principia vero demonstrationis possunt seorsum considerari, absque hoc quod considerentur conclusiones. Possunt etiam considerari simul cum conclusionibus, prout principia in conclusiones deducuntur. Considerare ergo hoc secundo modo principia, pertinet ad scientiam, quae considerat etiam conclusiones, sed considerare principia secundum seipsa, pertinet ad intellectum." This latter passage is concerned with the same issue as *in An.post.* lb.1 lect.10 ll.136–74 (§89). Note that Aristotle too sometimes employs the word συλλογισμός with—or, perhaps better, without excluding—the meaning 'conclusion': *An.pr.* i,9,30a16; *De an.* i,3,407a27.

At *in De.an.* §§400–402, Thomas discusses in particular Aristotle's remarks at *De an.* ii,7,418a29–31, which run (at least according to the Latin translation used by Thomas): "color is visible; it is such, however, insofar as it is *per se* visible—*per se*, however, not by virtue of its *ratio* but because it has in itself the cause of being visible."[23] Thomas comments that, according to Aristotle,

since color is something visible, to be visible pertains to it *per se* since color, insofar as it is color, is visible. *Per se*, however, is said in two ways. For in one way a proposition is said *per se* whose predicate falls in the definition of the subject—e.g. 'man is animal,' for animal falls in the definition of man. And because that which falls in the definition of something is in a way its cause, in those <propositions> where *per se* is said in this way, the predicate is a cause of the subject.

A proposition is said to be *per se* in another way whose subject, on the contrary, is placed in the definition of the predicate, as when it is said that 'nose is pug' or 'number is even'—for 'pug' is nothing other than a curved nose and 'even' is nothing other than a number having a middle; and in these the subject is the cause of the predicate. We are to understand, then, that color is visible *per se* in this second way, for visibility is a sort of passion of color like pug is a passion of nose. And this is why he says that color is *per se* visible and not by virtue of its *ratio*, that is, not such that visible is placed in its definition, but because it has in itself the cause of its being visible as the subject has in itself the cause of its proper passion.[24]

Many commentators, noting Aristotle's emphasis on causation here, hold that Aristotle is saying that "'visible' holds of 'color'" (i.e., the conclusion to the

23. "Visibile enim est color, hoc est in eo quod secundum se visibile; secundum se autem non ratione, sed quoniam in se habet causam essendi visibile" [*in De.an.*, p. 123; Latin translation of William of Moerbeke]. The now accepted Greek text of the pertinent passage (*De an.* ii,7,418a29–31) runs as follows: τὸ γὰρ ὁρατόν ἐστι χρῶμα, τοῦτο δ' ἐστὶ τὸ ἐπὶ τοῦ καθ' αὑτὸ ὁρατοῦ· καθ' αὑτὸ δὲ οὐ τῷ λόγῳ, ἀλλ' ὅτι ἐν ἑαυτῷ ἔχει τὸ αἴτιον τοῦ εἶναι ὁρατόν. For another Thomistic remark on the sense in which color is *per se* visible, see *ST* I q.87 a.1 ad 1.

24. *in De.an.* lb.2 cap.14 ll.40–59 (§§400–402): "Dicit ergo primo quod, cum color sit quoddam visibile, esse visibile convenit ei secundum se: nam color in eo quod est color est visibilis. Per se autem dicitur dupliciter. Uno enim modo dicitur propositio per se cuius praedicatum cadit in definitione subiecti, sicut ista: homo est animal; animal enim cadit in definitione hominis; et quia id quod est in definitione alicuius est aliquo modo causa eius, in hiis quae sic per se dicuntur, praedicatum est causa subiecti. Alio modo dicitur propositio per se, cuius e contrario subiectum ponitur in definitione praedicati, sicut si dicatur: nasus est simus, vel: numerus est par; simum enim nihil aliud est quam nasus curvus, et par nihil aliud est quam numerus medietatem habens; et in istis subiectum est causa praedicati. Intelligendum est ergo, quod color est visibilis per se hoc secundo modo et non primo: nam visibilitas est quaedam passio sicut simum est passio nasi. Et hoc est quod dicit quod color 'secundum se' est visibile 'non ratione,' idest non ita quod visibile ponatur in eius definitione, sed quia 'in se ipso habet causam' ut sit visibile, sicut subiectum in se

syllogism set out above) is not of type {1} or {2} but of type {4}.[25] Thomas, however, consistent with his ambivalent way of treating such matters in *in An.post.* §§82–89, chooses to attend to the directional-definitional rather than the causal aspect: i.e., he argues that Aristotle is interested in the disparate definitional directions of ways {1} and {2}. What Thomas says here, however, is in full accordance with the {4}-{1}-{2} structure set out in *in An.post.* §111: "'visible' holds of 'color'" could not be a type {4} proposition since it is not immediate. This suggests that, of the various aspects of type {4} predications identified above, immediacy is the most important.

---

ipso habet causam propriae passionis." Note that the Leonine text differs considerably from the Marietti.

25. See Hicks (1907), p. 367; Rodier (1900), p. 270 (although Rodier's use of {Simplicius}, *in De an.* 130.12 is questionable); Themistius, *in De an.* 58.29–32. Thomas certainly made use of Themistius's commentary: see Verbeke (1957), pp. ix–xxix.

THE DATING OF *DE MALO* Q.6

A comparison of *De malo* q.6 *(articulus unicus)* and *De veritate* q.24 a.1 suggests that the latter is a rewritten version of at least parts of the former, for *De ma.* q.6 contains several imperfections that do not appear in corresponding places in *De ver.* q.24 a.1, as well as other imperfections. Since *De ver.* was completed by 1259, i.e., during Thomas's first teaching assignment at Paris (1256–1259),[1] this would make *De ma.* q.6 quite an early work. If this is right, *De ma.* q.6 could have little directly to do with the Paris condemnations of 1270 (see above, chapter 5, section [1]).

In order to establish this thesis, it needs first to be established that the two articles are parallel. That is quite apparent, however, from the following factors:

1. *De ver.* q.24 a.1 is on a related, if not the same, topic as *De ma.* q.6: *De ver.* q.24 a.1 is "de libero arbitrio," *De ma.* q.6 "de electione humana." (Thomas makes the connection between *liberum arbitrium* and *libera electio* at *De ma.* q.6 obj.23.)

2. The first objection of *De ver.* q.24 a.1 is virtually identical to the first objection of *De ma.* q.6—i.e., they both cite Jeremiah 10.23, "Non est hominis via eius . . .". The respective responses differ only slightly.

3. Both articles begin with a series of objections having to do with divine action.

4. There are marked similarities between *De ver.* q.24 a.1 obj./ad 7 and *De*

---

1. Torrell (1996 <1993>), pp. 54–74, 334.

ma. q.6 obj./ad 23; between *De ver.* q.24 a.1 obj./ad 16 and *De ma.* q.6 obj./ad 3; between *De ver.* q.24 a.1 obj./ad 17 and *De ma.* q.6 obj./ad 11; between *De ver.* q.24 a.1 obj./ad 18 and *De ma.* q.6 obj./ad 10.

5. The initial sections of the bodies of both articles contain similar arguments, similarly structured. As pointed out in chapter 5, section [2], both speak about the opposed position's being incompatible with the Christian Faith—although *De ver.* q.24 a.1 makes it clear that what is incompatible is determinism, not the idea of freedom as non-coercion.[2] Both sections speak about the elimination of merit and demerit if the opposed position is maintained. Both sections say that the opposed position is contrary to reason, as well as to faith. Both then go through a series of similar divisions. In *De ver.* q.24 a.1, Thomas first distinguishes between things moved from within and things moved by force, the latter being defined as things "in quibus principium est extra, nil conferente vim passo."[3] Then he distinguishes between things that are moved from within but are not self-movers and things that are moved from within and are self-movers. He identifies the principle of action in things moved from within but not self-movers as their form. Then he distinguishes between self-movers without reason and self-movers with reason. In *De ma.* q.6, after the confusing section about determinism and coercion in which he also defines the *uiolentum* as "illud cuius principium est extra,"[4] Thomas distinguishes between man and other natural things that have within themselves their principle of action and motion. He identifies the principle of action in mere natural things as their form. Then he distinguishes between inanimate natural things and brute animals.

Assuming, then, that *De ver.* q.24 a.1 and *De ma.* q.6 are related to one another, there are reasons to believe that *De ver.* q.24 a.1 is the more finished version. Besides the difficulty about the object of the heresy charge (see note 2), notable are the following:

2. I argue in chapter 5 that the first section of the body of *De ver.* q.24 a.1 is better written than the corresponding section of *De ma.* q.6. The unfinished nature of this section of *De ma.* q.6 leads Bernard Lonergan astray; he reads it as if Thomas were condemning as heretical the idea that human freedom is freedom from coercion [Lonergan (1942), p. 533]. *De ver.* q.24 a.1 makes it apparent that the issue is not coercion but determinism in general. Further indication of the same comes in *De ma.* q.6 itself, for in ad 23 Thomas defends Augustine's position with respect to "libertatem que est a coactione" [l.721].

3. This definition is employed at *De ma.* q.6 obj.4.

4. *De ma.* q.6 ll.242–43. On the word *violentum,* see Appendix D, note 4.

1. The phrasing of the subtitle of *De ma.* q.6, "Et *primo* quaeritur . . . ," suggests either that Thomas originally planned more articles for this question or that it once was part of a question that contained more articles.[5]

2. In *De ma.* q.6 objection 18, Thomas begins by remarking that someone "was saying" [*dicebat*, l.164] something. In other objections in this aricle, this construction—"Sed dicebat . . . Sed contra"—signals a back-reference to an authority employed in the immediately preceding objection, an authority which, the first voice of the objection is saying, has been misinterpreted by the objector (the second voice). (See, for instance, objections 2 and 3: the first voice in obj. 2 attempts to clarify the Book of Jeremiah as used in obj. 1; the first voice in obj. 3 attempts to clarify Paul as used in obj. 2.) But in obj. 18, although it can be ascertained that in saying *dicebat* he means Aristotle, obj. 18 has nothing to do with obj. 17, which mentions no authority. The reference is rather to obj. 16 and Aristotle's *Metaph.* ix,5,1048a9–10, although even in obj. 16 Aristotle is not identified. Thus, obj./ad 18 is out of place (it should come after obj./ad 16); and obj. 16 is in an unfinished state.

3. In the body of *De ma.* q.6, at lines 263–68, Thomas says of "aberrant philosophical opinions" that "certain men are led to postulate such positions, partly out of impudence, partly on account of sophistical reasonings they are not able to resolve, as is said in *Metaphysics,* book 4." This, however, is a misreading of what Aristotle says at *Metaph.* iv,5,1009a17–22, which is that some put forward such positions out of impudence, some *others* out of honest puzzlement. Thomas gets this right, however, in his commentary on the *Metaphysics.*[6]

I conclude, therefore, that parts of *De ma.* q.6 constitute an earlier version of *De ver.* q.24 a.1. Perhaps q.6, "found in a drawer," was inserted into *De malo* in order to provide what was thought to be lacking in a work on evil: to wit, a treatment of the role of *voluntas.*

---

5. The Marietti version of *De ma.* q.6 begins, "Et unum quaeritur . . ."; but the Leonine version is the accepted critical edition. Normally (see, for instance, *Quodl.*), when there is only one article in a question, Thomas omits at the beginning his customary, *Ad primum sic proceditur. De ma.* q.6 is alone among the questions in *De ma.* to contain a single article.

6. *in Metaph.* §§663–64. The commentary was probably written after 1271 [Torrell (1996 <1993>), p. 344].

DE MALO Q.6

De electione humana

Questio est de electione humana. Et primo queritur utrum homo habeat liberam electionem suorum actuum aut ex necessitate eligat. Et uidetur quod non libere set ex necessitate eligat. Dicitur enim Ier. X "Non est hominis uia eius, nec uiri est ut ambulet et dirigat gressus suos." Set illud respectu cuius homo habet libertatem, eius est, quasi in ipsius dominio constitutum. Ergo uidetur quod homo suarum uiarum et suorum actuum liberam electionem non habeat.

2. Set dicebat quod hoc refertur ad exequtionem electionum, que interdum non sunt in hominis potestate. —Set contra est quod Apostolus dicit ad Ro. IX "Non est uolentis" scilicet uelle, "neque currentis" scilicet currere, "set miserentis Dei." Set sicut currere pertinet ad exteriorem exequtionem actuum, ita uelle ad interiorem electionem. Ergo etiam interiores electiones non sunt in hominis potestate, set sunt homini ex Deo.

DE MALO Q.6

About Human Choice[1]

The question is about human choice. And first it is asked whether man has the free choice of his acts or whether he chooses from necessity.

And it appears that he does not choose freely but from necessity [for the following reasons]:

1. It is said [5] in Jeremiah 10, "[T]he way of a man is not his: neither is it in a man to walk, and to direct his steps."[2] But, that with respect to which man has freedom is his as if placed in his dominion. Thus, it seems that man does not have [10] free choice of his ways and his actions.

2. But he was saying that this refers to the execution of choices, which occasionally are not within the capacity of a man. —But against this is the fact that the Apostle says in Romans 9: "[I]t is not of him that willeth" (namely, to will) [15] "nor of him that runneth" (namely, to run) "but of God that sheweth mercy."[3] But, as 'to run' pertains to the exterior execution of acts, so

---

1. This is a deliberately literal translation and one which attempts to follow the philosophical vocabulary and even the word order of the Latin. Some words I have chosen not to translate at all—notably, *voluntas* (on this word, see chapter 5, note 3). I also render many words by means of their English cognates, even if, in another context, such renderings might not be greatly enlightening. Thus, *principium* is translated throughout as simply 'principle.' Another example comes at l.374, where I translate *tandem consilio determinato* as, "the counsel once determined." In this case, translating *determinato* with, for instance, 'completed,' although better English, would sever the connection with Thomas's argument about liberty of determination. The numbers in square brackets correspond to the line numbering of the Leonine text.

2. Jeremiah 10.23; the English translation is from the Douay Version.

3. Romans 9.16 (Douay).

3. Set dicebat quod homo ad eligendum mouetur   20
quodam interiori instinctu, scilicet ab ipso Deo,
et immobiliter, non tamen hoc repugnat libertati.
—Set contra est quod cum omne animal moueat
se ipsum per appetitum, alia tamen animalia ab
homine non habent liberam electionem: quia   25
eorum appetitus a quodam exteriori mouente
mouetur, scilicet ex uirtute corporis celestis uel
ex actione alicuius alterius corporis. Si igitur
uoluntas hominis immobiliter mouetur a Deo,
sequitur quod homo non habeat liberam electio-   30
nem suorum actuum.

4. Preterea. Violentum est cuius principium
est extra nil conferente uim passo. Si igitur <in>
uoluntate electionis principium sit ab extra,
scilicet Deus, uidetur quod uoluntas per uiolentiam   35
et ex necessitate moueatur. Non ergo habet
liberam electionem suorum actuum.

5. Preterea. Impossibile est uoluntatem hominis
discordare a uoluntate Dei; quia sicut Augustinus
dicit in Encheridion, aut homo facit quod uult   40
Deus, aut Deus de eo suam uoluntatem implet.
Set uoluntas Dei est immutabilis, ergo et uoluntas
hominis. Omnes ergo humane electiones ex
immobili electione procedunt.

6. Preterea. Nullius potentie actus potest esse   45
nisi in suum obiectum; sicut uisus actio non
potest esse nisi circa uisibile. Set obiectum
uoluntatis est bonum, ergo uoluntas non potest
uelle nisi bonum. Ex necessitate ergo uult bonum
et non habet liberam electionem boni uel mali.   50

'to will' pertains to the interior choice. Thus, also, interior choices are not in the capacity of man but are man's from God.

3. But [20] he was saying that man is moved to choose by a certain interior instinct—i.e., God himself—and immovably, but this is not opposed to freedom. —But against this is the fact that every animal moves itself by means of appetite, for animals other than [25] man do not have free choice, since their appetite is moved by some exterior mover, which is to say under the influence of a celestial body or some other body. If, therefore, the *voluntas* of man is immovably moved by God [30], it follows that man does not have free choice of his actions.

4. Moreover, an instance of being forced is that whose "principle is outside, that which is acted upon contributing no force."[4] If, therefore, in *voluntas* of choice the principle is from without [35], i.e., from God, it seems that *voluntas* is moved by force and from necessity. It does not have, therefore, free choice of its actions.

5. Moreover, it is impossible for the *voluntas* of man to be discordant with the *voluntas* of God, for, as Augustine [40] says in the *Enchiridion*, either a man does what God wills or God completes his *voluntas* through him.[5] But the *voluntas* of God is immutable; so also therefore is the *voluntas* of man. Every human choice proceeds, therefore, from an unmovable choice.

6. Moreover [45], the act of no potency is possible except in its object, as the action of vision is not possible except with respect to the visible. But the

---

4. *EN* iii,1,1110a1–2. The awkward phrase "an instance of being forced" is occasioned by the fact that Thomas is referring to this passage in Aristotle (in Latin, "violentum autem est cuius principium extra, tale existens in quo nil confert operans vel patiens"). The phrase "violentum autem est cuius principium extra," which corresponds closely to the Greek βίαιον δὲ οὗ ἡ ἀρχὴ ἔξωθεν, makes it sound as if that which causes the violence (or force) has another principle outside of itself. Thomas, in his commentary on this passage [*in EN* lb.3 lect.1 ll.79–104 (§387)], makes it clear that the *violentum* is the forced movement (or "the instance of being forced").

5. Augustine, *Enchir.* c.100 (*Pat.Lat.* 40,279).

7. Preterea. Omnis potentia ad quam comparatur suum obiectum ut mouens ad mobile, est
potentia passiua, et suum operari est pati; sicut
sensibile mouet sensum, unde sensus est potentia
passiua et sentire est quoddam pati. Set obiectum   55
uoluntatis comparatur ad uoluntatem ut mouens
ad mobile: dicit enim Philosophus III De Anima
et IX Metaphisice quod appetibile est mouens
non motum, appetitus autem mouens motum.
Ergo uoluntas est potentia passiua, et uelle est   60
pati. Set omnis potentia passiua ex necessitate
mouetur a suo actiuo si sit sufficiens. Ergo
uidetur quod uoluntas de necessitate moueatur
ab appetibili, non ergo est liberum homini uelle
uel non uelle.   65

8. Set dicebat quod uoluntas habet necessitatem
respectu finis ultimi, quia omnis homo ex necessitate uult esse beatus, non autem respectu eorum
que sunt ad finem. —Set contra. Sicut finis est
obiectum uoluntatis, ita et id quod est ad finem;   70
quia utrumque habet rationem boni. Si igitur
uoluntas ex necessitate mouetur in finem, uidetur
etiam quod ex necessitate moueatur in id quod
est ad finem.

9. Preterea. Vbi est idem motiuum et idem   75
mobile, est idem modus mouendi. Set cum aliquis
uult finem et ea que sunt ad finem, idem est quod
mouetur, scilicet uoluntas, et idem est mouens:
quia ea que sunt ad finem non uult aliquis nisi
in quantum uult finem. Ergo est idem modus   80
mouendi, ut scilicet sicut aliquis ex necessitate
uult finem ultimum, ita ex necessitate uult ea que
sunt ad finem.

object of *voluntas* is the good; therefore, *voluntas* cannot will anything except the good. From necessity, therefore, it wills the good [50] and does not have free choice of good and evil.

7. Moreover, every potency whose object stands toward it as a mover toward a movable is a passive potency and for it to act is for it to suffer—as, for instance, the sensible moves a sense in such a way that the sense is a [55] passive potency and to sense is to suffer something. But the object of *voluntas* is compared to the *voluntas* as mover to movable, for the Philosopher says in *De anima*, book 3, and *Metaphysics*, book 9, that the appetible is a non-moved mover, appetite a moved mover.[6] Therefore [60], *voluntas* is a passive potency and to will is to suffer. But every passive potency is moved from necessity by its active factor if it be sufficient. Therefore, it seems that *voluntas* is moved of necessity by the appetible; therefore, to will [65] or not to will is not free for man.

8. But he was saying that *voluntas* has necessity with respect to the ultimate end (for every man wishes from necessity to be happy), not, however, with respect to those things that are for the end.[7] —But, to the contrary, as the end is [70] an object of *voluntas*, so also is that which is for the end, since both have the *ratio* of a good. If, therefore, *voluntas* is moved from necessity toward the end, it would seem also that it is moved from necessity toward that which is for the end.

9. Moreover [75], where the motive is the same and the movable thing is the same, the mode of moving is the same. But when someone wills the end and those things that are for the end, the same is that which is moved (i.e., *voluntas*) and the same is the mover, for no one wills those things that are for the end except [80] insofar as he wills the end. Therefore, the mode of moving is the same—that is to say, as someone from necessity wills the ultimate end, so also does he will those things that are for the end from necessity.

6. The first reference is *De an.* iii,10,433b11–18; the second is actually *Metaph.* xii,7,1072a24–27.
7. The phrase "eorum quae sunt ad finem" is a literal translation of the Greek τὰ πρὸς τὸ τέλος. See chapter 1, section [3].

10. Preterea. Sicut intellectus est potentia
separata a materia, ita et uoluntas. Set intellectus   85
ex necessitate mouetur a suo obiecto: cogitur
enim homo ex necessitate assentire alicui ueritati
per uiolentiam rationis. Ergo eadem ratione et
uoluntas necessario mouetur a suo obiecto.

11. Preterea. Dispositio primi mouentis relin-   90
quitur in omnibus sequentibus, quia omnia
secunda mouentia mouent in quantum sunt mota
a primo mouente. Set in ordine motuum uolun-
tariorum primum mouens est appetibile appre-
hensum. Cum igitur apprehensio appetibilis neces-   95
sitatem patiatur, si per demonstrationem probetur
aliquid esse bonum, uidetur quod necessitas
deriuetur ad omnes motus sequentes; et ita
uoluntas non libere set ex necessitate mouetur ad
uolendum.   100

12. Preterea. Res magis est motiua quam
intentio. Set secundum Philosophum in VI Metaphisice bonum est in rebus, uerum autem in
mente; et sic bonum est res, uerum autem
intentio; ergo magis habet rationem motiui   105
bonum quam uerum. Set uerum ex necessitate
mouet intellectum, ut dictum est. Ergo bonum
ex necessitate mouet uoluntatem.

13. Preterea. Dilectio, que pertinet ad uoluntatem, est uehementior motus quam cognitio,   110
que pertinet ad intellectum: quia cognitio
assimilat set dilectio transformat, ut uidetur per
Dionisium IV cap. De diuinis nominibus; ergo
uoluntas est magis mobilis quam intellectus.
Si ergo intellectus ex necessitate mouetur, uidetur   115
quod multo magis uoluntas.

10. Moreover, just as intellect is a potency [85] separate from matter, so also is *voluntas*. But intellect is moved by its object from necessity: for a man is compelled, from necessity, to assent to any truth by force of reason. Therefore, for the same reason, *voluntas* is necessarily moved by its object.

11. Moreover [90], the disposition of the first mover remains in everything that follows, for all secondary movements move insofar as they are moved by a first mover. But in the order of voluntary movements, the first mover is the [95] apprehended appetible. Since, therefore, apprehension of the appetible suffers necessity, if through a demonstration something should be proved to be good, it seems that necessity is imparted to every subsequent movement.[8] And, thus, *voluntas* is moved not freely but from necessity to [100] will.

12. Moreover, a thing is more a motive than is an intention. But, according to the Philosopher in *Metaphysics*, book 6, the good is in things, the true is in the mind;[9] and, so understood, the good is a thing, the true [105] an intention. Thus, the good has more of the *ratio* of a motive than the true. But the true moves the intellect from necessity, as was said. Thus, good moves *voluntas* from necessity.

13. Moreover, delight, which pertains to [110] *voluntas*, is a more vehement movement than thought, which pertains to intellect: for thought assimilates but delight transforms, as is seen in Dionysius's *De divinis nominibus*, chapter 4.[10] Thus, *voluntas* is more mobile than intellect. If [115], therefore, intellect is moved from necessity, it seems that so much the more is *voluntas*.

8. See *in An.post.* lb.1 lect.23 ll.98–116 (§198).
9. *Metaph.* vi,4,1027b25–27.
10. *Div.nom.* c.4 §13 (*Pat.Gr.* 3,712A).

14. Set dicebat quod actio intellectus est
secundum motum ad animam, actus autem uoluntatis est secundum motum ab anima; et sic
intellectus habet magis rationem passiui, uoluntas   120
autem magis rationem actiui: unde non necessitate
patitur a suo obiecto. —Set contra. Assentire
pertinet ad intellectum sicut consentire ad uoluntatem. Set assentire significat motum in rem cui
assentitur, sicut et consentire in rem cui consen-   125
titur. Ergo non magis est motus uoluntatis ab
anima quam motus intellectus.

15. Preterea. Si uoluntas respectu ad aliqua
uolita non ex necessitate moueatur, necesse est
dicere quod se habeat ad opposita: quia quod   130
non necesse est esse, possibile est non esse; set
omne quod est in potentia ad opposita, non
reducitur in actum alicuius eorum nisi per aliquod
ens actu quod facit illud quod erat in potentia
esse in actu; quod autem facit aliquid esse actu,   135
dicimus esse causam eius. Oportebit ergo, si
uoluntas aliquid determinate uult, quod sit aliqua
causa que faciat ipsam hoc uelle. Causa autem
posita necesse est effectum poni, ut Auicenna
probat: quia si causa posita adhuc est possibile   140
effectum non esse, indigebit adhuc alio reducente
de potentia in actum, et sic primum non erat
sufficiens causa. Ergo uoluntas ex necessitate
mouetur ad aliquid uolendum.

16. Preterea. Nulla uirtus se habens ad contraria   145
est actiua, quia omnis uirtus actiua potest agere
id cuius est actiua; possibili autem posito non
sequitur impossibile: sequeretur autem duo
opposita esse simul, quod est impossibile. Set
uoluntas est potentia actiua. Ergo non se habet   150
ad opposita, set de necessitate determinatur ad
unum.

14. But he was saying that the action of intellect is according to movement toward the soul, the act of *voluntas* according to movement from the soul; and in this sense [120] intellect has more the *ratio* of a passive thing, *voluntas* more of an active thing. Thus, it does not suffer from necessity from its object.[11] —But, to the contrary, to assent pertains to intellect just as to consent pertains to *voluntas*. But 'to assent' signifies a movement toward the thing [125] that is assented to, just as to consent <signifies a movement> toward the thing that is consented to. Thus, the movement of *voluntas* is not more from the soul than is the movement of intellect.

15. Moreover, if *voluntas* is not moved from necessity with respect to something willed, it is necessary [130] to say that it is open to opposites, for what not necessarily is, possibly is not. But everything that is in potency toward opposites is not reduced to act with respect to one of them unless through some being in act that makes that which was in potency [135] to be in act. That, however, which makes something to be in act, we say is its cause. It is necessary, therefore, if *voluntas* wills something in a determinate manner, that there be some cause that makes it to will this. A cause being posited, it is necessary to posit the effect, as Avicenna [140] proves: for if, when the cause is posited, it is still possible for the effect not to be, there will be yet lacking, something else that reduces potency into act, and thus the first thing was not a sufficient cause. Thus, *voluntas* from necessity is moved toward willing something.

16. Moreover [145], no power that is open to contraries is active, since every active virtue can bring about that for which it is active. For, if something possible is posited, something impossible does not follow, since that would be for two opposites to be at the same time—which is impossible. But [150] *voluntas* is an active potency. Thus, it is not open to opposites but is of necessity determined toward one.

11. Supplying *ex* before *necessitate*.

17. Preterea. Voluntas aliquando incipit eligere
cum prius non eligeret; aut igitur transmutatur a
dispositione in qua prius erat, aut non. Si non,   155
sequitur quod sicut prius non eligebat, ita nec
modo; et sic non eligens eligeret, quod est
impossibile. Si autem mutatur eius dispositio,
necesse est quod ab aliquo sit mutata, quia omne
quod mouetur ab alio mouetur. Mouens autem   160
imponit necessitatem mobili, alias non sufficienter
moueret ipsum. Ergo uoluntas ex necessitate
mouetur.

18. Set dicebat quod rationes iste concludunt
de potentia naturali, que est in materia, non autem   165
de potentia immateriali, que est uoluntas. —Set
contra. Principium totius humane cognitionis est
sensus; non ergo potest cognosci ab homine nisi
secundum quod cadit sub sensu uel ipsum uel
effectus eius. Set ipsa uirtus se habens ad opposita   170
non cadit sub sensu; in effectibus autem eius qui
sub sensu cadunt, non inueniuntur duo actus
contrarii simul existere, set semper uidemus quod
determinate unum procedit in actu. Ergo non
possumus iudicare esse in homine aliquam actiuam   175
potentiam ad opposita se habentem.

19. Preterea. Cum potentia dicatur ad actum,
sicut se habet actus ad actum, ita se habet potentia
ad potentiam. Set duo actus oppositi non possunt
esse simul. Ergo nec potest esse una potentia ad   180
duo opposita.

20. Preterea. Secundum Augustinum in I
De Trinitate, nichil est sibi ipsi causa ut sit, ergo
pari ratione nichil est sibi ipsi causa ut moueatur;
uoluntas ergo non mouet se ipsam. Set necesse   185
est quod ab aliquo moueatur, quia incipit agere
postquam prius non egerat, et omne tale aliquo

17. Moreover, *voluntas* sometimes begins to choose when it has not chosen previously; either, therefore, it is transformed from [155] the disposition in which it was previously, or it is not. If not, it follows that, as it was not choosing previously, neither does it choose now; and thus, not choosing, it was choosing—which is impossible. If, however, its disposition is changed, it is necessary that it be changed by something, for everything [160] that is moved is moved by another. The mover, however, imposes necessity on the moveable thing; otherwise it would not sufficiently move it. Thus, *voluntas* is moved from necessity.

18. But he was saying that these arguments are conclusive [165] with respect to natural potency,[12] which is in matter, not with respect to immaterial potency, which is *voluntas*. —But, to the contrary, the principle of all human thought is the senses; therefore, it cannot be known by man except insofar as it itself falls under the senses or [170] its effect does. But the power which itself is open to opposites does not fall under the senses; in its effects, however, which do fall under the senses, one does not find two contrary acts existing at the same time, but we always see that one precedes the other in act determinately. Thus [175], we cannot judge to be in man any active potency open to opposites.

19. Moreover, since a potency is attributed with respect to an act, as an act stands with respect to an act, so also stands a potency with respect to a potency. But two opposite acts cannot [180] be at the same time. Thus, there cannot be one potency that is open to two opposites.

20. Moreover, according to Augustine in *De Trinitate,* book 1,[13] nothing is the cause of its own being; thus, by like reasoning, nothing is the cause of its

---

12. As I argue in Appendix C, this objection is out of place. It should come after objection 16, which also talks about no capacity's being open to opposites. Thomas does not identify the author of the position discussed, but it is Aristotle. See *Metaph.* ix,2,1046b15–24 (and Thomas's *in Metaph.* §§1792–93) and *Metaph.* ix,5,1048a8–10 (and *in Metaph.* §1819).

13. *Trin.* lb.1 c.1 n.1 ll.35–36 (*Pat.Lat.* 42,820).

modo mouetur; unde et de Deo dicimus quod non
incipit uelle postquam noluerat, propter eius
immobilitatem. Ergo necesse est quod uoluntas 190
ab alio moueatur. Set quod ab alio mouetur,
necessitatem ab alio patitur. Ergo uoluntas necessario uult, et non libere.

21. Preterea. Omne multiforme reducitur ad
aliquid uniforme; set motus humani sunt uarii 195
et multiformes, ergo reducuntur in motum
<uniformem, qui est motus celi>, sicut in causam.
Set quod causatur ex motu celi ex necessitate
prouenit, quia causa naturalis ex necessitate
producit effectum suum nisi sit aliquid impediens, 200
motum autem celestis corporis non potest aliquid
impedire quin consequatur suum effectum, quia
oporteret quod etiam aliquid illius impedientis
reduceretur in aliquod principium celeste sicut
in causam. Ergo uidetur quod motus humani ex 205
necessitate proueniant, et non ex libera electione.
22. Preterea. Qui facit quod non uult, <non>
habet liberam electionem. Set homo facit quod
non uult, Ro. VII "Quod odi malum, illud facio."
Ergo homo non habet liberam electionem suorum 210
actuum.
23. Preterea. Augustinus dicit in Encheridion
quod "homo male utens libero arbitrio se
perdidit et ipsum." Set libere eligere non est nisi
habentis liberum arbitrium. Ergo homo non 215
habet liberam electionem.
24. Preterea. Augustinus dicit in VIII Confes-
sionum quod "dum consuetudini non resistitur,
fit necessitas." Ergo uidetur quod saltem in his
qui sunt assueti aliquid facere, uoluntas ex 220
necessitate moueatur.

own being moved. Thus [185], *voluntas* does not move itself. But it is necessary that it be moved by something, since it begins to act after first not acting, and everything is moved in some such way. (We also say, therefore, of God that he does not begin to will after having not willed, on account of [190] his immobility.) Thus, it is necessary that *voluntas* be moved by another. But what is moved by another, suffers necessity from the other. Thus, *voluntas* wills necessarily and not freely.

21. Moreover, every multiform thing is reduced to [195] something that is uniform. But human movements are various and multiform; therefore, they are reduced to a uniform movement—which is the movement of the heavens—as if to a cause. But what is caused by the movement of the heavens comes about from necessity, since a natural cause [200] produces its effect from necessity unless there be some impediment. But nothing can impede the movement of a heavenly body but that its effect follows, since it is necessary also that something of this impediment be reduced to some heavenly principle, as if to [205] a cause. Thus, it seems that human movements come about from necessity and not from free choice.

22. Moreover, he who does what he wills not, does not have free choice. But man does what he wills not: "the evil which I hate, that I do" (Romans 7).[14] Thus [210], man does not have free choice of his acts.

23. Moreover, Augustine says in the *Enchiridion*[15] that "the man ill using his free decision has ruined also himself." But to choose freely belongs to no one other than [215] to him who has free decision. Thus, man does not have free choice.

24. Moreover, Augustine says in *Confessions*, book 8,[16] that "when no resistence is made to custom, necessity arises." Thus, it seems that, at least

14. Romans 7.15 (Douay).
15. Augustine, *Enchir.* c.30 ll.37–38 (*Pat.Lat.* 40,246).
16. Augustine, *Conf.* viii c.5 n.10 ll.10–11 (*Pat.Lat.* 32,753).

Set contra est quod dicitur Eccli. XV "Deus ab
initio constituit hominem et reliquit eum in manu
consilii sui." Hoc autem non esset nisi haberet
liberam electionem, que est appetitus preconsiliati,   225
ut dicitur in III Ethicorum. Ergo homo habet
liberam electionem suorum actuum.

  2. Preterea. Potentie rationales sunt ad opposita;
secundum Philosophum. Set uoluntas est potentia
rationalis: est enim in ratione, ut dicitur in   230
III De Anima. Ergo uoluntas se habet ad opposita,
et non ex necessitate mouetur ad unum.

  3. Preterea. Secundum Philosophum in III et
VI Ethicorum, homo est dominus sui actus, et in
ipso est agere et non agere. Set hoc non esset si   235
non haberet liberam electionem. Ergo homo
habet liberam electionem suorum actuum.

Responsio. Dicendum, quod quidam posuerunt
quod uoluntas hominis ex necessitate mouetur ad
aliquid eligendum. Nec tamen ponebant quod   240
uoluntas cogeretur: non enim omne necessarium
est uiolentum, set solum illud cuius principium
est extra. Vnde et motus naturales inueniuntur
aliqui necessarii, non tamen uiolenti: uiolentum
enim repugnat naturali sicut et uoluntario, quia   245
utriusque principium est intra, uiolenti autem
principium est extra.

among those who are accustomed to doing something, *voluntas* is [220] moved from necessity.

But *against this* is the fact that it is said in Ecclesiasticus, chapter 15, "God made man in the beginning, and left him in the hand of his own counsel."[17] This would not be unless he had [225] free choice, which is the appetite of the pre-deliberated, as is said in book 3 of the *Ethics*.[18] Thus, man has free choice of his acts.

Moreover, rational potencies are for opposites, according to the Philosopher. But *voluntas* is a rational potency, for it is in reason, as is said in [230] *De anima*, book 3.[19] Thus, *voluntas* is open to opposites and it is not moved toward one thing from necessity.

Moreover, according to the Philosopher in books 3 and 6 of the *Ethics*, man is master of his own act and it is [235] up to him to act and not to act.[20] But this would not be if he did not have free choice. Thus, man has free choice of his acts.

Response. It needs to be said that some have assumed that man's *voluntas* is moved from necessity toward [240] something which is to be chosen. But neither were they assuming that *voluntas* is coerced—for not every instance of necessity is an instance of being forced but only that one whose principle is outside. Whence also natural movements are, some of them, discovered to be necessary but not instances of being forced, for an instance of being forced [245] is incompatible both with the natural and with the voluntary, since the principle of both of these is inside; the principle in an instance of being forced, however, is outside.

17. Ecclesiasticus 15.14 (Douay).
18. *EN* iii,2,1112a13–17.
19. *De an.* iii,9,432b5–6.
20. *EN* iii,1,1110a17; iii,5,1113b17–19; iii,5,1114a31–b16; vi,12,1144a10–11. See also *EE* ii,6,1223a4–5: ὥστε ὅσων πράξεων ὁ ἄνθρωπός ἐστιν ἀρχὴ καὶ κύριος.

Hec autem opinio est heretica. Tollit enim
rationem meriti et demeriti in humanis actibus:
non enim uidetur esse meritorium uel demerito-   250
rium quod aliquis sic ex necessitate agit quod
uitare non possit.

Est etiam annumeranda inter extraneas philosophie opiniones, quia non solum contrariatur
fidei, set subuertit omnia principia philosophie   255
moralis. Si enim non sit aliquid in nobis, set ex
necessitate mouemur ad uolendum, tollitur deli-
beratio, exhortatio, preceptum, et punitio et
laus et uituperium, circa que moralis philosophia consistit. Huiusmodi autem opiniones que   260
destruunt principia alicuius partis philosophie
dicuntur positiones extranee; sicut nichil moueri,
quod destruit principia scientie naturalis. Ad
huiusmodi autem positiones ponendas inducti
sunt aliqui homines partim quidem propter   265
proteruiam, partim propter aliquas rationes sophis-
ticas quas soluere non potuerunt, ut dicitur in
IV Metaphisice.

Ad euidentiam igitur ueritatis circa hanc ques-
tionem primo considerandum est quod sicut in   270
aliis rebus est aliquod principium propriorum
actuum, ita etiam in hominibus. Hoc autem
actiuum siue motiuum principium in hominibus
proprie est intellectus et uoluntas, ut dicitur in
III De Anima. Quod quidem principium partim   275
conuenit cum principio actiuo in rebus naturalibus,
partim ab eo differt. Conuenit quidem, quia sicut
in rebus naturalibus inuenitur forma, que est
principium actionis, et inclinatio consequens
formam, que dicitur appetitus naturalis, ex quibus   280
sequitur actio, ita in homine inuenitur forma
intellectiua et inclinatio uoluntatis consequens

This opinion, however, is heretical. It eliminates the reason for merit and demerit in human acts [250], for that seems not to be meritorious or demeritorious which someone does so much from necessity that he could not avoid it.

It is, furthermore, to be numbered among aberrant philosophical opinions, since it not only is contrary to [255] the Faith but also subverts every principle of moral philosophy. For, if there is not something that is up to us but rather we are moved to will from necessity, deliberation is eliminated, as are exhortation, precept, punishment, praise, and vituperation—in which moral [260] philosophy consists. Opinions of this sort which destroy the principles of a part of philosophy are called 'aberrant'—as, for instance, <the opinion> that nothing is moved, which destroys the principles of natural science.[21] Certain men are led to postulate such positions [265], partly out of impudence, partly on account of sophistical reasonings they are not able to resolve, as is said in *Metaphysics*, book 4.[22]

In order to bring to light the truth regarding this question, [270] *to be considered first* is that, just as in other things there is some principle of their proper acts, so also in men. This active or motivating principle in men properly, is intellect and *voluntas*, as is said in [275] *De anima*,[23] book 3—which principle partly coincides with the active principle in natural things, partly differs from it. It coincides with it since, just as in natural things is found form (which is the principle of action) and inclination following [280] the form (which is called 'natural appetite'), from which <two, i.e., form and inclination> issues the action, so also in man there is found intellectual form

21. The word 'aberrant' translates *extraneus* (ll.253,262). See *Top.* i,11,104b18–28, where Aristotle says that a thesis such as the thesis that there is no contradiction is παράδοξος [104b19]. See also *Phys.* i,3,186a4ff., where Parmenides and Melissus are both criticized for their position regarding the impossibility of movement and Melissus particularly is said to παραλογίζεσθαι [186a10–11]. In either case, one finds the idea of leading or going beyond (*extra*, παρά) the reasonable.

22. *Metaph.* iv,5,1009a17–22; see also *in Metaph.* §§663–64.

23. *De an.* iii,10,433a13–17.

formam apprehensam, ex quibus sequitur exterior
actio. Set in hoc est differentia, quia forma rei
naturalis est forma indiuiduata per materiam   285
unde et inclinatio ipsam consequens est determinata ad unum, set forma intellecta est uniuersalis,
sub qua multa possunt comprehendi. Vnde cum
actus sint in singularibus, in quibus nullum est
quod adequet potentiam uniuersalis, remanet   290
inclinatio uoluntatis indeterminate se habens ad
multa; sicut si artifex concipiat formam domus
in uniuersali, sub qua comprehenduntur diuerse
figure domus, potest uoluntas eius inclinari ad hoc
quod faciat domum quadratam uel rotundam uel   295
alterius figure.

Principium autem actiuum in brutis animalibus
medio modo se habet inter utrumque. Nam forma
apprehensa per sensum est indiuidualis sicut et
forma rei naturalis, et ideo ex ea sequitur inclinatio   300
ad unum actum sicut in rebus naturalibus. Set
tamen non semper eadem forma recipitur in
sensu, sicut est in rebus naturalibus, quia ignis
est semper calidus, set nunc una nunc alia: puta,
nunc forma delectabilis, nunc tristis. Vnde nunc   305
fugit, nunc persequitur. In quo conuenit cum
principio actiuo humano.

Secundo considerandum est quod potentia
aliqua dupliciter mouetur: uno modo ex parte
subiecti, alio modo ex parte obiecti. Ex parte   310
subiecti quidem, sicut uisus per immutationem
dispositionis organi mouetur ad clarius uel minus
clare uidendum; ex parte uero obiecti sicut uisus
nunc uidet album, nunc uidet nigrum. Et prima
quidem immutatio pertinet ad ipsum exercitium   315
actus, ut scilicet agatur uel non agatur, aut melius
uel debilius agatur; secunda uero immutatio

and the inclination of *voluntas* following the apprehended form, from which <two> issues the exterior action. But in the latter case there is a difference, for the form of a [285] natural thing is a form individuated by matter, so that also the inclination following it is determined toward one thing; but an intellectual form is a universal, under which many things can be comprehended. Thus, since acts are in singulars, in which there is nothing [290] that comes up to the potency of the universal, the inclination of *voluntas* remains indeterminately open to many things—just as, when an artificer conceives the form of a house in a universal under which are comprehended diverse shapes of a house, his *voluntas* can be disposed [295] to make the house square or round or of some other shape.

The active principle in brute animals stands midway between these two. For the form apprehended by the senses is individual, as is also [300] the form of a natural thing; and, therefore, the inclination issues from it toward one act, as in natural things. But it is not always the same form that is received into the senses (as in natural things, for fire is always hot) but at one time one, at another time another—for instance [305], at one time an agreeable form, at another time a disagreeable one; and thus, at one time something to avoid, at another time something to pursue. In this, it coincides with the human active principle.

To be considered secondly is that a potency is moved in two ways: one way is from the part [310] of the subject, the other way is from the part of the object. From the part of the subject: as when vision, due to a change of the disposition of the <visual> organ, is moved toward seeing more clearly or less clearly. From the part of the object: as when vision at one time sees white, at another time sees black. Indeed, the first [315] change pertains to the very exercise of the act—that is, that it might be brought into action or not brought into action, or be brought into action better or more weakly. The second change, however, pertains to the specification of the act, for the act is specified by its object.

pertinet ad specificationem actus, nam actus
specificatur per obiectum.

    Est autem considerandum quod in rebus natu-   320
ralibus specificatio quidem actus est ex forma,
ipsum autem exercitium est ab agente quod causat
ipsam motionem; mouens autem agit propter
finem; unde relinquitur quod primum principium
motionis quantum ad exercitium actus sit ex fine.   325
Si autem consideremus obiecta uoluntatis et
intellectus, inuenimus quod obiectum intellectus
est primum et precipuum in genere cause formalis,
est enim eius obiectum ens et uerum; set obiectum
uoluntatis est primum et precipuum in genere   330
cause finalis, nam eius obiectum est bonum, sub
quo comprehenduntur omnes fines sicut sub uero
comprehenduntur omnes forme apprehense. Vnde
et ipsum bonum in quantum est quedam forma
apprehensibilis, continetur sub uero quasi quod-   335
dam uerum, et ipsum uerum in quantum est finis
intellectualis operationis, continetur sub bono ut
quoddam particulare bonum.

    Si ergo consideremus motum potentiarum
anime ex parte obiecti specificantis actum, primum   340
principium motionis est ex intellectu: hoc enim
modo bonum intellectum mouet etiam ipsam
uoluntatem. Si autem consideremus motus potentiarum anime ex parte exercitii actus, sic principium motionis est ex uoluntate. Nam semper   345
potentia ad quam pertinet finis principalis mouet
ad actum potentiam ad quam pertinet id quod
est ad finem, sicut militaris mouet frenorum
factricem ad operandum. Et hoc modo uoluntas
mouet et se ipsam et omnes alias potentias: 350
intelligo enim quia uolo, et similiter utor omnibus
potentiis et habitibus quia uolo. Vnde et Commen-

It [320] is to be considered, however, that in natural things the specification indeed of the act is from the form; the exercise itself, however, is by the agent that causes the motion itself. The mover, however, acts for the sake of the end; thus, it remains that the first principle [325] of motion as to the exercise of the act is from the end. If, however, we consider the objects of *voluntas* and intellect, we discover that the object of intellect is primary and principal within the genus of formal cause, for its object is being and the true; but the object [330] of *voluntas* is primary and principal within the genus of final cause, for its object is the good, under which are comprehended all ends, as under the true are comprehended all apprehended forms. Thus, the good itself, insofar as it is an [335] apprehensible form, is contained under the true as something true; and the true itself, insofar as it is the end of the operation of the intellect, is contained under the good as a particular good.

If, therefore, we consider the movement of the potencies [340] of the soul from the part of the object specifying the act, the first principle of motion is from the intellect, for in this way the understood good moves even *voluntas* itself. If, however, we consider the movement of the potencies of the soul from the part of the exercise of the act, in this sense the principle of [345] motion is from *voluntas*. For the potency to which pertains the principal end always moves into act a potency to which pertains that which is for the end, as the soldier moves the maker of bridles into operation. And in this way *voluntas* [350] moves both itself and all other potencies: for I understand because I will, and similarly I use all my other potencies and habitual states because I will to do so. Thus, the Commentator defines habitual state in *De anima*, book 3, <saying that> it is an habitual state which someone uses when he wills.[24] Thus, so [355] to show that *voluntas* is not moved from necessity, one

24. Averroes, *in De an.* §18 (ll.26–29): "Haec enim est diffinitio habitus, scilicet ut habens habi-

tator diffinit habitum in III De Anima, quod
habitus est quo quis utitur cum uoluerit. Sic
igitur ad ostendendum quod uoluntas non ex   355
necessitate mouetur, oportet considerare motum
uoluntatis et quantum ad exercitium actus et
quantum ad determinationem actus, que est ex
obiecto.

Quantum ergo ad exercitium actus, primo   360
quidem manifestum est quod uoluntas mouetur
a se ipsa: sicut enim mouet alias potentias, ita et
se ipsam mouet. Nec propter hoc sequitur quod
uoluntas secundum idem sit in potentia et in
actu; sicut enim homo secundum intellectum   365
in uia inuentionis mouet se ipsum ad scientiam,
in quantum ex uno noto in actu uenit in aliquid
ignotum quod erat solum in potentia notum, ita
per hoc quod homo aliquid uult in actu, mouet
se ad uolendum aliquid aliud in actu. Sicut per   370
hoc quod uult sanitatem, mouet se ad uolendum
sumere potionem: ex hoc enim quod uult sani
tatem, incipit consiliari de his que conferunt ad
sanitatem, et tandem determinato consilio uult
accipere potionem; sic igitur uoluntatem acci-   375
piendi potionem precedit consilium, quod quidem
procedit ex uoluntate uolentis consiliari. Cum
igitur uoluntas se consilio moueat, consilium
autem est inquisitio quedam non demonstratiua
set ad opposita uiam habens, non ex necessitate   380
uoluntas se ipsam mouet. Set cum uoluntas non
semper uoluerit consiliari, necesse est quod ab
aliquo moueatur ad hoc quod uelit consiliari; et si
quidem a se ipsa, necesse est iterum quod motum
uoluntatis precedat consilium et consilium prece-   385
dat actus uoluntatis; et cum hoc in infinitum
procedere non possit, necesse est ponere quod

must consider the movement of *voluntas* both with respect to the exercise of the act and with respect to the determination of the act, which is from the object.

With [360] respect, therefore, to the exercise of the act, it is clear, first, that *voluntas* is moved by itself: as it moves the other potencies, so also it moves itself. Nor does it follow because of this that *voluntas* is, with regard to the same thing, both in potency and in [365] act. For, just as, with regard to the intellect, a man in the process of discovery moves himself to knowledge insofar as, from one thing known in act, he comes to something unknown which was known only in potency, so also, insofar as a man wills something in act, he moves [370] himself to willing something else in act. Just as, because he wills health, a man moves himself to willing to take medicine (because he wills health, he begins to take counsel about those things that bring one to health, and, this counsel once determined, he wills [375] to accept the medicine), so also the *voluntas* to accept medicine precedes counsel, which indeed proceeds from the *voluntas* of one who wills to take counsel. Since, therefore, *voluntas* moves itself to counsel but counsel is an enquiry that is not demonstrative [380] but oriented toward opposites,[25] *voluntas* does not move itself from necessity. But, since *voluntas* does not always will to take counsel, it is necessary that it be moved by something else so that it wills to take counsel; and if, indeed, by itself <it is so moved>, it is necessary again that a movement [385] of *voluntas* precede counsel and counsel precede the act of *voluntas*. And, since this cannot go on to infinity, it is necessary to suppose that, as to the first movement of *voluntas*, the *voluntas* [390] (of whoever is not forever actively willing) is moved by something external, by the prompting of which *voluntas* begins to will.

---

tum intelligat per ipsum illud quod est sibi proprium ex se et quando voluerit, absque eo quod indigeat in hoc aliquo extrinseco."

25. *EN* iii,3,1112b20–23.

quantum ad primum motum uoluntatis moueatur
uoluntas cuiuscumque non semper actu uolentis
ab aliquo exteriori, cuius instinctu uoluntas uelle   390
incipiat.

Posuerunt igitur quidam quod iste instinctus
est a corpore celesti. Set hoc esse non potest.
Cum enim uoluntas sit in ratione, secundum
Philosophum in III De Anima, ratio autem siue   395
intellectus non sit uirtus corporea, impossibile
est quod uirtus corporis celestis moueat ipsam
uoluntatem directe. Ponere autem quod uoluntas
hominum moueatur ex impressione celestis corpo-
ris, sicut appetitus brutorum animalium mouentur,   400
est secundum opinionem ponentium non differre
intellectum a sensu. Ad hos enim refert Philosophus in libro De Anima uerbum quorundam
dicentium quod talis est uoluntas in hominibus
"qualem in die ducit pater uirorum deorumque,"   405
id est celum uel sol.

Relinquitur ergo, sicut concludit Aristotiles in
capitulo De bona fortuna, quod id quod primo
mouet uoluntatem et intellectum sit aliquid supra
uoluntatem et intellectum, scilicet Deus. Qui cum   410
omnia moueat secundum rationem mobilium, ut
leuia sursum et grauia deorsum, etiam uoluntatem
mouet secundum eius conditionem, non ex
necessitate set ut indeterminate se habentem ad
multa. Patet ergo quod si consideretur motus   415
uoluntatis ex parte exercitii actus, non mouetur
ex necessitate.

Some suppose, therefore, that this prompting is from a heavenly body. But this cannot be. Since *voluntas* is in reason (according to [395] the Philosopher in *De anima*, book 3),[26] but reason or intellect is not a corporeal power, it is impossible that the power of a heavenly body should move *voluntas* itself directly. To suppose that the *voluntas* of man is moved by the impression of a heavenly [400] body, as the appetites of brute animals are moved, is, in the opinion of those so supposing, for the intellect not to differ from the senses. To these <thinkers> the Philosopher, in a book of the *De anima*, relates the maxim of those who say that thus is *voluntas* among men [405] "such as by day the father of men and gods" (i.e, the heavens or the sun) "directs."[27]

It remains, therefore, as Aristotle concludes in the chapter *De bona fortuna*,[28] that that which first moves *voluntas* and intellect is something above [410] *voluntas* and intellect—that is to say, God, who, since he moves everything according to the *ratio* of moveable things (e.g., light things upwards, heavy things downwards), also moves *voluntas* according to its condition: not from necessity but as something indeterminately open to [415] many things. It is obvious, therefore, that if the movement of *voluntas* is considered from the part of the exercise of the act, it is not moved from necessity.

26. *De an.* iii,9,432b5.
27. "Ad hos enim refert philosophus in libro De Anima verbum quorumdam dicentium, quod talis est voluntas in hominibus 'qualem in die ducit pater virorum deorumque,' id est caelum vel sol [ll.402–6]. This quotation, taken from the *translatio vetus* of De anima (at iii,3,427a26), appears a number of times in Thomas—but with variations. For instance, at *SCG* lb.3 cap.84 (§2591), he writes: "Talis est intellectus in diis et hominibus terrenis qualem in die ducit pater virorum deorumque"; at *in De an.* lb.3 cap.28 ll.66–68 (§619), "'Talis est intellectus in terrenis hominibus qualem pater virorumque deorumque,' id est sol, 'ducit in die'"; and at *ST* II–II q.95 a.5, "talis voluntas est in hominibus qualem in die inducit pater virorum deorumque." The quotation comes from Homer, *Odys.* xviii,136–37: τοῖος γὰρ νόος ἐστὶν ἐπιχθονίων ἀνθρώπων / οἷον ἐπ᾽ ἦμαρ ἄγῃσι πατὴρ ἀνδρῶν τε θεῶν τε.
28. *EE* viii,2,1248a16–29.

Si autem consideretur motus uoluntatis ex parte
obiecti determinantis actum uoluntatis ad hoc uel
illud uolendum, considerandum est quod obiectum   420
mouens uoluntatem est bonum conueniens appre-
hensum. Vnde si aliquod bonum proponatur
quod apprehendatur in ratione boni, non autem
in ratione conuenientis, non mouebit uoluntatem.
Cum autem consilia et electiones sint circa   425
particularia, quorum est actus, requiritur quod id
quod apprehenditur ut bonum et conueniens,
apprehenditur ut bonum et conueniens in particulari et non uniuersali tantum. Si igitur apprehendatur aliquid ut bonum conueniens secundum   430
omnia particularia que considerari possunt, ex
necessitate mouebit uoluntatem, et propter hoc
homo ex necessitate appetit beatitudinem, que
secundum Boetium est "status omnium bonorum
congregatione perfectus." Dico autem ex necessi-   435
tate quantum ad determinationem actus, quia non
potest uelle oppositum, non autem quantum ad
exercitium actus, quia potest aliquis non uelle
tunc cogitare de beatitudine, quia etiam ipsi actus
intellectus et uoluntatis particulares sunt.   440
    Si autem sit tale bonum quod non inueniatur
esse bonum secundum omnia particularia que
considerari possunt, non ex necessitate mouebit,
etiam quantum ad determinationem actus: poterit
enim aliquis uelle eius oppositum, etiam de eo   445
cogitans, quia forte est bonum uel conueniens
secundum aliquod aliud particulare consideratum;
sicut quod est bonum sanitati non est bonum
delectationi, et sic de aliis.

If, however, the movement of *voluntas* is considered from the part of the object that determines the act of *voluntas* to will [420] this or that, it is to be considered that the object moving *voluntas* is an apprehended suitable good. Thus, if some good is proposed, which is apprehended under the ratio of good but not under the ratio of something suitable, it does not move the *voluntas*. Since [425], however, counsels and choices are about particulars, among which is the act, it is required that that which is apprehended as good and suitable be apprehended as good and suitable in a particular and not only in a universal. If, therefore, [430] something is apprehended as a suitable good according to every particular it is possible to consider, it will move the *voluntas* from necessity; and for this reason man from necessity desires happiness, which is, according to Boethius, "the state that is perfect [435] by virtue of the assembly of all goods."[29] I mean, however, 'from necessity' with respect to the determination of the act (for it cannot will the opposite) not, however, with respect to the exercise of the act, for someone is able not to will to think of happiness at a given time—for also the acts [440] of intellect and *voluntas* are themselves particulars.

If, however, there is a good that is found not to be good with respect to every particular it is possible to consider, it will not be moved from necessity—even with regard to the determination of the act. For [445] someone can will its opposite, even while thinking of it, because, as might happen, it is good or suitable with respect to some other particular that is considered—as, for instance, what is good for the health is not good to the taste, and so also with other things.

29. Boethius, *Phil.cons.* bk.3 cap.2 p.47 ll.15–16 (*Pat.Lat.* 63,724A).

Et quod uoluntas feratur in id quod sibi offertur,   450
magis secundum hanc particularem conditionem
quam secundum aliam, potest contingere tripli-
citer. Vno quidem modo in quantum una prepon-
derat, et tunc mouetur uoluntas secundum rationem: puta cum homo preeligit id quod est utile   455
sanitati ei quod est utile uoluptati. Alio uero
modo in quantum cogitat de una particulari
circumstantia et non de alia, et hoc contingit
plerumque per aliquam occasionem, exhibitam
uel ab interiori uel ab exteriori, ut ei talis cogitatio   460
occurrat. Tertio uero modo contingit ex dispositione hominis: quia secundum Philosophum
"qualis unusquisque est, talis finis uidetur ei";
unde aliter mouetur ad aliquid uoluntas irati et
uoluntas quieti, quia non idem est conueniens   465
utrique, sicut etiam aliter acceptatur cibus a sano
et egro.

Si igitur dispositio per quam alicui uidetur
aliquid bonum et conueniens fuerit naturalis non
subiacens uoluntati, ex necessitate naturali uolun-   470
tas preeliget illud, sicut omnes homines naturaliter
desiderant esse, uiuere et intelligere. Si autem sit
talis dispositio que non sit naturalis, set subiacens
uoluntati, puta cum aliquis disponitur per habitum
uel passionem ad hoc quod sibi uideatur aliquid   475
uel bonum uel malum in hoc particulari, non ex
necessitate mouebitur uoluntas: quia poterit hanc
dispositionem remouere, ut sibi non uideatur
aliquid sic, ut scilicet cum aliquis quietat in se
iram ut non iudicet de aliquo tamquam iratus.   480
Facilius tamen remouetur passio quam habitus.

Sic igitur quantum ad aliqua uoluntas ex
necessitate mouetur ex parte obiecti, non autem
quantum ad omnia; set ex parte exercitii actus
non ex necessitate mouetur.   485

And [450] that the *voluntas* is drawn toward that which presents itself, more with respect to this particular condition than with respect to that other, can happen in three ways. One way, insofar as one condition preponderates—and, in this case, *voluntas* is moved according to [455] reason. For instance, a man chooses that which is useful for the health rather than that which is useful to carnal desire. Another way, however, insofar as he thinks of one particular circumstance and not of another—and this happens usually through some incident that is brought to bear [460] either from within or from without so that such a thought might occur to him. A third way, however, comes about due to the disposition of a man, for, according to the Philosopher, "as each is, so the end appears to him,"[30] so that the *voluntas* of an angry person and [465] that of a calm one are moved toward something in different ways, for the same thing is not suitable for each, as also food is regarded in different ways by a healthy person and a sick one.

If, therefore, the disposition by virtue of which something appears to someone good or suitable is natural and not [470] subject to *voluntas,* the *voluntas* prefers it from natural necessity, as all men naturally desire to be, to live, and to understand. If, however, the disposition be such that it is not natural but subject to *voluntas*—as when, for instance, someone is disposed by virtue of an habitual state [475] or a passion in such a way that something appears to him good or bad in this particular—the *voluntas* will not be moved from necessity, for it would be possible to remove this disposition so that something might not appear to him thus, as, for instance, when someone silences [480] anger in himself so that he might not judge something as would someone who is angry. For a passion is removed more easily than a habit.

In this way, therefore, with respect to some things, *voluntas* is moved from necessity from the part of the object, not however with respect to everything;

30. *EN* iii,5,1114a32–b1.

1. Ad primum ergo dicendum quod auctoritas
illa dupliciter potest intelligi: uno modo ut
loquatur propheta quantum ad exequtionem electionis: non enim est in potestate hominis ut
expleat in effectu quod mente deliberat. Alio modo   490
potest intelligi quantum ad hoc quod etiam
interior uoluntas mouetur ab aliquo superiori
principio quod est Deus; et secundum hoc
Apostolus dicit quod non est uolentis, scilicet
uelle, neque currentis, currere, sicut primi prin-   495
cipii, set Dei instigantis.

2. Vnde patet solutio ad secundum.

3. Ad tertium dicendum quod animalia bruta
mouentur per instinctum superioris agentis ad
aliquid determinatum secundum modum forme   500
particularis, cuius conceptionem sequitur appetitus
sensitiuus. Set Deus mouet quidem uoluntatem
immutabiliter propter efficaciam uirtutis mouentis,
que deficere non potest; set propter naturam
uoluntatis mote, que indifferenter se habet ad   505
diuersa, non inducitur necessitas set manet libertas.
Sicut etiam in omnibus prouidentia diuina infalli-
biliter operatur, et tamen a causis contingentibus
proueniunt effectus contingenter, in quantum
Deus omnia mouet proportionaliter, unumquod-   510
que secundum suum modum.

4. Ad quartum dicendum quod uoluntas aliquid
confert cum a Deo mouetur: ipsa enim est que
operatur, set mota a Deo. Et ideo motus eius
quamuis sit ab extrinseco sicut a primo principio,   515
non tamen est uiolentus.

5. Ad quintum dicendum quod uoluntas homi-

but from the part of the exercise of the act [485], it is not moved from necessity.

1. With respect to the first point, it needs to be said that that authority can be understood in two ways: one way, as if the prophet is speaking about the execution of the choice, for it is not in the capacity of man [490] to accomplish in effect what he deliberates about in his mind. Another way in which it can be understood is with respect to the fact that also the interior *voluntas* is moved by some superior principle—which is God. And in this sense the Apostle says that "it is not of him that willeth" (namely, [495] to will) "nor of him that runneth" (to run) as if he were the first principle, but rather it is of God who incites.

2. From this the solution to the second point is apparent.

3. With respect to the third point, it needs to be said that brute animals are moved through the prompting of a superior agent to [500] something determinate according to the mode of the particular form, the conception of which issues from the sensitive appetite. But God moves the *voluntas* immovably according to the efficacy of the power of the mover, which cannot fail; but, on account of the nature [505] of the *voluntas* moved, which is indifferently open to diverse things, necessity is not introduced but freedom remains. Even as divine providence operates in all things infallibly, nonetheless, from contingent causes, the effects come about contingently insofar as [510] God moves all things proportionately: each according to its own mode.

4. With respect to the fourth point, it needs to be said that *voluntas* contributes something when it is moved by God; for it is *voluntas* which acts, although moved by God. And, therefore, although its movement [515] is from without as from a first principle, this is not, however, an instance of being forced.

5. With respect to the fifth point, it needs to be said that the *voluntas* of

nis quodammodo discordat a Dei uoluntate, in
quantum scilicet uult aliquid quod Deus non uult
eam uelle, ut cum uult peccare; licet etiam non   520
uelit Deus uoluntatem hoc non uelle, quia si
uellet hoc Deus, fieret. Omnia enim quecumque
uoluit Dominus fecit. Et quamuis hoc modo
discordet uoluntas a Dei uoluntate quantum ad
motum uoluntatis, numquam tamen potest discor-   525
dare quantum ad exitum uel euentum, quia semper
uoluntas hominis hunc euentum sortitur, quod
Deus de homine suam uoluntatem implet. Set
quantum ad modum uolendi non oportet quod
uoluntas hominis Dei uoluntati conformetur, quia   530
Deus eternaliter et infinite uult unumquodque,
non tamen homo. Propter quod dicitur Ys. LV
"Sicut exaltantur celi a terra, ita sunt exaltate uie
mee a uiis uestris."

  6. Ad sextum dicendum quod ex hoc quod   535
bonum est obiectum uoluntatis potest haberi quod
uoluntas nichil uelit nisi sub ratione boni. Set
quia sub ratione boni multa et diuersa continentur,
non potest ex hoc haberi quod ex necessitate
uoluntas moueatur in hoc uel in illud.   540

  7. Ad septimum dicendum quod actiuum non
ex necessitate mouet nisi quando superat uirtutem
passiui. Cum autem uoluntas se habeat in potentia
respectu boni uniuersalis, nullum bonum superat
uirtutem uoluntatis quasi ex necessitate ipsam   545
mouens, nisi id quod est secundum omnem
considerationem bonum, et hoc solum est bonum
perfectum quod est beatitudo. Quod uoluntas non
potest non uelle, ita scilicet quod uelit oppositum;
potest tamen non uelle actu, quia potest auertere   550
cogitationem beatitudinis in quantum mouet
intellectum ad suum actum, et quantum ad hoc

man in a certain sense is discordant with the *voluntas* of God, insofar, that is, as it wills something that God does not will [520] it to will, as when it wills to sin—although it is also true that God does not will that *voluntas not* will this, for if God did will this, it would come about. For "whatsoever the Lord pleased, he hath done."[31] And, although *voluntas* might be in this way discordant with the *voluntas* of God with respect to [525] the movement of *voluntas*, it cannot ever be discordant with respect to the outcome or result, for the *voluntas* of man always receives as its lot this result, because God accomplishes his *voluntas* for man. But with respect to the mode of willing, it is not necessary that [530] the *voluntas* of man conform to the *voluntas* of God, for God eternally and infinitely wills every single thing—man does not. For this reason, it is said in Isaiah, chapter 55, "as the heavens are exalted above the earth, so are my ways exalted above your ways."[32]

6. With [535] respect to the sixth point, it needs to be said that since good is the object of *voluntas*, it is possible for it to be the case that *voluntas* wills nothing except under the *ratio* of good. But, since under the ratio of good many and diverse things are contained, it cannot be the case [540] that *voluntas* is moved from necessity toward this or toward that.

7. With respect to the seventh point, it needs to be said that the active factor does not move from necessity except when it overcomes the power of the passive. Since *voluntas* stands in an attitude of potency with respect to the universal good, no good exceeds [545] the power of *voluntas* as if moving it from necessity except that one that is good with respect to every consideration—and this is the perfect good alone, which is happiness. What the *voluntas* cannot not will—in such a way, that is, that it wills its opposite—it [550] can, however, not will actively, for it can divert the thought of happiness since it moves the intellect toward its act; and, in this respect, neither is happiness

31. Psalms 134.6 (Douay).
32. Isaiah 55.9 (Douay).

nec ipsam beatitudinem ex necessitate uult. Sicut
etiam aliquis non ex necessitate calefieret, si posset
calidum a se repellere cum uellet.   555

8. Ad octauum dicendum quod finis est ratio
uolendi ea que sunt ad finem; unde non similiter
se habet uoluntas ad utrumque.

9. Ad nonum dicendum quod quando ad finem
non posset perueniri nisi una uia, tunc eadem   560
ratio est uolendi finem et ea que sunt ad finem.
Set ita non est in proposito, nam multis uiis ad
beatitudinem perueniri potest. Et ideo, licet homo
ex necessitate uelit beatitudinem, nichil tamen
eorum que ad beatitudinem ducunt ex necessitate   565
uult.

10. Ad decimum dicendum quod de intellectu
et uoluntate quodammodo est simile et quodammodo dissimile. Dissimile quidem quantum ad
exercitium actus, nam intellectus mouetur a   570
uoluntate ad agendum, uoluntas non ab alia
potentia set a se ipsa. Set ex parte obiecti est
utrobique similitudo. Sicut enim uoluntas mouetur
ex necessitate ab obiecto quod est omnifariam
bonum, non autem ab obiecto quod potest accipi   575
secundum aliquam rationem ut malum, ita etiam
intellectus ex necessitate mouetur a uero necessario, quod non potest accipi ut falsum, non autem
a uero contingenti, quod potest accipi ut falsum.

11. Ad undecimum dicendum quod dispositio   580
primi mouentis manet in his que ab eo mouentur
in quantum mouentur ab ipso: sic enim eius
similitudinem recipiunt. Non tamen oportet quod
totaliter eius similitudinem consequantur: unde
primum principium mouens est immobile, non   585
autem alia.

12. Ad duodecimum dicendum quod ex hoc

itself willed from necessity. Similarly, someone would not be warmed from necessity if he could [555] repel heat from himself when he would.

8. With respect to the eighth point, it needs to be said that the end is the reason for willing those things that are for the end; thus, *voluntas* does not stand in the same way with respect to each.

9. With respect to the ninth point, it needs to be said that, when [560] it is not possible to arrive at an end except by one route, then there is the same reason for willing the end and the things that are for the end. But it is not this which is being proposed, for it is possible to arrive at happiness by many routes. And, therefore, granted that man wills happiness from necessity, none [565] of those things that lead to happiness does he will from necessity.

10. With respect to the tenth point, it needs to be said that, with respect to intellect and *voluntas*, things are, in a way, similar, in a way, dissimilar. Dissimilar with respect to [570] the exercise of the act, for the intellect is moved by the *voluntas* to act, the *voluntas* not by another potency but by it-self. But from the part of the object, there is a similarity with respect to both. For, just as the *voluntas* is moved from necessity by an object that is in every way [575] good but not by an object that can be regarded according to some ratio as bad, so also is the intellect moved from necessity by something that is true and necessary, which cannot be regarded as false, but not by something that is true and contingent, which can be regarded as false.

11. With [580] respect to the eleventh point, it needs to be said that the dis-position of the first mover remains in those things that are moved by it inso-far as they are moved by it: in this way they acquire its likeness. It is not, how-ever, necessary that they totally follow its likeness. Thus [585], the first mov-ing principle is immobile, but not the others.

12. With respect to the twelfth point, it needs to be said that due to the

ipso quod uerum est intentio quedam quasi in
mente existens, habet quod sit magis formale
quam bonum et magis motiuum in ratione obiecti;   590
set bonum est magis motiuum secundum rationem
finis, ut dictum est.

13. Ad tertium decimum dicendum quod amor
dicitur transformare amantem in amatum in
quantum per amorem mouetur amans ad ipsam   595
rem amatam, cognitio uero assimilat in quantum
similitudo cogniti fit in cognoscente. Quorum
primum pertinet ad immutationem que est ab
agente quod querit finem, secundum uero pertinet
ad immutationem que est secundum formam.   600

14. Ad quartum decimum dicendum quod
assentire non nominat motum intellectus ad rem,
set magis ad conceptionem rei que habetur in
mente; cui intellectus assentit dum iudicat eam
esse ueram.   605

15. Ad quintum decimum dicendum quod non
omnis causa ex necessitate inducit effectum etiam
si sit causa sufficiens, eo quod causa potest
impediri ut quandoque effectum suum non consequatur, sicut cause naturales, que non ex necessi-   610
tate producunt suos effectus, set ut in pluribus,
quia in paucioribus impediuntur. Sic igitur illa
causa que facit uoluntatem aliquid uelle, non
oportet quod ex necessitate hoc faciat, quia
potest per ipsam uoluntatem impedimentum   615
prestari, uel remouendo talem considerationem
que inducit eum ad uolendum, uel considerando
oppositum, scilicet quod hoc quod proponitur ut
bonum secundum aliquid non est bonum.

16. Ad sextum decimum dicendum quod   620
Philosophus in VIII Metaphisice ostendit per
illud medium, non quod aliqua potentia non sit

very fact that the true is an intention, existing as it were in the mind, it possesses something that is more formal than the good and more motivating in the ratio of the object [590]; but the good is more motivating according to the ratio of the end, as was said.

13. With respect to the thirteenth point, it needs to be said that love is said to transform the lover into the loved [595] insofar as, through love, the lover is moved toward the thing loved itself; thought, however, assimilates insofar as a likeness of the thing known comes to be in the knower. Of which, the first pertains to a change that is by the agent that seeks the end; the second, however, pertains [600] to a change that is according to the form.

14. With respect to the fourteenth point, it needs to be said that 'to assent' does not name a movement of the intellect toward the thing but rather toward the conception of the thing that is held in the mind. It is to this that the intellect assents when it judges it [605] to be true.

15. With respect to the fifteenth point, it needs to be said that not every cause induces its effect from necessity, even if it is a sufficient cause, for a cause can be impeded so that sometimes its effect does not [610] follow—as with natural causes that do not produce their effects from necessity but for the most part, since in a few cases they are impeded. So, that cause that makes the *voluntas* to will something need not do this from necessity, for [615] it is possible for an impediment to be set up by the *voluntas* itself, either by removing that consideration that induces him to will or by considering its opposite—i.e., that that which is proposed as good, in a certain respect is not good.

16. With [620] respect to the sixteenth point, it needs to be said that the Philosopher, in *Metaphysics,* book 8, shows by that means not that a potency that is open to contraries is not active but that an active potency open to con-

actiua ad contraria se habens, set quod potentia
actiua ad contraria se habens non ex necessitate
producit suum effectum. Hoc enim posito mani-   625
feste sequeretur quod contradictoria essent simul.
Si autem detur quod aliqua potentia actiua ad
opposita se habeat, non sequitur opposita esse
simul: quia etsi utrumque oppositorum ad quod
potentia se habet sit possibile, unum tamen est   630
incompossibile alteri.

  17. Ad septimum decimum dicendum quod
uoluntas quando de nouo incipit eligere, transmutatur a sua priori dispositione quantum ad hoc
quod prius erat eligens in potentia et postea fit   635
eligens actu. Et hec quidem transmutatio est ab
aliquo mouente, in quantum ipsa uoluntas mouet
se ipsam ad agendum et in quantum etiam mouetur
ab aliquo exteriori agente, scilicet Deo. Non
tamen ex necessitate mouetur, ut dictum est.   640

  18. Ad duodeuicesimum dicendum quod principium humane cognitionis est a sensu, non
tamen oportet quod quicquid ab homine cognoscitur sit sensui subiectum, uel per effectum
sensibilem immediate cognoscatur. Nam et ipse   645
intellectus intelligit se ipsum per actum suum qui
non est sensui subiectus; similiter autem et
interiorem actum uoluntatis intelligit in quantum
per actum intellectus quodammodo mouetur
uoluntas, et alio modo actus intellectus causatur   650
a uoluntate, ut dictum est, sicut effectus cognosci-
tur per causam et causa per effectum. Dato tamen
quod potentia uoluntatis ad opposita se habens
non possit cognosci nisi per effectum sensibilem
adhuc ratio non sequitur. Sicut enim uniuersale   655
quod est ubique et semper, cognoscitur a nobis
per singularia que sunt hic et nunc, et materia

traries does not from necessity [625] produce its effect.³³ For, supposing this, it clearly follows that contradictories could be at the same time. If, however, it should be granted that some active potency is open to opposites, it does not follow that the opposites are at the same time: for, although both of the opposites toward which [630] a potency is open are possible, the one is not compatible with the other.

17. With respect to the seventeenth point, it needs to be said that when the *voluntas* begins newly to choose, it is transformed from its previous disposition insofar as [635] previously it was choosing in potency and afterwards it comes to be choosing actively. And this transformation is by some mover, insofar as the *voluntas* itself moves itself to act and insofar as it is also moved by an exterior agent, namely God. It is not [640], however, moved from necessity, as was said.

18. With respect to the eighteenth point, it needs to be said that the principle of human thought is from the senses; it is not, however, necessary that whatever is known by man be subject to the senses or that it be known [645] immediately by virtue of a sensible effect. For the intellect itself understands itself by virtue of its act,³⁴ which is not subject to the senses; similarly, however, it also understands the interior act of the *voluntas* insofar as, in a certain sense, the *voluntas* is moved by an act of the intellect [650] and, in another sense, the act of the intellect is caused by the *voluntas*, as was said, as an effect is known from its cause and a cause from its effect. Granted, however, that the potency of the *voluntas*, which is open to opposites, cannot be known except through its sensible effect, [655] even still the argument does not follow.

33. The citation is actually *Metaph.* ix,5,1047b31–1048a10 (and particularly 1048a9–10: ὥστε ἅμα ποιήσει τὰ ἐναντία· τοῦτο δὲ ἀδύνατον). See also above, note 12.

34. *ST* I q.87 a.1 c. See also *in De an.* lb.3 cap.3 ll.61–106 (§§724–26); also *ST* I q.14 a.2 ad 1, which is, however, to be interpreted in the light of *in Lib.caus.* lect.15 (§310), where he says that the phrase *sciens essentiam suam* means to know the essence through its operation. (That is also what the *Liber de causis* itself says: see corresponding proposition in the same volume: proposition 15, n.125.)

prima que est in potentia ad diuersas formas
cognoscitur a nobis per successionem formarum
que tamen non sunt simul in materia, ita et   660
potentia uoluntatis ad opposita se habens cognoscitur a nobis, non quidem per hoc quod actus
oppositi sint simul, set quia successiue sibi
inuicem succedunt ab eodem principio.

19. Ad undeuicesimum dicendum quod ista   665
propositio 'sicut se habet actus ad actum, ita se
habet potentia ad potentiam' quodammodo est
uera et quodammodo falsa. Si enim accipiatur
actus ex equo respondens potentie ut uniuersale
obiectum ipsius, ueritatem habet propositio: sic   670
enim se habet auditus ad uisum sicut sonus ad
colorem. Si autem accipiatur id quod continetur
sub obiecto uniuersali sicut particularis actus, sic
propositio ueritatem non habet: una est enim
potentia uisiua, cum tamen album et nigrum non   675
sint idem. Licet ergo simul insit homini potentia
uoluntatis ad opposita se habens, tamen opposita
illa ad que se habet uoluntas non sunt simul.

20. Ad uicesimum dicendum quod idem secundum idem non mouet se ipsum; set secundum   680
aliud potest se ipsum mouere. Sic enim intellectus
in quantum intelligit actu principia, reducit se
ipsum de potentia in actum quantum ad conclusiones, et uoluntas in quantum uult finem, reducit
se in actum quantum ad ea que sunt ad finem.   685

21. Ad uicesimum primum dicendum quod
motus uoluntatis cum sint multiformes, reducuntur ad aliquod principium uniforme. Quod
tamen non est corpus celeste set Deus, ut dictum
est, si accipiatur principium quod directe uolun-   690
tatem mouet; si autem loquamur de motu
uoluntatis secundum quod mouetur ab exteriori

Just as a universal, which is everywhere and always, is known by us through singulars, which are here and now, and <just as> primary matter, which is in potency toward diverse forms, is known by us through the succession of forms [660] which, however, are not in the matter at the same time, so also the potency of *voluntas*, which is open to opposites, is known by us—not, indeed, because the opposite acts are at the same time but because they succeed one another successively from the same principle.

19. With [665] respect to the nineteenth point, it needs to be said that this proposition 'as an act stands with respect to an act, so also stands a potency with respect to a potency' is in a certain sense true, in a certain sense false. For if we regard the act as corresponding *ex aequo* to the potency, as a universal [670] object of itself, the proposition is true: 'as hearing stands with respect to vision, so also stands sound with respect to color.'[35] If, however, that which is contained under the universal object is regarded as a particular act, so taken the proposition is not true, for [675] the potency of sight is one, while white and black are not the same. Thus, although there is present in man at the same time the potency of *voluntas*, which is open to opposites, nonetheless, these opposites with respect to which *voluntas* is open, are not at the same time.

20. With respect to the twentieth point, it needs to be said that the same thing [680] does not move itself in the same respect; in a different respect, however, it can move itself. For in this way intellect, insofar as it actively understands the principles, reduces itself from potency into act with respect to conclusions; and *voluntas,* insofar as it wills the end, reduces [685] itself to act with respect to those things that are for the end.

21. With respect to the twenty-first point, it needs to be said that the move-

---

35. Thomas's *ex aequo* corresponds to Euclid's δι᾽ ἴσου, as at *Elem.* v, definition 17 (6.7), proposition 22 (60.20), etc. The idea is that, in order for the proportion to be valid, there must be parity among the elements coming into the proportion. Thus, vision (the act) corresponds equally to color (the potentially seen) when both are considered universally—i.e., not yet determinately— and, in particular, when the potency is considered as a universal object of the act. If, however, on the potency side, we substitute determinate things such as white and black (i.e., determinate instances of color), the proportion is not valid, for the elements are not equal: on the act side, there is a universal act (vision); on the potency side, there are two determinate potencies.

sensibili per occasionem, sic motus uoluntatis
reducitur in corpus celeste. Nec tamen ex necessitate uoluntas mouetur: non enim est necessarium   695
quod presentatis sibi delectabilibus uoluntas appetat ipsa. Nec tamen uerum est quod ea que directe
causantur a corporibus celestibus ex necessitate
ab ipsis proueniant. Vt enim Philosophus dicit in
VI Metaphisice, si omnis effectus ex aliqua causa   700
procederet et omnis causa ex necessitate produ-
ceret suum effectum, sequeretur quod omnia
essent necessaria Set utrumque istorum est falsum,
quia alique cause etiam cum sint sufficientes, non
ex necessitate producunt suos effectus, quia   705
possunt impediri, sicut patet in omnibus causis
naturalibus. Nec iterum uerum est quod omne
quod fit, habeat causam naturalem: ea enim que
fiunt per accidens non fiunt ab aliqua causa actiua
naturali, quia quod est per accidens non est ens   710
et unum. Sic igitur occursus impedientis, cum sit
per accidens, non reducitur in corpus celeste
sicut in causam: agit enim corpus celeste per
modum agentis naturalis.

    22. Ad uicesimum secundum dicendum quod   715
ille qui facit quod non uult, non habet liberam
actionem, set potest habere liberam uoluntatem.

    23. Ad uicesimum tertium dicendum quod
homo peccans liberum arbitrium perdidit quantum
ad libertatem que est a culpa et miseria, non autem   720
quantum ad libertatem que est a coactione.

    24. Ad uicesimum quartum dicendum quod
consuetudo facit necessitatem non simpliciter set
in repentinis precipue. Nam ex deliberatione
quantumcumque consuetus potest tamen contra   725
consuetudinem agere.

ment of *voluntas,* since it is multiform, is reduced to some uniform principle, but that, nonetheless, it is not a heavenly body but God, as was said [690]—if what is meant is the principle that moves the *voluntas* directly. If, however, we speak of the movement of *voluntas* insofar as it is moved by an exterior sensible in an occasional manner, in this sense the movement of the *voluntas* is reduced to a heavenly body. Neither, however, is [695] *voluntas* moved from necessity, for that is not necessary which, delectable things being presented, the *voluntas* desires. Neither, however, is it true that those things that are directly caused by heavenly bodies come from them from necessity. As the Philosopher says in [700] *Metaphysics,* book 6, if every effect proceeded from some cause and every cause produced its effect from necessity, it would follow that everything is necessary.[36] But both of these are false,[37] for some causes, even when they are sufficient, do not [705] produce their effects from necessity, for they can be impeded, as is clear in all natural causes. Nor, again, is it true that everything that comes about has a natural cause, for those things that come about accidentally do not come about due to any active [710] natural cause, since what is accidental is not being and one.[38] Thus, the occurrence of an impediment, when it is accidental, is not reduced to a heavenly body as if to a cause, for a heavenly body acts in the mode of a natural agent.

22. With [715] respect to the twenty-second point, it needs to be said that he who does what he wills not does not have freedom of action, but he can have a free *voluntas.*

23. With respect to the twenty-third point, it needs to be said that the man who sins loses his free decision with respect to [720] that freedom that is from guilt and misery but not with respect to that freedom that is from coercion.

24. With respect to the twenty-fourth point, it needs to be said that custom creates necessity not *simpliciter* but principally in unexpected occurrences. For, with deliberation [725], however accustomed a person might be, he can nevertheless act against the custom.

36. *Metaph.* vi,3,1027a29ff.
37. That is, both points in Aristotle's protasis: 'every effect proceeds from some cause' and 'every cause produces its effect from necessity.'
38. See *in Metaph.* §§2419–21; *ST* I q.39 a.3 c.

BIBLIOGRAPHY

Primary Sources

See also "Abbreviations, Texts, Conventions, Sigla," near the front of the present volume.

Curly brackets signify that the attribution of a work to the author in the brackets is at least uncertain. In this regard, for the Greek commentators, I follow Sorabji (1990b), pp. 27–29.

A date given in round brackets is the date of the work I cite in the text. If the work has been published previously and if I think this would be good for the reader to know, I add another date in pointed backets, as in: "Anscombe, G. E. M. (1981 <1961>)," etc. (see below). Sometimes I also add bibliographical information pertaining to the earlier publication, as in: "Chisholm, R. (1978 <Blackwell, *Practical Reason, Körner*, S. (ed.), 1974>)," etc. (see below).

Albert the Great. *in An.post.: Libri posteriorum analyticorum.* In *Opera omnia:* vol. 2, pp. 1–232. Paris: Vivès (1890).

————. *Quin.prob.: De quindecim problematibus* (B. Geyer, ed.). In *Opera omnia:* vol. 17.1, pp. 31–44. Aschendorff: Monasterium Westfalorum (1975).

Alexander of Aphrodisias. *De an.: Liber de anima* (I. Bruns, ed.). In Commentaria in Aristotelem Graeca: vol. 2.1 (supplement), pp. 1–100. Berlin: Reimer (1887).

————. *De fat.: De fato* (I. Bruns, ed.). In Commentaria in Aristotelem Graeca: vol. 2 (supplement), pp. 164–212. Berlin: Reimer (1892).

————. *in An.pr.: In Aristotelis Analyticorum priorum librum I commentarium* (M. Wallies, ed.). In Commentaria in Aristotelem Graeca: vol. 2.1. Berlin: Reimer (1883).

————. *in Metaph.: In Aristotelis Metaphysica commentaria* (M. Hayduck, ed.). In Commentaria in Aristotelem Graeca: vol. 1. Berlin: Reimer (1891).

————. *in Top.: In Aristotelis topicorum libros octo commentaria* (M. Wallies, ed.). In Commentaria in Aristotelem Graeca: vol. 2.2. Berlin: Reimer (1891).

{Alexander of Aphrodisias}. *Mant.: De anima libri mantissa* (I. Bruns, ed.). In Commentaria in Aristotelem Graeca: vol. 2.1 (supplement), pp. 101–86. Berlin: Reimer (1887).

———. *Quaest.: Quaestiones* (I. Bruns, ed.). In Commentaria in Aristotelem Graeca: vol. 2.2 (supplement), pp. 1–163. Berlin: Reimer (1892).

Augustine. *Conf.: Confessiones* (P. Knöll, ed.). In Corpus Scriptorum Ecclesiasticorum Latinorum: vol. 33. Prague/Vienna/Leipzig: Tempsky/Tempsky/Freytag (1896).

———. *De lib.arb.: De libero arbitrio* (W. Green, ed.). In Corpus Scriptorum Ecclesiasticorum Latinorum: vol. 74 (*Sancti Aurelii Augustini Opera*, 6.3). Vienna: Hoelder-Pichler-Tempsky (1956).

———. *Enchir.: Enchiridion ad Laurentium de fide et spe et caritate* (E. Evans, ed.). In Corpus Christianorum (series latina): vol. 46. *Aurelii Augustini Opera*, 13.2: pp. 21–114. Turnhout, Belgium: Brepols (1969).

———. *Trin.: De Trinitate* (W. J. Mountain, ed.). In Corpus Christianorum (series latina): vols. 50/50A. *Aurelii Augustini Opera*, 16.1–2. Turnhout, Belgium: Brepols (1968).

Averroes. *in An.post.: In librum de demonstratione Aristotelis maxima expositio. Aristotelis Opera cum Averrois Commentariis:* vol. 1. Venice (1552).

———. *in De an.: Commentarium magnm in Ariotelis De anima libros* (F. S. Crawford, ed.). In Corpus Commentariorum Averrois in Aristotelem (H. A. Wolfson, D. Baneth, and F. H. Fobes, eds.): vol. 6.1. Cambridge, MA: Mediaeval Academy of America (1953).

Avicenna. *Phil.pr.: Libe de philosphia prima sive scientia divina* (S. Van Riet, ed.). In Avicenna Latinus. Louvain/Leiden: E. Peeters/E. J. Brill (1977–1983).

Boethius. *Phil.cons.: Philosophiae consolatio* (G. Weinberger, ed.). In Corpus Scriptorum Ecclesiasticorum Latinorum: vol. 47. Vienna/Leipzig: Hoelder-Pichler-Tempsky/Akademische Verlagsgesellschaft (1934).

Cajetan (Cajetanus), Thomas de Vio. *in An.post.: Super Aristotelis Posteriorum libros commentaria.* In *Super praedicabilia Porphyrii & Aristotelis praedicamenta, ac Posteriorum libros & opusculum S. Thomae De ente & essentia praeclarissima commentaria, annotationes, ac quaestiones. Eiusdem de totius naturalis scientiae subjecto absolutissima quaestio, et tractatus de variis cambiorum generibus.* Venice: H. Scotus (1554).

Calcidius. *in Ti.: Commentarius in Timaeum Platonis.* In *Timaeus a Calcidio translatus commentarioque instructus* (J. H. Waszink, ed.). In Plato Latinus: vol. 4. London/Leiden: Warburg Institute/E. J. Brill (1962).

Cicero. *De inv.: De inventione* (G. Achard, ed. and trans., *Cicéron: De l'invention*). Paris: Les Belles Lettres (1994).

Damascene (John). *De fide orth.: De fide orthodoxa* [in the Versions of Burgundio and Cerbanus] (E. M. Buytaert, ed.). St. Bonaventure, NY: Franciscan Institute (1955).

Dionysius (pseudo-). *Div.nom.: De divinis nominibus* (B. R. Suchla, ed.). In Corpus Dionysiacum: vol. 1, pp. 107–231. Berlin: De Gruyter (1990).

Euclid. *Elem.: Elementa* (J. L. Heiberg, ed.). Leipzig: B. G. Teubner (1883–1888). See also Heath (1956 <1925>) in secondary bibliography.

Gellius, A. *Noct.Att.: Noctes Atticae* (P. K. Marshall, ed.). Oxford: Clarendon Press (1968).

Grosseteste, R. *in An.post.: Commentarius in Posteriorum analyticorum libros* (P. Rossi, ed.). Florence: Olschki (1981).

{Heliodorus}. *in EN: In Ethica Nicomachea paraphrasis* (G. Heylbut, ed.). In Commentaria in Aristotelem Graeca: vol. 19.2. Berlin: Reimer (1889).

Homer. *Odys.: Odyssea* (T. W. Allen, ed.). *Opera:* vols. 3–4. Oxford: Clarendon (1917).

Maximus Confessor. *Opus.th.polem.: Opuscula theologica et polemica ad Marinum* (F. Combefis, ed. and trans.). In *Opera omnia:* vol. 91, pp. 9–286. Patrologia Graeca. Paris: Migne (1860).

Michael of Ephesus. *in MA: In librum animalium motione commentarium* (M. Hayduck, ed.). In Commentaria in Aristotelem Graeca: vol. 22.2, pp. 461–620. Berlin: Reimer (1904).

Nemesius (Emesenus). *De nat.hom.: De natura hominis* (M. Morani, ed.). Leipzig: Teubner (1987). See also *De natura hominis Graece et Latine* (C. F. Matthaei, ed.). Hildesheim: Georg Olms (1967 <1802>). See also Verbeke and Moncho (1975).

Pappus Alexandrinus. *Collec.: Collectionis quae supersunt* (F. Hultsch, ed.). Berlin: Weidmann (1876–1888). See also Jones (1986).

Philoponus (John). *in De an.: in Aristotelis De anima I–II commentaria* (M. Hayduck, ed.). In Commentaria in Aristotelem Graeca: vol. 15, pp. 1–445. Berlin: Reimer (1897).

———. *in An.pr.: in Aristotelis Analytica priora librum I commentarium* (M. Wallies, ed.). In Commentaria in Aristotelem Graeca: vol. 13.2, pp. 1–386. Berlin: Reimer (1905).

———. *in An.post.: in Aristotelis Analytica posteriora in librum I commentarium* (M. Wallies, ed.). In Commentaria in Aristotelem Graeca: vol. 13.3, pp. 1–333. Berlin: Reimer (1909).

Proclus. *Elem.: The Elements of Theology: A Revised Text with Translation, Introduction and Commentary* (E. Dodds, ed.) (2d ed.). Oxford: Clarendon (1963).

Simplicius. *in Phys.: In Aristotelis Physica commentaria* (H. Diels, ed.). In Commentaria in Aristotelem Graeca: vol. 9 (books 1 to 4) and vol. 10 (books 5 to 8). Berlin: Reimer (1882, 1895).

{Simplicius}. *in De an.: In libros Aristotelis De anima commentaria* (M. Hayduck, ed.). In Commentaria in Aristotelem Graeca: vol. 11. Berlin: Reimer (1882).

Themistius. *in De an.: Librorum De anima libros paraphrasis* (R. Heinze, ed.). In Commentaria in Aristotelem Graeca: vol. 5.3. Berlin: Reimer (1899). See also Verbeke (1957).

Zabarella, J. *De prop.nec.: De propositionibus necessariis libri duo.* In *Opera logica: Quorum argumentum, seriem et utilitatem ostendet tum versa pagina, tum affixa praefatio Ioannis Lodovici Havvenrevteri doctoris medici, et philosophi, in Argentoratensi Academia professoris* (4th ed.), pp. 345–412. Cologne (1602).

———. *De praecogn.: De tribus praecognitis.* Also in *Opera logica* (see above), pp. 497–530.

———. *in An.post.: In duos Aristotelis libros Posteriores analyticos commentarii.* Also in *Opera logica* (see above), pp. 615–1283.

Secondary Sources

Aertsen, J. A. (1989). "Method and Metaphysics: The *via resolutionis* in Thomas Aquinas." *New Scholasticism,* 63, pp. 405–18.

Allan, D. J. (1953). "Aristotle's Account of the Origin of Moral Principles." In *Actes du XIème Congrès International de Philosophie/Proceedings of the XIth International Congress of Philosophy,* 12. Amsterdam/Louvain: North-Holland Publishing/Éditions E. Nauwelaerts, pp. 120–27.

—— (1955). "The Practical Syllogism." In *Autour d'Aristote: Recueil d'études de philosophie ancienne et médiévale, offert à Monseigneur A. Mansion* (pp. 325–40). Bibliothèque philosophique de Louvain, 16. Louvain: Publications Universitaires de Louvain.

—— (1961). "Quasi-mathematical Method in the *Eudemian Ethics.*" In S. Mansion (ed.), *Aristote et les problèmes de méthode: Communications présentées au Symposium Aristotelicum tenu à Louvain du 24 août au 1ᵉʳ septembre 1960.* Louvain/Paris: Publications Universitaires de Louvain/Éditions Béatrice-Nauwelaerts, pp. 303–18.

—— (1962). *Aristote: Le philosophe* (C. Lefèvre, trans.). Louvain/Paris: Publications Universitaires/Béatrice-Nauwelaerts.

Annas, J. (1976). *Aristotle's "Metaphysics," Books M and N: Translated with Introduction and Notes.* Oxford: Clarendon.

Anonymous ("S."). (1937–1939). "Corrections textuelles, n.77." *Bulletin Thomiste,* 5, pp. 53–61.

Anscombe, G. E. M. (1981 <1961>). "War and Murder." In *Collected Philosophical Papers of G. E. M. Anscombe* (3 vols.), vol. 3: *Ethics, Religion and Politics* (pp. 51–61). Minneapolis/Oxford: University of Minnesota Press/Basil Blackwell.

—— (1982). "Action, Intention and 'Double Effect.'" *Proceedings of the American Catholic Philosophical Association,* 56, pp. 12–25.

Armstrong, R. A. (1966). *Primary and Secondary Precepts in Thomistic Natural Law Teaching.* The Hague: Martinus Nijhoff.

Aubert, J.-M. (1955). *Le droit romain dans l'oeuvre de saint Thomas.* Bibliothèque thomiste, 30. Paris: Librairie Philosophique J. Vrin.

Baker, G. P., and P. M. S. Hacker (1984). *Frege: Logical Excavations.* New York/Oxford: Oxford University Press/Basil Blackwell.

Barnes, J. (1969). "Aristotle's Theory of Demonstration." *Phronesis,* 14, pp. 123–52.

—— (1981). "Proof and the Syllogism." In E. Berti (ed.), *Aristotle on Science: "The Posterior Analytics"* [Proceedings of the Eighth Symposium Aristotelicum held in Padua from September 7 to 15, 1978] (pp. 17–59). Studia Aristotelica, no. 9. Padua: Antenore.

—— (1982). "Sheep Have Four Legs." In *Proceedings of the World Congress on Aristotle, Thessaloniki, August 7–14, 1978,* vol. 3 (pp. 113–19). Athens: Ekdosis Ypoyrgeiou.

—— (ed.) (1984). *The Complete Works of Aristotle: The Revised Oxford Translation.* Princeton: Princeton University Press.

———— (1990a). "Aristotle and Political Liberty." In G. Patzig (ed.), *Aristoteles' 'Politik'*: *Akten des XI Symposium Aristotelicum* (pp. 249–63). Göttingen: Vandenhoeck and Ruprecht.

———— (1990b). "Logical Form and Logical Matter." In A. Albrti (ed.), *Logica, Mente e Persona* (pp. 7–119). Florence: Leo S. Olschki.

———— (1994 <1975>). *Aristotle, "Posterior Analytics": Translated with a Commentary* (2d ed.). Clarendon Aristotle Series. Oxford: Clarendon.

Barnes, J., S. Bobzien, K. Flannery, and K. Ierodiakonou (trans.). (1991). *Alexander of Aphrodisias: On Aristotle "Prior Analytics" 1.1–7*. London: Duckworth.

Becker, A. (1933). *Die Aristotelische Theorie der Möglichkeitsschlüsse*. Berlin: Junker und Dünnhaupt.

Belmans, T. G. (1982). "Autour du problème de la défense légitime chez Saint Thomas." In *Morale e diritto nella prospettiva tomistica: Atti dell'VIII Congresso Tomistico Internazionale* [no editor given] (pp. 162–70). Studi tomistici, 15. Rome: Libreria Editrice Vaticana.

Bennett, J. (1995). *The Act Itself*. Oxford: Clarendon.

Berti, E. (1983). "Differenza tra il metodo risolutivo degli aristotelici e la *resolutio* dei matematici." In L. Olivieri (ed.), *Aristotelismo veneto e scienza moderna* (pp. 435–57). Padua: Antenore.

Beth, E. W. (1955). "Semantic Entailment and Formal Derivability." *Mededelingen der Koninklijke Nederlandse Akademie van Wetenschappen, afd. Letterkunde*, Nieuwe Reeks, Deel 18, no. 13, pp. 309–42. Amsterdam: N. V. Noord-Hollandsche Uitgevers Maatschappij [reprinted in J. Hintikka, *The Philosophy of Mathematics* (Oxford University Press, 1969)].

Bochenski, I. M. (1951). *Ancient Formal Logic*. Studies in Logic and the Foundations of Mathematics. Amsterdam: North-Holland Publishing.

———— (1956). *Formale Logik*. Orbis Academicus. Freiburg/Munich: Karl Alber.

———— (1961). *A History of Formal Logic* (I. Thomas, trans. and ed.). Notre Dame: University of Notre Dame Press [translation of Bochenski (1956)].

Bonitz, H. (1961 <1870>). *Index Aristotelicus. Aristotelis opera*, vol. 5. Berlin: De Gruyter.

Bourke, V. J. (1964). *Will in Western Thought: An Historico-Critical Study*. New York: Sheed and Ward.

Boyle, J. (1977). "Double-Effect and a Certain Type of Craniotomy." *Irish Theological Quarterly*, 44, pp. 303–18.

———— (1978). "*Praeter intentionem* in Aquinas." *Thomist*, 42, pp. 649–65.

———— (1991a). "Who Is Entitled to Double-Effect?" *Journal of Medicine and Philosophy*, 16, pp. 475–94.

———— (1991b). "Further Thoughts on Double-Effect: Some Preliminary Responses." *Journal of Medicine and Philosophy*, 16, pp. 565–70.

———— (1994). "The Personal Responsibility Required for Mortal Sin." In L. Gormally (ed.), *Moral Truth and Moral Tradition: Essays in Honour of Peter Geach and Elizabeth Anscombe* (pp. 149–62). Dublin: Four Courts.

Boyle, J., G. Grisez, and J. Finnis (1990). "Incoherence and Consequentialism (or

Proportionalism): A Rejoinder." *American Catholic Philosophical Quarterly,* 64, pp. 271–77.

Boyle, J., G. Grisez, and O. Tollefsen (1976). *Free Choice: A Self-Referential Argument.* Notre Dame/London: University of Notre Dame Press.

Brandon, E. P. (1978). "Hintikka on ἀκολουθεῖν." *Phronesis,* 23, pp. 173–78.

Brennan, T. (1997). "Aristotle's Modal Syllogistic: A Discussion of R. Patterson, *Aristotle's Modal Logic.*" *Oxford Studies in Ancient Philosophy,* 15, pp. 207–30.

Broadie, S. (1990). "Nature and Craft in Aristotelian Teleology." In D. Devereux, and P. Pellegrin (eds.), *Biologie, logique et métaphysique chez Aristote* (pp. 389–403). Paris: Éditions du Centre National de la Recherche Scientifique.

Brock, D. W. (1973). "Recent Work in Utilitarianism." *American Philosophical Quarterly,* 10, pp. 241–69.

Brock, S. L. (1991). "*Ars imitatur naturam:* Un aspecto descuidado de la doctrina de la ley natural en S. Tómas de Aquino." In R. Alvira (ed.), *El hombre, transcendencia y imanencia: Actas del XXV Congreso Filosóico* (vol. 1, pp. 383–95). Pamplona: Servicio de Publicaciones de la Universidad de Navarra.

———— (1998). *Action and Conduct: Thomas Aquinas and the Theory of Action.* Edinburgh: T. and T. Clark.

Broome, J. (1991). *Weighing Goods.* Oxford: Blackwell.

Burnyeat, M. F. (1981). Review of Martha Craven Nussbaum's *Aristotle's "De Motu Animalium."* *Archiv für Geschichte der Philosophie,* 3, pp. 184–89.

———— (1987). "Platonism and Mathematics: A Prelude to Discussion." In *Mathematics and Metaphysics in Aristotle/Mathematik und Metaphysik bei Aristotles: Akten des X.Symposium Aristotelicum, Sigriswil, 6–12 September 1984* (pp. 213–40). Bern/Stuttgart: Paul Haupt.

Byrne, P. (1997). *Analysis and Science in Aristotle.* Albany: State University of New York Press.

Cai, R. (ed.) (1953). *S. Thomae Aquinatis super epistolas S. Pauli lecturas* (8th ed.). Turin/Rome: Marietti.

Cavanaugh, T. A. (1997). "Aquinas's Account of Double Effect." *Thomist,* 61, pp. 107–21.

Charles, D. (1984). *Aristotle's Philosophy of Action.* London: Duckworth.

———— (1990). "Comments on M. Nussbaum." In G. Patzig (ed.), *Aristoteles' "Politik": Akten des XI Symposium Aristotelicum* (pp. 187–201). Göttingen: Vandenhoeck and Ruprecht.

Charlton, W. (1992). *Aristotle, "Physics," Books I and II: Translated with Introduction, Commentary, Note on Recent Work, and Revised Bibliography.* Oxford: Clarendon.

Cherniss, H. (1944). *Aristotle's Criticism of Plato and the Academy.* Baltimore: Johns Hopkins.

Chisholm, R. (1978 <Blackwell, *Practical Reason,* Körner, S. (ed.), 1974>). "Practical Reason and the Logic of Requirement." In J. Raz (ed.), *Practical Reasoning* (pp. 118–27). Oxford: Oxford University Press.

Cleary, J. J. (1995). *Aristotle and Mathematics: Aporetic Method in Cosmology and Metaphysics.* Philosophia antiqua, no. 67. Leiden/New York/Cologne: Brill.

Composta, D. (1975). "Le *inclinationes naturales* e il diritto in S. Tommaso d'Aquino."

In *San Tommaso e la filosofia del diritto oggi: Saggi*. Studi Tomistici, 4 (pp. 40–53). Rome: Pontificia Accademia Romana Di S. Tommaso D'Aquino.

Connery, J. (1977). *Abortion: The Development of the Roman Catholic Perspective.* Chicago: Loyola University Press.

Cook Wilson, J. (1904). "On the Platonist Doctrine of the *asymblētoi arithmoi.*" *Classical Review,* 18, pp. 247–60.

Cooper, J. M. (1982). "Aristotle on Natural Teleology." In *Language and Logos: Studies in Ancient Greek Philosophy* (M. Schofield and M. Nussbaum, eds.) (pp. 197–222). Cambridge: Cambridge University Press.

———— (1986 <1975>). *Reason and Human Good in Aristotle.* Indianapolis: Hackett.

Corcoran, J. (1973). "A Mathematical Model of Aristotle's Syllogistic." *Archiv für Geschichte der Philosophie,* 55, pp. 191–219.

———— (1974). "Aristotle's Natural Deduction Theory." In J. Corcoran (ed.), *Ancient Logic and Its Modern Interpretations* (pp. 83–131). Dordrecht: Reidel.

———— (1994). "The Founding of Logic: Modern Interpretations of Aristotle's Logic." *Ancient Philosophy,* 14, pp. 9–24.

Corcoran, J., and M. Scanlon (1982). "The Contemporary Relevance of Ancient Logical Theory" [critical study of *Aristotle and Logical Theory* by Jonathan Lear]. *Philosophical Quarterly,* 32, pp. 76–86.

Crombie, A. C. (1994). *Styles of Scientific Thinking: The History of Argument and Explanation Especially in the Mathematical and Biomedical Sciences and Arts.* London: Duckworth.

Dancy, R. M. (1975). *Sense and Contradiction: A Study in Aristotle.* Dordrecht: D. Reidel.

Daniel, W. (1979). "Double Effect and Resisting Evil." *Australasian Catholic Record,* 56, pp. 377–87.

D'Arcy, E. (1961). *Conscience and Its Right to Freedom.* London and New York: Sheed and Ward.

Denifle, H., and A. Chatelain (1889). *Chartularium Universitatis Parisiensis.* Paris: Delalain.

Dewan, L. (1985). "Saint Thomas and the Principle of Causality." In *Jacques Maritain: Philosophe dans la cité,/A Philosopher in the World* (pp. 153–71). Ottawa: Éditions de L'Université D'Ottawa (University of Ottawa Press).

———— (1995). "St. Thomas, James Keenan, and the Will." *Science et esprit,* 47, pp. 153–76.

———— (1997). "Saint Thomas, Physics, and the Principle of Metaphysics." *Thomist,* 61, pp. 549–66.

Diels, H., and W. Kranz (eds. and trans.) (1951). *Die Fragmente der Vorsokratiker* (6th ed.). Dublin/Zurich: Weidmann.

Dolan, J. V. (1960). "Natural Law and the Judicial Function." *Laval théologique et philosophique,* 16, pp. 94–141.

Dolan, S. E. (1950). "Resolution and Composition in Speculative and Practical Discourse." *Laval théologique et philosophique,* 6, pp. 9–62.

Donagan, A. (1977). *The Theory of Morality.* Chicago: University of Chicago Press.

Düring, I. (1969). *"Der Protreptikos" des Aristoteles: Einleitung, Text, Übersetzung und Kommentar.* Frankfurt am Main: Vittorio Klostermann.

Einarson, B. (1936). "On Certain Mathematical Terms in Aristotle's Logic." *American Journal of Philology,* 57, pp. 33–54, 151–72.

Elders, L. (1987). *Autour de Saint Thomas d'Aquin: Recueil d'études sur sa pensée philosophique et théologique* [vol. 1: Les commentaires sur les oeuvres d'Aristote, la métaphysique de l'être; vol. 2: L'agir moral, approches théologiques]. Paris/Brugge: FAC-Éditions/Tabor.

Elders, L., and K. Hedwig (eds.) (1984). *The Ethics of St. Thomas Aquinas: Proceedings of the Third Symposium on St. Thomas Aquinas' Philosophy, Rolduc, November 5 and 6, 1983.* Studi tomistici, 25. Vatican City: Libreria Editrice Vaticana.

Finnis, J. (1968). "Natural Law and *Humanae Vitae.*" *Law Quarterly Review,* 84, pp. 467–71.

—— (1970). "Natural Law and Unnatural Acts." *Heythrop Journal,* 11, pp. 365–87.

—— (1980). *Natural Law and Natural Rights.* Oxford: Clarendon.

—— (1981). "Natural Law and the 'Is'-'Ought' Question: An Invitation to Professor Veatch." *Catholic Lawyer,* 26, pp. 266–77.

—— (1983). *Fundamentals of Ethics.* Washington, DC: Georgetown University Press.

—— (1990a). "Natural Law and Legal Reasoning." *Cleveland State Law Review,* 38, pp. 1–13.

—— (1990b). "Allocating Risks and Suffering." *Cleveland State Law Review,* 38, pp. 193–207.

—— (1990c). "Concluding Reflections." *Cleveland State Law Review,* 38, pp. 231–50.

—— (1991a). "Intention and Side-Effects." In *Liability and Responsibility: Essays in Law and Morals* (R. G. Frey and C. W. Morris, eds.) (pp. 32–64). Cambridge: Cambridge University Press.

—— (1991b). *Moral Absolutes: Tradition, Revision and Truth.* Washington, DC: The Catholic University of America Press.

—— (1992 <*Thomist,* 55, 1991>). "Object and Intention in Moral Judgments According to St. Thomas Aquinas." In J. Follon and J. McEvoy (eds.), *Finalité et intentionnalité: Doctrine thomiste et perspectives modernes* (pp. 127–48). Paris/Louvain: Librairie Philosophique J. Vrin/Éditions Peeters.

—— (1996). "The Truth in Legal Positivism." In Robert P. George (ed.), *The Autonomy of Law* (pp. 195–214). Oxford: Clarendon.

—— (1998). *Aquinas: Moral, Political and Legal Theory.* Oxford: Oxford University Press.

Finnis, J., J. Boyle, and G. Grisez (1987). *Nuclear Deterrence, Morality and Realism.* Oxford: Clarendon.

Finnis, J., and G. Grisez (1981). "The Basic Principles of Natural Law: A Reply to Ralph McInerny." *American Journal of Jurisprudence,* 26, pp. 21–31.

Flannery, K. L. (1987). "A Rationale for Aristotle's Notion of Perfect Syllogisms." *Notre Dame Journal of Formal Logic,* 28, pp. 455–71.

—— (1991). Review article on Robin Smith's *Aristotle: "Prior Analytics."* *Ancient Philosophy,* 11, pp. 187–93.

—————— (1993a). "Alexander of Aphrodisias and Others on a Controversial Demonstration in Aristotle's Modal Syllogistic." *Journal of the History and Philosophy of Logic*, 14, pp. 210–14.

—————— (1993b). "What Is Included in a Means to an End?" *Gregorianum*, 74, pp. 499–513.

—————— (1995a). "Natural Law *mens rea* v. the Benthamite Tradition." *American Journal of Jurisprudence*, 40, pp. 377–400.

—————— (1995b). Review of Daniel Westberg's *Right Practical Reason: Aristotle, Action and Prudence in Aquinas*. *Gregorianum*, 76, pp. 623–24.

—————— (1995c). Review of *Moral Truth and Moral Tradition: Essays in Honour of Peter Geach and Elizabeth Anscombe*, by Luke Gormally (ed.). *International Philosophical Quarterly*, 35, pp. 497–501.

—————— (1995d). *Ways into the Logic of Alexander of Aphrodisias*. Philosophia Antiqua, 62. Leiden/New York/Cologne: Brill.

—————— (1995e). "The Aristotelian First Principle of Practical Reason." *Thomist*, 59, pp. 441–64.

—————— (1996). "Robinson's Łukasiewiczian *Republic* IV,435–439." *Gregorianum*, 77, pp. 705–26.

—————— (1997). "Ancient Philosophical Theology." In *A Companion to the Philosophy of Religion* (P. Quinn and C. Taliaferro, eds.) (pp. 73–79). Oxford: Blackwell.

—————— (1998a). "Aquinas on Analogy." *Gregorianum*, 79, pp. 381–84.

—————— (1998b). "Practical Reason and Concrete Acts." In R. P. George (ed.), *Natural Law and Moral Inquiry: Ethics, Metaphysics and Politics in the Work of Germain Grisez* (pp. 107–34). Washington, DC: Georgetown University Press.

—————— (1999). "The Synonymy of Homonyms." *Archiv für Geschichte der Philosophie*, 81, pp. 268–89.

—————— (2000). "Dui sensi della logica in Aristotele." In S. L. Brock (ed.), *L'attualità di Aristotele* (pp. 73–84). Rome: Armando Editore.

Flannery, K. L., and P. Moser (1985). "Kripke and Wittgenstein: Intention without Paradox." *Heythrop Journal*, 26, pp. 310–18.

Foot, P. (1978 <1967>). "The Problem of Abortion and the Principle of Double Effect." In P. Foot (ed.), *Virtues and Vices* (pp. 19–32). Berkeley/Los Angeles: University of California Press.

Frede, D. (1970). *Aristoteles und die 'Seeschlacht': Das Problem der "contingentia futura" in "De interpretatione" 9*. Hypomnemata, 27. Göttingen: Vandenhoeck and Ruprecht.

—————— (1974). "Comment on Hintikka's Paper 'On the Ingredients of an Aristotelian Science.'" *Synthese*, 28, pp. 79–89.

Friedberg, A. (ed.) (1881). *Corpus Iuris Canonici* (2d ed.): vol. 2. *Decretalium Collectiones*. Leipzig: B. Tauchnitz.

Gabbay, D., and F. Guenthner (1994). *Handbook of Philosophical Logic* (vol. 1: Elements of classical logic; vol. 2: Extensions of classical logic; vol. 3: Alternatives to classical logic; vol. 4: Topics in the philosophy of language). Dordrecht: Kluwer Academic Publishers.

Gallagher, D. M. (1994a). "Aquinas on Goodness and Moral Goodness." In D. M. Gallagher (ed.), *Thomas Aquinas and His Legacy* (pp. 37–60). Studies in Philosophy and the History of Philosophy, vol. 28. Washington, DC: The Catholic University of America Press.

———— (1994b). "Free Choice and Free Judgment in Thomas Aquinas." *Archiv für Geschichte der Philosophie*, 76, pp. 247–77.

Gauthier, R.-A. (1954). "Saint Maxime le Confesseur et la psychologie de l'acte humain." *Recherches de théologie ancienne et médiévale*, 21, pp. 51–100.

Gauthier, R. -A., and J. Y. Jolif (1958–1959). *"L'Éthique à Nicomaque": Introduction, traduction et commentaire* (2 vols.). Louvain: Publications Universitaires de Louvain; Paris: Éditions Béatrice-Nauwelaerts.

Geach, P. (1972). *Logic Matters*. Oxford: Basil Blackwell.

Gentzen, G. (1934). "Untersuchungen über das logische Schliessen." *Mathematische Zeitschrift*, 39, pp. 176–210, 405–31.

———— (1955 <1934>). *Recherches sur la déduction logique (Untersuchungen über das logische Schliessen)* (R. Feys and J. Ladrière, eds.). Paris: Presses Universitaires de France [French translation of Gentzen (1934), plus commentary].

George, R. P. (1988). "Recent Criticism of Natural Law Theory." *University of Chicago Law Review*, 55, pp. 1371–1429.

———— (1993). *Making Men Moral: Civil Liberties and Public Morality*. Oxford: Clarendon Press.

———— (ed.) (1992). *Natural Law Theory: Contemporary Essays*. Oxford: Clarendon Press.

———— (ed.) (1998). *Natural Law and Moral Inquiry: Ethics, Metaphysics and Politics in the Work of Germain Grisez*. Washington, DC: Georgetown University Press.

Gilby, T. (1966). *St. Thomas Aquinas, "Summa theologiae": vol. 28. Law and Political Theory: 1a 2ae 90–97*. London/New York: Blackfriars/Eyre and Spottiswoode/McGraw-Hill.

Gómez-Lobo, A. (1978). "Aristotle's First Philosophy and the Principles of Particular Disciplines: An Interpretation of *Metaph*. E,1,1025b10–18." *Zeitschrift für philosophische Forschung*, 32, pp. 183–94.

———— (1985). "Natural Law and Naturalism." *Proceedings of the American Catholic Philosophical Association*, 59, pp. 232–49.

Gosling, J. C. B., and C. C. W. Taylor (1982). *The Greeks on Pleasure*. Oxford: Clarendon.

Grabmann, M. (1929). *Mittelalterliche lateinische Übersetzungen von Schriften der Aristoteles-Kommentatoren Johannes Philoponos, Alexander von Aphrodisias und Themistios*. Munich. Sitzungsberichte der Bayerischen Akademie der Wissenschaften.

Grant, A. (1885). *The Ethics of Aristotle: Illustrated with Notes and Essays*. London: Longmans, Green, and Co.

Greenwood, L. H. G. (1973 <Cambridge University Press, 1909>). *Aristotle: Nicomachean Ethics, Book Six, with Essays, Notes and Translation*. New York: Arno.

Grisez, G. (1964). *Contraception and the Natural Law*. Milwaukee: Bruce Publishing.

———— (1965). "The First Principle of Practical Reason: A Commentary on the *Summa theologiae*, 1–2, Question 94, Article 2." *Natural Law Forum*, 10, pp. 168–201.

———— (1970). "Toward a Consistent Natural-Law Ethic of Killing." *American Journal of Jurisprudence*, 15, pp. 64–96.

———— (1978). "Against Consequentialism." *American Journal of Jurisprudence*, 23, pp. 21–72.

———— (1983). *The Way of the Lord Jesus:* vol. 1. *Christian Moral Principles.* Chicago: Franciscan Herald.

———— (1988a). "The Structures of Practical Reason: Some Comments and Clarifications." *Thomist*, 52, pp. 269–91.

———— (1988b). "A Critique of Russell Hittinger's Book *A Critique of the New Natural Law Theory*." *New Scholasticism*, 62, pp. 438–65.

———— (1993). *The Way of the Lord Jesus:* vol. 2. *Living a Christian Life.* Quincy, IL: Franciscan.

———— (1997). *The Way of the Lord Jesus:* vol. 3. *Difficult Moral Questions.* Quincy, IL: Franciscan.

Grisez, G., and J. Boyle (1979). *Life and Death with Liberty and Justice: A Contribution to the Euthanasia Debate.* Notre Dame/London: University of Notre Dame Press.

Grisez, G., J. Boyle, and J. Finnis (1987). "Practical Principles, Moral Truth, and Ultimate Ends." *American Journal of Jurisprudence*, 32, pp. 99–151.

Gulley, N. (1958). "Greek Geometrical Analysis." *Phronesis*, 3, pp. 1–14.

Gury, J. P. (1890). *Compendium theologiae moralis* (revised by H. Dumas). Lyons/Paris: Delhomme et Briguet/Victor Lecoffre.

Hall, P. M. (1994). *Narrative and the Natural Law: An Interpretation of Thomistic Ethics.* Notre Dame/London: University of Notre Dame Press.

Hardie, W. F. R. (1968). *Aristotle's Ethical Theory.* Oxford: Clarendon Press.

Hare, R. M. (1981). *Moral Thinking: Its Levels, Method and Point.* Oxford: Clarendon.

Hart, H. L. A. (1968 <1967>). "Intention and Punishment." In *Punishment and Responsibility: Essays in the Philosophy of Law* (pp. 113–35). Oxford: Clarendon.

———— (1983). *Essays in Jurisprudence and Philosophy.* Oxford: Clarendon.

———— (1994 <1961>). *The Concept of Law* (2d ed.). Oxford: Clarendon.

Heath, T. L. (1956 <Cambridge University Press, 1925>). *Euclid, the Thirteen Books of the "Elements": Translated with Introduction and Commentary* (2d ed.). New York: Dover.

———— (1981 <Clarendon, 1921>). *A History of Greek Mathematics.* New York: Dover.

Henle, R. J. (1956). *Saint Thomas and Platonism: A Study of the "Plato" and "Platonici" Texts in the Writings of St. Thomas.* The Hague: Martinus Nijhoff.

Hicks, R. D. (1907). *Aristotle, "De Anima": with Translation, Introduction and Notes.* Cambridge: Cambridge University Press.

Hintikka, J. (1959). "Aristotle and the Ambiguity of Ambiguity." *Inquiry*, 2, pp. 137-51. [A more developed version of this paper appears in Hintikka (1973), chapter 1.]

———— (1972). "On the Ingredients of an Aristotelian Science." *Nous*, 6, pp. 55-69.

———— (1973). *Time and Necessity.* Clarendon: Oxford.

———— (1974). "Reply to Dorothea Frede." *Synthese*, 28, pp. 91-96.

Hintikka, J., and U. Remes (1974). *The Method of Analysis: Its Geometrical Origin and Its General Significance.* Boston Studies in the Philosophy of Science, 25. D. Reidel: Dordrecht/Boston.

———— (1976). "Ancient Geometrical Analysis and Modern Logic." In *Essays in Memory of Imré Lakatos* (R. S. Cohen, P. K. Feyerabend, and M. W. Wartofsky, eds.) (pp. 253-76). Boston Studies in the Philosophy of Science, 39. Reidel: Dordrecht.

Hittinger, R. (1987). *A Critique of the New Natural Law Theory.* Notre Dame: University of Notre Dame Press.

Hoenen, P. (1952). *Reality and Judgment according to St. Thomas* (H. Tiblier, trans.). Chicago: Henry Regnery.

Inciarte, F. (1994a). "Aristotle's Defense of the Principle of Non-Contradiction." *Archiv für Geschichte der Philosophie,* 76, pp. 129-50.

———— (1994b). "Die Einheit der Aristotelischen Metaphysik." *Philosophisches Jahrbuch,* 101, pp. 1-21.

Irwin, T. H. (1977). *Plato's Moral Theory: The Early and Middle Dialogues.* Oxford: Clarendon.

———— (1995). *Plato's Ethics.* New York/Oxford: Oxford University Press.

Janssens, L. (1994). "Teleology and Proportionality." In *The Splendor of Accuracy* (J. Selling and J. Jans, eds.) (pp. 99-113). Kampen, Netherlands: Kok Pharos Publishing.

Jenkins, J. I. (1996). "Expositions of the Text: Aquinas's Aristotelian Commentaries." *Medieval Philosophy and Theology,* 5, pp. 39-62.

———— (1997). *Knowledge and Faith in Thomas Aquinas.* Cambridge: Cambridge University Press.

Joachim, H. H. (1951). *Aristotle: "The Nicomachean Ethics."* Oxford: Clarendon.

Johnstone, B. V. (1986). "The Structures of Practical Reason: Traditional Theories and Contemporary Questions." *Thomist,* 50, pp. 417-46.

Jones, A. (1986). *Pappus of Alexandria, Book 7 of "The Collection": Text, Translation and Commentary.* Sources in the History of Mathematics and Physical Sciences, 8. Berlin: Springer.

Judson, L. (1991). "Chance and 'Always for the Most Part' in Aristotle." In L. Judson (ed.), *Aristotle's "Physics": A Collection of Essays* (pp. 73–99). Oxford: Clarendon.

Kahn, C. (1990). "The Normative Structure of Aristotle's *Politics.*" In G. Patzig (ed.), *Aristoteles' 'Politik': Akten des XI Symposium Aristotelicum* (pp. 369–84). Göttingen: Vandenhoeck and Ruprecht.

Kass, L. R. (1980). "The Hippocratic Oath: Thoughts on Medicine and Ethics" [address delivered November 12, 1980, University of Chicago].

———— (1992). "I Will Give No Deadly Drug: Why Doctors Must Not Kill." *American College of Surgeons Bulletin,* 77, pp. 6–17.

Keenan, J. F. (1992). *Goodness and Rightness in Thomas Aquinas's "Summa Theologiae."* Washington, DC: Georgetown University Press.

Kenny, A. (1963). *Action, Emotion and Will.* London/New York: Routledge and Kegan Paul/Humanities Press.

———— (1966). "The Practical Syllogism and Incontinence." *Phronesis,* 11, pp. 163–84.

———— (1975). *Will, Freedom and Power*. Oxford: Basil Blackwell.

———— (1979). *Aristotle's Theory of the Will*. London: Duckworth.

———— (1992). *Aristotle on the Perfect Life*. Oxford: Clarendon.

Kirwan, C. (1993 <1971>). *Aristotle, "Metaphysics," books Γ, Δ and E: Translation with Notes* (2d ed.). Oxford: Clarendon.

Klibansky, R. (1982 <1939, 1943>). *The Continuity of the Platonic Tradition During the Middle Ages, with a New Preface and Four Supplementary Chapters, together with "Plato's 'Parmenides' in the Middle Ages and the Renaissance," with a New Introductory Preface*. Milwood, New York/London/Nendeln: Kraus International Publications.

Klubertanz, G. P. (1961). "The Root of Freedom in St. Thomas's Later Works." *Gregorianum*, 42, pp. 701–24.

Kluxen, W. (1964): *Philosophische Ethik bei Thomas von Aquin* (Mainz: Matthias-Grünewald-Verlag).

Kneale, W., and M. Kneale (1962). *The Development of Logic*. Oxford: Clarendon Press.

Kraut, R. (1989). *Aristotle on the Human Good*. Princeton: Princeton University Press.

Kretzmann, N. (1988). "Warring Against the Law in My Mind: Aquinas on Romans 7." In T. V. Morris (ed.), *Philosophy and the Christian Faith* (pp. 172–95). Notre Dame: University of Notre Dame Press.

Krueger, P., and T. Mommsen (1900–1905). *Corpus Iuris Civilis* [vol. 1: *Institutiones* (pp. 1–56) (P. Krueger, ed., 1905), *Digesta* (pp. 1–873) (T. Mommsen, ed., 1905); vol. 2: *Codex Iustinianus* (P. Krueger, ed., 1900); vol. 3: *Novelle* (R. Schoell, ed, 1904)]. Berlin: Weidmann.

Kung, J. (1982). "Aristotle's *De motu animalium* and the Separability of the Sciences." *Journal of the History of Philosophy*, 20, pp. 65–76.

Lauer, R. Z. (1954). "St. Thomas's Theory of Intellectual Causality in Election." *New Scholasticism*, 28, pp. 299–319.

Lear, J. (1980). *Aristotle and Logical Theory*. Cambridge, England: Cambridge University Press.

Lee, P. (1996). *Abortion and Unborn Human Life*. Washington, DC: The Catholic University of America Press.

———— (1997). "Is Thomas a Natural Law Theory Naturalist?" *American Catholic Philosophical Quarterly*, 71, pp. 567–87.

Leibniz, G. W. (1966 <1903>). *Opuscules et fragments inédits extraits des manuscrits de la Bibliothèque royale de Hanovre* (L. Couturat, ed.). Hildesheim: Georg Olms.

Lemmon, E. J. (1978 <1965>). *Beginning Logic*. Indianapolis: Hackett.

Lonergan, B. (1942). "St. Thomas' Thought on *gratia operans*." *Theological Studies*, 3, pp. 533–78.

Lottin, O. (1924). "L'ordre moral et l'ordre logique d'après saint Thomas d'Aquin." *Annales de l'Institut Supérieur de Philosophie*, 5, pp. 301–99.

———— (1925). "La définition classique de la loi: Commentaire de la 1a 2ae, q.90." *Revue néo-scolastique de philosophie*, 27, pp. 129–45, 243–73.

———— (1928). "La date de la question disputée *De malo* de saint Thomas d'Aquin."

Revue d'histoire ecclésiastique, 24, pp. 373–88. [Reprinted, with additional remarks, at Lottin (1942–1960), vol. 6, pp. 353–72.]

———— (1929 <*Revue thomiste*, 32–34, 1927–1929>). *La théorie du libre arbitre depuis S. Anselme jusqu'à S. Thomas d'Aquin*. Saint-Maximin (Var)/Louvain: École de Théologie/Abbaye du Mont-César.

———— (1931 <*Ephemerides theologicae Lovanienses*, 1924–1926>). *Le droit naturel chez Saint Thomas d'Aquin et ses prédécesseurs* (2d ed.). Bruges: Ch. Beyaert.

———— (1942-1960). *Psychologie et morale aux XIIᵉ et XIIIᵉ siècles* [vol. 1, Problèmes de psychologie, 1942; vol. 2, Problèmes de morale (première partie), 1948; vol. 3.1, Problèmes de morale (seconde partie, I), 1949; vol. 3.2, Problèmes de morale (seconde partie, II), 1949; vol. 4.1, Problèmes de morale (troisième partie, I), 1954; vol. 4.2, Problèmes de morale (troisième partie, II), 1954; vol. 5: Problèmes d'histoire littéraire, L'école d'Anselme de Laon et de Guillaume de Champeaux, 1959; vol. 6: Problèmes d'histoire littéraire de 1160 à 1300, 1960]. Louvain/Gembloux: Abbaye du Mont-César/J. Duculot.

———— (1950). "La valeur des formules de S. Thomas d'Aquin concernant la loi naturelle." In *Mélanges Joseph Maréchal* [no editor given] (vol. 2, pp. 345–77). Museum Lessianum, section philosophique, 31. Brussels/Paris: Édition Universelle/ Desclée De Brouwer.

———— (1954). *Morale fondamentale*. Bibliothèque de théologie, série 2, Théologie morale, 1. Paris: Desclée.

———— (1956a). "La preuve de la liberté humaine chez saint Thomas d'Aquin." *Recherches de théologie ancienne et médiévale*, 23, pp. 323–30.

———— (1956b). Short notice on R. Z. Lauer, "St. Thomas's Theory of Intellectual Causality in Election." *Bulletin de théologie ancienne et médiévale*, 7, pp. 580–81 (§2201).

Luban, D. (1990). "Incommensurable Values, Rational Choice, and Moral Absolutes." *Cleveland State Law Review*, 38, pp. 65–84.

Łukasiewicz, J. (1910). "Über den Satz des Widerspruchs bei Aristoteles." *Bulletin international de l'Académie des Sciences de Cracovie*, pp. 15–38.

———— (1957). *Aristotle's Syllogistic from the Standpoint of Modern Formal Logic* (2d ed.). Oxford: Clarendon.

———— (1975 <1910>). "Aristotle on the Law of Contradiction" [translation by J. Barnes of Łukasiewicz (1910)]. In *Articles on Aristotle* (J. Barnes, M. Schofield, and R. Sorabji, eds.), vol. 3: *Metaphysics* (pp. 50–62). London: Duckworth.

MacIntyre, A. (1981). *After Virtue*. London: Duckworth.

———— (1990a). *First Principles, Final Ends and Contemporary Philosophical Issues*. The Aquinas Lecture, 1990. Milwaukee: Marquette University Press.

———— (1990b). *Three Rival Versions of Moral Enquiry: Encyclopaedia, Genealogy, and Tradition: Being Gifford Lectures Delivered in the University of Edinburgh in 1988*. Notre Dame: University of Notre Dame Press.

Maier, H. (1936 <1896–1900>). *Die Syllogistik des Aristoteles* (2d ed.). Leipzig: K. F. Koehler.

Mangan, J. T. (1949). "An Historical Account of the Principle of Double Effect." *Theological Studies*, 10, pp. 40–61.

Mansion, A. (1925). "Pour l'histoire du commentaire de Saint Thomas sur la *Métaphysique.*" *Revue néo-scolastique de philosophie,* 27, pp. 274–95.

Mansion, S. (1946). *Le jugement d'existence chez Aristote.* Louvain/Paris: Éditions de L'Institut Supérieur de Philosophie/Desclée de Brouwer.

Maritain, J. (1943). *The Rights of Man and Natural Law.* New York: Scribner.

——— (1947 <New York: Éditions de la Maison Française, 1942>). *Les droits de l'homme et la loi naturelle.* Paris: Paul Hartmann.

May, W. E. (1984). "Aquinas and Janssens on the Moral Meaning of Human Acts." *Thomist,* 48, pp. 566–606.

——— (1991). *An Introduction to Moral Theology* (2d ed.). Huntington, IN: Our Sunday Visitor.

McCormick, R. A. (1978). "A Commentary on the Commentaries." In *Doing Evil to Achieve Good: Moral Choice in Conflict Situations* (R. A. McCormick and P. Ramsey, eds.) (pp. 193–267). Chicago: Loyola University Press.

McInerny, R. M. (1961). *The Logic of Analogy: An Interpretation of St. Thomas.* The Hague: Martinus Nijhoff.

——— (1968a). "The *ratio communis* of Analogical Names." In *Studies in Analogy* (see below) (pp. 2–66). The Hague: Martinus Nijhoff.

——— (1968b). *Studies in Analogy.* The Hague: Martinus Nijhoff.

——— (1980). "The Principles of Natural Law." *American Journal of Jurisprudence,* 25, pp. 1–15.

——— (1982). *Ethica Thomistica: The Moral Philosophy of Thomas Aquinas.* Washington, DC: The Catholic University of America Press.

——— (1984). "On Knowing Natural Law." In *The Ethics of St. Thomas Aquinas: Proceedings of the Third Symposium on St. Thomas Aquinas' Philosophy, Rolduc, November 5 and 6, 1983* (L. J. Elders and K. Hedwig, eds.) (pp. 133–42). Studi tomistici, 25. Vatican City: Libreria Editrice Vaticana.

——— (1986). *Being and Predication: Thomistic Interpretations.* Studies in Philosophy and the History of Philosophy, no. 16. Washington, DC: The Catholic University of America Press.

——— (1990). *Boethius and Aquinas.* Washington, DC: The Catholic University of America Press.

——— (1992). *Aquinas on Human Action: A Theory of Practice.* Washington, DC: The Catholic University of America Press.

——— (1996). *Aquinas and Analogy.* Washington, DC: The Catholic University of America Press.

——— (1998). "Portia's Lament: Reflections on Practical Reason." In R. P. George (ed.), *Natural Law and Moral Inquiry: Ethics, Metaphysics and Politics in the Work of Germain Grisez* (pp. 82–103). Washington, DC: Georgetown Univerity Press.

McKim, R., and P. Simpson (1988). "On the Alleged Incoherence of Consequentialism." *New Scholasticism,* 62, pp. 349–52.

McKirahan, R. D., Jr. (1992). *Principles and Proofs: Aristotle's Theory of Demonstrative Science.* Princeton: Princeton University Press.

Mignucci, M. (1969). *Aristotele, gli "Analitici primi": Traduzione, introduzione, commento.* Naples: Loffredo.

———— (1975). *L'Argomentazione dimostrativa in Aristotele: Commento agli "analtici secondi."* Padua: Antenore.

———— (1981). "Ὡς ἐπὶ τὸ πολύ et nécessaire." In E. Berti (ed.), *Aristotle on Science: The "Posterior Analytics"* (pp. 173-203). Proceedings of the eighth Symposium Aristotelicum held in Padua from September 7 to 15, 1978. Padua: Antenore.

———— (1987). "Aristotle's Arithmetic." In A. Graeser (ed.), *Mathematics and Metaphysics in Aristotle/Mathematik und Metaphysik bei Aristoteles: Akten des X.Symposium Aristotelicum, Sigriswil, 6–12 September 1984* (pp. 175–211). Bern and Stuttgart: Paul Haupt.

———— (1991). "Expository Proofs in Aristotle's Syllogistic." *Oxford Studies in Ancient Philosophy* (supplementary volume), pp. 9–28.

Morrison, D. (1987). "The Evidence for Degrees of Being in Aristotle." *Classical Quarterly,* 37, pp. 382–401.

Mueller, I. (1974). "Greek Mathematics and Greek Logic." In J. Corcoran (ed.), *Ancient Logic and Its Modern Interpretations* (pp. 35–70). Dordrecht: Reidel.

———— (1976). Review of *The Method of Analysis: Its Geometrical Origins and Its General Significance* by Jaakko Hintikka and Unto Remes. *Journal of Philosophy,* 73, pp. 158–62.

Narcy, M. (1978). "Aristote et la géométrie." *Les études philosophiques,* 53, pp. 13–24.

Nelson, D. M. (1992). *The Priority of Prudence: Virtue and Natural Law in Thomas Aquinas and the Implications for Modern Ethics.* University Park: The Pennsylvania State University Press.

Newman, W. L. (1988 <Clarendon, 1887–1902>). *The "Politics" of Aristotle.* Salem, NH: Ayer.

Nussbaum, M. (1978). *Aristotle's "De motu animalium".* Princeton: Princeton University Press.

———— (1990). "Nature, Function, and Capability: Aristotle and Political Distribution." In G. Patzig (ed.), *Aristoteles' 'Politik': Akten des XI Symposium Aristotelicum* (pp. 152–86). Göttingen: Vandenhoeck and Ruprecht.

———— (1992). *Love's Knowledge: Essays on Philosophy and Literature.* New York/Oxford: Oxford University Press.

Owen, G. E. L. (1960). "Logic and Metaphysics in Some Earlier Works of Aristotle." In I. Düring and G. E. L. Owen (eds.), *Aristotle and Plato in the Mid-Fourth Century* (pp. 163–90). Göteberg: Elanders Boktryckeri Aktiebolag [reprinted in *Logic, Science and Dialectic: Collected Papers in Greek Philosophy,* ed. M. Nussbaum (London: Duckworth, 1986)].

Owens, J. (1978). *The Doctrine of Being in the Aristotelian "Metaphysics": A Study in the Greek Background of Mediaeval Thought* (3d ed.). Toronto: Pontifical Institute of Mediaeval Studies.

Pakaluk, M. (1992). "Friendship and the Comparison of Goods." *Phronesis,* 37, pp. 111–30.

Pangallo, M. (1997). *Legge di Dio, sinderesi e coscienza nelle "Questiones" di S. Alberto Magno.* Studi tomistici, 63. Vatican City: Libreria Editrice Vaticana.

Patterson, R. (1989). "The Case of the Two Barbaras: Basic Approaches to Aristotle's Modal Logic." *Oxford Studies in Ancient Philosophy,* 7, pp. 1–40.

——— (1995). *Aristotle's Modal Logic: Essence and Entailment in the Organon.* Cambridge: Cambridge University Press.

Patzig, G. (1963). *Die aristotelische Syllogistik: Logisch-philosophische Untersuchungen über das Buch A der "Ersten Analytiken"* (2d ed.). Göttingen: Vandenhoeck and Ruprecht.

——— (1968 <1963>). *Aristotle's Theory of the Syllogism: A Logico-Philological Study of Book A of the "Prior Analytics"* (J. Barnes, trans.). Dordrecht: Reidel [translation and revision of Patzig (1963)].

Pelster, F. (1936). "Die Uebersetzungen der aristotelischen Metaphysik in den Werken des hl. Thomas von Aquin—IV: Weitere Ergebnisse und Fragen." *Gregorianum,* 17, pp. 377–406.

——— (1949). "Neuere Forschungen über die Aristotelesübersetzungen des XII und XIII Jahrhunderts." *Gregorianum,* 30, pp. 46–77.

Penner, T. (1990). "Plato and Davidson: Parts of the Soul and Weakness of Will." *Canadian Journal of Philosophy,* 16 (supplementary volume), pp. 35–74 [=D. Copp (ed.), *Canadian Philosophers: Celebrating Twenty Years of the Canadian Journal of Philosophy*].

——— (1992). "Socrates and the Early Dialogues." In R. Kraut (ed.), *The Cambridge Companion to Plato* (pp. 121–69). Cambridge: Cambridge University Press.

Penner, T., and C. J. Rowe (1994). "The Desire for Good: Is the *Meno* Inconsistent with the *Gorgias?*" *Phronesis,* 39, pp. 1–25.

Preller, V. (1967). *Divine Science and the Science of God: A Reformulation of Thomas Aquinas.* Princeton: Princeton University Press.

Rackham, H. (1975 <1934>). *Aristotle: "Nicomachean Ethics," with an English Translation* (2d ed.). Cambridge, MA/London: Harvard University Press/William Heinemann.

Rawls, J. (1971). *A Theory of Justice.* Cambridge, MA: Belknap Press of Harvard University Press.

Reale, G. (1993 <Naples: Loffredo, 1968>). *Aristotele, "Metafisica": Saggio introduttivo, testo greco con traduzione a fronte e commentario* ["edizione maggiore rinnovata"]. Milan: Vita e Pensiero.

Rhonheimer, M. (1987). *Natur als Grundlage der Moral: eine Auseinandersetzung mit autonomer und teleologischer Ethik.* Innsbruck/Vienna: Tyrolia.

——— (1994). *Praktische Vernunft und Vernünftigkeit der Praxis: Handlungstheorie bei Thomas von Aquin in ihrer Entstehung aus dem Problemkontext der aristotelischen Ethik.* Berlin: Akademie.

Robinson, R. (1937). "The Discourse on Method in *Republic* (510–511)." In *L'unité de la science; la méthode et les méthodes,* ed. R. Bayer (vol. 5, pp. 108–13). Travaux du IXe Congrès international de philosophie. Paris: Hermann.

——— (1953). *Plato's Earlier Dialectic* (2d ed.). Oxford: Clarendon.

——— (1969 <*Mind*, 1936>). "Analysis in Greek Geometry." In *Essays in Greek Philosophy* (pp. 1–15). Oxford: Claredon Press.

Rodier, G. (1900). *Aristote, "Traité de l'Ame": traduit et annoé*. Paris: Ernest Leroux.

Romiti, J. (1949). *De processu evolutivo doctrinae de actu humano completo in operibus S. Thomae Aquinatis* [excerpt of a dissertation submitted in 1948 to the Philosophy Faculty of the Pontifical Gregorian University]. Milan: P.I.M.E.

Ross, W. D. (ed. and trans.) (1925). *Ethica Nicomachea*. In *The Works of Aristotle:* vol. 9. Oxford: Clarendon.

——— (1936). *Aristotle's "Physics": A Revised Text with Introduction and Commentary*. Oxford: Clarendon.

——— (1949). *Aristotle's "Prior and Posterior Analytics."* Oxford: Clarendon.

——— (1953 <1924>). *Aristotle's "Metaphysics": A Revised Text with Introduction and Commentary* (2d ed.). Oxford: Clarendon.

Rowan, J. P. (trans.). (1995 <1961>). *St. Thomas Aquinas, Commentary on Aristotle's "Metaphysics."* Notre Dame, IN: Dumb Ox Books.

San Cristóbal-Sebastián, A. (1958). *Controversias acerca de la voluntad desde 1270 a 1300: Estudio histórico-doctrinal*. Madrid: Editorial y Libreria Co.Cul.S.A.

Schiaparelli, A. (1994). "Aspetti della critica di Jan Lukasiewicz al principio aristotelico di non contraddizione." *Elenchos*, 15, pp. 43–77.

Schofield, M. (1990). "Ideology and Philosophy in Aristotle's Theory of Slavery." In G. Patzig (ed.), *Aristoteles' 'Politik': Akten des XI Symposium Aristotelicum* (pp. 1–27). Göttingen: Vandenhoeck and Ruprecht.

Schultz, J. L. (1985). "Is-Ought: Prescribing and a Present Controversy." *Thomist*, 49, pp. 1–23.

——— (1986). "The Ontological Status of Value Revisited." *Modern Schoolman*, 63, pp. 133–37.

——— (1987). "'Ought'-Judgements: A Descriptivist Analysis from a Thomistic Perspective." *New Scholasticism*, 61, pp. 400–426.

——— (1988a). "St. Thomas Aquinas on Necessary Moral Principles." *New Scholasticism*, 62, pp. 150–78.

——— (1988b). "Thomistic Metaethics and a Present Controversy." *Thomist*, 52, pp. 40–62.

Schuster, J. (1933). "Von den ethischen Prinzipien: eine Thomasstudie zu *S.Th.* Ia IIae, q.94, a.2." *Zeitschrift für katholische Theologie*, 57, pp. 44–65.

Sharples, R. W. (1978). "Alexander of Aphrodisias *De fato:* Some Parallels." *Classical Quarterly*, 28, pp. 243–66.

——— (ed. and trans.) (1983). *Alexander of Aphrodisias "On Fate": Text, Translation and Commentary*. London: Duckworth.

Smart, J. J. C. (1967). "Utilitarianism." In P. Edwards (ed.), *Encyclopedia of Philosophy* (vol. 8, pp. 206–12). New York/London: Macmillan/Collier-Macmillan.

Smiley, T. J. (1973). "What Is a Syllogism?" *Journal of Philosophical Logic*, 2, pp. 136–54.

Smith, R. (1982). "What Is Aristotelian Ecthesis?" *History and Philosophy of Logic*, 3, pp. 113–27.

———— (1983). "Completeness of an Ecthetic System." *Notre Dame Journal of Formal Logic*, 24, pp. 224–32.

———— (trans.) (1989). *Aristotle, "Prior Analytics".* Indianapolis/Cambridge: Hackett.

Sorabji, R. (1980). *Necessity, Cause and Blame: Perspectives on Aristotle's Theory.* London: Duckworth.

———— (1990a). "Comments on J. Barnes." In G. Patzig (ed.), *Aristoteles' 'Politik': Akten des XI Symposium Aristotelicum* (pp. 264–76). Göttingen: Vandenhoeck and Ruprecht.

———— (ed.) (1990b). *Aristotle Transformed: The Ancient Commentators and Their Influence.* London: Duckworth.

Stewart, J. A. (1892). *Notes on the "Nicomachean Ethics" of Aristotle.* Oxford: Clarendon Press.

Susemihl, F. (1883). *Aristotelis, "Magna Moralia."* Leipzig: Teubner.

Szabó, A. K. (1974). "Working Backwards and Proving by Synthesis." In J. Hintikka and U. Remes, *The Method of Analysis: Its Geometrical Origin and Its General Significance* (pp. 118–30). Boston Studies in the Philosophy of Science, 25. D. Reidel: Dordrecht/Boston.

Te Velde, R. A. (1995). *Participation and Substantiality in Thomas Aquinas.* Studien und Texte zur Geistesgeschichte des Mittelalters, 46. Leiden/New York/Cologne: Brill.

Théry, G. (1926). *Autour du décret de 1210, II: Alexandre d'Aphrodise, aperçu sur l'influence de sa noétique.* Bibliothèque Thomiste, 7. Kain, Belgium.

Thom, P. (1981). *The Syllogism.* Munich: Philosophia Verlag.

———— (1996). *The Logic of Essentialism: An Interpretation of Aristotle's Modal Syllogistic.* The New Synthese Historical Library, 43. Dordrecht/Boston/London: Kluwer Academic Publishers.

Thillet, P. (1963). *Alexandre d'Aphrodise "De fato ad Imperatores," version de Guillaume de Moerbeke.* Paris: Vrin.

Torrell, J.-P. (1996 <1993: Fribourg, Switzerland/Paris>). *Saint Thomas Aquinas: Vol. 1: The Person and His Work.* Washington, DC: The Catholic University of America Press.

Toth, I. (1997). *Aristotele e i fondamenti assiomatici della geometria: Prolegomeni alla comprensione dei frammenti non euclidei nel "Corpus Aristotelicum" nel loro contesto matematico e filosofico.* Milan: Vita e Pensiero.

Tugwell, S. (1988). *Albert and Thomas: Selected Writings.* New York/Mahwah, NJ: Paulist.

Tuninetti, L. F. (1996). *"Per se notum": Die logische Beschaffenheit des Selbstverständlichen im Denkens des Thomas von Aquin.* Studien und Texte zur Geistesgeschichte des Mittelalters, 47. Leiden: Brill.

Van Overbeke, P.-M. (1957). "La loi naturelle et le droit naturel selon S. Thomas." *Revue thomiste*, 57, pp. 53–78, 450–95.

Van Steenberghen, F. (1991). *La philosophie au XIIIᵉ siècle* (2d ed.). Louvain-la-neuve/Louvain-Paris: Éditions de L'Institut Supérieur de Philosophie/Éditions Peeters.

Veatch, H. (1981). "Natural Law and the 'Is'-'Ought' Question: Queries to Finnis and Grisez." In *Swimming Against the Current in Contemporary Philosophy* (pp. 293–311). Studies in Philosophy and the History of Philosophy, Vol. 20. Washington, DC: The Catholic University of America Press.

Verbeke, G. (ed.) (1957). *Thémistius, "Commentaire sur le 'Traité de l'Ame' d'Aristote": Traduction de Guillaume de Moerbeke, édition critique et étude sur l'utilisation du commentaire dans l'œuvre de Saint Thomas.* Corpus Latinum Commentarium in Aristotelem Graecorum. Louvain: Publications Universitaires de Louvain.

Verbeke, G., and J. R. Moncho (eds.) (1975). *Némésius d'Émèse, "De natura hominis": Traduction de Burgundio de Pise.* Corpus Latinum Commentarium in Aristotelem Graecorum. Leiden: Brill.

Vlastos, G. (1975). *Plato's Universe.* Seattle: University of Washington Press.

von Arnim, H. F. (1964). *Stoicorum Veterum Fragmenta.* Stuttgart: Teubner.

Walton, W. M. (1952). "The Second Mode of Necessary or *per se* Propositions according to St. Thomas Aquinas." *Modern Schoolman,* 29, pp. 293–306.

Weinreb, L. L. (1987). *Natural Law and Justice.* Cambridge, MA/London: Harvard University Press.

Weisheipl, J. A. (1983 <1974>). *Friar Thomas D'Aquino: His Life, Thought, and Works.* Washington, DC: The Catholic University of America Press.

Westberg, D. (1994a). "Did Aquinas Change His Mind about the Will?" *Thomist,* 58, pp. 41–60.

——— (1994b). *Right Practical Reason: Aristotle, Action, and Prudence in Aquinas.* Oxford: Clarendon Press.

Wiggins, D. (1980 <*Proceedings of the Aristotelian Society* 76 (1975–1976), 29–51>). "Deliberation and Practical Reason." In A. O. Rorty (ed.), *Essays on Aristotle's Ethics* (pp. 221–40). Berkeley/Los Angeles/London: University of California Press.

Wippel, J. (1977). "The Condemnations of 1270 and 1277 at Paris." *Journal of Medieval and Renaissance Studies,* 7, pp. 169–201.

Wittgenstein, L. (1981 <1921>). *Tractatus Logico-philosophicus* (C. K. Ogden, trans.). London/ Boston/Henley: Routledge and Kegan Paul.

——— (1968 <1953>). *Philosophical Investigations/Philosophische Untersuchungen* (G. E. M. Anscombe, trans.) (3d ed.). Oxford: Basil Blackwell.

——— (1956). *Bemerkungen über die Grundlagen der Mathematik/Remarks on the Foundations of Mathematics* (G. H. Von Wright, R. Rhees, and G. E. M. Anscombe, eds.). Oxford: Basil Blackwell.

——— (1978 <1956>). *Remarks on the Foundations of Mathematics* (G. H. V. Wright, R. Rhees, and G. E. M. Anscombe, eds.) (2d ed.). Oxford: Basil Blackwell.

Woods, M. (1992). *Aristotle's "Eudemian Ethics," Books I, II and VIII* (2d ed.). Oxford: Clarendon.

Zanatta, M. (1989). *Aristotele, "le Categorie": Introduzione, traduzione e note.* Milan: Rizzoli.

Indices

INDEX OF ARISTOTELIAN
AND THOMISTIC PASSAGES CITED[1]

Aristotle

An.post.: 11, 19–20, 23, 39
  i: 237
  i,1: 20, 34, 36, 211
  i,2: 17, 19, 32–35, 38, 75, 209
  i,4: 31, 236, 240, 243
  i,6: 19
  i,7: 54, 59
  i,9: 38, 51–53
  i,10: 37–38, 54, 75
  i,11: 38
  i,12: 17, 19–20, 56
  i,13: 16, 59–60, 212
  i,14: 201, 205, 209
  i,15: 207
  i,21: 201
  i,22: 39
  i,24: 15
  i,28: 59
  i,32: 54–56
  i,33: 38, 55

  ii: 237
  ii,2–6: 211
  ii,14: 99
  ii,16: 20
  ii,17: 20, 211, 243
  ii,18: 243
  ii,19: 30, 88

An.pr.
  i,1: 127, 196–97, 199–201
  i,2: 148
  i,4: 197, 203
  i,5: 201
  i,6: 202–3, 241
  i,7: 201, 241
  i,9: 38, 244
  i,10: 211
  i,23: 202, 219
  i,28: 9
  i,32: 200

  ii,21: 11, 206

Cael.
  ii,5: 104

  iv,1: 75

Cat.: 85, 103
  i: 95–96
  ii: 88
  v: 94–95, 97, 105, 149
  vi: 105
  vii: 105
  xi: 28
  xii: 104

De an.: 144
  i,3: 244

  ii,3: 102
  ii,4: 161
  ii,5: 130
  ii,7: 245

  iii: 113
  iii,2: 201
  iii,3: 119, 127, 271–75
  iii,4: 124, 142
  iii,6: 41, 201
  iii,7: 132–33, 201, 233, 245
  iii,9: 125, 128, 144, 264–65, 274–75
  iii,10: 12, 125–28, 132, 140–41, 157, 254–55, 266–67
  iii,11: 105–6
  iii,19: 124

EE: 137
  i,8: 21, 86
  i,12: 22

  ii,3: 15
  ii,4: 233
  ii,6: 16, 265

1. For abbreviations used here, see pp. xix–xxii.

(EE: 137 continued)
ii,7: 129
ii,10: 16, 127
ii,11: 16

vii,2: 105
vii,6: v
vii,11: 105

viii,2: 136–39, 274–75
viii,3: 13

EN

i,1: 87, 144, 211
i,2: 5, 189
i,3: 14, 17,
i,4: 17, 28,
i,6: 28–29, 42, 86, 88, 96,
    212
i,7: 14
i,9: 189
i,12: 22–23
i,13: 189

ii,2: 14, 18, 211
ii,4: 14
ii,6: 15, 82, 162
ii,9: 49

iii: 12–13
iii,1: 15, 118, 152, 158, 164,
    252–53, 264–65
iii,2: 5–6, 13, 70, 128, 133,
    152, 264–65
iii,3: 13, 16, 69, 136, 213,
    233
iii,4: 127, 133
iii,5: 164, 264–65, 278–
    79
iii,7: 136

v,1: 127
v,2: 162, 189
v,7: 80
v,9: 128, 213
v,10: 83

vi: 6, 13, 22
vi,2: 133, 163
vi,5: 13, 17
vi,7: 22, 125
vi,8: 189
vi,9: 13

vi,10: 126
vi,11: 17, 130
vi,12: 6, 13, 264–65
vi,13: 13, 22, 125, 128

vii: 119
vii,2: 124, 189
vii,3: 16, 124, 130, 135
vii,8: 16, 17
vii,11: 180
vii,12: 180
vii,13: 44

viii,3: 134
viii,5: 134
viii,7: 134
viii,11: 105

ix,2: 18
ix,4: 43, 134
ix,7: 134
ix,8: 43, 134

x,2: 29
x,3: 29, 97

Int.
vii: 197
ix: 135–36, 140
xiii: 96

MA: 3
i: 21
ii: 21
vi: 21, 125, 128
vii: 6–9, 12

Metaph.: 103, 145
i,1: 130, 184, 211
i,2: 22, 29, 125
i,6: 93

ii,1: 12, 35
ii,2: 211

iii,1: 37
iii,2: 37, 161
iii,3: 29–30, 87–88
iii,4: 93

iv: xvi, 40
iv,1: 58
iv,2: 28, 96–97, 179

iv,3: 37, 41, 78, 145–47,
    150, 219, 230–31
iv,4: 41, 145–153, 157
iv,5: 38, 249, 266–67
iv,6: 147

v,1: 30, 52, 58
v,10: 88
v,11: 104
v,15: 140
v,18: 240–41

vi,1: 20
vi,2: 179, 181
vi,3: 138–39, 141–42,
    292–93
vi,4: 201, 256–57

vii,8: 130
vii,12: 105

ix,1: 142
ix,2: 127–28, 260–61
ix,4: 126
ix,5: 127, 141, 249, 260–61,
    286–89
ix,7: 140
ix,8: 184
ix,10: 142

x,1: 88

xi,4: 37, 54, 211

xii,7: 140
xii,9: 211
xii,10: 22, 28

xiii: 57, 85, 90
xiii,1: 85
xiii,6: 88, 90
xiii,7: 88, 90–94,
    254–55
xiii,8: 90
xiii,9: 88

xiv: 85
xiv,1: 86, 88

MM
i,10: 16
i,34: 13

ii,6: 130
ii,11: 130

PA

    i,4: 99

    iv,10: 46

Phys.

    i,1: 33–35

    i,3: 267

    ii,3: 9, 16, 181, 205–6

    ii,5: 134

    ii,6: 139

    ii,8: 181–82

    ii,9: 16

    iii,2: 182, 184

    iii,3: 181, 184

    iii,5: 75

    v,4: 182, 184

    vii,2: 184

    vii,4: 95, 106

    viii,1: 127

Pol.

    i,1: 102

    i,4: 105

    i,9: 211

    i,13: 103–5

    ii,8: 190, 211

    iii,1: 103

    iii,6: 184

    iii,9: 189

    iii,12: 103, 106

    iii,13: 103

    iv,1: 75

    vii: 102

    vii,1: 102

    vii,2: 102

    vii,3: 102

    vii,4: 102

    vii,8: 181

    viii: 102

Protr.

    B81–82: 95–86

Rhet.

    i,2: 189

    i,4: 189

    i,7: 99, 102

    i,10: 127

    ii,4: 134

    iii,6: 34

    iii,15: 134

SE

    i,11: 37

Top.

    i,11: 134, 267

    i,15: 28, 95

    iv,5: 165

Thomas Aquinas

De carit.

    q.un a.3: 114–15

De div.nom.

    §572: 161–62

De ma.: 113

    q.2 a.4: 158, 162, 184

    q.2 a.5: 159

    q.2 a.7: 162

    q.2 a.9: 162

    q.3 a.3: 137

    q.3 a.13: 165

    q.4 a.1: 162

    q.6: xvi, xviii, 112–144,

      165, 247–293

    q.8 a.1: 162

    q.9 a.2: 159

    q.10 a.1: 162

    q.16 a.6: 162

De pot.

    q.1 a.3: 244

    q.7 a.8: 106

    q.10 a.2: 117

De princ.nat.

    cap.3: 238

De ver.: 112–13, 115, 247

    q.2 a.8: 144

    q.3 a.3: 12

    q.12 a.1: 68

    q.14 a.1: 68

    q.14 a.4: 144

    q.14 a.5: 237

    q.16 a.1: 43

    q.21 a.1: 144

    q.21 a.2: 144

    q.22 a.2: 44

    q.22 a.6: 11, 113, 115

    q.22 a.7: 117

    q.22 a.10: 144

    q.22 a.12: 115

    q.22 a.14: 115

    q.22 a.15: 163

    q.23 a.4: 117

    q.23 a.5: 141

    q.24 a.1: xviii, 112, 117–19,

      131, 165, 247–49

    q.24 a.3: 122

in I Tim.

    cap.1 lect.3: 76

in An.post.

    lb.1 lect.1: 16, 20, 158

    lb.1 lect.3: 34

    lb.1 lect.4: 16, 19, 31,

      33–34, 38

    lb.1 lect.5: 58

    lb.1 lect.6: 51

    lb.1 lect.10: 39, 236–46

    lb.1 lect.11: 243

    lb.1 lect.13: 242, 246

    lb.1 lect.15: 59

    lb.1 lect.17: 51–52, 54, 56,

      59

    lb.1 lect.18: 38, 54, 56

(in An.post. continued)
  lb.1 lect.20: 30, 38, 54
  lb.1 lect.21: 56
  lb.1 lect.23: 242, 257
  lb.1 lect.25: 213
  lb.1 lect.26: 207, 236, 242
  lb.1 lect.27: 51
  lb.1 lect.31: 242
  lb.1 lect.33: 39
  lb.1 lect.35: 241, 242
  lb.1 lect.36: 41, 88
  lb.1 lect.41: 16, 213
  lb.1 lect.43: 38, 54–55, 68
  lb.1 lect.44: 16, 38, 41

  lb.2 lect.4: 68
  lb.2 lect.16: 16
  lb.2 lect.19: 243
  lb.2 lect.20: 88

in De an.
  lb.2 cap.5: 102
  lb.2 cap.6: 161
  lb.2 cap.14: 244–46

  lb.3 cap.3: 142, 289
  lb.3 cap.5: 41
  lb.3 cap.6: 134
  lb.3 cap.8; 144
  lb.3 cap.9: 42, 125–26, 157
  lb.3 cap.10: 106
  lb.3 cap.28: 275

in De cael.
  lb.2 lect.4: 68

in De hebdom.
  lect. 2: 35

in EN
  lb.1 lect.1: 28–29
  lb.1 lect.3: 14, 69
  lb.1 lect.4: 34
  lb.1 lect.6: 28–29, 42, 86
  lb.1 lect.7: 28, 87
  lb.1 lect.8: 42

  lb.2 lect.7: 162

  lb.3 lect.1: 253
  lb.3 lect.3: 158

  lb.3 lect.8: 69, 136

  lb.5 lect.12: 80, 235
  lb.5 lect.16: 80, 83

  lb.6 lect.9: 130

  lb.7 lect.12: 180
  lb.7 lect.13: 44

  lb.8 lect.11: 105

in Int.
  lb.1 lect.1: 153
  lb.1 lect.5: 153
  lb.1 lect.8: 153
  lb.1 lect.14: 115, 135–36,
    140–41

in Lib.caus.
  lect.15: 289

in Metaph.
  prooem.: 32, 68
  §21: 184
  §42: 29
  §49: 40
  §70: 241
  §278: 35, 69
  §§437–38: 30, 88
  §595: 35, 145
  §§596–610: 40
  §603: 41, 78, 231
  §605: 37, 41
  §606: 146
  §658: 145
  §§663–64: 249, 267
  §§692–707: 38
  §764: 238
  §§766–70: 115
  §771: 161
  §§833–35: 238
  §840: 241
  §899: 238
  §§1023–25: 140
  §1056: 240–41
  §1057: 237, 240–41
  §1149: 52
  §1177: 179
  §§1192–93: 141
  §§1207ff.: 79
  §1212: 139

  §§1216–22: 138
  §1218: 139
  §1563: 105
  §1787: 128
  §§1792–93: 261
  §1819: 261
  §§1820–21: 141
  §§2419–21: 293
  §2464: 238
  §§2468–70: 238
  §2488: 85
  §2663: 85

in Phys.
  lb.1 lect.1: 33–34

  lb.2 lect.5: 161, 207
  lb.2 lect.14: 183

  lb.3 lect.5: 237–38

  lb.8 lect.5: 54

in Pol.
  lb.1 cap.10: 103

  lb.3 cap.1: 103

in Rom.
  §§564–82: 129

in Sent.: 122
  lb.1 prolog. q.1 a.2: 22
  lb.1 d.1 q.1 a.2: 19
  lb.1 d.3 q.1 a.2: 38
  lb.1 d.19 q.5 a.1: 241
  lb.1 d.45 q.1 a.3: 241
  lb.1 d.48 q.1 a.2: 158
  lb.1 d.48 q.1 a.4: 47

  lb.2 d.7 q.1 a.1: 115, 122,
    129
  lb.2 d.9 q.1 a.8: 68
  lb.2 d.24 q.1 a.1: 163
  lb.2 d.25 q.1 a.1: 122
  lb.2 d.25 q.1 a.4: 117
  lb.2 d.36 q.1 a.1: 141, 184
  lb.2 d.36 q.1 a.5: 158

  lb.3 d.12 q.2 a.1: 122, 165
  lb.3 d.18 q.1 a.2: 122
  lb.3 d.23 q.2 a.3: 144

lb.3 d.27 q.1 a.1: 140
lb.3 d.30 q.1 a.4: 45, 244
lb.3 d.33 q.3 a.4: 82
lb.3 d.37 q.1 a.2: 45, 76–77
lb.3 d.37 q.1 a.3: 79–80
lb.3 d.37 q.1 a.4: 82–83

lb.4 d.9 q.1 a.4: 68
lb.4 d.15 q.3 a.1: 76, 82
lb.4 d.15 q.3 a.2: 76
lb.4 d.26 q.1 a.1: 47, 235
lb.4 d.26 q.2 a.2: 216
lb.4 d.28 q.1 a.4: 184
lb.4 d.31 q.1 a.2: 184
lb.4 d.33 q.1 a.1: 43, 47, 216
lb.4 d.33 q.1 a.2: 47
lb.4 d.49 q.3 a.5: 34

in Trin.

q.1 a.3: 44, 68
q.5 a.1: 12
q.6 a.1: 52

Perf.

§562: 43, 45
§626: 45

Quodl.: 249

V q.10 a.1: 13
VII q.5 a.5: 28
VII q.7 a.1: 46

SCG: 112

lb.2 cap.31: 237
lb.2 cap.48: 115
lb.2 cap.81: 237

lb.3 cap.13: 237
lb.3 cap.38: 44
lb.3 cap.41: 68
lb.3 cap.44: 68
lb.3 cap.73: 115
lb.3 cap.84: 275
lb.3 cap.88: 115
lb.3 cap.89: 138
lb.3 cap.117: 43
lb.3 cap.123: 77
lb.3 cap.125: 73

lb.4 cap.92: 70

ST

I : 112

q.2 a.1: 31, 44
q.2 a.2: 44
q.3 a.3: 157
q.5 a.1: 42, 144
q.6 a.2: 106
q.13 a.12: 241
q.14 a.2: 289
q.14 a.8: 141
q.14 a.13: 132
q.14 a.16: 12
q.17 a.4: 144
q.33 a.1: 30
q.39 a.1: 157
q.39 a.2: 157
q.39 a.3: 293
q.42 a.1: 37
q.77 a.6: 239
q.79 a.11: 144, 199
q.82 a.2: 123
q.82 a.4: 115–16
q.87 a.1: 245, 289
q.115 a.6: 141

I–II: 112, 114, 145

q.1 a.3: 237
q.4 a.4: 81, 161
q.5 a.5: 28
q.6 a.1: 30
q.7 a.2: 179
q.7 a.3: 158
q.9 a.4: 138
q.10 a.1: 47
q.12 a.1: 171
q.13 a.3: 16
q.13 a.4: 163
q.13 a.6: 11
q.14 a.5: 70–71
q.15 a.3: 163–64
q.16 a.1: 19
q.17 a.4: 159
q.18 a.1: 144, 179
q.18 a.2: 140, 158, 160, 179
q.18 a.3: 179
q.18 a.4: 162
q.18 a.6: 158–59, 162
q.18 a.7: 158
q.18 a.8: 154
q.18 a.9: 154
q.18 a.11: 162

q.19 a.6: 162
q.19 a.7: 162
q.20 a.2: 159
q.20 a.3: 159
q.23 a.8: 114
q.54 a.2: 239
q.55 a.4: 158
q.57 a.2: 67, 244
q.60 a.2: 158
q.63 a.1: 157
q.65 a.2: 158
q.71 a.5: 162
q.72 a.1: 168
q.72 a.3: 158
q.72 a.9: 162
q.73 a.3: 158
q.74 a.7: 67, 163
q.75 a.1: 141
q.75 a.4: 158
q.89 a.6: 44
q.90 a.1: 229
q.90 a.2: 28, 68, 131
q.91 a.3: 71, 229
q.92 a.2: 27–28, 229
q.93 a.3: 4, 83
q.94 a.1: 31
q.94 a.2: xv–xvi, xviii, 25–50, 84–85, 105, 107–8, 145, 228–35
q.94 a.3: 46
q.94 a.4: 31, 43, 72, 81–82
q.94 a.5: 31
q.94 a.6: 31
q.95 a.1: 28
q.95 a.2: 71–75, 78, 188
q.95 a.3: 73
q.95 a.4: 31, 73, 188
q.96 a.1: 14
q.96 a.6: 82
q.99 a.1: 28, 43, 45
q.99 a.5: 28
q.100 a.3: 42, 43
q.100 a.5: 28
q.100 a.11: 43

II–II: 114

q.2 a.3: 49
q.4 a.2: 144
q.25 a.1: 45
q.25 a.12: 43, 45
q.43 a.3: 168

(ST II–II continued)
  q.44 a.1: 28
  q.47 a.9: 14
  q.51 a.4: 81
  q.57 a.2: 73, 80–81
  q.60 a.3: 14
  q.64 a.3: 169

q.64 a.7: xvii, 167–176,
  186–88, 191–92
q.70 a.2: 14
q.85 a.1: 216
q.95 a.5: 275
q.120 a.1: 82
q.154 a.2: 46

q.154 a.12: 47

III
  q.16 a.7: 237

Tab.
  B118

INDEX OF NAMES

Aertsen, J., 69
Albert the Great, 15, 27, 119, 237, 242
Alexander of Aphrodisias, xiv, 9, 75, 127, 131–32, 146, 148–49, 165, 184, 208, 213, 238
Alexander of Aphrodisias (pseudo–), 132
al-Fārābī, 238
Allan, D., 5–8, 12–13, 69, 113
Annas, J., 86, 90, 93
Anscombe, G., 168, 170, 173
Anselm of Laon, 27
Armstrong, R., 26, 31, 43, 47–48, 50, 72, 74
Aspasius, 15
Aubert, J.-M., 77, 83
Augustine, 169, 188, 248, 253, 260–63
Averroes, 118, 238, 270–71,
Avicenna, 141, 258–59

Baker, G., 147
Barnes, J., 11, 20, 36–39, 60, 75, 102, 158, 200–1, 210, 213, 223, 243
Becker, A., 209
Belmans, T., 168
Bennett, J., 174
Beth, E., 203, 219–20
Bobzien, S., 200–1
Bochenski, I., 219
Boethius, 35, 37, 118, 132, 230–31, 276–77
Bonitz, H., 75, 197, 206, 210–11

Bourke, V., 113
Boyle, J., 25–26, 48, 85, 164, 168, 173–76, 183
Brandon, E., 62
Brennan, T., 209
Broadie, S., 182
Brock, D., 85
Brock, S., 25, 45, 182, 184
Broome, J., 108
Bryson, 54
Burgundio di Pisa, 165
Burnyeat, M., 8, 89
Byrne, P., 69

Cai, R., 76
Cajetan (Cajetanus), Thomas de Vio, 31, 239, 244
Calcidius, 75
Cavanaugh, T., 168
Caverot, D., 174
Charles, D., 102, 181
Charlton, W., 34
Charmides, 177
Chatelain, A., 112
Cherniss, H., 89
Chisholm, R., 10
Cicero, 76
Cleary, J., 89
Colvert G., 120
Composta, D., 235
Connery, J.,173
Cook Wilson, J., 89
Cooper, J., 8, 87, 182
Corcoran, J., 202–3, 219
Critias, 177
Crombie, A., 66

D'Arcy, E., 49–50, 78
Damascene (John), 233
Dancy, R., 146–48
Daniel, W., 168
Denifle, H., 112
Dewan, L., 22, 44, 114, 182
Diels, H., 75, 177
Dionysius (pseudo–), 161–62, 256, 257
Dionysodorus, 180
Dodds, E. R., 53
Dolan, J., 35
Dolan, S., 66
Donagan, A., 108

Einarson, B., 69
Elders, L., 31, 69
Euclid, 20, 36–37, 58, 61–62, 66, 99, 243, 291
Eudoxus, 62, 98

Figulus, N., see 'Nigidius Figulus'
Finnis, J., 15, 25–26, 45, 48, 73, 75, 77, 161, 163, 165, 168, 187–88, 194, 233, 235
Flannery, K., 9, 11, 23, 43, 48, 95, 98, 121, 128, 147, 148, 157–58, 164, 168, 174, 179, 200–1, 203, 208, 214
Foot, P., 168, 172–73
Frede, D., 165, 211
Frege, G., 90
Friedberg, A., 168

Gabbay, D., 218
Gallagher, C., 169

Gallagher, D., 28, 42, 112, 121
Gauthier, R.-A., 86, 180–81, 233
Geach, P., 10
Gellius, A., 75
Gentzen, G., 218–19
George, R., 25, 85
Gilby, T., 74
Gosling, J., 29
Grabmann, M., 132
Grant, A., 13
Gratian, 43
Greenwood, L., 13
Grisez, G., xv, 25–26, 28, 30, 43–44, 47–49, 84–85, 164, 168, 174, 188, 229
Grosseteste, R., 15, 238
Guenthner, F., 218
Gulley, N., 61
Gury, J., 174
Gómez-Lobo, A., 25, 52–53, 58, 60

Hacker, P., 147
Hall, P., 48
Hardie, W., 13, 15
Hare, R., 108
Hart, H., 168, 174, 188
Heath, T., 36, 54, 58, 61–64, 66, 98, 243
Heliodorus (pseudo-), 134
Heiberg, J., 62
Henle, R., 29
Heraclitus, 146
Heron, 62
Hicks, R., 246
Hintikka, J., 9, 59, 61–62, 66–67, 70, 211, 218, 220
Hittinger, R., 25, 84–85
Hoenen, P., 237, 239, 242
Homer, 275
Hugh of St. Victor, 77

Ierodiakonou, K., 200–1
Inciarte, F., 145–46
Irwin, T., 179

Jaeger, W., 149
James of Venice, 51
Janssens, L., 160–61
Jenkins, J., 33

Johnstone, B., 25
Jolif, J., 86, 180–81
Jones, A., 61
Judson, L., 210

Kahn, C., 102
Kass, L., 185
Keenan, J., 114–15
Kenny, A., 7–8, 10–12, 14, 138, 185, 198, 213
Kirwan, C., 240
Klibansky, R., 75
Klubertanz, G., 114–15
Kluxen, W., 144
Kneale, M., 219
Kneale, W., 219
Kranz, W., 75, 177
Kraut, R., 87
Kretzmann, N., 129
Krueger, P., 233
Kung, J., 60

Ladrière, J., 218
Lauer, R., 114–15
Lear, J., 218
Lee, P., 25, 168
Leibniz, G., 67, 219
Lombard, P., 76–77, 122
Lonergan, B., 117, 248
Lottin, O., xvi, 13, 25, 27, 31, 43, 47, 111–17, 122, 165
Luban, D., 85
Łukasiewicz, J., 146–47, 219

MacIntyre, A., 20, 38–39, 176, 223
Maier, H., 197
Mandonnet, P., 76
Mangan, J., 168
Mansion, A., 85
Mansion, S., 52
Maritain, J., 3–4
Maximus Confessor, 165
May, W., 25, 43, 159
McCormick, R., 84
McInerny, R., 25, 28, 32, 35–36, 42, 47, 98, 107, 144, 163, 241
McKim, R., 85
McKirahan, R., 60, 243
Melissus, 267

Michael of Ephesus, 21
Mignucci, M., 52, 88, 197, 201, 203, 208–11, 213
Moerbeke, W., see 'William of Moerbeke'
Mommsen, T., 233
Moncho, J., 165
Morrison, D., 95–96
Moser, P., 11
Mueller, I., 36, 61–62
Mure, G., 52

Narcy, M., 69
Nelson, D., 26, 33, 50, 74
Nemesius (Emesenus), 132, 165
Newman, W., 102
Nigidius Figulus, 75
Nussbaum, M., xiv–xv, 3–5, 7–8, 11–12, 14, 19, 21, 23, 50, 60, 102

Owen, G., 28
Owens, J., 28, 96

Pakaluk, M., 86–87, 95, 107
Pappus Alexandrinus, 61, 70
Parmenides, 267
Patterson, R., 209
Patzig, G., 201
Pelster, F., 85
Penner, T., 106, 124, 135, 155, 197, 236
Philoponus (John) 34, 52,
Plato, 27, 35, 53, 57, 75, 86–87, 90, 93, 95, 102, 105, 124, 157, 167, 177–79, 181, 183–89, 219
Preller, V., 33
Proclus, 53, 70, 132

Rackham, H., 13
Rawls, J., 5, 23
Reale, G., 90, 92, 93, 149
Remes, U., 9, 61, 66, 67, 70, 218, 220
Rhonheimer, M., 25, 47, 66, 72
Robinson, R., 53, 62
Rodier, G., 246

Ross, W., 6, 34, 90, 91, 93, 96, 149, 201, 240
Rowan, J., 85
Rowe, C., 106
Russell, B., 219

San Cristóbal-Sebastián, A., 112
Schiaparelli, A., 150
Schofield, M., 105
"Scholiast, the," 15
Schultz, J., 25, 241
Schuster, J., 30, 33, 41, 47, 55
Sharples, R., 131, 132, 165
Simplicius, 9, 75
Simplicius (pseudo–), 246
Simpson, P., 85
Smart, J., 107–8
Smiley, T., 202, 203
Smith, R., 201, 203
Socrates, 27, 35, 57, 177, 178, 179, 184
Sorabji, R., 102, 210
Speusippus, 86
Stewart, J., 13, 17
Szabó, A., 70

Taylor, C., 29
Tempier, É., 111, 112, 115, 116, 117, 118, 143
Te Velde, R., 29
Theaetetus, 62
Themistius, 246
Theon, 62
Théry, G., 132
Thierry of Chartres, 77
Thillet, P., 132
Thom, P., 203, 208, 218

Thrasymachus, 178
Tollefsen, O., 164
Torrell, J.-P., 76, 112, 115, 247, 249
Toth, I., 20
Tricot, J., 52
Tugwell, S., 76, 112
Tuninetti, L., 26, 32, 35, 242

Van Overbeke, P.-M., 25, 27, 47, 48
Van Steenberghen, F., 112
Veatch, H., 25
Verbeke, G., 165, 246
Vlastos, G., 184
von Arnim, H., 233
von Wright, G., 8

Xenocrates, 86

Walton, W., 237
Weinreb, L., 188
Weisheipl, J., 76, 112, 145
Westberg, D., 112, 121, 163
Whitehead, A., 219
Wiggins, D., 8
William of Conches, 77
William of Moerbeke, 16, 50, 51, 245
Wippel, J., 112
Wittgenstein, L., 11, 151
Woods, M., 128

Zabarella, J., 52, 60, 244
Zanatta, M., 96
Zenobius, 75

SUBJECT INDEX

analogy: 97–100
analysis (analysis/synthesis method): 9–10, 35, 50, 53, 55, 60–71, 75, 217–23

boulēsis (see *voluntas*)

capital punishment: 169, 171–72, 175–76, 186–87, 190–92
causality (*see also* cause): assigned to will or intellect: 112–15, 121, 131, 133–34, 136–41; in-trinisic/extrinsic: 237–41
cause: 23, 32, 61, 76, 79, 136, 138–39, 141, 161–62, 181–82, 192, 204–5, 211, 236–41, 258–59, 260–63, 286–93; efficient: 9, 112, 182, 236–40; final: 112, 114–15, 121, 131, 133–34, 206, 237–40; formal: 112, 114–15, 121, 133, 236, 238, 270–71; material: 9, 236, 238, 240–41; sufficient, 141, 259, 286–87
choice [*prohairesis, electio*]: 6; free choice, 111–13, 116–23, 129–35, 162–66
commensurability/incommensurability: xv–xvi, 49, 84–108
common notions (common axioms): 36–39, 41–42, 51–60
consequence [*akolouthon*] (concomitant): 60–62, 198
consequentialism (weighing of goods): 49, 84–85, 105–8, 114
craft [*technē*]: 180–85, 189–90, 193, 206–8, 210–17, 224
craniotomy: 173–176, 183–85, 190, 192, 214, 223–26

decision procedure: 66–67
deduction, natural: 217–23
deductivism: 3–4, 50–83; in Neoplatonism, 53, 73

deposits (to be returned): 43, 49, 79–83
determinism: 112–13, 115, 117–20, 129, 131, 136–43, 248
divine, the (*see also* God): 22–23

ecthesis [*ekthesis*]: 148, 203–4, 219, 221
elenchic demonstrations: xvi–xvii, 145–57, 160
epistemology: 32–35, 37–39, 49

first principle of practical reason (FPPR): 42–45, 48, 84, 144–46, 149, 151–57, 199, 212–17, 223–24, 233; FPPR for medicine (FPPR^m): 212–14, 223–24
fixed paths (*see also* craft): 48, 167–94, 206–17, 223–26
force [*violentia*] (see also *violentum*): 116–18, 139, 168–69, 175, 186, 188, 225–26

genus (genera, universals, common ideas): 20, 27–29,33–34, 38–39, 55, 59, 86–89, 106, 129–30, 197
geometry: 16–20, 36–39, 52–54, 56–59, 62–71, 75, 98–99, 108, 205, 218; as pertinent to ethics: 16–20, 69–71, 108
God (*see also* divine): 4, 43–46, 136–40; his existence, 43; natural inclination toward: 107, 234–35
grace: 136–38

homononyms: 94–97
hysterectomy: 173–76, 183–85, 190, 193, 214, 225–26

inclinations, human: 25–26, 28, 46–49, 107, 232–35
indefinite propositions: 196–98

indivisibles [*atomoi*] (relative indistinguishables): 87–94, 100–102
intellect, inseparable from *voluntas:* 121
intensity-more-and-less: 95, 97–105

law: 27–29, 187–91, 217, 224; positive (posited), 71–78; law-making (legislating): 189
Lesbian rules: 83
liberty of exercise/liberty of specification:
  112–13, 115, 120–21, 124, 132–135, 143, 165–66
lying: 77, 160–62

"mapping on": 203–8, 216, 223–25
materia circa quam: 157–62
means to an end: 6, 10–14, 19, 206, 255
metaphysics: 20–22, 32, 37, 50–60, 67, 145, 181
moral absolutes (the immorality of attacking
  basic human goods): 14–24, 49, 108, 172,
  191–94, 223–ͅ 26
more-and-less [*to mallon kai to hētton*] (*see*
  intensity-more-and-less *and* position-
  more-and-less)

Neoplatonism: 53, 57, 73
numbers: 91–94

order (ordering): 29, 71, 85–108

per (the preposition): 236–39
per se (see also '*per se notum*'):236–46
per se notum (see also *per se*): 26, 31–39, 216,
  219, 231
physicalism (physical events in ethics): 150,
  157–58, 181–83, 192–93, 213–14
political science [*politikē*]: 189
position-more-and-less: 95, 97–105, 108
practical reason (*see* reason)
practical syllogism: 5–12, 71, 131, 195–226; direction of: 9–12, 17; defeasibility of: 10–12,
  17, 195–96; "good preserving": 12, 198
practices (*see* fixed paths)
precepts: 25–49; as distinct from principles,
  xxiii, 30–1, 50; higher and lower, 41–48,
  50–83, 105–8; common, 42–48, 216

principle of double effect: xiii, xvii, 48,
  167–94, 223–26
principle of non-contradiction (PNC):
  39–41, 45, 144–52, 154, 156–57, 199, 212–14,
  231; for medicine (PNC^m): 212, 214
principles [*archai*] (*see also* common notions): 16–19, 30; as distinct from precepts, xxiii, 30–31
prosequendum(a): 153–55, 159–63, 166
psychologism: 147

reason (practical and theoretical): 12, 30–31,
  39–45, 152–57; practical reason, as an "extension" of theoretical: 144, 197, 199,
  203–08, 215–16, 225; reason (rationality)
  and freedom: 130–32

self-defense: 168–72, 175–76, 186–87, 191–92,
  224
sex: 232–33
signification(s): 145–56, 166
slavery: 104–5
syllogism (*see also* practical syllogism): 9–10,
  78, 195–96, 199–203, 208–10, 244; as "a
  gathering together": 223; perfect and perfected: 199–203; modal: 208–10
synonyms: 94–97
synthesis (*see* analysis)

technē (*see* craft)
translatio vetus of Aristotle's *De anima:* 275

universal intellectual forms (*see also* genus):
  119–20, 123, 130–31, 134–35

violentum ("instance of being forced"; *see
  also* force): 252–53
voluntas [*boulēsis*] (will): 6, 111–143; 'will' vs.
  voluntas: 113, 143; inseparable from intellect: 121; predominance of, 124–29

will (see *voluntas*)

Acts Amid Precepts: The Aristotelian Logical Structure of Thomas Aquinas's Moral Theory was designed and composed in Minion with Cataneo display type by Kachergis Book Design, Pittsboro, North Carolina, and printed on sixty-pound Glatfelter Natural Smooth and bound by Sheridan Books, Ann Arbor, Michigan.